A-LEVEL AND AS-LEVEL   PHYSICS

GUIDES

LONGMAN A-LEVEL AND AS-LEVEL REVISE GUIDES

Series editors
Geoff Black and Stuart Wall

Titles available
Biology
Chemistry
Economics
English
Geography
Mathematics
Physics

Forthcoming
Art
Computing
French
History
Sociology

A-LEVEL
AND AS-LEVEL

LONGMAN

REVISE

GUIDES

PHYSICS

Stephen Grounds
Edwin Kirby

Longman

Longman Group UK Limited,
Longman House, Burnt Mill, Harlow,
Essex CM20 2JE, England
and Associated Companies throughout the world.

© Longman Group UK Limited 1990

First published 1990

British Library Cataloguing in Publication Data

Grounds, Stephen
  Physics.
  1. England. Secondary schools. Curriculum subjects.
  Physics. G.C.E. (A level) examinations
  I. Title   II. Kirby, Edwin
  530′.76

  ISBN 0-582-05169-X

Designed and produced by the Pen & Ink Book Company Ltd,
Huntingdon, Cambridgeshire

Set in 10/12pt Century Old Style

Printed and bound in Great Britain by
William Clowes Limited, Beccles and London

EDITORS' PREFACE

Longman A Level Revise Guides, written by experienced examiners and teachers, aim to give you the best possible foundation for success in your course. Each book in the series encourages thorough study and a full understanding of the concepts involved, and is designed as a subject companion and study aid to be used throughout the course.

Many candidates at A Level fail to achieve the grades which their ability deserves, owing to such problems as the lack of a structured revision strategy, or unsound examination technique. This series aims to remedy such deficiencies, by encouraging a realistic and disciplined approach in preparing for and taking exams.

The largely self-contained nature of the chapters gives the book a flexibility which you can use to your advantage. After starting with the background to the A, AS Level and Scottish Higher courses and details of the syllabus coverage, you can read all other chapters selectively, in any order appropriate to the stage you have reached in your course.

Geoff Black and Stuart Wall

ACKNOWLEDGEMENTS

The authors and publishers are grateful to the following Examination Boards for permission to reproduce past examination questions:

Associated Examination Board (AEB)
Joint Matriculation Board (JMB)
Northern Ireland Schools Examinations Council (NI)
Oxford and Cambridge Schools Examination Board (O & C)
Oxford Delegacy of Local Examinations (Oxford)
Scottish Examination Board (Scottish)
Southern Universities' Joint Board (Southern)
University of Cambridge Local Examinations Syndicate (Cambridge)
University of London Schools Examinations Board (London)
Welsh Joint Education Committee (Welsh).

The comments, outline answers and tutor's answers are entirely the responsibility of the authors and have neither been provided nor approved by the examining boards. The University of Cambridge Local Examinations Syndicate bears no responsibility for the example answers to questions taken from its past question papers which are contained in this publication. The University of London Schools Examination Board accepts no responsibility whatsoever for the accuracy or method of working in the answers given.

We are most grateful to Reg Phillips for his valuable suggestions concerning the text of this book.

We also acknowledge the patience shown by our families whilst this book was in preparation.

CONTENTS

NAMES AND ADDRESSES OF THE EXAM BOARDS

Associated Examining Board (AEB)
Stag Hill House
Guildford
Surrey GU2 5XJ

University of Cambridge Local Examinations Syndicate (UCLES)
Syndicate Buildings
1 Hills Road
Cambridge CB1 1YB

Joint Matriculation Board (JMB)
Devas St
Manchester M15 6EU

University of London Schools Examination Board (ULSEB)
Stewart House
32 Russell Square
London WC1B 5DN

Northern Ireland Schools Examination Council (NISEC)
Beechill House
42 Beechill Road
Belfast BT8 4RS

Oxford and Cambridge Schools Examination Board (OCSEB)
10 Trumpington Street
Cambridge CB2 1QB

Oxford Delegacy of Local Examinations (ODLE)
Ewert Place
Summertown
Oxford OX2 7BX

Scottish Examination Board (SEB)
Ironmills Road
Dalkeith
Midlothian EH22 1BR

Welsh Joint Education Committee (WJEC)
245 Western Avenue
Cardiff CF5 2YX

EXAM BOARDS AND SYLLABUS COVERAGE

GETTING STARTED

The table of contents contained in this chapter is based on the published A Level (Higher grade for Scottish) and AS Level syllabuses for the 1990 examinations.

A LEVEL

A large percentage of all these A Level syllabuses is similar, much of it being based on the *common core* at A Level which was introduced in 1987. Most of the items mentioned in Table 1 are included in these syllabuses, either explicitly or implicitly. The text of this book concentrates mainly on this common ground. Some examination boards use an *extended core* and others a *core* plus a small percentage of *options*. For 1990, the Cambridge, JMB, London and Scottish boards have included options, but all syllabuses are regularly reviewed. As well as the common core, the text also covers almost all the extended material and parts of the options, though the options consider the subject matter in much more detail. Examination boards often publish booklets or recommend specific reading for the option topics.

AS LEVEL

Most boards offer an AS Level in Physics and these usually comprise a *core* plus *options*. The AS Levels are intended to occupy half the study and teaching time of an A Level. Clearly the content is less than A Level, but the core material, and in some cases the options, are similar to A Level. The book covers the core of the AS syllabuses and parts of the options.

If you wish to be certain of the details of your particular examination, you should obtain a syllabus for the specific year from the examination board of the course you are following. The addresses of these boards are set out overleaf.

SYLLABUS COVERAGE

Table 1.1 will give you a brief overview of the topics included in your syllabus. For more detail, check with the syllabus of your own exam board.

When you come across the topic areas outlined in Table 1.1 in this book, you can check the table to make sure that the topic appears on your course and syllabus.

Table 1: Syllabus coverage

TOPICS	CORE	Cam	So	Ox	AEB	NI	Nuff	JMB	O&C	We	Lon	AEB	Ox	Lon	Cam O&C So	SEB
Physical quantities and units																
S.I. Units	✓	✓	✓	✓	✓	✓	✓	✓	✓	✓	✓	✓	✓	✓	✓	✓
Avogadro constant	✓	✓	✓	✓	✓	✓	✓	✓	✓	✓	✓	✓	✓	✓	✓	✓
Dimensions (homogeneity of equations)	✓	✓	✓	✓	✓	✓	✓	✓	✓	✓	✓	✓	✓			
Scalars and vectors	✓	✓	✓	✓	✓	✓	✓	✓		✓	✓	✓	✓		✓	✓
Composition and resolution	✓	✓		✓	✓	✓	✓			✓	✓	✓	✓		✓	✓
Static forces																
Equilibrium of forces	✓	✓	✓		✓	✓	✓	✓		✓	✓	✓			✓	
Closed polygon	✓	✓	✓		✓	✓	✓			✓	✓				✓	
Centre of gravity		✓	✓		✓	✓	✓									
Moment of a force	✓	✓	✓		✓	✓	✓				✓	✓			✓	
Principle of moments	✓	✓	✓		✓	✓	✓				✓	✓			✓	
Couple and torque	✓	✓	✓		✓	✓	✓		✓	✓					✓	
Frictional forces	✓	✓				✓										
Pressure in fluids		✓	✓	✓	✓				✓							
$P = \rho gh$	✓	✓	✓	✓	✓		✓					✓				
Manometer	✓			✓	✓											
Buoyancy effect		✓	✓	✓	✓											
Dynamics																
Rectilinear motion	✓	✓	✓	✓	✓	✓	✓	✓	✓	✓	✓	✓	✓	✓	✓	✓
Uniformly accelerated motion	✓	✓	✓	✓	✓	✓	✓	✓	✓	✓	✓	✓	✓	✓	✓	✓
Newton's laws of motion	✓	✓	✓	✓	✓	✓	✓	✓	✓	✓	✓	✓	✓	✓	✓	✓
Momentum	✓	✓	✓	✓	✓	✓	✓	✓	✓	✓	✓	✓	✓	✓	✓	✓
Conservation of momentum	✓	✓	✓	✓	✓	✓	✓	✓	✓	✓	✓	✓	✓	✓	✓	✓
Elastic and inelastic collisions	✓	✓	✓	✓	✓	✓	✓	✓	✓	✓	✓					✓
Projectiles	✓	✓			✓	✓	✓		✓	✓	✓					✓
Work, energy, power																
Conservation of energy	✓	✓	✓	✓	✓	✓	✓	✓	✓	✓	✓	✓	✓	✓	✓	
Renewable and non-renewable sources		✓	✓	✓			✓					✓				
Potential energy	✓	✓	✓	✓	✓	✓	✓	✓	✓	✓	✓	✓	✓			✓
Kinetic energy	✓	✓	✓	✓	✓	✓	✓	✓	✓	✓	✓	✓	✓		✓	✓
Work	✓	✓	✓	✓	✓	✓	✓	✓	✓	✓	✓	✓	✓	✓	✓	✓
Power	✓	✓	✓	✓	✓	✓	✓	✓	✓	✓	✓	✓	✓	✓	✓	✓
Motion in a circle																
Uniform circular motion	✓	✓		✓	✓	✓	✓		✓	✓	✓				✓	
Angular velocity	✓	✓	✓		✓	✓	✓		✓	✓	✓				✓	
Centripetal acceleration	✓	✓			✓	✓	✓		✓	✓	✓				✓	
Angular motion			✓		✓				✓	✓						
Angular acceleration			✓		✓				✓							
Moment of inertia			✓		✓				✓	✓						
Angular momentum			✓		✓				✓	✓						
Conservation of angular momentum			✓		✓				✓	✓						
Rotational kinetic energy					✓				✓	✓						

TOPICS	CORE	A LEVEL Cam	So	Ox	AEB	NI	Nuff	JMB	O&C	We	Lon	AS LEVEL AEB	Ox	Lon	Cam O&C So	SCOTTISH HIGHER SEB
Simple harmonic motion																
Acceleration, velocity and displacement	✓	✓	✓	✓	✓	✓	✓	✓	✓	✓	✓	✓				
Period, frequency, amplitude			✓	✓	✓	✓	✓	✓	✓	✓	✓	✓	✓			
Simple pendulum		✓	✓	✓	✓	✓			✓	✓	✓		✓			
Mass-spring system		✓	✓	✓	✓	✓	✓	✓	✓	✓	✓	✓				
Cylinder in water			✓	✓												
Energy in SHM		✓			✓			✓	✓	✓	✓					
Free and forced oscillations																
Resonance and damping	✓	✓	✓	✓	✓	✓	✓	✓	✓	✓	✓	✓	✓			
Waves																
Progressive waves	✓	✓	✓	✓	✓	✓	✓	✓	✓	✓	✓		✓		✓	
Amplitude, speed, frequency and phase	✓	✓	✓	✓	✓	✓	✓	✓	✓	✓	✓		✓		✓	
Measurement of frequency, wavelength and speed	✓		✓	✓		✓	✓				✓					
$c = f\lambda$	✓	✓			✓	✓	✓	✓	✓	✓	✓		✓		✓	
Longitudinal and transverse waves																
Polarisation	✓	✓	✓		✓	✓	✓	✓	✓		✓		✓			
Speed of sound using stationary waves		✓	✓	✓	✓	✓		✓		✓	✓		✓			
Frequency of sound using c.r.o.		✓	✓			✓	✓		✓				✓			
Stroboscope				✓									✓			✓
Vibrations of strings			✓	✓	✓	✓	✓		✓	✓	✓		✓			
Air columns			✓	✓	✓	✓			✓	✓			✓			
Superposition of waves																
Interference	✓	✓	✓	✓	✓	✓	✓	✓	✓		✓				✓	
Two-source patterns	✓	✓	✓	✓	✓	✓	✓	✓	✓		✓					
Lloyd's mirror								✓								
Beats			✓	✓											✓	
Diffraction	✓	✓	✓	✓	✓	✓	✓	✓	✓		✓					
Single slit	✓	✓	✓	✓	✓	✓	✓	✓	✓		✓					
Diffraction grating	✓	✓	✓	✓	✓	✓	✓	✓	✓		✓					
Stationary waves	✓	✓	✓	✓	✓	✓	✓	✓	✓		✓					
Electromagnetic spectrum																
Characteristics and orders of magnitude	✓	✓	✓	✓	✓	✓	✓	✓	✓		✓	✓	✓	✓		
Reflection	✓		✓	✓				✓	✓		✓	✓	✓			✓
Refraction	✓		✓	✓		✓		✓	✓		✓	✓	✓			✓
Snell's law					✓	✓		✓	✓		✓	✓	✓			✓
Total internal reflection					✓		✓		✓		✓	✓	✓			✓
Optical fibres							✓									✓
Doppler effect			✓	✓					✓							
Concave mirrors			✓	✓									✓			
Convex lens			✓	✓		✓		✓					✓			✓
Refracting telescope			✓	✓				✓								✓
Magnifying power			✓	✓				✓								✓
Eye ring			✓	✓												✓

TOPICS	CORE	A LEVEL Cam	So	Ox	AEB	NI	Nuff	JMB	O&C	We	Lon	AS LEVEL AEB	Ox	Lon	Cam O&C So	SCOTTISH HIGHER SEB
Electric Current																
Charge		✓	✓	✓	✓	✓	✓	✓	✓	✓	✓	✓	✓	✓	✓	✓
Current as rate of flow of charged particles	✓	✓	✓	✓	✓	✓	✓	✓	✓	✓	✓	✓	✓	✓	✓	
Conductors, semiconductors and insulators	✓	✓	✓		✓	✓		✓			✓					
$I = nAev$	✓	✓			✓	✓		✓	✓		✓					
Typical carrier drift speeds	✓	✓	✓	✓	✓	✓		✓								
E.m.f.	✓	✓	✓	✓	✓	✓	✓	✓	✓	✓	✓	✓	✓	✓	✓	
Potential difference	✓	✓	✓	✓	✓	✓	✓	✓	✓	✓	✓	✓	✓	✓	✓	
Resistance	✓	✓	✓	✓	✓	✓	✓	✓	✓	✓	✓	✓	✓	✓	✓	
Resistivity	✓	✓	✓	✓	✓	✓	✓	✓	✓	✓	✓	✓				
Temperature coefficient of resistance				✓	✓		✓	✓	✓	✓			✓		✓	
Internal resistance of sources	✓			✓	✓		✓	✓		✓	✓		✓		✓	✓
Diode		✓					✓		✓		✓	✓				
LDR				✓			✓				✓	✓				
Thermistor				✓			✓				✓	✓				
Energy & power		✓		✓		✓				✓	✓	✓		✓		✓
D.C. circuits																
Resistors in series	✓	✓	✓	✓	✓	✓	✓	✓	✓	✓	✓	✓	✓	✓	✓	✓
Resistors in parallel	✓	✓	✓	✓	✓	✓	✓	✓	✓	✓	✓	✓	✓	✓	✓	✓
Kirchhoff's laws	✓	✓	✓	✓	✓	✓	✓	✓	✓	✓	✓	✓				✓
Potential divider		✓	✓	✓	✓	✓	✓	✓	✓	✓	✓					✓
Balanced potentials		✓	✓	✓	✓	✓	✓	✓	✓	✓	✓					✓
Null method's				✓	✓		✓		✓							✓
Capacitors																
Capacitance	✓	✓	✓	✓	✓	✓	✓	✓	✓	✓	✓	✓		✓		✓
Capacitors in series		✓	✓	✓	✓	✓	✓	✓	✓	✓	✓					
Capacitors in parallel		✓	✓	✓	✓	✓	✓	✓	✓	✓	✓					
Energy stored	✓	✓	✓	✓	✓	✓	✓	✓	✓	✓	✓	✓				
Charge and discharge	✓	✓	✓	✓	✓	✓	✓	✓	✓	✓	✓			✓		✓
Reed switch		✓				✓		✓			✓					
Inverse square law fields																
Electric field	✓	✓		✓	✓	✓	✓	✓	✓	✓	✓			✓		✓
Inverse square law	✓	✓		✓	✓	✓	✓	✓	✓	✓	✓			✓		
Field of a point charge	✓	✓		✓	✓	✓	✓	✓	✓	✓	✓			✓		
Electric potential	✓	✓		✓	✓	✓	✓	✓	✓	✓	✓			✓		✓
Gravitational field	✓	✓		✓	✓	✓	✓	✓	✓	✓	✓	✓		✓		✓
Gravitational potential	✓	✓		✓	✓	✓	✓	✓	✓	✓	✓			✓		
Newton's law	✓	✓		✓	✓	✓	✓	✓	✓	✓	✓			✓		
Relation between g and G		✓		✓	✓	✓	✓	✓	✓							
Motion of satellites in circular orbits		✓		✓	✓	✓	✓	✓	✓		✓					
Uniform field between parallel plates		✓			✓	✓				✓						
Parallel plate capacitor				✓	✓		✓		✓							✓
Magnetic effects of electric currents																
Straight wire	✓	✓	✓	✓		✓	✓	✓	✓	✓	✓		✓		✓	
Plane coil	✓	✓	✓	✓	✓	✓	✓	✓	✓	✓	✓		✓			✓
Solenoid	✓	✓	✓	✓	✓	✓	✓	✓	✓	✓	✓	✓	✓			

TOPICS	CORE	Cam	So	Ox	AEB	NI	Nuff	JMB	O&C	We	Lon	AEB	Ox	Lon	Cam O&C So	SEB
		A LEVEL										AS LEVEL				SCOTTISH HIGHER
Magnetic flux density	✓	✓	✓	✓	✓	✓	✓	✓	✓	✓	✓		✓			
Magnetic flux		✓	✓	✓	✓	✓	✓	✓	✓	✓	✓		✓			
Force on current-carrying conductor		✓	✓	✓	✓	✓	✓	✓	✓	✓	✓	✓	✓	✓	✓	✓
Torque on coil				✓	✓	✓		✓					✓			
Force between current-carrying conductors	✓	✓	✓	✓	✓	✓	✓	✓	✓	✓	✓					
Definition of the ampere	✓			✓	✓	✓	✓	✓	✓	✓	✓					
The current balance		✓	✓					✓								
Force on moving charge		✓		✓	✓				✓	✓	✓					
Hall effect		✓			✓			✓	✓		✓					
Electromagnetic induction																
Magnitude of induced e.m.f.	✓	✓		✓	✓	✓	✓	✓	✓	✓	✓	✓	✓	✓	✓	✓
Direction of induced e.m.f.	✓	✓		✓	✓	✓	✓	✓	✓	✓	✓	✓	✓	✓	✓	✓
Self induction	✓		✓	✓	✓	✓	✓	✓	✓	✓	✓					✓
Mutual induction	✓		✓	✓	✓	✓	✓	✓	✓	✓	✓					
The transformer				✓	✓	✓		✓	✓	✓	✓	✓				✓
Alternating currents																
Frequency, amplitude, phase	✓			✓		✓		✓	✓			✓	✓			
R.M.S.	✓	✓	✓	✓	✓		✓	✓	✓	✓	✓	✓	✓			✓
Energy and power	✓		✓	✓		✓	✓	✓	✓	✓	✓	✓				
Rectification	✓	✓	✓	✓	✓	✓		✓		✓	✓					
Transmission of energy	✓											✓				
Reactance				✓	✓	✓	✓	✓	✓	✓	✓					✓
Inductors				✓	✓	✓	✓	✓	✓	✓	✓					✓
Capacitors				✓	✓		✓	✓	✓	✓	✓					✓
Resonance					✓	✓		✓	✓	✓	✓					✓
Electronics																
Logic gates, truth tables (NOT, AND, NAND, NOR, OR, EX-NOR)	✓	✓	✓	✓	✓	✓	✓	✓		✓						✓
Bistable		✓	✓			✓	✓			✓						✓
Half-adder		✓			✓											✓
Operational amplifier	✓	✓	✓	✓		✓	✓	✓	✓	✓						✓
Inverting amplifier		✓	✓	✓	✓	✓	✓	✓	✓							✓
Non-inverting amplifier		✓	✓	✓	✓	✓	✓	✓	✓							
Differential amplifier		✓	✓	✓	✓	✓	✓	✓	✓							
Comparator		✓			✓	✓	✓	✓	✓							
Feedback	✓	✓	✓	✓	✓	✓	✓	✓	✓	✓						✓
Oscillator	✓			✓	✓	✓	✓	✓	✓	✓						
States of matter																
Solids, liquids, gases	✓	✓	✓	✓	✓	✓	✓		✓	✓	✓					✓
Crystalline and glassy solids	✓	✓	✓	✓	✓	✓	✓	✓	✓						✓	
Amorphous and polymeric solids	✓	✓	✓	✓	✓	✓	✓	✓	✓							
Deformation of solids																
Elastic and plastic behaviour	✓	✓	✓	✓	✓	✓	✓		✓	✓	✓	✓				
Hooke's law		✓	✓	✓	✓	✓	✓	✓	✓	✓	✓	✓				
Force-extension graphs	✓	✓	✓	✓	✓	✓	✓	✓	✓	✓	✓	✓	✓			
Stress and strain	✓	✓	✓	✓		✓	✓	✓	✓	✓	✓	✓	✓			
Young's modulus	✓	✓	✓	✓	✓	✓	✓	✓	✓	✓	✓	✓	✓			
Strain energy		✓	✓	✓	✓	✓	✓	✓	✓	✓	✓		✓			

TOPICS	CORE	A LEVEL										AS LEVEL			Cam O&C So	SCOTTISH HIGHER
		Cam	So	Ox	AEB	NI	Nuff	JMB	O&C	We	Lon	AEB	Ox	Lon		SEB
Kinetic theory of gases																
Basic assumptions	✓	✓	✓	✓	✓	✓	✓	✓	✓	✓	✓	✓				✓
Derivation of equations		✓				✓	✓	✓	✓							✓
Pressure of a gas		✓					✓	✓	✓	✓	✓	✓				✓
Kinetic energy of a molecule		✓					✓	✓	✓	✓	✓					
Temperature and energy	✓	✓			✓			✓	✓	✓	✓					
Boltzmann constant	✓	✓		✓	✓			✓	✓	✓	✓					
Temperature scales																
Resistance thermometer	✓	✓	✓	✓	✓			✓			✓	✓	✓		✓	
Liquid-in-glass thermometer	✓	✓	✓	✓				✓		✓		✓	✓		✓	
Thermocouple thermometer	✓	✓	✓	✓				✓		✓					✓	✓
Thermodynamic temperature	✓	✓	✓	✓								✓	✓	✓		✓
Celsius temperature	✓	✓		✓		✓		✓	✓	✓		✓	✓	✓		✓
Heat																
Heat capacity	✓	✓	✓	✓				✓	✓	✓	✓		✓	✓	✓	✓
Latent heat	✓	✓	✓					✓	✓	✓	✓	✓	✓		✓	✓
Internal energy	✓	✓	✓	✓				✓								
First law of thermodynamics	✓	✓				✓	✓	✓	✓	✓	✓		✓		✓	
Thermal conduction	✓	✓	✓	✓	✓	✓	✓	✓	✓	✓	✓	✓	✓		✓	
Thermal conductivity	✓	✓	✓	✓	✓	✓	✓	✓	✓	✓	✓	✓	✓		✓	
Convection	✓	✓		✓	✓				✓		✓				✓	
Radiation	✓	✓		✓	✓		✓		✓	✓					✓	
Isothermal expansion				✓	✓				✓	✓	✓				✓	
Adiabatic expansion				✓	✓				✓	✓	✓				✓	
Work expended on expansion				✓	✓			✓	✓							
Linear expansion	✓			✓	✓											
Charged particles																
Electrons	✓	✓	✓	✓	✓	✓		✓	✓	✓	✓					✓
Millikan's experiment		✓	✓	✓	✓			✓	✓	✓						
Beams of charged particles		✓	✓	✓	✓	✓	✓	✓	✓	✓						✓
Deflection by magnetic fields	✓	✓	✓	✓	✓	✓	✓	✓	✓	✓	✓					✓
Deflection by electric fields	✓	✓	✓	✓	✓	✓	✓	✓	✓	✓						✓
Cathode-ray oscilloscope		✓	✓	✓	✓	✓	✓	✓	✓	✓		✓				✓
Radioactivity																
α, β, γ radiation	✓	✓	✓	✓				✓	✓	✓	✓	✓	✓	✓	✓	✓
Ionising effects of particles		✓		✓				✓	✓	✓	✓					✓
Deflection by fields		✓		✓				✓	✓	✓	✓					✓
Detection of particles		✓						✓	✓	✓						✓
Hazards and safety precautions		✓				✓	✓	✓		✓		✓				✓
Radioactive decay				✓	✓	✓	✓	✓	✓	✓	✓	✓	✓	✓	✓	✓
Random nature of decay	✓			✓	✓	✓	✓	✓	✓	✓		✓	✓	✓		✓
Decay constant and half-life	✓			✓	✓	✓	✓	✓	✓	✓	✓	✓	✓		✓	✓
Photons and energy levels																
Energy of a quantum	✓	✓	✓	✓	✓	✓		✓	✓	✓	✓		✓	✓		✓
Photoelectric effect	✓	✓	✓	✓	✓	✓		✓	✓	✓	✓		✓	✓		✓

TOPICS	CORE	A LEVEL										AS LEVEL				SCOTTISH HIGHER
		Cam	So	Ox	AEB	NI	Nuff	JMB	O&C	We	Lon	AEB	Ox	Lon	Cam O&C So	SEB
Energy levels in atoms	✓	✓	✓	✓	✓	✓	✓	✓	✓	✓	✓		✓	✓		✓
Emission line spectra	✓	✓	✓	✓	✓	✓	✓	✓	✓	✓	✓		✓	✓		✓
Absorption line spectra			✓	✓	✓				✓	✓	✓					✓
Wave-particle duality	✓	✓	✓	✓	✓		✓	✓	✓							✓
Diffraction of electrons		✓		✓												
X-rays			✓	✓			✓		✓		✓					
Nuclear atom	✓	✓	✓	✓	✓	✓		✓	✓	✓	✓	✓	✓	✓	✓	✓
Isotopes		✓	✓	✓	✓		✓	✓		✓	✓	✓	✓	✓	✓	✓
Binding energy		✓		✓		✓			✓					✓		✓
Mass defect		✓		✓		✓		✓						✓		✓
Nuclear fission		✓		✓	✓	✓		✓		✓	✓			✓		✓
Nuclear fusion		✓		✓	✓	✓	✓			✓				✓		✓

EXAMINATION TECHNIQUES

SUCCESSFUL STUDY

REVISION FOR THE EXAMINATION

AT THE EXAMINATION

GETTING STARTED

You will probably have come to A Level Physics after studying Physics to GCSE level, or more likely, after studying Physics as an element in a double certificated Science course. In Scotland you will have studied Standard Grade Physics, and will be going on to the Scottish Higher or a Sixth year study course. Scottish readers should note that although the term 'A level' is used in this book the treatment is intended to cover much of the work for Higher and Sixth year studies examinations.

You will have chosen A Level Physics for all sorts of reasons. You probably see it as an interesting and exciting subject concerned with the theories, models, experiments, and facts about the physical world. You recognise that it has a practical value through its application in science and technology on the way we live. Maybe you see it as a necessary subject for a career, if not in a Physics-based subject, then in engineering or in medicine. Or perhaps you ultimately have your sights on a career in commerce and see A Level Physics as a good qualification for activities in which a good deal of mathematical manipulation and modelling is required. Maybe you have enjoyed the experimental side of your previous science work and wish to extend this further in your A Level study. Whatever your reasons, it is important at the outset to be clear about the way A Level Physics is *different* from what you will have done earlier on.

ESSENTIAL PRINCIPLES

In spite of changes to A Level syllabuses, and some reduction in the amount of content, many students have found the transition from GCSE studies difficult. An obvious difference is in the *volume* and *breadth* of knowledge required. Although your GCSE studies may have been wide-ranging, you will often have had all the information you needed *supplied to you*. In A Level work, by contrast, it will be assumed that you already have a broad background of factual knowledge, and that you can fill in any gaps in that knowledge yourself.

Another difference is that A Level work is more *specialised*. For example in GCSE you may have studied mechanics in an indirect way, e.g. by analysing some topics in transport. At A Level you will need to approach mechanics by understanding the basic laws and vocabulary of the physics specialist. So you will need to be familiar with the basic equations and formulae, and more importantly, to thoroughly understand the fundamental principles and concepts. Interestingly, in a survey completed some years ago, Physics teachers themselves ranked the thorough understanding of the main principles of Physics as their number one aim in successful A Level teaching.

A Level Physics also requires much more use of *arithmetic*. You will see this by comparing any A Level Physics paper with its equivalent at GCSE. A good example is the inverse square law of gravity. At GCSE level you will simply encounter this as the way the gravitational force of an attracting body diminishes as you move away from it. However, at A Level you will be expected to think quickly and *quantitatively*, for instance, about questions such as:

- what happens when you move to a point twice as far away as your initial position?
- what about the energy changes?
- what would be the change in the orbiting time?

The key thing here is that you begin to see at A Level that to a large extent the physical world is governed by laws which can be put in a single mathematical form. So you need to develop your arithmetical and mathematical skills in parallel with your understanding of the Physics concepts. You need to have a good grasp of proportionality and inverse proportionality and you must be able to carry out complex computations quickly and accurately, making sensible use of your electronic calculator.

Progress through GCSE Physics has been compared to a steady tramp up a uniformly sloping incline, requiring effort of course, but without being too arduous or laborious. By contrast, progress in A Level Physics is much more like a scramble over rough country to the top of a mountain. Occasionally there are some very steep climbs before you can get your breath on an upland plateau. The mental leap upward at each of these barriers is as demanding as, say, the mastery of multiplication tables, or trigonometry, but with the comfort that once aloft, the scenery becomes much clearer and progress turns into a rapid canter with the summit in sight.

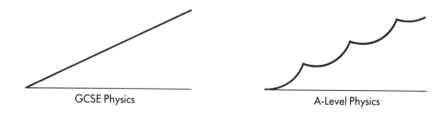

GCSE Physics   A-Level Physics

Fig. 2.1

There are two other ways in which A Level work is different from GCSE. First, *practical* work at GCSE will have generally been rather qualitative. The emphasis at A Level is much more on careful measurements of a quantitative kind in order to test out the mathematical patterns mentioned earlier. And secondly, there is a much greater need at A Level to be able to read and write fluently. Communication in Physics is important and hard. You will need to read from a variety of sources including text-books, magazines, and special articles, and one of the most difficult tasks for physicists is being able to put into words what they understand. Skills like this are only touched on in GCSE, but at A Level they are put to a full test in exercises like the comprehension papers of a number of Boards.

Whether you are studying for your A Level Physics at college (F.E or sixth form), school, evening class or at home, you will be working a good deal of time on your own, probably without much of the kind of guidance you have been used to. Sometimes students find this transition to advanced work difficult. And there are all sorts of traps in store for you. Perhaps you arrive home from school or college with a pile of books intending to get your head down to do your Physics homework. But it has been a hard day at school and you feel like a change of scene and remember that you promised to mend that puncture on your brother's bicycle. Unfortunately you run out of rubber solution and so call round at a friend's to borrow some. The friend is pleased to see you and shows you a new tape he has bought and you decide to listen to it on his hi-fi system. By the time you get home it's supper time. It's a pleasant meal and you linger on after it drinking a coffee with your older sister who has just come in from work. When you finish you remember there is still the bicycle. By the time that's done you need to clean up with a shower. Time is running on and eventually you decide that you must get down to work, so there is another cup of coffee and then you settle down and start to read your Physics text book. But after twenty minutes you realise that you are still on the same page. Not much has gone in and your eyes are starting to glaze over. You decide to get up and have a stroll round the house, and as you do so you hear that the 'Nine O'clock News' has begun. . . How do you avoid this kind of snare?

TIMING

You need to plan a *timetable* of work and to keep a record (a diary) of it. You need also to analyse when your *best time* for working is. Some students find that working early in the evening is the best: some prefer to work later in the evening, and for some early in the morning seems much better. Find out when *your* best time is.

You must also organise yourself so that you *do* have periodic breaks. After about forty minutes most people's concentration begins to wane. *Plan* for this kind of break and set yourself a mini-target of work to be done before it comes up. Ten minutes rest will help you to refresh yourself, enabling you to continue your studying more effectively.

LOCATION

Where you work is also very important. Try to find somewhere which can be your base, where you can work without being disturbed, and where you can keep your books and papers. Avoid eye strain by making sure that it is a well-lit environment, and make sure that it is comfortable and warm but not overheated. Have everything you need ready at hand: writing paper, pens, a highlighting pencil, calculator, etc.

ENGAGING IN ACTIVE LEARNING

Once you start work you must work *effectively*. You will do this if you are interested in what you are doing and if you are well motivated. Above all you need to be *active* in your approach to learning. Just reading a text-book is not enough. That is where this book comes in. One of our aims is that it should be a study-aid, i.e. that you can use it to try to teach yourself a topic or to research material which you were not clear about when it was tackled at school or college.

When you start a new topic, the 'Getting Started' sections are to help you map out the topic and the learning goals that you should aim for. Be clear about these objectives: you will concentrate much more when you know where you are going and what your endpoints are. You can then use this book as a starter to map out precisely what you need to know. The text has been written after carefully researching what is in the common syllabuses, and more importantly, what is regularly tested in A Level exams. The temptation to go down interesting side-streets or diversions has been largely avoided. Once you have established a good 'overview' of the topic area, you should go on to your text-book which will provide further detail and the necessary background reading needed at A Level.

You need to try to keep an accurate, organised, and systematic set of notes, expressed in your own words and intelligible to you when you come to revise for the exam. But make sure they are *notes*: you already have a text-book and there is no point trying to rewrite it. The use of a highlighting pencil with your notes or with this book is a recommended idea. If possible, use specialist books for background reading. If you find a paragraph particularly relevant or which puts into words an idea you have had difficulty with, then copy it out (or paraphrase it) and keep it at an appropriate place in your notes. It will refresh your memory later when time is short.

One of the best ways of being active in your approach to learning Physics is to *try problems*. Start by doing exercises on the simpler and more straightforward applications of the theory. We recommend starting with shorter questions or parts of longer questions which have been broken down into structured sub-questions. We also recommend starting on the mathematical parts of a question first, identifying any formulae you will need to use, and sorting out the steps necessary to pursue the calculation to its endpoint. Then move on to the non-mathematical parts of the question. You will find lots of practice questions at the end of each chapter in this book.

When you get to the end of a topic, go back to the text of this book and make sure that there are no parts missing that you should understand. At this stage it would be useful to engage in another exercise which will help you to be active in your learning. This is to draw out a *map* of the topic to show how its various parts are connected. A map such as the one in Fig. 2.2 shows the principle of identifying the important areas and the links between them. As you make progress in Physics, you will find that the subject is like a spider's web, with each part somehow connected to something else in an apparently different area. Paradoxically, rather than getting more difficult, this makes the subject easier as you make progress through it.

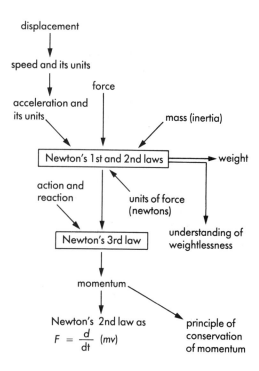

Fig. 2.2 Topic map for motion

REVISION FOR THE EXAMINATION

The second purpose of this book is to help you in your *revision* as the examination approaches. We presume you will have access to a number of recent past papers from your Board. As the exam approaches make sure you will be undisturbed and try to work on some questions from these, giving yourself the same time that you will have in the exam.

ANSWERING A STRUCTURED QUESTION PAPER

Most Boards set a long paper with a number of extended *structured* questions, not all of which need to be answered. In the examination you will need to scan the paper quickly and to select those questions which you think you can answer fairly painlessly. These will not necessarily be the questions which are only one or two sentences long. Questions which appear long are sometimes much easier to answer than those which can be read quickly, mainly because the longer questions help you through the exercise and give you more information.

Make sure you have read the question fully and understand all the parts of it. Read right through to the end of a question before deciding to try it. An easy first part may conceal a sting in the tail which may well carry a high proportion of the marks.

In essay type questions, allow yourself a little time to *plan* your response in order that your answer might have fluency and cohesion.

Once you are clear about what you are going to do and how you will answer a question, then start work on it. The following list is useful for checking whether you have omitted any important features.

1 If you have drawn a *diagram*, make sure it contains everything that is necessary and relevant. Diagrams should be drawn when specifically asked for, or when you feel that a diagram would be more appropriate and easier than providing a lengthy description. Make sure it is of a reasonable size. Check that the labelling is complete and that key distances are clearly and unambiguously labelled.

2 *Definitions* should be precise and complete. Do not leave out any constraints or special conditions which should be mentioned.

3 Ensure that any *theory* is relevant and that any *conclusions* that you draw follow logically from your argument. Be concise and try to use each sentence to make a relevant point, avoiding both waffle and repetition.

4 In *calculations* make sure you include sufficient working and explanation to show the steps in your answer. If you make a calculator error and there is no *evidence* as to what you have attempted to do, then the available marks cannot be awarded. When you have reached your final numerical answer, check:
   a) that you have quoted a sensible number of significant figures (2, 3 or 4 at the most would be normal at A Level);
   b) that you have included the appropriate units and have used scientific notation with correct powers of ten;
   c) that your answer is sensible and is clearly not absurd by referring back to the question and seeing if your answer is approximately near to what you would expect.

5 *Graphs* are used increasingly at A Level. If you are asked to draw a detailed graph, make sure that your axes are clearly labelled and that the units and powers of ten are shown. Choose a convenient scale, plot the points carefully, and draw a 'best-fit' smooth line. Show clearly how any readings, extrapolations, intercepts, or gradients are taken from the graph. When taking readings, remember to include units. Remember that the area under a graph is significant and that its units are the product of those on the axes. (See, as an example, Chapter 18, page 216.)

6 If you are asked for, or decide yourself to include *sketch graphs*, then make sure the axes are clearly labelled.

MULTIPLE CHOICE TESTS

The most common form of *multiple choice* question is one which consists of a short statement which is to be completed by selecting one of five responses. Only one of the responses is correct and the others are called distractors. These are designed to trap candidates by making commonly occurring errors. But there are other types such as the *multiple completion* type. Here you have first to decide whether each of (usually) three statements is correct and then choose an answer which corresponds to the correct *combination* of these statements.

Normally about fifty questions need to be completed in an hour. Multiple choice questions are very good for doing revision as you can quickly find out whether you have understood the topic. Remember you can learn as much from your mistakes as from your correct responses. This book contains a number of selected questions from a variety of Boards, together with some comments which will help you if you run into difficulties.

COMPREHENSION QUESTIONS

It is quite common for a *comprehension* or *passage analysis* test to be set, the aim being to find out about your communication skills and the way you can apply the concepts you have learned in your course. A passage, sometimes edited from a scientific text, might be presented. As well as having to show whether you know enough Physics to follow the author's ideas, you may be asked some questions about the consequences of the idea, or you may have to suggest alternative methods or strategies to those in the passage.

Read through the text at a reasonably normal reading speed in order to get an *overview* of what it is about. Then work through the questions in order. Where necessary, refer back to the passage for greater comprehension. Try to avoid quoting the passage back to the examiners by putting the answer into your own words. With each question you may find it useful to jot down on rough paper any formulae which may seem applicable. As with the long questions, aim for clear and concise answer which use your knowledge of Physics. Don't be tempted to write long rambling sentences.

It is common to find that as you get toward the end of the test your understanding increases to a point where you notice mistakes in the answers you had written first. You can then go back and correct these.

PRACTICAL TESTS AND DATA ANALYSIS QUESTIONS

Unless your experimental work is examined by a form of continuous assessment, it is likely that part of your examination will be a *practical test*. The types of test used by A Level boards vary considerably. Some Boards set a *data analysis* question where candidates are provided with some data from an experiment already carried out which they must analyse. Both these kinds of test are considered in detail in Chapter 21.

AT THE EXAMINATION

When you come to the examination itself you will need to employ all the question answering techniques you have been developing. In addition you will need to give close attention to *timing*. On a multiple choice paper, for example, you should remember that only one mark is allocated to each question. Don't therefore spend too much time on any one question. The questions do not necessarily get more difficult and so you should not allow yourself to get stuck on any single question. With the harder questions it is useful to make brief notes on rough paper of your thoughts and decisions. Then, when you come to check over your answers at the end, you won't have to rethink the question from scratch.

With other kinds of paper you should note the number of questions that you are expected to do and compare this with the total time for the examination. It is very useful to have worked out an approximate time allocation for each question, with some allowance for checking at the end. Remember that you should be scoring marks at a regular rate throughout the examination. The examiner will have a mark scheme that allows marks to be allocated to you for specific points as you make them: remember this and let it caution you against working too slowly on parts of the paper with which you find difficulty.

Lastly, remember that examiners are human beings. Increasingly they are trying hard to construct tests which enable you to demonstrate what you know and what you can do, rather than to trap you into showing where you are at your weakest. So think positively and do your best!

GETTING STARTED

Mechanics has been described as a well-developed yet changing subject, constantly being reconstructed to explain *movement* in the extremes of nature, from the composition of the nucleus to the structures of stars and galaxies. All other branches of Physics incorporate some mechanics. The kind of modelling and mathematical manipulation used in mechanics is regarded as the working method for the whole subject — put another way, the kinds of *process* skills you learn in mechanics are then applied everywhere else in Physics. That is why it's important to start here.

The basic ideas of mechanics are introduced in GCSE, but in some GCSE courses the use of mathematics, and in particular the use of *algebra*, may be very limited. In more advanced Physics, the application of algebra is a most important skill, which makes it another reason for starting with mechanics.

The very basic idea used in mechanics is that of **force**. Indeed mechanics is that part of Physics concerned with the action of forces on a system of particles. The particles may be able to move freely, as in a gas or a liquid, or they may be bound together in a rigid body. When the forces are not in equilibrium there is accelerated motion and the subject is called **dynamics**. This branch of mechanics is studied in Chapter 4. If they are in equilibrium then no motion ensues and the subject is called **statics**.

You should begin by looking back at your course notes for GCSE, or Chapter 3 of the Longman *GCSE Physics Revise Guide* (Forces and Structures). The topics in statics that find their way into A Level Physics are rather a series of 'bits and pieces' selected because of the need to meet the requirements of the common-core. Unlike other sections of the syllabus you may therefore find the topic rather 'bitty'. Don't worry about that.

ESSENTIAL PRINCIPLES

SCALARS AND VECTORS

A scalar quantity has *magnitude only* and is completely described by a certain number of appropriate units. Examples are mass (e.g. $m = 26.0$ kg) or temperature (e.g. $\theta = 292$ K). *Force* is an example of a vector quantity, and needs the specification of magnitude *and* direction.

ADDING VECTORS

> In GCSE exams scale drawings suffice for adding vectors, but at A Level you may wish to use geometry.

Vectors don't add arithmetically, but by the parallelogram rule (Fig. 3.1). The **parallelogram rule** states that if two vectors acting at a point are represented in magnitude and direction by the sides of a triangle, their **resultant** (R) is represented by the diagonal of the parallelogram drawn from the point.

In the special case of two vectors at right angles to each other you can either use a scale drawing or solve the problem by geometry (Fig. 3.2).

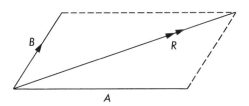

Fig. 3.1 Finding the resultant, using the parallelogram rule

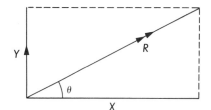

Fig. 3.2 Finding the resultant of two vectors at right angles

Using Pythagoras' theorem:
$$R = \sqrt{Y^2 + X^2}$$
and $\tan\theta = Y/X$

RESOLVING VECTORS

This is an 'opposite' procedure (Fig. 3.3). A *single* vector is regarded as the *resultant* of two vectors, usually at right angles. The two vectors are called **components**. In many problems it is much easier to work in terms of the single vector broken down into these two components.

$$X = R\cos\theta$$
$$Y = R\sin\theta$$

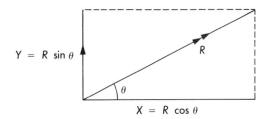

Fig. 3.3 Resolving vectors into two components at right angles

TYPES OF FORCES IN SITUATIONS WHERE THERE IS STATIC EQUILIBRIUM

FORCES AND EQUILIBRIUM

A simple example would be that of a book resting on a table. The usual types of forces at A Level are:

i) **Weight** (W) – always considered to act at the centre of mass (centre of gravity).
ii) **Normal reaction forces** (N) – these result from the solidity of an object when another is pushing into it. They act at 'right angles' to the surface. (This is what is meant by the adjective 'normal'.)

iii) **Friction** (F) – these act between surface when they move or try to move relative to each other. Friction acts parallel to a surface and is proportional to the weight or normal force.

iv) **Tension** (T) (or Compression) – these are forces acting along the direction of a strut or a pillar.

EQUILIBRIUM WITH SEVERAL NON-PARALLEL FORCES

An object is said to be in **equilibrium** if it remains at rest even though it is acted on by several forces.

The two forces in Fig. 3.4 added by the parallelogram rule produce R. The body would be in equilibrium if a third force equal to R, but in the *opposite direction* was also acting (Fig. 3.5). A diagram with the 3 forces acting at a point is called a **space diagram**. If the diagram is re-drawn so that the 'head' of each arrow lies on the 'tail' of the next then a closed triangle is formed (Fig. 3.6). With more than three forces a closed polygon results (Fig. 3.7). An example of three forces in equilibrium is the method of supporting the conducting cable on overhead-wire electrified railways (Fig. 3.8).

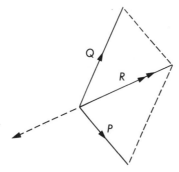

Fig. 3.4 Equilibrium situation

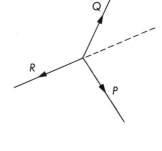

Fig. 3.5 Space diagram of body in equilibrium

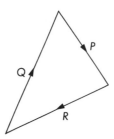

Fig. 3.6 Closed triangle of forces

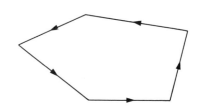

Fig. 3.7 Closed polygon of forces

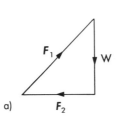

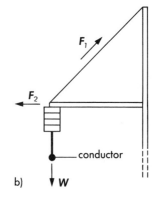

Fig. 3.8

EQUILIBRIUM WITH SEVERAL PARALLEL FORCES

A see-saw is in equilibrium when acted on by a set of parallel forces (Fig. 3.9). Each force on its own produces a **torque** or moment about a fixed axis. The **moment** is defined as the force × perpendicular distance from the line of the force to the axis.

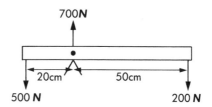

Note that the unit of torque is newton metres (Nm) rather than joules, as the force is perpendicular to the distance and no work is done (see Chapter 4). For equilibrium to be achieved in this situation, the sum of the clockwise moments about *any point* on the body must be equal to the sum of the anticlockwise moments. This is the **principle of moments**. (Note that in the see-saw example, any point could be used for the analysis, not just the pivot. If a point *other than the pivot* is chosen, then the upward normal reaction force of 700 N has to be included.)

CENTRE OF GRAVITY (CENTRE OF MASS)

The weight of an object behaves *as if* the object was a point mass with the weight acting at that point. For an object with a distributed mass, the **centre of gravity** (or centre of mass) is the point at which, for the purpose of calculations, all the mass of the body can be considered to act. This is the point which is used in moment calculations. For example, a man standing on the plank produces an anticlockwise moment at the pivot which is counteracted by the moment Wx of the plank if W, the weight of the plank, acts through the centre of gravity (Fig. 3.10).

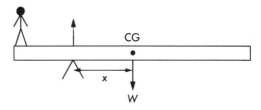

Fig. 3.10

TACKLING EQUILIBRIUM PROBLEMS

In dealing with equilibrium problems, it is best to adopt the following procedures:

i) Start with a sketch diagram showing all the forces acting on a body.
ii) *Resolve* the forces into two components in two mutually perpendicular directions chosen at your convenience (e.g. along a slope and normal to it).
iii) Then apply the rule that the *nett* (resultant) force in any particular direction is zero. At this stage if you find an unbalanced force then either you have missed out one or more forces at step i), or else you don't have equilibrium.
iv) Apply the principle of moments through the most convenient axis.

NON-EQUILIBRIUM SITUATIONS

When step iii) above yields a truly unbalanced force, then the body will accelerate in a straight line in the direction of that force. If on the other hand step iv) suggests an unbalanced moment, the body will undergo rotational acceleration in the same rotational sense, i.e. clockwise or anticlockwise, as the moment (see Chapter 5).

COUPLE

This is defined as two equal and opposite parallel forces whose lines of action do not coincide. The moment of a **couple** is always the same about any fixed point and is always equal to the product of one of the forces and the distance between them. Note that if, in

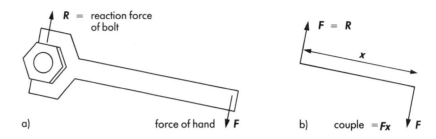

Fig. 3.11 Example of a couple: turning a nut on to a bolt

a) force of hand ▼ F

b) couple = **Fx** ▼ F

Fig. 3.11, the nut is tight on the bolt due to friction, then the couple will be opposed by the frictional forces (see Chapter 5).

PRESSURE IN FLUIDS

Pressure is Force ÷ Area. The application of this principle to a right circular cylinder (Fig. 3.12) leads to the **manometer formula**. If this cylinder is filled with a liquid of density ρ, and A is the area of the cylinder, we get

$$\text{mass} = \text{volume} \times \text{density}$$
$$= Ah \times \rho$$
$$\text{weight} = Ah\rho g \text{ where } g \text{ is } 9.8 \text{ Nkg}^{-1}, \text{ so}$$
$$\text{Pressure } (p) = \frac{Ah\rho g}{A} = h\rho g$$

Empirically it is found that:

i) $p = h\rho g$ applies for all geometries (Fig. 3.13), not just a right circular cylinder.
ii) the pressure acts equally in all directions (Fig. 3.14).
iii) the same results hold for gases.
Note that because of iii) the term 'fluids' is used which means both liquids and gases.

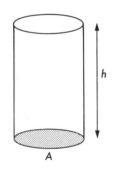

Fig. 3.12 Right circular cylinder

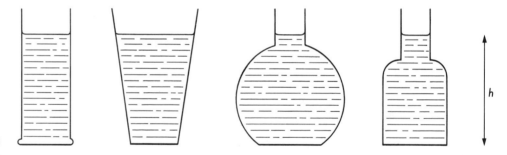

Fig. 3.13 Containers of various geometries

The **Manometer** is an instrument comprising a U-tube, a liquid, and a rubber bung leading to a gas supply. It is used to measure gas pressure (Fig. 3.15). Since the gas pressure is greater than atmospheric pressure, the liquid is forced upwards.
Then gas pressure $p = h\rho g + p_A$ where p_A is the atmospheric pressure.

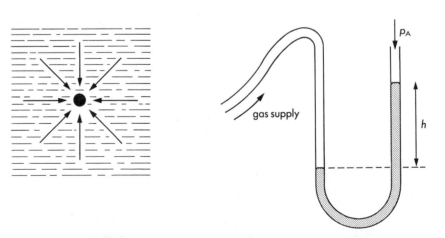

Fig. 3.14 Pressure acts equally in all directions

Fig. 3.15 Manometer used to measure gas pressure

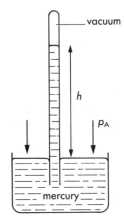

Fig. 3.16 Barometer

In a *barometer* (Fig. 3.16) the same formula is used. It is common in this case to use a very dense liquid, e.g. mercury. Here, $p_A = h\rho g$ + pressure of a vacuum, i.e.

$$p_A = h\rho g + 0 = h\rho g.$$

Pressure is properly measured in *pascals* (Pa), where $1 \text{ Pa} = 1 \text{ N m}^{-2}$. It is common for pressure to be expressed in liquid column equivalents, e.g. 760 mm of mercury, but they can always be converted to pascals using $p = h\rho g$.

PRESSURE AND UPTHRUST IN A LIQUID

An object immersed in a fluid experiences a nett force which tends to push it upwards and, if possible, out of the fluid (Fig. 3.17). This resultant force arises from the fact that the pressure in a fluid increases with depth. The resultant force is called the **upthrust**. **Archimedes' principle** states that the upthrust is equal to the weight of liquid displaced. The object may, of course, be only partially immersed in the liquid.

In Fig. 3.18 the drum floating in a liquid of density ρ displaces a volume of liquid Ad and hence a mass of $Ad\rho$ and a weight of $Ad\rho g$. For a *floating* object the weight of the object equals the weight of liquid displaced. This is called **buoyancy**.

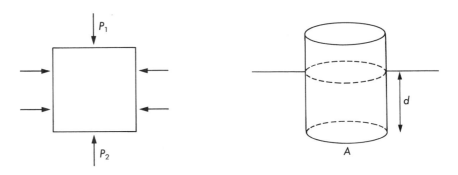

Fig. 3.17 Fully immersed object   Fig. 3.18 Partially immersed object

EXAMINATION QUESTIONS

MULTIPLE CHOICE QUESTIONS

1   Each of the diagrams below represents the forces acting in a vertical plane on a body X (which is considered to be a point). No external forces are omitted and all are, by convention, drawn as arrows acting away from the body along the lines of action of the forces.

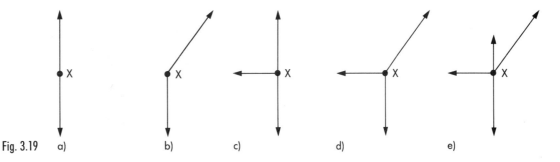

Fig. 3.19   a)   b)   c)   d)   e)

Which diagram best illustrates the forces acting on:

a)   a sledge, pulled at a steady speed over rough horizontal ground by a rope held over the puller's shoulder;

b)   a pendulum bob, at one extreme of its oscillation;

c)   a charged sphere, supported on a nylon thread, in equilibrium alongside a second similarly charged sphere;

d)   a mass rotating at constant speed in a horizontal circle, and supported by a rope?

(London 1987)

2 A rigid body acted upon by a set of forces is in equilibrium if:

  a) the resultant force acts through the centre of mass;
  b) each force acts through the centre of mass;
  c) the resultant force is zero;
  d) the resultant couple is zero;
  e) both the resultant force and the resultant couple are zero.

(Oxford 1986)

3 The uniform rod shown below is supported on two knife-edges, X and Y, at P and S. The distances PQ, QR, RS, and ST are equal. What is the consequence of sliding the knife-edge X from P to Q?

Fig. 3.20

  a) The upward force on the rod due to X increases.
  b) The upward force on the rod due to X decreases.
  c) There is a change in the total upward force on the rod due to X and Y.
  d) The rod starts to rotate anticlockwise.
  e) The rod starts to rotate clockwise.

4 Fig. 3.21 below shows a load of mass M supported by a wire PR and by a light bar QR pivoted at Q. The arrangement can be changed in the ways listed below, but in each case so that the bar QR remains horizontal.

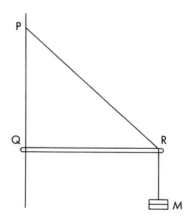

Fig. 3.21

  1 Increase the length of the bar and the wire, keeping P and Q at their original positions, with the mass at the end of the rod.
  2 Increase the length of the wire and move P upwards, keeping the length of the bar constant.
  3 Increase M, the other dimensions being held constant.

  Which of the above changes will cause an increase in the tension in the wire PR.

  a) 3 only   d) 2 and 3 only
  b) 1 and 2 only   e) 1, 2 and 3
  c) 1 and 3 only

(NI 1988)

5 In the J tube shown in Fig. 3.22 both ends are sealed and the liquid density is ρ kg m^{-3}. The thick arm has twice the cross-sectional area of the thin arm.

  Pressure P_1 is given by:

  a) $P_2 + \dfrac{\rho g y}{2}$

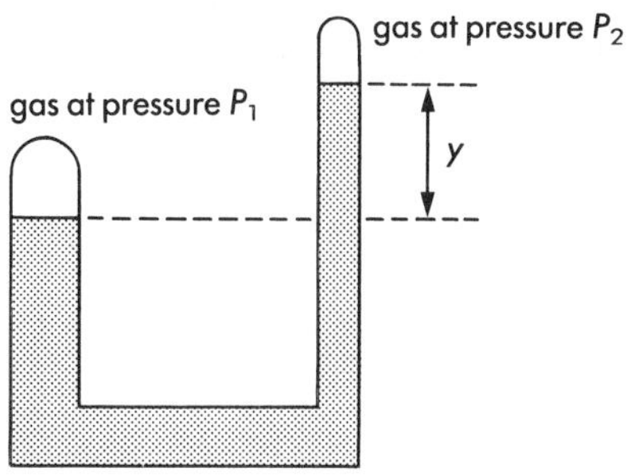

gas at pressure P_2

gas at pressure P_1

y

b) $P_2 + \rho g y$
c) $P_2 - \rho g y$
d) $P_2 + 2\rho g y$
e) $P_2 - 2\rho g y$

Fig. 3.22

(Scottish Paper Specimen 1986)

ANSWERS AND COMMENTS

QUESTION	1a)	1b)	1c)	1d)	2	3	4	5
Answer	e)	b)	d)	b)	e)	a)	c)	b)

1   This is fairly straightforward. Remember that when the forces are in equilibrium they must produce a zero resultant (e.g. 1a) and 1c)) but when accelerating, the forces must produce an unbalanced force in the direction of acceleration (1b) and 1d)). Question 1a) is the hardest. Don't be distracted by answer d) which ignores the ground's normal reaction.

2   Remember to look for conditions for both *rotational* and translational equilibrium.

3   The weight acts about the centre, so taking moments about the centre gives $2F_x = F_y$ or $F_x = F_y/2$. With X moved to Q we get $F_x = F_y$. Hence moving the position increases the forces.

4   If T is the tension in the wire, then $T \cos \theta$ represents the only upward force opposing the weight Mg, θ being the angle of the wire to the vertical. Hence if θ gets larger $\cos \theta$ gets smaller and so T, itself, is increased. This is what happens in case 1). In case 2) the opposite occurs. θ gets smaller and so T is decreased.

5   The difference in the thickness of the arms has no effect on the pressure. So the pressure at the level of the bottom hatched line is the same on both arms. At the bottom of the right one it is the pressure exerted by the gas above plus $\rho g y$.

STRUCTURED QUESTIONS

6   a)   i) Explain what is meant by the *moment* of a force.
         ii) State the conditions under which a body will be in equilibrium when acted upon by a set of coplanar forces.

   b) Describe an experiment which makes use of standard masses, cords and pulleys to demonstrate the condition for the equilibrium of **three** non-parallel, coplanar forces which act at a point. Explain how the readings obtained would be used to demonstrate the condition. Indicate any precautions which should be taken to ensure that the experiment is as accurate as possible, giving a reason for each precaution you suggest.

   c) A lever in a weighing machine is made from a uniform metal rod LM of mass 1.0 kg which is 0.40 m long. It is freely pivoted from a fixed bearing at L. The end M is suspended by a light spring. The other end of the spring is supported at X. A force of 2.5 N is required to extend the spring by 0.010 m. When the lever is in equilibrium it makes an angle of 30° with the horizontal, the angle between the lever and the spring being 90°.

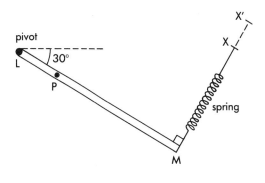

Fig. 3.23

   i) Calculate the tension in the spring and its extension when the system is arranged in this way.

ii) An additional force of 30 N is then applied vertically downwards on the lever at point P, 0.10 m from L. In order to return the reading of the weighing machine to zero, the supported end X of the spring is then moved to X', so that the lever is in its original position with the angle between the lever and the spring again 90°. Calculate the distance XX' through which the end of the spring is moved, assuming it continues to obey Hooke's law.

(JMB 1988)

7   A steel ball falls vertically into a flask filled with thick oil. The ball hits the oil surface at speed and slows down almost to a halt after falling 10 cm within the oil.

Show on a free-body diagram the three principal forces which act on the steel ball when it is about 5 cm below the oil surface. Explain the origin of each of these forces.

(London 1987)

OUTLINE ANSWERS AND COMMENTS

6   a) i) and ii) are considered in the text and as a 'Student's Answer' (p. 24). The experimental arrangement required for b) is shown in Fig. 3.24. The pulley wheels are lightly oiled and equilibrium is carefully found. Typical masses might be 300 g and 400 g for the left and right masses respectively and 500 g for the centre one. The directions of the cords transmitting the forces away from O are recorded on the sheet of paper behind. It is useful to use a small mirror held flat against the paper and to mark points on the paper when a cord is seen in line with its image (the no-parallax method). The parallelogram rule is then employed with two of the forces. The resultant should be equal and opposite to the third force.

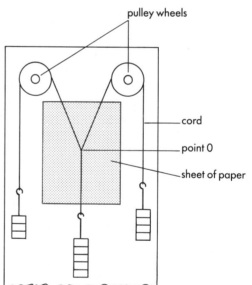

Fig. 3.24

In c)

i) begin by drawing the force diagram. An unknown force acts through L and so moments should be taken about this point. Let T be the tension in the spring.

$10 \times 0.2\cos30° = 0.4\ T$

hence $T = 4.33$N and the extension $= 0.0173$m.

ii) $T = 10.83$N giving XX' $= 0.025$m.

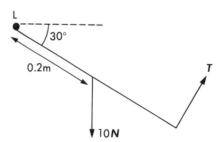

Fig. 3.25

7 At A Level, a 'free-body diagram' is one in which the body can be treated as a point, and where only the forces acting on it are included (i.e. forces on neighbouring or interacting objects are excluded). A diagram for question 7 should therefore show:
  i) the frictional (viscous) upward force
  ii) the weight acting downwards
  iii) the upward buoyancy force.

TUTOR'S QUESTION AND ANSWER

QUESTION

8 In Fig. 3.26 AB represents the raised bonnet of a car, hinged freely at A. The bonnet is of mass 12 kg and its weight acts through the point G.

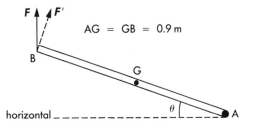

Fig. 3.26

  a) Calculate the value of the vertical force F that will just maintain the position of the bonnet.
  b) Instead of applying a vertical force to raise the bonnet, a force F' is applied perpendicular to the surface of the bonnet.
    i) Calculate F' for $\theta = 24°$.
    ii) Hence explain why it is easier to raise the bonnet by applying a force in the direction of F' than by applying a force in the direction of F.

(London 1988)

ANSWER

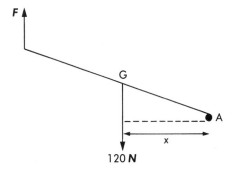

Fig. 3.27

8 To answer part a), draw the force diagram as shown in Fig. 3.27. The diagram omits an unknown force at A. So taking moments about A, with x the horizontal distance shown, we have:

$2xF = 120x$

(The unknown force contributes no moment about A.)

$F = 60N.$

For part b), with $\theta = 24°$, then $x = 0.9 \cos 24° = 0.822$. Again taking moments about A:

$F' \times 1.8 = 120 \times 0.822$

giving $F' = 54.8N$

In ii), it is easier to raise the bonnet by applying a force in the direction of F' than by applying a force in the direction of F, because then the distance of the line of action of the force from A is increased and so, as the product of this and the force is constant, so the force is decreased.

STUDENT'S ANSWER WITH EXAMINER COMMENTS

STUDENT'S ANSWER TO QUESTION 6a) AND b)

6a) i) The moment of a force is the product of the force times the distance from the point.

ii) The conditions for equilibrium are that the sum of anticlockwise moments must equal the sum of clockwise moments, about any point.

b) The experiment uses three pieces of string all tied at a point and with each other end attached to a standard weight. Two of the strings are passed over pulley wheels attached to a wooden board. The system is allowed to come to equilibrium. The lines of action are copied on to a piece of paper behind the strings.

A parallelogram of forces is then drawn using two of the forces. The resultant should be equal to the third force.

> Weak on explanation. Needs to explain 'point' and refer it to a sketch diagram. The distance should be referred to as the perpendicular distance.

> Weak on explanation. What masses are to be used? A diagram would be much better.

> Equal in magnitude but opposite in direction.

> No precautions mentioned.

> More explanation is needed, e.g. sides drawn in direction of forces and of length proportional to magnitude.

Overall Comment: This piece of work suggests that the candidate probably knows the Physics but he/she has not been exact enough in the account. Typical of a grade C or D piece of work.

DYNAMICS AND ENERGY

GETTING STARTED

When the forces acting on a body are *not* in equilibrium, acceleration results and the subject is called **dynamics**. A study of dynamics has to be preceded by a good working knowledge of **kinematics**. You should therefore begin by understanding terms like **displacement**, **velocity** and **acceleration** and their formulae. You should be able to use these terms and to handle the algebra, even if these were topics which lacked emphasis in your GCSE course. Newton's laws link force and motion and lead to the important principle of the **conservation of linear momentum**, one of the most important of a number of conservation laws in physics.

Dynamics is also a useful starting point for the quantitative study of **energy**, **work** and **power**. You will probably have studied these ideas in a wide and general way at GCSE level. Here it will be necessary to begin a firm quantitative treatment. The understanding you have of energy is then used throughout the rest of A Level physics.

It cannot be emphasised how important a thorough understanding of mechanics is. You will not be able to make much progress in other topics such as waves and oscillations, until you understand mechanics.

ESSENTIAL PRINCIPLES

KINEMATICS

Kinematics is just a Greek word meaning the science or study of motion. Before starting it is important to distinguish between the scalar and vector terms used in the subject:

SCALAR TERMS	VECTOR TERMS
distance travelled	displacement
speed	velocity
	acceleration

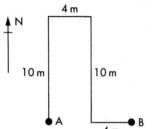

Fig. 4.1

Displacement is the distance 'as the crow flies' from some starting point to the finishing point, with the direction also specified. Consider a shopper in a supermarket going from A to B (Fig. 4.1). The **distance travelled** is *28m* but the **displacement** is *8m east of A*. Similarly consider a child on a roundabout (Fig. 4.2). Here, her **speed** may be constant at, say, 4 ms^{-1}. But **velocity** is speed in a particular direction and the velocity is constantly changing because the child's direction of motion is changing. At one instant her velocity is 4 ms^{-1} due east. Half a revolution later it is 4 ms^{-1} due west.

To summarise:

- *Displacement* is distance measured in a particular direction
- *Velocity* is the rate of change of displacement
- *Acceleration* is the rate of change of velocity.

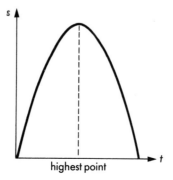

Fig. 4.2

UNIFORM ACCELERATION IN A STRAIGHT LINE

This is an important case, the most common of which is the uniform acceleration of a body under gravity. If the velocity of a body increases from an initial value u to a final value v, with a constant acceleration a, in a time t, then

$$a = \frac{v - u}{t}, \text{ giving}$$
$$v = u + at.$$

If the displacement is s, then the following equations can be derived:

- $s = \frac{1}{2}(u + v)t$
- $s = ut + \frac{1}{2}at^2$, and
- $v^2 = u^2 + 2as$

Take care with units when using these equations. Units are: s (m); v (ms^{-1}); a (ms^{-2}); and t (s).

Questions will often be set using s,t and v,t graphs. The only problem which generally occurs is in the sign convention used. In Physics, **vector** quantities are often treated by taking their magnitudes as positive and describing the direction by quoting an angle with respect to a fixed direction e.g. north. However in one dimensional motion there are only two possible directions, forwards and backwards, and the obvious way to indicate directions is by signs. The graphs (Figs 4.3 and 4.4) show displacement and velocity for a

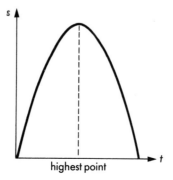

Fig. 4.3 Graph of displacement against time

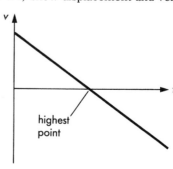

Fig. 4.4 Graph of velocity against time

stone thrown in the air. Here, upward is taken as positive and so when v goes negative it implies the stone is moving downwards. With this sign convention, the acceleration a is constant at -9.8 ms^{-2}.

AVERAGE AND INSTANTANEOUS VELOCITY AND ACCELERATION

The formulae used for calculating average and instantaneous velocity are:

- **Average velocity** $= \dfrac{\text{final displacement } - \text{ initial displacement}}{\text{total time}}$

- **Instantaneous velocity** $= v = \dfrac{\Delta s}{\Delta t}$,

  where Δs is the small change in displacement which occurs in a small instant of time Δt. More strictly, using the notation of calculus, we have:

  $$v = \lim_{\Delta t \to 0} \left(\frac{\Delta s}{\Delta t} \right) = \frac{ds}{dt}$$

  Graphically, ds/dt is the slope of an s, t graph at a particular instant in time. Acceleration is defined using similar equations:

- **Average acceleration** $= \dfrac{\text{change in velocity}}{\text{time taken for the change}}$

- **Instantaneous acceleration** $= \lim_{\Delta t \to 0} \left(\dfrac{\Delta v}{\Delta t} \right) = \dfrac{dv}{dt}$

Graphically, $\dfrac{dv}{dt}$ is the slope of a v, t graph at a particular instant in time.

MOMENTUM

NEWTON'S LAWS OF MOTION

Newton's laws use the concept of momentum.

Momentum, p, is defined as mass $\times$ velocity i.e. $p = m \times v$.

As mass is a scalar quantity and velocity a vector quantity, momentum is a vector with units of kg m s^{-1} or, from Newton's 2nd law (see below), Ns.

Newton's laws of motion are:

1 The basic kind of motion is uniform motion in a straight line and a body has this motion unless a resultant force acts on it.

2 If a resultant force acts on a body, the momentum of the body changes and its rate of change of momentum is equal to the resultant force and in the direction of that force.

3 Forces between bodies act in pairs, i.e. when one exerts a force (attractive or repulsive) on a second body, the second exerts an equal and opposite force on the first (e.g. the earth attracts me, but I attract the earth with an equal and opposite force).

> The usual textbook definitions are direct translations from Latin, and obscure the physics, particularly the translation of the third law.

Using the definition of momentum and in the notation of calculus, the second law gives us the equation:

$$F = \frac{d\,(mv)}{dt} .$$

Normally the mass is constant, and so:

$$F = m\,\frac{dv}{dt} \text{ or } F = ma$$

which is the usual form of Newton's 2nd law encountered in GCSE science.

The **Impulse**, I, of a force is defined as the force multiplied by its time of action. So when a force acts for a short time Δt, we get:

$$I = \bar{F}\Delta t = \Delta p$$

where $\bar{F}$ is the average force acting over the time interval Δt, and Δp is the momentum

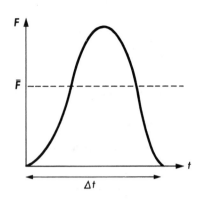

Fig. 4.5 Force-time graph

change it produces. Hence, when a golf club strikes a golf ball, the manner in which the force on the ball varies with time is shown by the F,t graph (Fig. 4.5).

The impulse I = the area under the graph, and the average force $\bar{F}$ acting is such that:

$\bar{F}\Delta t$ = area under the graph
     = change in momentum of the golf ball.

Note from the force-time graph that the same change in momentum can either result from a large force acting for a very short time or a much smaller force acting for a much longer time (Fig. 4.6).

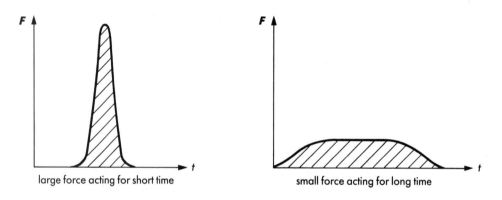

Fig. 4.6   large force acting for short time   small force acting for long time

PRINCIPLE OF THE CONSERVATION OF LINEAR MOMENTUM

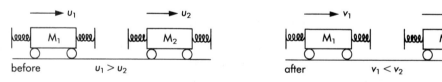

Fig. 4.7 Momentum conservation with colliding trucks

before $u_1 > u_2$ after $v_1 < v_2$

Consider two colliding trucks (Fig. 4.7). If the impact time is Δt, then:

- average force due to truck M_1 on truck M_2 = $\dfrac{\Delta p_2}{\Delta t} = m_2 \dfrac{(v_2 - u_2)}{\Delta t}$

- average force due to truck M_2 on truck M_1 = $\dfrac{\Delta p_1}{\Delta t} = m_1 \dfrac{(v_1 - u_1)}{\Delta t}$

By Newton's third law, these forces are equal but opposite, so:

$\Delta p_1 = -\Delta p_2$

giving $m_1 u_1 + m_2 u_2 = m_1 v_1 + m_2 v_2$

i.e. the total momentum remains unchanged. Note that:

1   The principle applies only if the two trucks interact only with each other, i.e. *providing no external force* component acts along the direction of motion.
2   Momentum is a vector quantity. For one dimensional problems the final value of a calculation will be + or − according to the sign convention you have adopted.

> **In examination, candidates often forget to mention the need for external forces to be zero.**

The principle of the conservation of momentum applies to *all* collisions, *elastic* and *inelastic* (see the energy section, page 30 below).

WEIGHT AND INERTIA

Newton's second law allows an understanding to be given to **weight**. The weight W of a body is the force of gravity acting on it and acts towards the centre of the earth. As such it is a force and is not to be confused with mass, which is independent of the presence or absence of the earth. The mass of a body is a measure of its reluctance to change its motion when a force acts, and is sometimes called its **inertia**. Imagine a body falling under gravity.

$$a = g$$
and $F = W$, its weight. Therefore
$$F = ma \text{ gives } W = mg.$$

For a second body, $W' = m'g'$. Dividing these two results we get $W'/W = m'/m$, showing that the weight of a body is proportional to its mass.

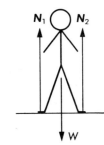

Fig. 4.8

FREE FALL

Note that we don't actually 'feel' the force of gravity, but instead the normal (reaction) forces which occur. Hence a man standing on the ground experiences normal (reaction) forces N_1 and N_2 at his feet (Fig. 4.8). By Newton's first law:

$$N_1 + N_2 = W$$

as he does not move. If the ground were not there he would accelerate downwards with acceleration g. His experience would be the 'weightless' experience of free fall. He would still have weight but would have lost the forces N_1 and N_2 which were what he *felt*.

PROJECTILE MOTION

Projectile motion is handled by treating the horizontal (x) motion separately from the vertical (y) motion. Assuming negligible air resistance, the horizontal motion is the constant velocity motion associated with Newton's first law. The vertical motion is motion with a constant downwards gravitational acceleration, g. Suppose the projectile is launched with a velocity u at angle θ to the horizontal (Fig. 4.9).

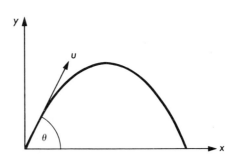

Fig. 4.9

VERTICAL MOTION	HORIZONTAL MOTION
Initial velocity $= u \sin \theta$	Initial velocity $= u \cos \theta$
Acceleration $= -g$ (minus, since positive is taken as upwards)	Acceleration $= 0$
Time taken $= t$	Time taken $= t$
Displacement $= y$	Displacement $= x$
Using $s = ut + \frac{1}{2}at^2$	Using $s = ut + \frac{1}{2}at^2$
we get $y = u \sin \theta . t - \frac{1}{2}gt^2$	we get $x = u \cos \theta . t$

Eliminating t between these two equations gives the equation of the parabola shown in Fig. 4.9.

WORK, ENERGY, POWER

Energy is often defined as that which enables a 'job' to be done, a 'job' being the raising of a weight, the acceleration of a mass, etc. In the complete theory of energy and in thermodynamics, it is regarded as a *conserved quantity* following the pattern of momentum, where changes in energy are merely changes from one form to another. It is measured in terms of *potential* and *kinetic* energy.

In mechanics, **work** is the amount of energy transferred. If energy is likened to money, then work is like a cheque measuring the money transferred from one account to another. Work done, W, is defined as the component of the force in the direction of the distance moved × the distance moved. The units of work and therefore energy are joules, the joule being the work done when a force of 1 newton moves through a distance of 1 m, given by the equation $W = F \times s$.

Power is the rate of doing work. Its unit is the watt, which is a rate of doing work of 1 J s^{-1}. When a force moves forward at a constant velocity v, then:

■ Power $= F \times v$.

Potential energy, U, is the energy due to the position of a body in a gravitational field, and referred to some level chosen as zero.

■ $U = mgh$ where h is the height above the (arbitrary) zero position.

More generally it also includes other types of stored energy, e.g. energy stored in a spring, in an electric field, or in a magnetic field. All these will be dealt with later.

Kinetic Energy, T, is the energy a body has by virtue of its velocity, given by the equation:

■ $T = \frac{1}{2}mv^2$.

You need to look up a proof of this formula in your textbook.

ENERGY IN COLLISION PROBLEMS

In the collision problem referred to earlier it was emphasised that momentum conservation *always* holds, i.e.,

$$m_1u_1 + m_2u_2 = m_1v_1 + m_2v_2.$$

But the conservation of energy in its kinetic form, i.e.,

$$\tfrac{1}{2}m_1u_1^2 + \tfrac{1}{2}m_2u_2^2 = \tfrac{1}{2}m_1v_1^2 + \tfrac{1}{2}m_2v_2^2$$

only holds in the case of **elastic** collisions. These are collisions in which there is no transfer of energy from the motion of the trucks into 'internal energy', that is into the microscopic motion of the molecules of the trucks with a small accompanying temperature rise. If there is such an energy transfer, then the energy conservation equation becomes:

> " Note the terminology and don't call this heat. "

$$\tfrac{1}{2}m_1u_1^2 + \tfrac{1}{2}m_2u_2^2 = \tfrac{1}{2}m_1v_1^2 + \tfrac{1}{2}m_2v_2^2 + Q,$$

where Q is the kinetic energy converted into internal energy. Note that Q can always be found if the speeds can be measured. Such a collision is called an **inelastic** collision. In calculations it is important not to assume without good reason that Q is zero. An example of an inelastic collision is one where the two trucks lock together. In such cases $v_1 = v_2$.

EXAMINATION QUESTIONS

MULTIPLE CHOICE QUESTIONS

1   A body of mass 4 kg is accelerated from rest by a steady force of 9 N. What is its speed when it has travelled a distance of 8 m?

a) 3.6 m s^{-1} d) 118.0 m s^{-1}
b) 4.5 m s^{-1} e) 36.0 m s^{-1}
c) 6.0 m s^{-1}

(London 1985)

2 A block of mass 3 kg is held at rest on a friction-free surface inclined at 30° to the horizontal. Two seconds after the block is released, the component of the weight (F) acting down the slope, and the distance (d) travelled are

    F   d

  a) 15 N   10 m
  b) 15 N   5.0 m
  c) 26 N   2.5 m
  d) 26 N   5.0 m
  e) 30 N   5.0 m   (Scottish 1986)

3 A small smooth sphere is released from rest just below the surface of the liquid in a tall vessel of large diameter. The sphere, whose density exceeds that of the liquid, is observed until it reaches its terminal speed.
During the period of observation, its *downward* acceleration is

  a) constant and positive   d) negative
  b) positive and increasing   e) zero
  c) positive and decreasing   (London 1988)

4 A wheel nut falls straight down from a helicopter which is descending vertically at a constant speed of 5m s^{-1}. The wheel nut strikes the ground 5 s later. Assuming that the effect of air resistance on the nut is negligible, how far does the nut drop?

  a) 50 m   d) 125 m
  b) 55 m   e) 150 m
  c) 100 m   (Scottish 1986)

5

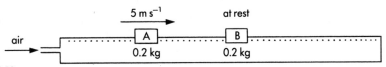

Fig. 4.10

Fig. 4.10 shows two vehicles on a linear air track. After colliding they move off separately to the right. Vehicle A moves with a speed of 2 m s^{-1} and vehicle B with a speed of 3 m s^{-1}. Which one of the following correctly describes this collision?

	Kinetic Energy	Momentum	Type of Collision
a)	Conserved	Lost	Elastic
b)	Lost	Conserved	Elastic
c)	Conserved	Conserved	Inelastic
d)	Conserved	Lost	Inelastic
e)	Lost	Conserved	Inelastic

                                   (Scottish Specimen Paper 1986)

6 A mass is projected horizontally from the top of a cliff with velocity v. Three seconds later the direction of the velocity of the mass is 45° to the horizontal. Assuming air resistance to be negligible and taking the acceleration of free fall g to be 10 m s^{-2}, the value of the projection velocity v, in m s^{-1}, is

  a) 3.3   d) 45
  b) 15   e) 90
  c) 30   (NI 1988)

7 Two masses of 5.00 kg and 10.00 kg are connected by a light inextensible string passing over a frictionless pulley, as shown in Fig. 4.11. Initially the masses are held at rest, but when they are released they move under the action of gravity. Taking the acceleration of free fall g to be 10 m s^{-2}, the tension in the string, in newtons, when the masses are in motion is

  a) 0   d) 75.0
  b) 50.0   e) 150.0
  c) 66.7   (NI 1988)

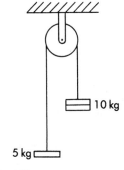

Fig. 4.11

8 An astronaut of mass m is launched from the surface of the Earth in a capsule having an initial vertical acceleration of $4g$, where g is the acceleration of free fall. The initial push of the capsule on the astronaut is

a) zero
b) mg
c) $3mg$
d) $4mg$
e) $5mg$

(London 1988)

9 Which of the following pairs contains one vector and one scalar quantity?

a) Displacement, acceleration
b) Power, speed
c) Work, potential energy
d) Force, kinetic energy
e) Momentum, velocity

(London 1988)

ANSWERS AND COMMENTS

Question	1	2	3	4	5	6	7	8	9
Answer	c)	a)	c)	e)	e)	c)	c)	e)	d)

1 This is a straightforward calculation using first $F = ma$ and then $v^2 = u^2 + 2as$.

2 You need to recognise that down the slope the force is gravity scaled down by the factor $\sin \theta$. The acceleration is similarly scaled down. Here $\sin \theta = 0.5$, and so the use of:
$$s = ut + \tfrac{1}{2}at^2, \text{ gives } d = 10 \text{ m (if } g \text{ is taken as 10 m s}^{-2}).$$

3 This is about terminal velocity.

4 Again you need the formula $s = ut + \tfrac{1}{2}at^2$. Take all downward vectors as positive. Note that unlike Question **2**, u is non-zero: it is 5 m s^{-1}.

5 If necessary this can be solved using equations for the conservation of momentum and energy. It ought however to be a familiar example which can be answered by recall.

6 If the mass falls at 45° to the vertical, then the horizontal and vertical components of velocity must be equal. The vertical component can be calculated using
$$v = u + at, \text{ with } a = 10 \text{ m s}^{-2}.$$

7 Arguably the hardest question. You need to treat each mass separately and to suppose the tension in the string to be T N and the acceleration to be a. For the 5 kg mass:
$$T - 50 = 5a.$$
For the 10 kg mass
$$100 - T = 10a.$$
Solving these two simultaneous equations gives:
$$T = \tfrac{200}{3} \text{ N} = 66\tfrac{2}{3} \text{ N}.$$

8 Apply Newton's 2nd law: $F - mg = ma$. Hence,
$$F = 5mg, \text{ and } a = 4g.$$

9 Requires recall of scalars and vectors.

STRUCTURED QUESTIONS

10 a) A linear air-track is a length of metal track along which objects (gliders) can move with negligible friction, supported on a cushion of air. A glider of mass 0.40 kg is stationary near one end of a level air-track and an air-rifle is mounted close to the glider with its barrel aligned along the track. A pellet of mass 5.0×10^{-4} kg is fired from the rifle and sticks to the glider which acquires a speed of 0.20 m s^{-1}. Calculate the speed with which the pellet struck the glider.

b) Describe an experimental arrangement you would use to verify the above result.

c) A student using an air-track fails to level it correctly. The speed of a glider along the track near its centre is 0.20 m s^{-1} and when it has moved to a further distance of 0.90 m it is 0.22 m s^{-1}. Determine the angle made by the track to the horizontal.

d) A glider reaches the end of a level air-track and rebounds from a rubber band stretched across the track. Assuming that, whilst in contact with the band, the force exerted on the glider is proportional to the displacement of the band from the point of impact, sketch a graph showing how the velocity of the glider varies with time. Explain the shape of the graph.

(JMB 1987)

11 a) State the law of conservation of energy and the law of conservation of momentum and show how the latter can be deduced from Newton's second and third laws of motion.
   b) Carefully apply the law of conservation of energy to the motion of a rubber ball bouncing up-and-down vertically on a cement floor in such a way that when the ball drops from a height h it bounces to a height of 0.8 h.
   c) The mass of the nucleus of a carbon atom is twelve times that of a neutron. Calculate the energy transfer when a 2 MeV neutron makes a perfectly elastic head-on collision with a carbon nucleus initially at rest.

(Welsh 1987)

12 A vehicle has a mass of 600 kg. Its engine exerts a tractive force of 1500 N, but motion is resisted by a constant frictional force of 300 N. Calculate:
   a) the acceleration of the vehicle;
   b) its momentum 10 s after starting to move;
   c) its kinetic energy 15 s after starting to move.

(Southern 1987)

13 The gravitational force acting on an astronaut travelling in a space vehicle in low earth orbit is only slightly less than if he were standing on earth.
   a) Explain why the force is only slightly less.
   b) Explain why, when travelling in the space vehicle, the astronaut appears to be 'weightless'.

(London 1988)

14 Two identical steel balls hang with their centres on a horizontal line (Fig. 4.12a)). Ball A is pulled to one side in a vertical plane, as shown in the diagram, and then released. It collides elastically with B.

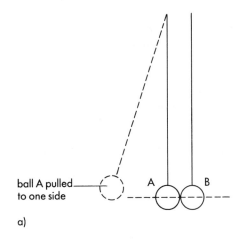
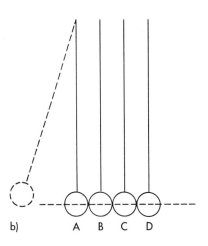

ball A pulled to one side

a)

b)   A B C D

Fig. 4.12

   a) State the law of conservation of linear momentum.
   b) Give the meaning of the term *elastic collision*.
   c) Describe the motion of the balls immediately after the collision. Apply appropriate conservation laws to the collision to justify your answer.
   d) Fig. 4.12b) shows a similar arrangement but with four identical balls, almost touching one another. Ball A is pulled to one side and then released. Describe and account briefly for the subsequent motion of the balls.

(Oxford and Cambridge 1988)

OUTLINE ANSWERS AND COMMENTS

10 a) $v = 160.2$ ms^{-1}.

b) See the Student's Answer.

c) $u = 0.20$ ms^{-1}, $v = 0.22$ ms^{-1}, $s = 0.90$ m. Using
$v^2 = u^2 + 2as$, then $a = 4.76 \times 10^{-3}$ ms^{-2}

The acceleration is $g \sin \theta$, giving:

$\sin \theta = 4.75 \times 10^{-4}$, taking g as 9.81 ms^{-2}

$\theta = 0.0273$ degrees

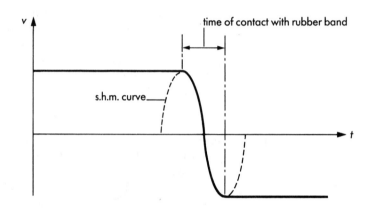

Fig. 4.13

d) The motion of the trolley once in contact with the band, is that of a simple harmonic oscillator. See the tethered trolley described in Chapter 6.

11 a) See the text (pp. 28–30).

b) Your account needs to focus on the energy changes in a bounce, e.g. potential to kinetic as ball falls. Hence kinetic to strain energy as it hits with ground, with 20% of energy converted into internal energy of ball and ground, then strain to kinetic, etc.

c) Let u = initial velocity of neutron and m its mass

v_c = velocity of carbon atom after collision

v_n = velocity of neutron after collision.

Applying the conservation of momentum and kinetic energy we obtain:

$mu = 12mv_c + mv_n$

and $\frac{1}{2}mu^2 = \frac{12}{2} mv_c^2 + \frac{1}{2}mv_n^2$.

These equations can be simplified to give:

i) $v_n = u - 12 v_c$

and ii) $v_n^2 = u^2 - 12 v_c^2$.

Squaring i) and equating it to ii) gives:

$u^2 + 144v_c^2 - 24uv_c = u^2 - 12v_c^2$,

which gives $v_c = \frac{2}{13} u$.

$$\frac{\text{Energy of carbon atom after collision}}{\text{Initial neutron energy}} = \frac{\frac{1}{2}.12m.\frac{4}{169}u^2}{\frac{1}{2}mu^2}$$

$$= 0.28.$$

Hence energy transferred $= 0.57$ MeV.

12 a) 2 ms^{-2} b) 1.2×10^4 kg ms^{-1}

c) 2.7×10^5 J

In this question be very careful about units.

13 a) The gravity is inversely proportional to the square of the distance from the centre of the earth. So a low orbit will only fractionally increase the distance from the earth's centre.

b) This is explained in the text (see page 29).

14 See the text. Fig. 4.12b) refers to the well-known Newton's cradle. Eventually the right hand ball bounces off alone with the original momentum of the left hand ball.

TUTOR'S QUESTION AND ANSWER

15 a) State Newton's laws of motion. Explain how the newton is defined from these laws.

b) A rocket is propelled by the emission of hot gases. It may be stated that both the rocket and the emitted hot gases each gain kinetic energy and momentum during the firing of the rocket. Discuss the significance of this statement in relation to the laws of conservation of energy and momentum, explaining the essential difference between these two quantities.

c) A bird of mass 0.5 kg hovers by beating its wings of effective area 0.3 m².
   i) What is the upward force of the air on the bird?
   ii) What is the downward force of the bird on the air as it beats its wings?
   iii) Estimate the velocity imparted to the air, which has a density of 1.3 kg m⁻³, by the beating of the wings.

Which of Newton's laws is applied in each of i), ii) and iii) above?

(London 1983)

15 a) Newton's 1st law. If a body is at rest or if it is in motion it moves with uniform velocity (i.e. constant speed in a straight line) unless it is acted upon by a resultant force.

2nd Law. The rate of change of momentum of a body is proportional to the resultant force and occurs in the direction of the force.

3rd Law. If body A exerts a force on body B, then body B exerts an equal and opposite force on body A.

The newton is defined from the 2nd law. If mass is measured in kilograms and velocity in metres per second, momentum is measured in kg m s⁻¹. A newton is therefore defined as the force acting if the momentum is changing at a rate of 1 kg m s⁻¹ every second.

b) The exhaust gases are propelled out of the rocket by the combustion of fuel. They gain kinetic energy as a result of energy transfer from the chemical energy content of the fuel. As they shoot out of the rocket they exert a reaction force on the rocket. It accelerates in the opposite direction. The momentum acquired by the rocket (in one direction) is equal in magnitude to the momentum acquired by the gases (but in the opposite direction). The net momentum of the rocket and exhaust gases is zero, as no external forces act on the system. Because of its movement the rocket also acquires kinetic energy. Both the rocket and the exhaust gases, therefore, acquire kinetic energy.

c) i) For the bird to hover, the upward force exerted must equal the weight downwards. This is 0.5×10 N (assuming $g = 10$ N kg⁻¹). This is by the application of Newton's first law.

ii) By Newton's third Law the downward force of the bird on the air must be 5 N.

iii) If the wings beat over an area of 0.3 m² and the air is moved at v ms⁻¹ then in 1 second a volume of air $v \times 0.3$ m³ is moved.

The mass moved in 1 second
$$= v \times 0.3 \times 1.3 \text{ kg}$$
The momentum acquired = mass × v
$$= v \times 0.3 \times 1.3 \times v$$
$$= 0.39 \, v^2 \text{ kg m s}^{-1}.$$
But this occurs in 1 second and so is the rate of change of momentum in kg m s⁻².
By Newton's 2nd law this is the force exerted.
Therefore $5 = 0.39 \, v^2$
$$v^2 = \frac{5}{0.39} = 12.82$$
So $v = 3.6$ m s⁻¹ (to 2 significant figures.)

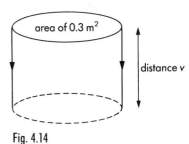
area of 0.3 m²

distance v

Fig. 4.14

STUDENT'S ANSWER WITH EXAMINER COMMENTS

STUDENT'S ANSWER TO QUESTION 10a) AND b)

“Indicate units to be used.”

“Physical principle not stated. Here the candidate has used the conservation of energy, which is invalid, the collision being inelastic.”

10 a) Let initial velocity of pellet be v.

Then initial kinetic energy $= \frac{1}{2} \times (5 \times 10^{-4})v^2$

Final kinetic energy $= \frac{1}{2}$ (total mass) $\times (0.2)^2$

$\qquad = \frac{1}{2} (0.4005) \times (0.2)^2$

$\therefore \quad v^2 = \dfrac{0.4005 \times (0.2)^2}{5 \times 10^{-4}} = 32.04$

$v = 5.66$ m/s.

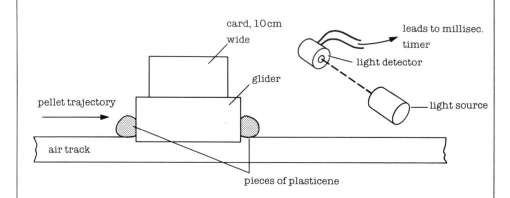

Fig. 4.15

b) To verify the above result the arrangement shown in Fig. 4.15 should be used. The glider should have two pieces of plasticene fixed to each end, one to which the pellet can adhere, and one of roughly equal mass to balance the glider. It should also have a piece of card, 10 cms wide, attached at the top. This is to intersect the beam of a light gate mounted further down the track. The total mass of the glider, card, and plasticene should be found by weighing on a top-pan balance. The glider should be placed on the track which should then be levelled so that the glider can remain stationary on it. The glider should then be mounted near the air-rifle and the light gate should be moved so that the card will begin to obstruct the beam as soon as the glider begins to move. The timer should be switched on. The velocity of the glider is found from

$$v = \frac{0.10}{\text{time in seconds}} \text{ m/s.}$$

The mass of a pellet is found by weighing several, say 50, and dividing the balance reading by the total number of pellets.

“An extremely good account of the experimental details. However the candidate needs to conclude the account by showing how the measurements would be put together to verify the principle.”

Overall Comment: There would be poor marks for the calculation of v because of the employment of the wrong physical principle. The *experimental* account, however, is typical of that of a grade B candidate.

CIRCULAR MOTION

GETTING STARTED

All syllabuses include some work on **circular motion**. Here you need to be really clear about the need to employ vectors in Physics. Unless you have done the rotational motion option in a Nuffield GCSE course, nearly all the problems in dynamics that you will have handled will have been what some teachers call 'tram-line problems', i.e. one dimensional problems, such as that of trucks colliding along a straight line. The vector nature of force, momentum, etc. is usually obscured. In circular motion however, not only do particles move in two dimensions, but the *direction* of a vector (e.g. velocity) may be changing whilst its *magnitude* remains constant.

The key idea is found in Newton's 2nd law of motion, in the form: force is equal to the rate of change of momentum. It is also important to understand that this law also applies to situations where momentum changes in direction but not in magnitude.

This chapter also includes some work on the projection of circular motion into two directions at right angles, and so links with **simple harmonic motion** treated in Chapter 6. Some extension work on the rotation of rigid bodies is also included, as at least three A Level syllabuses include it as a topic.

ESSENTIAL PRINCIPLES

MOTION IN A CIRCLE

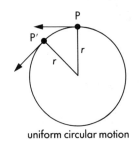

uniform circular motion

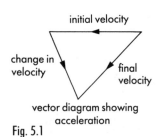

vector diagram showing acceleration

Fig. 5.1

Uniform circular motion is a kind of motion where the *magnitude* of the velocity vector is constant whilst the *direction* steadily changes. Fig. 5.1 shows two positions of a particle, P and P', when it is moving in a circle. The vector diagram shows how the velocity at P', the *final velocity*, is obtained from adding a vector representing the *change in velocity* to the initial velocity vector. The acceleration is given by this change in velocity divided by the time taken for the change. Note that it is directed inwards, towards the centre of the circle. By Newton's 2nd law, there must be a physical force inwards that is responsible for this acceleration. This force is called a **centripetal** force. It always has a physical cause. In the case of the planets revolving round the sun it is gravitational attraction.

FORMULAE

The **angular speed** ω of a particle in a circle is equal to the angle of a complete revolution in radians divided by the time T for a complete revolution in seconds.

- So the **angular speed** ω of the particle is given by:

  $$\omega = 2\pi/T.$$

- The **velocity** v of the particle is given by:
  $$v = \omega r.$$

- The **inward acceleration** is $a = v^2/r = \omega^2 r$.

- The **centripetal force** is $m\omega^2 r$.

Note that because motion is at right angles to the force, the force does not act in the direction of the motion and so no work is done by it. As an example of circular motion, consider a conical pendulum, i.e. a mass hanging on a thread set in motion so that it moves in a horizontal circle of radius r with an angular velocity ω (Fig. 5.2. See also Multiple Choice Question 3). The centripetal force comes from the tension in the thread. Resolving forces vertically and applying Newton's 2nd Law, we have:

$$F \cos \theta = mg$$

(i.e. the net upward force is zero as the mass doesn't have vertical acceleration). Resolving horizontally:

$$F \sin \theta = m\omega^2 r.$$

Dividing the second equation by the first we get:

$$\tan \theta = \omega^2 r/g$$

i.e. the angle θ is related to the angular speed ω. The periodic time T is:

$$2\pi/\omega = 2\pi \sqrt{g \tan \theta/r}$$

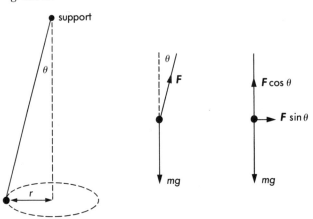

Fig. 5.2 Conical pendulum

ROTATIONAL MOTION OF RIGID BODIES

MOMENT OF INERTIA

Consider a rigid body rotating about a fixed axis at an angular velocity ω (Fig. 5.3). Now imagine one of the particles of matter making up the body. Suppose this has a mass m and is at a distance r from the axis (Fig. 5.3).

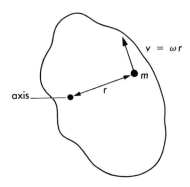

Fig. 5.3 Rigid body rotating about a fixed axis

Its **kinetic energy** $= \frac{1}{2}mv^2$
$$= \frac{1}{2}m\,(r\omega)^2$$
$$= \frac{1}{2}mr^2\omega^2.$$

The *total* kinetic energy of the body is found by adding these results for all the particles of the body i.e.

$$E = \frac{1}{2}(m_1 r_1^2)\,\omega^2 + \frac{1}{2}(m_2 r_2^2)\omega^2 + \dots\,$$

$$= \sum_{i=1}^{N} \frac{1}{2}(m_i r_i^2)\omega^2 = \frac{1}{2}\omega^2 \left(\sum_{i=1}^{N} m_i r_i^2 \right)$$

where the summation runs over all the particles of the body.

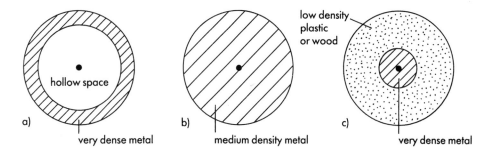

Fig. 5.4 Cylinders of same mass but with different distributions of mass inside

The quantity $\sum_{i=1}^{N} m_i r_i^2$ is called I, the **moment of inertia** of the body. This is a scalar quantity which depends on the mass distribution of the body and the position of the axis of rotation. For example, it is possible to construct three cylinders each of the same mass but with a different distribution of mass inside (Fig. 5.4). If the axis of rotation is the central axis of the cylinders, then a) has the largest value of moment of inertia, because all the mass is away from the axis (in $\Sigma\,mr^2$, all the values of r are large). By contrast, c) has the lowest values of r.

Our energy formula is $E = \frac{1}{2}I\omega^2$. This is analogous to the $\frac{1}{2}mv^2$ energy formula of straight line motion in Chapter 4.

STRAIGHT LINE MOTION	RIGID BODY ROTATION
mass m	moment of inertia I
velocity v	angular velocity ω

Notice how for a rotating body we have the above equivalent quantities. To increase the angular velocity of a rotating body, a *couple* or *torque* must be applied (see Chapter 3). The torque, T, takes the place of force in straight line motion, and instead of Newton's 2nd law in the form:

$$F = \frac{dv}{dt} = ma,$$

we have:

$$T = I\ \frac{\mathrm{d}\omega}{\mathrm{d}t} = I\alpha$$

where α, the angular acceleration (measured in radians s^{-1}) takes the place of acceleration.

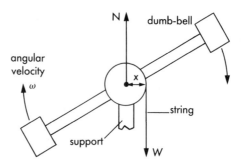

Fig. 5.5 Weight acting on a string wrapped around an axle

> **Don't confuse angular acceleration here with the centripetal acceleration described on page 38**

As an example consider a weight acting on a string wrapped around an axle so that it angularly accelerates a dumb-bell of moment of inertia I (Fig. 5.5). Because there is no upward or downwards motion, the downward force W must be balanced by the upward normal reaction force N at the support. So $N = W$. These two forces form a *couple*, the torque T of which is Nx, where x is the distance between the lines of action, i.e. the radius of the axle. So,

$$T = I\ \frac{\mathrm{d}\omega}{\mathrm{d}t}\ ,$$

where ω is the angular velocity of the dumb-bell. Note that measurements made in this experiment could be used to determine the moment of inertia of the dumb-bell. For many common shapes, however, formulae for moments of inertia are quoted in textbooks.

CONSERVATION OF ANGULAR MOMENTUM

Angular momentum (L) is defined as the product of moment of inertia and angular velocity, given by the equation:

$$L = I\omega \qquad (\text{cf momentum} = mv).$$

The **conservation of angular momentum** is thus a principle which goes alongside the conservation of linear momentum. Provided no external couple acts on a system, its total angular momentum remains constant.

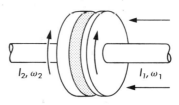

Fig. 5.6 Activating clutch mechanism between two rotating discs

An example of something akin to a collision in straight line motion is what happens when a clutch mechanism between two rotating discs is activated so that they come together and subsequently rotate together (see Fig. 5.6).

$$I_1\omega_1 + I_2\omega_2 = (I_1 + I_2)\omega_3,$$

where ω_3 is the new angular velocity after the discs have come together. (Note that we have not proved any of the above formulae. You should look up any proofs that you may need in your textbook.)

SUMMARY OF EQUIVALENCES BETWEEN LINEAR AND ROTATIONAL MOTION

QUANTITY OR FORMULA IN LINEAR MOTION	EQUIVALENT IN RIGID BODY ROTATION
Displacement (s)	Angular displacement (θ)
Velocity (v)	Angular velocity (ω)
Acceleration ($a = \dfrac{dv}{dt}$)	Angular acceleration ($\alpha = \dfrac{d\omega}{dt}$)
Mass (m)	Moment of inertia (I)
Force (F)	Torque (T)
Momentum (mv)	Angular momentum ($L = I\omega$)
Kinetic Energy ($\frac{1}{2}mv^2$)	Kinetic energy ($\frac{1}{2}I\omega^2$)
Work done Fs	Work done $T\theta$
$F = ma$	$T = I\alpha$
$m_1v_1 + m_2v_2 =$ constant	$I_1\omega_1 + I_2\omega_2 =$ constant
$v = u + at$	$\omega_{\text{final}} = \omega_{\text{initial}} + \alpha t$
etc	etc

CIRCULAR MOTION AND OSCILLATIONS

Consider a particle moving anti-clockwise in a circle at an angular velocity ω (Fig. 5.7a)). Suppose that at $t = 0$ the particle is at P. Consequently, if it is at P′ t seconds later, then $\theta = \omega t$.

Represented graphically, with x and y axes drawn through the origin O, we can look at the projection of the position of P′ on the y axis. Experimentally we can do this as shown in Fig. 5.7b), where a distant horizontal light casts a shadow on a screen of a ball on a rotating turntable.

$$y = a \sin \theta,$$
$$\text{so } y = a \sin \omega t.$$

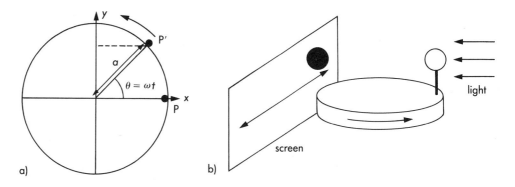

Fig. 5.7 Particle moving anti-clockwise in a circle   a)

b)

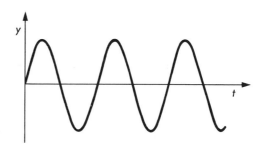

Fig. 5.8

The graph of y against t (Fig. 5.8) is sinusoidal, with a period $T = 2\pi/\omega$; a, the radius of the circle, becomes the amplitude of the motion. This connection between circular motion and sinusoidal motion is important both in simple harmonic motion (Chapter 6) and alternating current theory (Chapter 15).

EXAMINATION QUESTIONS

**MULTIPLE
CHOICE
QUESTIONS**

1 A spacecraft of mass 500 kg travelling through space at 30 m s^{-1} fires its rockets so that the direction of its path changes by 90°, the craft continuing at the same speed. The magnitude of the change in momentum of the spacecraft, in kg m s^{-1}, is:

a) 0

b) 15×10^3

c) 21×10^3

d) 30×10^3

e) 225×10^3

(NI 1986)

2 A stone attached to a string of length r is whirled in a vertical circle with constant speed v. Fig. 5.9 below shows its position at various times. Which ONE of the following statements is *incorrect*?

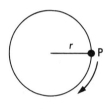 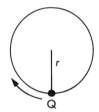 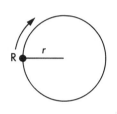 

Fig. 5.9

1) The tension in the string is equal at P. Q, R and S.
2) The tension in the string is a maximum at Q.
3) The tension in the string is a minimum at S.
4) The centripetal acceleration of the stone is v^2/r.
5) The stone makes one revolution in a time $2\pi r/v$.

(NI 1987)

3 A small bob of mass m hangs from a light string. The bob is set into motion so that it moves in a horizontal circle of radius r with angular velocity ω and the string makes an angle θ with the vertical. Which one of the following is equal to tan θ? [The acceleration of free fall is g.]

a) $m\omega^2 r$

b) $\dfrac{m\omega^2 r}{g}$

c) $\dfrac{\omega}{g}$

d) $\dfrac{\omega^2 r}{g}$

e) $\dfrac{\omega r^2}{g}$

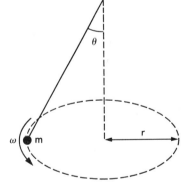

Fig. 5.10

(Oxford 1987)

4 A particle moves with constant speed in a circular path of radius r and completes one revolution in time T. The magnitude of the particle's acceleration is:

a) zero
b) proportional to r/T
c) proportional to r^2/T
d) proportional to r/T^2
e) proportional to r^2/T^2

(Oxford 1988)

5 A coin of mass m is placed on a freely-rotating turn-table at a distance r from the centre. The maximum frictional force between the coin and the table is $\dfrac{mg}{2}$.   The table's angular velocity is steadily increased. The coin will begin to slide when the table's angular velocity is:

a) $\sqrt{\dfrac{g}{2r}}$ d) $\dfrac{gr}{2}$

b) $\sqrt{\dfrac{mg}{2r}}$ e) $\sqrt{\dfrac{mgr}{2}}$

c) $\dfrac{g}{2r}$

(AEB 1987 Specimen Paper)

6 A boy jumps on to a rotating playground roundabout. Which of the following statements is untrue?

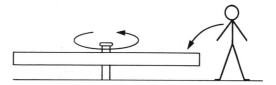

Fig. 5.11

1) The angular momentum of the system remains the same.
2) The angular velocity of the playground roundabout is reduced.
3) The kinetic energy of the system is unchanged.
4) The moment of inertia of the roundabout is unchanged.
5) The moment of inertia of the body about the axis is his mass multiplied by the square of his distance from the axis.

7 The following objects have the same mass and the same external radius, r

a) A solid sphere
b) A hollow sphere
c) A hollow cylinder of length $2r$
d) A solid cylinder of length $2r$
e) A solid cylinder of length $4r$
If rolled down an incline which will reach the bottom last?

ANSWERS AND COMMENTS

Question	1	2	3	4	5	6	7
Answer	c)	1)	d)	d)	a)	3)	c)

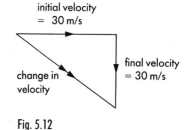

Fig. 5.12

1 The vector diagram for velocity is:
Hence the change in velocity = 30 $\sqrt{2}$ ms^{-1}, and the change in momentum is 21×10^3 kg m s^{-1}.

2 As the stone travels at constant speed, the centripetal force must be constant. This force is provided by gravity and the tension of the string. As the angle between these varies, so must the tension vary.

3 See text.

4 The acceleration is usually written $a = \omega^2 r$.
$T = 2\pi/\omega$ and so $2\pi/T$ can be substituted for ω giving:
$a = 4\pi^2 r/T^2$.

5 The centripetal force $= m\omega^2 r$. Equating this to $mg/2$ gives the result.

6 Demands recall of theory.

7 As each item falls, the loss of potential energy equals $\frac{1}{2}mv^2 + \frac{1}{2}I\omega^2$. c) has the largest value of I, and hence the smallest values of v and ω.

STRUCTURED
QUESTIONS

8 a) Define angular momentum.

   b) Describe briefly how you would demonstrate (using a simple experiment) the principle of conservation of angular momentum.

   c) A stationary horizontal hoop of mass 0.04 kg and mean radius 0.15 m is dropped from a small height centrally and symmetrically onto a gramophone turntable which is *freely* rotating at an angular velocity of 3.0 rad s^{-1}. Eventually the combined turntable and hoop rotate together with an angular velocity of 2.0 rad s^{-1}. Calculate:

   i) the moment of inertia of the turntable about its rotation axis;

   ii) the original kinetic energy of the turntable;

   iii) the eventual kinetic energy of the combined hoop and turntable.

   Account for any change in kinetic energy which has occurred.

(Welsh 1988)

9 The turntable of a record player is a uniform disc of moment of inertia 1.2×10^{-2} kg m^2. When the motor is switched on it takes 2.5 s for the turntable to accelerate uniformly from rest to 3.5 rad s^{-1} ($33\frac{1}{3}$ r.p.m.).

   a) What is the angular acceleration of the turntable?

   b) What torque must the motor provide during this acceleration?

OUTLINE ANSWERS

8 a) See the text and the Student's Answer (p. 45).

   b) Part c) itself provides a framework for demonstrating the principle.
   An answer would need to fully describe the experimental details.

   c) i) Moment of inertia of hoop is given by
$$I_h = mr^2 = 9 \times 10^{-4} \text{ kg m}^2.$$
   In the collision which ensues:
$$I_t\omega_i = I_t\omega_f + I_h\omega_f,$$
   where I_t is the turntable moment of inertia. Hence:
$$I_t = 1.8 \times 10^{-3} \text{ kg m}^2.$$

   ii) $E = \frac{1}{2}I_t\omega_i^2 = 0.0081$ J.

   iii) 0.0054 J with a loss to internal energy because of the inelastic collision.

9 Use the equations for constant angular acceleration which are like the equations for constant translational motion.

   a) 1.4 radians s^{-2}.

   b) 0.0168 N m.

> Take particular care with unfamiliar units in these rotational problems.

TUTOR'S QUESTION AND ANSWER

QUESTION

A bobsleigh rises up the side of an ice track when it follows a *horizontal circular path* at speed. Figure 5.13a) shows a cross section of the ice track and Figure 5.13b) is a free body diagram showing the forces which act on the bobsleigh.

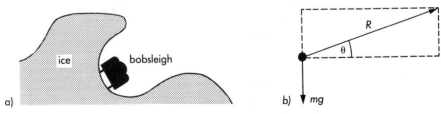

Fig. 5.13   a)   b) mg

a) Explain why the kinetic energy of the bobsleigh is conserved but not its linear momentum.

b) What effect does the horizontal component of the push, R, of the ice track on the bobsleigh have on the motion of the bobsleigh?

c) Calculate the value of tan θ for a speed of 25 m s^{-1} if the radius of the circular path the bobsleigh follows is 20 m.

(London 1987 Part question)

ANSWER

a) The kinetic energy is conserved because no force acts instantaneously with a component parallel to the velocity, to increase or decrease the kinetic energy. On the other hand a force acts at right angles to the velocity. This changes the direction of the velocity and hence the linear momentum.

b) The horizontal component of R changes the direction of the velocity vector. It holds the bobsleigh in a circle by providing the centripetal force.

c) Using the free body diagram (Fig. 5.13b)), and resolving forces vertically, we have:
   i) $mg = R \sin \theta$.
   Resolving horizontally, then:
   ii) $R \cos \theta = mv^2/r$.
   Dividing equation ii) by equation i), and taking g as 9.81 ms^{-2}, we have:
   $$\tan \theta = gr/v^2 = \frac{9.81 \times 20}{25^2}$$

   $$= 0.314$$

STUDENT'S ANSWER WITH EXAMINER COMMENTS

STUDENT'S ANSWER TO QUESTION 8a) AND b)

" Good statement. Useful to include the units of angular momentum, also to mention that it is a conserved quantity in physics, and is a vector. "

8 a) The angular momentum of a particle needs to be defined about a particular axis. It is the product of the momentum of the particle multipled by the perpendicular distance of the momentum vector from the axis. For an extended body it is the sum of all the angular moments of the component masses.

   b) To demonstrate the principle of the conservation of angular momentum I would stand on a turntable holding two weights in my hands. When I moved my arms outwards I would slow down.

" Weak on description. Note that the question asks only for a *demonstration* not for a verification. But the account needs to mention:
   how you start to rotate,
   moment of inertia,
   how changing the position of the arms changes the moment of inertia,
   angular velocity. "

" The diagram should at least be labelled. It adds little to the account. "

Overall Comment: The answer, particularly the descriptive part, shows a number of weaknesses. The answer begins well but then deteriorates. The experimental description is typical of a grade D/E candidate.

OSCILLATIONS AND RESONANCE

GETTING STARTED

Waves are a means of transferring energy from one place to another and appear in nature in a variety of forms, e.g. sound, heat, light, X- and γ-rays. It is now also quite clear that at the atomic level, matter itself often behaves in a wave-like manner. It is for these sorts of reasons that the study of waves is prominent in any advanced course in Physics. All waves are essentially complicated oscillating systems; for example sound waves in air involve the oscillations of local pockets of air, and light waves involve oscillating electric and magnetic fields. Hence it is necessary to begin with a good understanding of oscillations.

Once you have begun to master mechanics, oscillations is a good topic to go on to. This is because A Level examinations often test your ability to apply your knowledge of mechanics to oscillatory problems. Simple harmonic motion (SHM) should be firmly grasped in your understanding, but you should remember that most real oscillatory behaviour only approximates to SHM. You will also need to study damped oscillations and resonance. The ideas and nomenclature started in this chapter are then needed in the theory of travelling waves which is considered in Chapter 7. When two such travelling waves move through each other in opposite directions, a stationary or standing wave is produced. In bounded systems such as the string of a musical instrument, or the air column in an organ pipe, standing waves occur only at certain frequencies and so themselves are an example of resonance. Since resonance is linked with oscillation we shall consider them in this chapter.

ESSENTIAL PRINCIPLES

■ **Oscillation**: a repeated cycle of motion about an equilibrium position (but note that this idea extends to electrical oscillations where a p.d., charge, or current varies cyclically about an equilibrium value). The graphs in Fig. 6.1 show possible displacement/time graphs for an oscillation. Note that at the equilibrium position, the displacement x has been taken as zero.

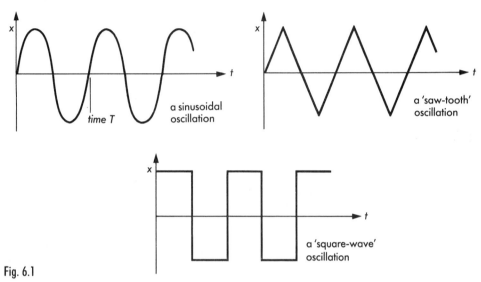

Fig. 6.1

■ **Period** (T): the time for one complete cycle (or return journey from and to an extreme position) of the oscillation.

■ **Frequency** (f): the number of cycles of oscillation per second; and note that:
$f = 1/T$

■ **Amplitude** (x_o): the maximum value of the displacement from equilibrium.

■ **Simple Harmonic Motion** (SHM): a special class of oscillation where the period (T) is the same for *all* amplitudes, be they large or small. *If and only if* an oscillator has this property then it follows that:
  i) the oscillation is sinusoidal;
  ii) the acceleration is proportional to the magnitude of the displacement but directed always towards the equilibrium position, that is the mid-point of the motion.

■ **Anharmonic Motion**: an oscillation where the period changes as the amplitude changes.

SHM CONSIDERED MATHEMATICALLY

The simplest example of SHM is the idealised motion of a trolley tethered by two springs. In the ideal case there is no friction and so the oscillation goes on indefinitely: the motion is horizontal and the only horizontal forces acting are the restoring forces of the springs (Fig. 6.2). The displacement/time graph for this is shown in Fig. 6.3; on page 48 there are the corresponding velocity/time (Fig. 6.4), and acceleration/time (Fig. 6.5) graphs.

Note that in the special case of SHM, all the three graphs are sinusoidal. The velocity/time, and acceleration/time graphs are 90° and 180° out of phase, respectively,

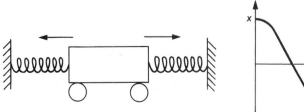

Fig. 6.2 Tethered trolley

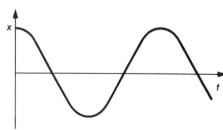

Fig. 6.3 Displacement in SHM

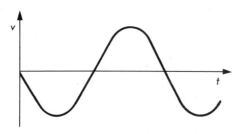 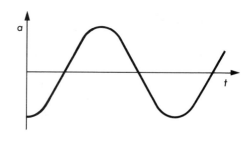

Fig. 6.4 Velocity in SHM   Fig. 6.5 Acceleration in SHM

with the displacement/time graph. Also, note the term **phase**. The sine and cosine functions are *circular* functions, repeating themselves every 360° (or 2π radians). A complete cycle of oscillation is therefore 360°; and a quarter of a cycle, 90°. When two oscillations are '90° out of phase' we mean that they are out of step by a quarter of a complete cycle.

Because of **Hooke's law**, the elasticity of the springs provides a restoring force, F, given by:

$$F = -kx,$$

where k is the force per unit displacement. The value for k is found experimentally by displacing the trolley from its equilibrium position, measuring the restoring force with a Newtonmeter, and then dividing the force by the displacement.

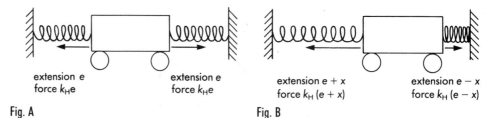

extension e extension e extension $e + x$ extension $e - x$
force $k_\mathrm{H}e$ force $k_\mathrm{H}e$ force $k_\mathrm{H}(e + x)$ force $k_\mathrm{H}(e - x)$

Fig. A   Fig. B

In the account of the trolley k is taken simply as the constant which relates the displacement to the nett force. The force, of course, arises from the separate extensions of both springs. In equilibrium the trolley is as shown in Fig. A.

If both springs are the same then each exerts a force of amount $k_\mathrm{H}e$, where k_H is the constant which relates force to extension in Hooke's law, i.e. force $= k_\mathrm{H}$ times extension, and e is the extension. One spring pulls to the left and the other to the right. Forces are vectors and so as usual we need to set up a sign convention (see Chapter 4). If we take forces to the right as positive, and those to the left as negative, the nett force to the right is $k_\mathrm{H}e - k_\mathrm{H}e = 0$.

When the trolley is displaced to the right by an amount x (Fig. B), the left hand spring exerts a greater force, and one to the left, (i.e. a negative one) and the right hand one a smaller one to the right. If e is the original extension the force of the left hand spring is $-k_\mathrm{H}(e+x)$, and the force of the right hand spring is $k_\mathrm{H}(e-x)$.

The nett force is therefore $- k_\mathrm{H}(e+x) + k_\mathrm{H}(e-x) = 2k_\mathrm{H}x$.

This shows that k, the constant used to describe the resultant behaviour of the two springs, is equal to $2k_\mathrm{H}$.

$F = ma$ by Newton's 2nd law, giving:

$a = -\dfrac{k}{m}x$, which is usually simplified as:

$a = -\omega^2 x.$

> **What initial conditions would give the solution $x = x_0 \sin \omega t$?**

Note that as the trolley is displaced more and more to the right, the net force to the left gets more and more. Because of the vector nature of force this means that the net force in the direction of increasing x is negative, and hence so is the acceleration. In simple language, it means the trolley decelerates. (See also the spring constants box.)

Assuming that the trolley is released with a displacement

$x = x_0$ at $t = 0$, the solution of this equation is:

$x = x_0 \cos \omega t$

where x_0 is the amplitude of oscillation.

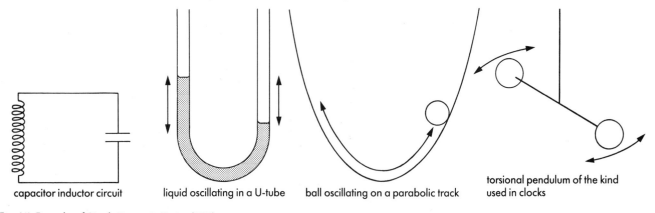

capacitor inductor circuit   liquid oscillating in a U-tube   ball oscillating on a parabolic track   torsional pendulum of the kind used in clocks

Fig. 6.6 Examples of Simple Harmonic Motion (SHM)

The graphs that result are those shown in Figures 6.4 and 6.5 and described by the equations below:

- **velocity** $v = \omega x_o \sin \omega t = v_{max} \sin \omega t = \omega \sqrt{x_o^2 - x^2}$
- **acceleration** $a = -\omega^2 x_o \cos \omega t = -\omega^2 x$

with $T = 2\pi/\omega$ and $f = 1/T = \omega/2\pi$. Once all these equations can be written down, with known values for the variables, we have a complete mathematical description of the oscillation. Notice the link with circular motion described in Chapter 5.

Other mechanical examples of SHM include the various types of pendulum, including torsional ones, a mass rolling on a parabolic track, liquids oscillating in a U-tube, and so on. Capacitor-inductor circuits are an electrical example.

The particular systems which you should learn will be given in your syllabus, but others may be asked in a structured question. In these cases you need to establish the relationship between the restoring force F and the displacement in order to set up an equation corresponding to $F = -kx$. Then using $F = ma$ you can obtain $a = \omega^2 x$ and find T from $\omega^2 = k/m$.

Your value of ω can then be substituted into the other equations. Note that in all these cases you 'idealise' the problem by ignoring frictional forces. The method is further illustrated for a mass hanging from a spring and a simple pendulum.

MASS HANGING FROM A SPRING

This is more difficult to calculate than the tethered trolley because now there are two types of forces acting in the direction of motion; spring forces where the force is proportional to the extension, and gravity.

Three diagrams help (Fig. 6.7). The first shows the spring of length, l, unloaded. The second shows the spring loaded but in its equilibrium (rest) position, the spring extended by a distance e. The third is a 'snapshot' at a point in the cycle of oscillation with a displacement, x, from the rest position of the second diagram.

Applying **Hooke's law** to the second diagram we obtain:

$F_s = ke$

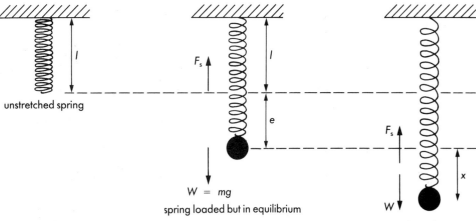

unstretched spring

$W = mg$

spring loaded but in equilibrium

Fig. 6.7 Mass hanging from a spring

mass in motion
A 'snapshot' diagram

where F_s is the force exerted by the spring. Because of equilibrium, F_s = the weight of the mass m, giving:

$ke = mg$, or $k = mg/e$.

In the third diagram F_s, acting upwards, is given by:

$F_s = k (e + x)$.

As before, with up-and-down motion we need to establish a sign convention. Let us regard x as positive when increasing in a downward direction from the equilibrium position. The net force F in the direction of increasing x is then:

$$\begin{aligned} F &= mg - k(e + x) \\ &= mg - ke - kx \\ &= -kx \end{aligned}$$

Note that it is this result which *proves* that the motion is SHM. We have a *restoring* force proportional to the displacement.

$$F = ma,$$

so:

$$\begin{aligned} ma &= -kx \\ a &= -\frac{k}{m} x \end{aligned}$$

or $a = -\omega^2 x$, where $\omega^2 = k/m$;

so $x = x_0 \cos \omega t$

$T = 2\pi/\omega$, hence $T = 2\pi \sqrt{m/k}$.

THE SIMPLE PENDULUM

The term 'simple' is used to describe a pendulum where all the mass acts at one point at the end of the pendulum. In this case the analysis is a bit harder than that of the tethered trolley because of the need to resolve forces in the direction of motion and to make a small angle approximation.

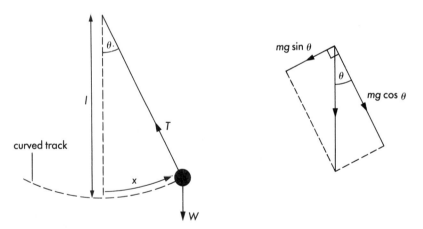

Fig. 6.8 Simple pendulum

The fixed length of the string, l, constrains the motion of the bob, to the arc of a circle (Fig. 6.8). It is helpful therefore to think of the bob moving on a curved track, the steepness of which increases as the distance from the equilibrium position increases. Two forces act on the bob; the tension T in the string and the weight W. The tension is always at right angles to the 'track', whilst W has to be resolved into two components as shown in the smaller diagram. Here the component along the 'track' is $W \sin \theta$, or $mg \sin \theta$.

Let x be the distance along the arc of the track. Then in radians:

$\theta = x/l$.

For small angles, $\sin \theta \approx \theta$ and so $\sin \theta = x/l$.
The restoring force, in the direction of increasing x, is therefore $-mgx/l$.

$$F = ma,$$

so $ma = -mgx/l$

or $\quad a = -\omega^2 x$, where $\omega^2 = g/l$

so $\quad x = x_o \cos \omega t$, and the period T is given by:

$\quad T = 2\pi \sqrt{l/g}$.

SHM AND ENERGY CONSIDERATIONS

In SHM there is a constant interchange of energy between the kinetic and potential forms, the total energy staying constant. If $x = x_o \cos \omega t$, then the **kinetic energy** is given by:

$\quad E_k = \frac{1}{2}mv^2 = \frac{1}{2}mv^2_{max} \sin^2\omega t = \frac{1}{2}m\omega^2(x_o^2 - x^2)$,

and the **potential energy** is given by:

$\quad E_p = \frac{1}{2}m\omega^2 x^2$.

E_k is a maximum at the equilibrium position where it is $\frac{1}{2}mv^2_{max}$. The total energy is constant and is always the sum of E_k and E_p. Hence:

$\quad$ total energy $= \frac{1}{2}m\omega^2 x_o^2$

Fig. 6.9 shows the behaviour as the oscillator goes through a complete cycle. Note the dependence on amplitude squared. If the amplitude is doubled, the system stores quadruple the energy.

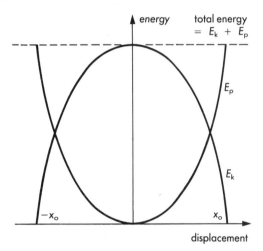

Fig. 6.9 Behaviour of oscillator going through a complete cycle

DAMPED SHM

Most real oscillators are **damped**, i.e. there is a steady loss of energy as this is converted to other forms. Usually it will be to internal energy through friction, but energy may also be radiated away (e.g. a vibrating tuning fork loses energy by sound radiation). When the damping forces are proportional to the velocity, v, the period remains constant as the amplitude diminishes and the oscillator is called **isochronous**. A graph of displacement against time is as shown with the dotted curve being an exponentially diminishing curve. This is a very common case (Fig. 6.10). Unless the damping is considerable, the frequency is not appreciably different from what it would be without any damping.

With heavier damping there are no oscillations and the displacement exponentially diminishes to zero (Fig. 6.11).

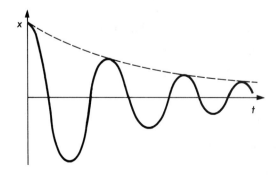

Fig. 6.10 Small damping

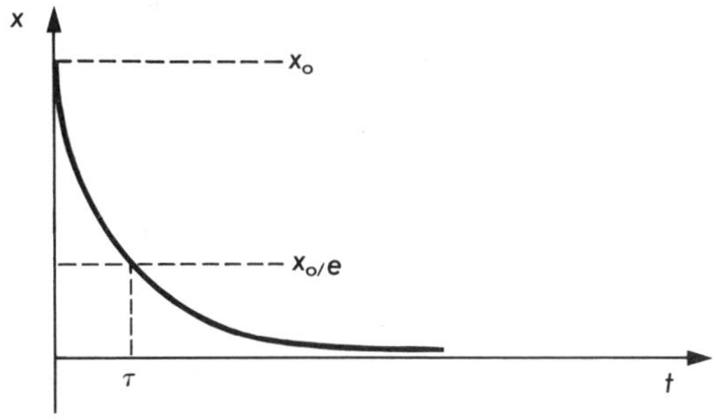

Fig. 6.11 Heavy damping sharing the significance of the time constant τ

In this graph, $x = x_o e^{-t/\tau}$ where τ is the time-constant of the system. Here τ is the time taken for the displacement x to fall to x_o/e, i.e. $0.37\ x_o$.

A *critically* damped oscillator is one where the time constant τ takes the minimum value it can without oscillations taking place (Fig. 6.12).

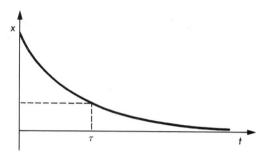

Fig. 6.12 Critical damping

<table>
<tr><td>

FORCED OSCILLATIONS AND RESONANCE

</td><td>

Here a periodic force at a given frequency is applied to an oscillator. Initially the system exhibits **transient** behaviour and then settles down with oscillations at the frequency of the driving force. When the driving frequency is the same as the natural frequency of the oscillator, the amplitude of oscillation is at its greatest. This is called **resonance.**

</td></tr>
</table>

Fig. 6.13 shows the steady state amplitude of a resonant system for different driving frequencies and with different amounts of damping. For a simple harmonic oscillator there will only be one frequency of resonance.

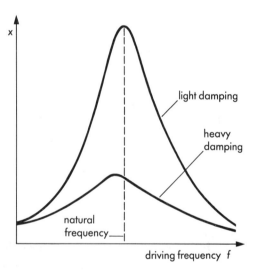

Fig. 6.13 Steady state amplitude of a resonant system for different amounts of damping

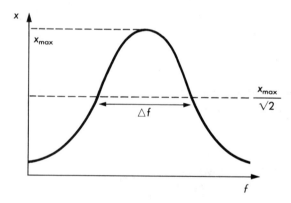

Fig. 6.14 Finding the *Q*-Factor of a resonant system

ENERGY CONSIDERATIONS

Whether or not a body is at or close to resonance, the oscillator settles down in a **steady state** where the energy supplied from the driver per cycle is equal to the energy dissipated per cycle. The **sharpness of the resonance**, called the **Q-factor**, is equal to:

$$\frac{\text{energy lost per cycle}}{\text{energy at the start of the cycle}}$$

It is also given by:

$Q = f_o/\Delta f,$

where Δf is the width of the resonance curve when

$x = x_{max}/\sqrt{2}$

x_{max} being the maximum value of x, and where f_o is the resonant frequency.

PHASE

At resonance, an oscillator lags behind the driver by 90°, i.e. it is 90° out of **phase** with the driver. When the driver is at a much lower frequency than the oscillator's natural frequency ($f_d < f_N$) the oscillator is in step with the driver. When the driver frequency is much higher than the natural frequency ($f_d > f_N$) the driver and the oscillator are 180° out of phase.

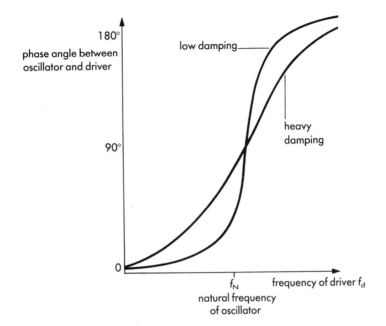

Fig. 6.15 Phase relationship between driver and oscillator for different amounts of damping

SHM AND WAVE MOTION

Consider ripples on water (Fig. 6.16). Here, each point on the surface oscillates with SHM but the oscillations of adjacent points (e.g. A and B) are slightly out of phase. The profile of the water becomes sinusoidal and this profile moves across the surface (see diagram). Note it is the pattern which moves across: the water itself moves only locally and vertically. Ripples like these are an example of a **transverse** wave i.e. a wave in which the local movement is at right angles to the wave motion. In **longitudinal** (or compressional) waves the local movement is parallel to the wave motion.

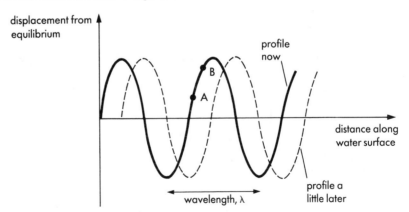

Fig. 6.16 Travelling waves (ripples) on water

STATIONARY WAVES

An example of this is what happens when a guitar string is plucked. The disturbance which is created travels along the string and is reflected back at the ends. At any point in time there are waves travelling in opposite directions in the string. **Standing** or **stationary waves** are what results when two progressive waves of the same amplitude travel in the same medium in opposite directions and interact. A typical sequence in time is shown in Fig. 6.17.

Note the following:

1 Points of maximum amplitude (A_1, A_2, A_3) are called **antinodes**.
2 Points of no motion (N_1, N_2, N_3, N_4) are **nodes**.
3 The distance between adjacent nodes is $\lambda/2$, i.e. $N_1N_2 = A_1A_2 = \lambda/2$, where λ is the **wavelength**.

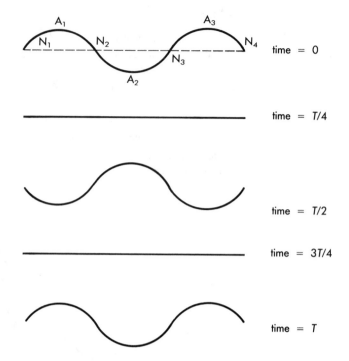

Fig. 6.17 'Snapshots' of a standing wave system

4   Adjacent antinodes oscillate in **antiphase**.
5   The **travelling wave equation**, $c = f\lambda$, can be used (c is the speed of the associated progressive wave).
6   Only certain values of λ are permitted if nodes are to appear at the ends. The simplest example is the guitar string mentioned above. The system vibrates at the frequency given by $f = c/\lambda$.
7   If an external vibration corresponding to such a value of f is applied, then the standing wave may be set up in a further example of resonance.
8   Unlike the case of the resonance of the simple harmonic oscillator there will be several resonant frequencies.

STANDING WAVES IN SOUND

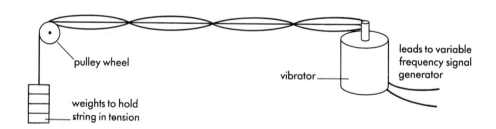

Fig. 6.18 Melde's apparatus

Standing waves on strings can be set up using **Melde's apparatus** (Fig. 6.18). The frequency of the vibrator is adjusted until a resonance is obtained, i.e. a stationary wave pattern is produced. The speed of such waves (c) is given by:

$$c = \sqrt{T/\mu}$$

where T is the tension in the string and μ the mass per unit length. Using the fact that l, the node-to-node distance, is $\lambda/2$, and $c = f\lambda$, we find:

$$f = \frac{l}{2l} \sqrt{T/\mu.}$$

Another way of producing this type of resonance is to send a.c. from a variable frequency signal generator along a wire with a magnetic field across the wire at its centre (Fig. 6.19). Oscillations will be induced through the $F = BIl$ force (see Chapter 13) at the centre. Note that only resonances associated with nodes at the ends and an antinode at the centre will be obtained.

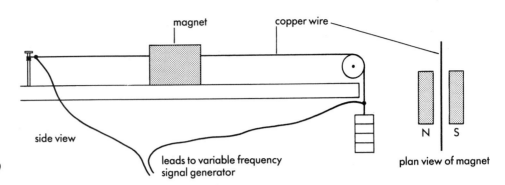

Fig. 6.19

side view

magnet

copper wire

leads to variable frequency
signal generator

plan view of magnet

N | S

AIR COLUMNS

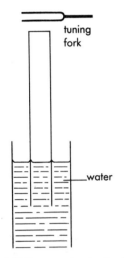

tuning
fork

water

Fig. 6.20 Resonance in tube closed
at one end

Fig. 6.21 Standing waves in a pipe
closed at one end

A simple example of resonance in a tube closed at one end is obtained using the equipment shown in Fig. 6.20. A typical stationary wave pattern of nodes and antinodes of displacement is shown. Because sound waves are *compressional*, it is common to show the equivalent pattern for a *transverse system*. This is illustrated in Fig. 6.21a).

The open end is an *antinode* because the air can freely oscillate there. N is a node because there the oscillation is impeded by the end. Fig. 6.21b) shows the actual pattern of air oscillation at some intermediate positions. Because adjacent antinodes oscillate in antiphase, the movement of air will sometimes be in opposite directions *away* from a node (see Fig. 6.21c)) whereas at other times the air will converge on a node. As a result, *pressure* variations have antinodes at displacement nodes and vice-versa. Microphones will usually detect pressure variations, not displacements.

Typical equivalent transverse stationary wave patterns for a pipe open at one end are shown in Fig. 6.22. Note that the antinode at the open end of the pipe will actually be a little way out from the end of the pipe, by a distance *e* called the end correction.

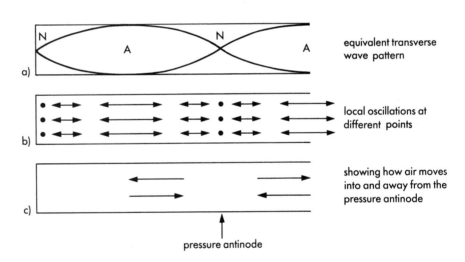

a)
equivalent transverse
wave pattern

b)
local oscillations at
different points

c)
showing how air moves
into and away from the
pressure antinode

pressure antinode

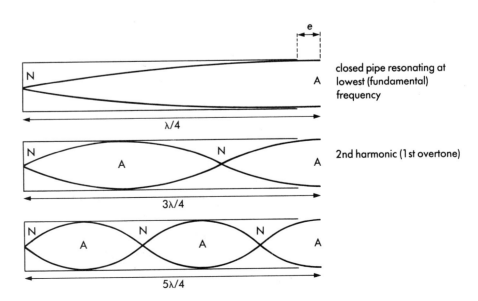

closed pipe resonating at
lowest (fundamental)
frequency

$\lambda/4$

2nd harmonic (1st overtone)

$3\lambda/4$

$5\lambda/4$

Fig. 6.22 Equivalent transverse
wave configurations for standing
waves in a pipe closed at one end.
The diagram shows three possible
resonances

Similar patterns for a pipe open at both ends are shown in Fig. 6.23.

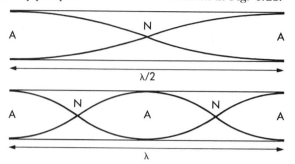

Fig. 6.23 Two possible resonances
for a pipe open at both ends

EXAMINATION QUESTIONS

**MULTIPLE
CHOICE
QUESTIONS**

1 When a particle oscillates in a straight line with simple harmonic motion, the period of the oscillation is:

a) directly proportional to the displacement of the particle from the origin;
b) directly proportional to the square root of the displacement of the particle from the origin;
c) directly proportional to the acceleration of the particle;
d) independent of the frequency of oscillation;
e) independent of the amplitude of oscillation.

$a = -\frac{4\pi^2}{T^2} x \qquad T^2 = -\frac{4\pi^2 x}{a}$

$T\omega = 2\pi$
$\omega = \frac{2\pi}{T}$

(NI 1985)

2 A particle moves with simple harmonic motion in a straight line. Which ONE of the graphs in Fig. 6.24 best represents the way in which the force F acting on the particle depends on the displacement r? (By convention, a force acting in the direction of $+r$ is taken as a *positive* force.)

(NI 1985)

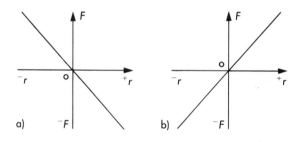

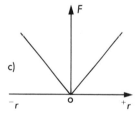
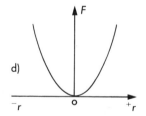
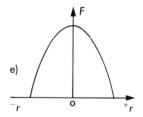

Fig. 6.24

(For questions **3** and **4** select your answer using the following code)
a) if **1**, **2** and **3** are all correct
b) if **1** and **2** only are correct
c) if **2** and **3** only are correct
d) if **1** only is correct
e) if **3** only is correct

3 A particle oscillates so that its displacement x from a fixed point is related to time t, by the equation $x = 3 \sin 5\pi t$. If x is in cm and t is in s, we can deduce that the particle:

1 Moves with simple harmonic motion.
2 Has a frequency of 2.5 Hz.
3 Has an amplitude of 1.5 cm.

(AEB 1986)

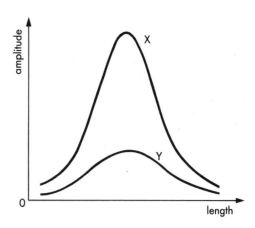

Fig. 6.25

4   Two pendulums, X and Y, are identically coupled to a much more massive pendulum, Z. The length of Z is varied. Graphs of the amplitude of oscillation of X and Y against the length of Z are shown. Which of the following is/are correct?

1   The pendulums X and Y have equal length.
2   Y is more heavily damped than X.
3   X and Y will always vibrate in phase with Z.

(AEB 1986)

5   A light helical spring is suspended from a beam, and a mass, m, is attached at its lower end, causing the spring to extend through a distance a. The mass is now caused to execute vertical oscillations of amplitude a. When the mass is at its lowest point, the energy stored in the spring is

a) 0
b) $\frac{1}{2}mga$
c) mga
d) $2mga$
e) $4mga$

(London 1987)

6   Two identical helical springs are suspended from fixed points. A mass $2M$ is attached to the lower end of one spring and a mass M to the lower end of the other. The masses are given small vertical displacements to produce simple harmonic motion of the same amplitude for each mass. The ratio:

$$\frac{\text{maximum acceleration of mass } 2M}{\text{maximum acceleration of mass } M}$$

is

a) $\frac{1}{4}$
b) $\frac{1}{2}$
c) 1
d) 2
e) 4

(NI 1988)

7   An organ pipe of length 0.80 m is closed at one end and open at the other. What are the two lowest resonant frequencies of the air in the pipe? (Neglect end corrections, and take the speed of sound in air to be $320 \, \text{ms}^{-1}$.)

a) 100 Hz and 200 Hz
b) 100 Hz and 300 Hz
c) 200 Hz and 400 Hz
d) 200 Hz and 600 Hz
e) 400 Hz and 800 Hz.

(Oxford 1987)

ANSWERS AND COMMENTS

Question	1	2	3	4	5	6	7
Answer	e)	a)	b)	b)	d)	b)	b)

1 and **2** Note the distractors which are intended to trip candidates who get the SHM formulae muddled up. For example the answer d) in question **2** would be correct if the question had been about the dependence of potential energy on *r*, and e) correct if it had been about the dependence of kinetic energy on *r*.

3   The formula $x = a \sin 2\pi ft$ is needed. 3 is a distractor for candidates who think the 3 in $3 \sin 5\pi t$ refers to the 'peak to peak' distance.

4   This arrangement is sometimes called Barton's pendula. A massive pendulum is used to act as a driver of a pendula of small mass.

5   At the lowest position the mass extends the spring by $2a$. There is no kinetic energy, so the stored energy must equal *mgh*, the loss of potential energy, with $h = 2a$.

6   To answer this it is best to forget about SHM formulae and just use Newton's 2nd Law. Here $a = -\dfrac{k}{m}x$ and as k and x are the same for both springs, $a \propto \dfrac{l}{m}$.

7   See the text (pp. 55–6).

STRUCTURED
QUESTIONS

8   What is meant by *simple harmonic motion*?
A wire of mass per unit length $5.0\,\text{g m}^{-1}$ is stretched between two points 30 cm apart. The tension in the wire is 70 N. Calculate the frequency of the sound emitted by the wire when it oscillates in its fundamental mode.
Explain, with reference to this example, the term *damped harmonic motion*.

(London 1989)

9   A helical spring requires a force, *k*, to produce unit extension. When it is suspended vertically a mass, *M*, attached to its lower end performs <u>simple harmonic motion</u> with a time period, *T*, when given a small vertical displacement and released. The time period is independent of the <u>amplitude</u>.

a) Define the terms underlined and write down an expression for *T* in terms of *M* and *k*.

b) The diagrams below show helical springs connected in series (Fig. 6.26a)) and in parallel (Fig. 6.26b)). All four springs are identical and each arrangement has a mass, *M*, attached to its lower end. In each case determine, in terms of *T*, the new time period and explain your reasoning.

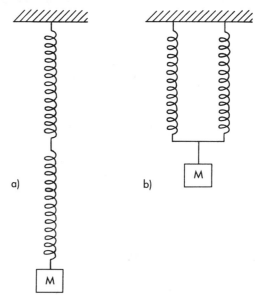

Fig. 6.26

(JMB 1987)

10   a) Fig. 6.27 shows a section of a stationary transverse wave.

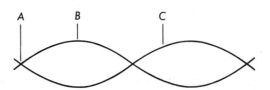

Fig. 6.27

     i) Explain how such a wave may be formed from two progressive waves, making clear any conditions which must be fulfilled.

     ii) Compare the amplitudes of particle vibrations at A, B and C and the phases at B and C.

  b) Stationary waves are set up in an air column contained in a tube closed at one end. A small loudspeaker connected to a signal generator is placed near the open end of the tube in order to produce the sound. The tube has a length of 50.0 cm.

     i) At certain precise frequencies a loud sound is emitted from the tube. Give the reasons for this.

     ii) The lowest frequency that will cause this effect is 165 Hz. Assuming that any end correction may be neglected calculate the speed of sound.

     iii) The frequency of the generator is increased until the next loud sound occurs. Calculate the frequency at which this happens.

  c) The pitch of a certain wind instrument is found to increase slightly with temperature.

     i) Suggest why this is so.

     ii) At 20°C a wind instrument produces a note of frequency 440 Hz. When the air temperature rises to 30°C the frequency increases. Calculate this increase. You may ignore any expansion of the instrument.

                                            (Southern 1987)

11 a) A vibrating system which is made to undergo *forced vibrations* may exhibit *resonance*. Explain the terms in italics.

  b) What is meant by *damping*? Indicate how the amount of damping can influence resonance.

                                            (JMB 1988)

12 'Resonance is a Mixed Blessing.'

Discuss this statement. Include in your answer an explanation of what is meant by resonance and describe *four* examples of resonance. *At least one* example should show how resonance can be helpful and *at least one* should show how it can be a nuisance.

  In *at least one* example explain quantitatively how the resonant frequency is related to other properties of the system.

                                  (O and C (Nuffield), 1986)

OUTLINE ANSWERS

8 The calculation needs the formula $f = \dfrac{1}{2l}\sqrt{\dfrac{T}{\mu}}$ (see text).

Care is needed in conversion to SI units. $T = 70\,\text{N}$, $\mu = 5.0\,\text{g m}^{-1} = 5 \times 10^{-3}\,\text{kg m}^{-1}$ and $l = 0.3\,\text{m}$; hence $f = 197.2\,\text{Hz}$.

9 a) See text (p. 47). $T = 2\pi\sqrt{\dfrac{M}{k}}$

  b) In case a) the arrangement gives twice the original extension for the same load, and in case b), half the extension. So $k_a = \dfrac{k}{2}$ and $k_b = 2k$, (using an obvious notation). Hence using the formula given in a) $T_a = \sqrt{2}\,T$ and $T_b = T/\sqrt{2}$.

10 a) i) See text (p. 53).

     ii) B is an antinode, there is no vibration at A and that at C is in antiphase with that at B, but with a smaller amplitude.

  b) i) See text (p. 55).

     ii) $\lambda/4 = 0.50\,\text{m}$ $v = f\lambda$ gives $v = 330\,\text{ms}^{-1}$

     iii) $3 \times 165\,\text{Hz} = 495\,\text{Hz}$

  c) The pitch increases because the speed of sound is proportional to the square root of the absolute temperature i.e. $v \propto \sqrt{T}$. In a wind instrument the time for sound to travel up and down the instrument is reduced. The length of the instrument is unchanged. Hence the observed frequency increases and a rise in pitch is noticed.

i.e. $\dfrac{f_2}{f_1} = \dfrac{\sqrt{T_2}}{\sqrt{T_1}}$ so $\dfrac{f_2}{440} = \dfrac{\sqrt{273+30}}{\sqrt{273+20}} \Rightarrow f = 447.45 \text{ Hz}$

11 and **12**. See text.

TUTOR'S QUESTION AND ANSWER

QUESTION

a) One end of a light spring is attached to a fixed point and a body is hung on the other end. Show that, if Hooke's law is obeyed and the body is displaced vertically from its equilibrium position, it will oscillate with simple harmonic motion. Derive an expression for the period of oscillation.

b) A car suspension system consists of four springs together with dampers (shock absorbers) to damp oscillations when the car goes over a bump. The damper consists of a piston moving through a cylinder which contains oil. An experimental car, fitted with springs but not dampers, is lowered onto the ground and as a result the springs are 10 cm shorter than their unstressed length. The effective mass of the car is 1000 kg.
 i) In one test the car is forced downwards by a further 8 cm, released and allowed to oscillate. What is the period of oscillation?
 ii) What would be the effect on the period of oscillation if the test were repeated with the car carrying an evenly distributed load of 250 kg?
 iii) Dampers are now fitted. Sketch graphs on the same axes to compare the oscillations of the car in tests with and without dampers.

c) Oscillations similar to those in b) could have been obtained by raising the car body.
 i) Estimate the external work required to raise the car body (without the 250 kg load) through a height of 8 cm. Show your working clearly.
 ii) Discuss the energy changes which occur during the oscillations if dampers are not fitted.
 iii) Discuss the energy changes if dampers are fitted.

(AEB 1987 Specimen Paper)

ANSWER

a) Three diagrams have been drawn (Fig. 6.28).

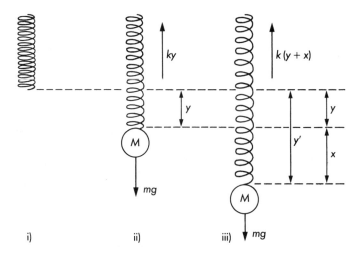

Fig. 6.28

 i) shows the spring unloaded and unstretched;
 ii) shows the spring loaded with the mass m and stretched in its equilibrium position;
 iii) shows the spring displaced away from equilibrium by an amount x.
 In ii) the force of gravity equals the force due to the spring which obeys Hooke's law.

This gives

$mg = ky$, where k is the Hooke constant.

In iii) there is a net upward force of amount:

$ky' - mg = ky + kx - mg$

and as $ky = mg$, this is kx.

Taking the direction of increasing x (downwards) as positive, this is $-kx$.

This force acts on the mass m.

Applying Newton's 2nd law we have:

$ma = -kx,$

giving $a = -\dfrac{k}{m} x$

where a is the acceleration (i.e we have acceleration proportional to displacement from equilibrium). This proves that the mass subsequently oscillates with simple harmonic motion.

$$a = -\omega^2 x \text{ where } \omega = \sqrt{\frac{k}{m}}.$$

The period $T = \dfrac{2\pi}{\omega} = 2\pi \sqrt{\dfrac{m}{k}}$

b) In equilibrium each of the four springs is subjected to the effective weight of 250 kg; i.e. for each spring,

force applied $= 250 \times 10$ N

displacement $x = 0.10$ m

$$k = \frac{F}{x} = \frac{250 \times 10}{0.10} = 2.5 \times 10^4 \text{ Nm}^{-1}$$

i) If displaced further, each spring will oscillate with effectively 250 kg of the car body

$$T = 2\pi \sqrt{\frac{m}{k}} = 2\pi \sqrt{\frac{250}{2.5 \times 10^4}}$$

$$= 0.63 \text{ s}$$

ii) With an evenly distributed load of 250 kg each spring carries an additional mass of 62.5 kg

T is now given by $T = 2\pi \sqrt{\dfrac{(62.5) + 250}{2.5 \times 10^4}}$

$$= 0.70 \text{ s}.$$

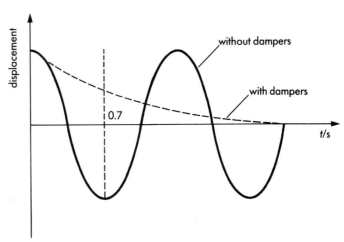

Fig. 6.29

iii) The graph with dampers assumes damping at least equal to that needed to provide critical damping.

c) i) When the car is lowered on to the ground each spring stores energy of amount $\frac{1}{2}kx^2$ where x is the displacement from equilibrium, i.e. 0.1 m. When the car is raised by 0.08 m the displacement is only 0.02 m,

amount of energy released $= 4 \times |\frac{1}{2}k(0.10)^2 - \frac{1}{2}k(0.02)^2|$
$= 2 \times 2.5 \times 10^4 ((0.10)^2 - (0.02)^2)$
$= 480$ J

In raising the car, work done against gravity $= mgh$
$= 1000 \times 10 \times 0.08 = 800$ J

Net external work required $= 800 - 480$ J
$= 320$ J.

ii) Consider the energy changes from the moment in the cycle of oscillations that the car is in the upper position. Here it has no kinetic energy. As it falls towards the equilibrium position gravitational potential energy is converted into kinetic energy and potential energy in the springs. As it descends to the bottom position there is further conversion of gravitational potential energy into spring potential energy together with conversion of kinetic energy into spring potential energy. All the energy changes are then reversed as the car moves upwards.

iii) With dampers fitted, the car very quickly reaches its maximum speed, and the speed then steadily falls. So initially there is a conversion of gravitational potential energy into kinetic energy and then a progressive loss of kinetic energy and gravitational potential energy into spring potential energy and internal energy of the pistons/oil etc.

STUDENT'S ANSWER WITH EXAMINER COMMENTS

STUDENT'S ANSWER TO QUESTION 11

> **There may be more than one frequency of resonance.**

> **Answer is correct but rather too general. It would be helpful to give an example.**

> **This sentence is true of a system oscillating freely: here the question is about one being driven.**

An oscillating system has a natural frequency of oscillation. However it may be connected to an external system which can cause it to vibrate at any frequency. Such oscillations are called forced oscillations. At resonance these are at a maximum. The frequency of resonance is the same as the natural frequency.

Damping is when the oscillations die away due to frictional forces. The diagram shows the effect on resonance.

> **The student needs to clearly state that the *forced oscillations* are not the oscillations of the driver but those of the *driven* system.**

> **The diagram needs to be much clearer and needs to be labelled. It needs to clearly show that damping broadens the resonance curve and reduces the maximum amplitude produced.**

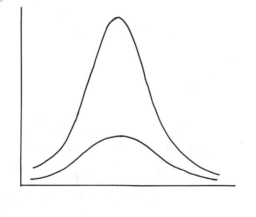

Overall Comment: This answer is typical of a candidate who probably knows the physics, but is not capable of describing ideas in the kind of detail needed for high marks at A-Level. The answer is typical of a C-grade candidate.

WAVES

GETTING STARTED

The general ideas of longitudinal and transverse, progressive and stationary waves and the basic terminology which accompanies them are mentioned in all A Level syllabuses. Stationary waves and the examples of vibrating strings and air columns are dealt with in detail in Chapter 6. The stroboscope, Doppler effect and beats are mentioned in only a few syllabuses.

ESSENTIAL PRINCIPLES

TRAVELLING (PROGRESSIVE) WAVES

TRANSVERSE WAVES

An understanding of the way in which a wave travels is useful before considering other wave properties. Let us consider the example of ripples on water. Such a wave motion consists of a series of crests and troughs travelling across the surface. It is useful to sketch a graph of such a wave (Fig. 7.1) The y axis represents the **displacement** of the water from its horizontal level and the x axis the distance along the water surface from some arbitrary point. The maximum displacement of the water is known as the **amplitude** (A) and the distance between the tops of two crests is the **wavelength** (λ). The diagram represents a picture of the water surface at a certain time; shortly afterwards the wave will have moved forward (to the right) so that location P is no longer the top of a crest. The locations P and Q, one wavelength apart, will, however, always have the same displacement and be moving in the same vertical direction – they are said to be **in phase**.

> **❝Always label axes of graphs.❞**

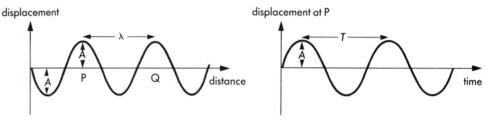

Fig. 7.1 Ripples on water   Fig. 7.2 Displacement against time

As time progresses, a point on the water surface (e.g. at location P) oscillates up and down with a regular frequency. Hence a graph of the displacement of P against *time* can be drawn (Fig. 7.2). The y axis once again represents displacement from the equilibrium position, but the x axis represents time. On this graph the 'distance' between two peaks is the time for one complete oscillation at P. This time is called the **period** T, and if this is $\frac{1}{6}$ second then the **frequency** is 6 waves per second or 6 Hz. The 6 waves will stretch over a distance of 6 wavelengths and this is the distance the wave travels in 1 second.

Hence: speed = frequency × wavelength

$$c = f\lambda.$$

A wave motion, where the displacements are *perpendicular* to the direction in which the wave travels, is called a **transverse** wave. All electromagnetic waves, including light are transverse. In this case the electric and magnetic field vectors (corresponding to displacement in the water waves just considered), are both perpendicular to the direction in which the wave is travelling.

LONGITUDINAL WAVES

Sound is a wave motion, and it travels by means of the local oscillations of the medium of propagation, for instance, air. However, these oscillations are to and fro (Fig. 7.3), along the direction of travel, and the wave is said to be **longitudinal**.

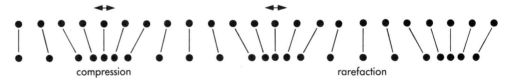

compression   rarefaction

Fig. 7.3 Longitudinal wave

Graphs of displacement against distance or displacement against time can be plotted for longitudinal waves, though it is to be remembered that the actual displacements are along the direction of travel.

Take the case of sound travelling in air; in the regions (called **compressions**) where the air molecules are more densely packed than usual, the pressure is greater than atmospheric pressure. In the regions where the molecules are less densely packed (called rarefactions), the pressure is less than atmospheric. The distance between adjacent compressions or adjacent rarefactions is one wavelength.

Longitudinal and transverse waves show the properties of rectilinear propagation, reflection, refraction, interference and diffraction, but polarisation is exhibited only by transverse waves.

MEASURING FREQUENCIES

"Remember the x axis of an oscilloscope is a *time* axis."

MEASURING SPEED AND FREQUENCY OF SOUND WAVES

The **frequency** of a note can be measured by using a microphone and amplifier to display the waveform on a Cathode Ray Oscilloscope (cro). The time for one cycle and thus the number of cycles per second can be measured if the cro is suitably calibrated.

The **wavelength** of a note can be obtained from a stationary wave pattern. Interference between two waves travelling in opposite directions can produce such a pattern, for example, by connecting two loudspeakers to the same signal generator and placing the speakers opposite each other. If a microphone is moved along the line joining the speakers, the amplitude will be observed to rise and fall regularly. The distance between two adjacent maxima (antinodes) is half the wavelength of the progressive sound waves. One speaker facing a reflector will achieve a similar effect. The minima (nodes) are not zero, because one wave is usually bigger than the other, say if you are nearer one speaker than the other.

Once the wavelength and frequency are known the **speed** can be found from $c = f\lambda$.

MEASURING FREQUENCY OF VIBRATION OR ROTATION WITH A STROBOSCOPE

A **Xenon stroboscope** is a device which produces a very short flash of light at regular intervals. The frequency is the number of flashes per second. The aim is to adjust the frequency of the strobe until it is flashing once per vibration or rotation, so that the object will always be in the same place when you see it and so appear stationary. In practice you have to be careful, because the object may have rotated/vibrated twice between flashes. However, if the object is illuminated twice per revolution/rotation, it will appear stationary in two different positions.

DOPPLER EFFECT

The **Doppler effect** is a phenomenon where the *observed* frequency of a source is less or more than the true frequency as a result of either the source or the observer or both moving.

SOUND

If the source is stationary, the f waves it emits in one second will be spread out over a distance equal to c (c is the speed of sound).

Moving observer

If an observer is *moving towards* a stationary source (Fig. 7.4), then he will pass through more complete waves than if he were stationary. The diagram shows the waves the observer will pass through in one second. The observer moving at speed v will travel a

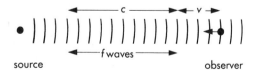

Fig. 7.4 Observer moving towards a stationary source

distance v to meet the wave which has travelled forward a distance c. There are f waves in a distance c, so the number of waves in a distance $c + v$ is given by:

$\dfrac{(c + v)}{c} f$, which is the apparent frequency heard. This is greater than f.

If the observer is *moving away* from the source, the *apparent* frequency is given by:

$\dfrac{(c - v)}{c} f$, which is less then the true frequency.

A passenger on a train hears a sudden fall in the frequency of the warning bell when passing a crossing.

Moving source

The effect of moving the source (Fig. 7.5) is to change the wavelength of the travelling waves. The source moves a distance u in 1 second, and so the f waves will be contained in

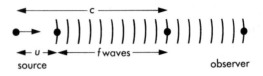

Fig. 7.5 Effect of moving the source

a distance $(c - u)$. The wavelength will be $(c - u)/f$ and so the apparent frequency will be:

$$\frac{cf}{(c - u)}$$ which is greater than f.

If the source is moving away from the observer, the apparent frequency will be:

$$\frac{cf}{(c + u)}$$ which is less than f.

A person standing on the platform hears a sudden drop in the frequency of the train's siren as the train passes by.

Moving source and observer

For instance, a moving object reflecting a wave back towards the transmitter. The speed of the moving observer (the object moving through the waves) and the moving source (the object bouncing back the waves) are both w and so the apparent frequency is given by

$$\frac{(c + w)}{(c - w)} f.$$

If the reflected wave is combined with a wave direct from the transmitter a beat frequency is heard.

LIGHT

The treatment of the Doppler effect for *light* is somewhat different, as light travels at the same speed relative to any source. However, a source moving towards an observer will result in an apparent increase in frequency and consequent decrease in wavelength, known as the *red shift*.

BEATS

If the sounds from two sources of slightly different frequency are combined, the *amplitude* of the resultant note will be heard to rise and fall at a **beat frequency**. If the frequency of one source is f and the frequency of the other is $(f + x)$, then at some instant the two sources will be in phase and so produce a loud note. $1/x$ seconds later one source will have emitted $f(1/x) = f/x$ waves, and the other $(f + x)(1/x) = f/x + 1$.

This means that the second source will have emitted one more complete wave and so the sources will be back in phase. They will therefore be in phase every $1/x$ seconds or x times per second. So the **beat frequency** is x, the difference between the frequencies of the two sources.

EXAMINATION QUESTIONS

1   The diagrams in Fig. 7.6 show an instantaneous photograph of a *transverse* wave on water in a ripple tank. The wave is travelling from left to right. The arrows on the diagrams are intended to indicate the direction of motion of the surface of the water at the instant the photograph was taken. Which ONE of the diagrams is correct?

(NI 1987)

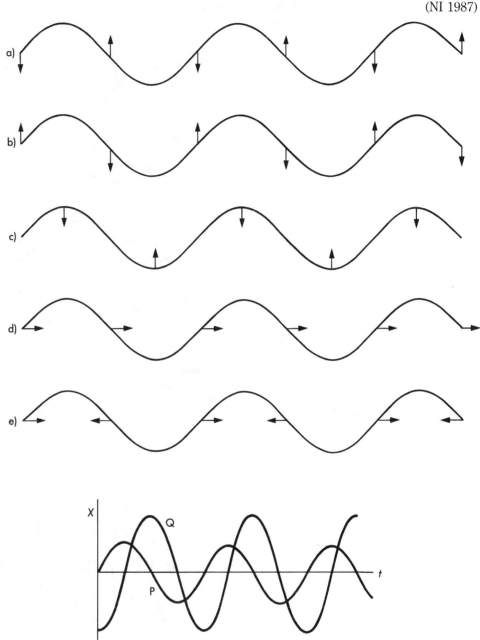

Fig. 7.6

Fig. 7.7

2   Two progressive waves, P and Q, meet at a point. The variation of the displacement, X, of each wave with time, t, is shown on the graph above. Which of the following statements is true?

   a) The waves are 180° out of phase and the amplitude of Q is twice that of P.

   b) The frequency of Q is twice that of P and both waves travel at the same speed.

   c) Both waves are of the same frequency but Q lags 90° behind P in phase.

   d) Constructive interference will occur at the point and the amplitude of the resulting wave will be three times the amplitude of P.

   e) Destructive interference will occur at the point and the amplitude of the resultant wave will be zero.

(London 1988)

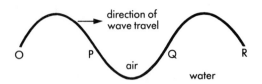

Fig. 7.8

3 At a particular instant the profile of a surface wave on water is as indicated in Fig. 7.8. Which of the graphs in Fig. 7.9 best represents the vertical velocities of the water surface layer at this instant, upward velocities being considered as positive?

(London 1988)

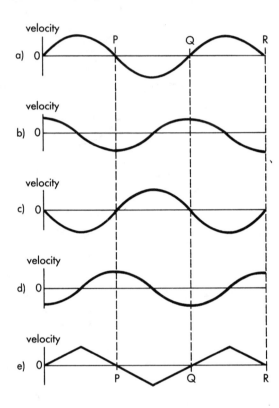

Fig. 7.9

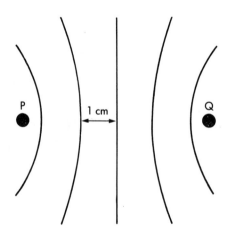

Fig. 7.10

4 The diagram in Fig. 7.10 shows the interference pattern in a ripple tank when the probes P and Q are vibrating in phase and at a frequency of 10 Hz. The lines of the pattern are equally spaced between P and Q and are 1.0 cm apart. The speed of the water waves in the ripple tank is

a) 0.025 m s^{-1} d) 0.20 m s^{-1}
b) 0.050 m s^{-1} e) 0.40 m s^{-1}
c) 0.10 m s^{-1}

(London 1987)

5 Fig. 7.11 shows an experiment to investigate the sound wave emitted from a certain source. The screen of the cathode-ray oscilloscope has a graticule ruled in 1 cm

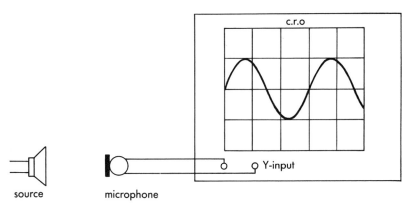

Fig. 7.11

squares. The time-base is set at '2 ms/cm' and the Y-sensitivity at '5 V/cm'. A student makes the following deductions from the trace on the screen:
1) The frequency of the sound wave is 166⅔ Hz.
2) The wavelength of the sound wave is 3 cm.
3) The amplitude of the sound wave is 5 V.

Which of these deductions is (are) correct?

a) 1 only   d) 2 and 3 only
b) 2 only   e) 1, 2 and 3
c) 1 and 2 only

(NI 1987)

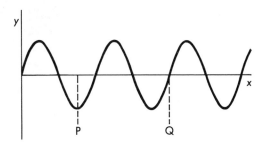

Fig. 7.12

6 The graph in Fig. 7.12 represents the displacement y at different points along a wave travelling in the direction x at a particular instant of time. P and Q are two points along the wave. The phase relationship between the displacements at these points is:

a) Q is 90° ($\pi/2$ rad) in advance of P.
b) Q is 90° ($\pi/2$ rad) behind P.
c) Q is 180° (π rad) in advance of P.
d) Q is in phase with P.
e) There is no constant phase relationship.

(London 1987)

7 A wave of frequency 2 Hz travels through a medium at a speed of 8 m s^{-1}. At any instant the separation of adjacent points where the displacement is zero will be:

a) 1 m   d) 8 m
b) 2 m   e) 16 m
c) 4 m

(London 1989)

ANSWERS AND COMMENTS

Question	1	2	3	4	5	6	7
Answer	a)	c)	d)	d)	a)	b)	b)

1 The diagram shows the direction of motion of the points.
2 Remember t is plotted on x axis.
3 The graphs represent the velocity of the points. At the instant shown, P is moving at its fastest speed upwards.
4 A stationary wave is set up between P and Q. The distance between two antinodes = 1 cm, so the wavelength of the progressive waves = 2 cm.
   Speed $= 2 \times 10 = 20$ cm s^{-1} = 0.2 m s^{-1}.
5 1) Time for 1 cycle = 3 cm = 6 ms. Frequency = 1000/6 = 166⅔ Hz.
   2) Wavelength = speed/frequency which is not equal to 3 cm.
   3) Amplitude of trace = 1 cm = 5V, but this is not the amplitude of the sound wave.
6 The point Q is 1¼ cycles behind P.
7 The wavelength = speed/frequency = 8/2 = 4 m.

STRUCTURED QUESTIONS

8 A black disc with a white dot rotates clockwise at a uniform speed of 30 revolutions per second (see Fig. 7.13). The disc is viewed in light which flashes at a frequency f (produced by a stroboscope with a calibrated frequency dial).

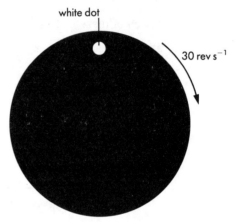

white dot

30 rev s^{-1}

Fig. 7.13

a) State three values of f for which a stationary pattern (as shown in Fig. 7.13) would be seen. (2)
b) Explain how you would confirm from observations of the disc and readings of the stroboscope dial that the disc was rotating at 30 revolutions per second. (2)
c) Describe what would be seen if the stroboscope flashes at a frequency of:
   i) 90 Hz; (2)
   ii) 31 Hz. (3)

(Oxford 1988)

OUTLINE ANSWERS

a) The three values for f are: i) 30 Hz ii) 15 Hz iii) 7.5 Hz.
b) Double the strobe frequency to 60 Hz and two dots will be seen opposite each other because the disc is being illuminated twice per revolution.
c) i) Three equally spaced dots as the disc is being illuminated three times per revolution.
   ii) A disc with one dot which appears to be rotating slowly backwards as the disc is being illuminated just before it completes one revolution.

CHAPTER 8

INTER-FERENCE, DIFFRACTION AND POLAR-ISATION

GETTING STARTED

When two progressive waves meet they **interfere**, and the **resultant effect** is found by algebraically adding the two waves together using the principle of superposition. With two coherent sources, fixed regions of constructive and destructive interference occur and a pattern is observed.

Diffraction is a phenomenon which occurs when an obstacle or slit in some way restricts the passage of a wave. Without the obstruction, the plane wave propagates forward as a plane wave, and so the light travels in a straight line. However, if part of the wavefront is restricted, then diffraction will occur and the plane wave will spread and produce a pattern of varying intensity. These effects can all be explained by **Huygen's principle of secondary sources** which can also be used to explain **rectilinear propagation, reflection** and **refraction. Polarisation** is mentioned in the core syllabus as a phenomenon affecting transverse waves, particularly electromagnetic waves.

ESSENTIAL PRINCIPLES

INTERFERENCE

When two waves meet, their displacements *add up* to produce a resultant displacement. If a crest of amplitude A meets a similar crest then the result will be a crest of amplitude $2A$. Two troughs will produce a trough of amplitude $2A$ but a crest and trough will cancel to produce no displacement (Fig. 8.1).

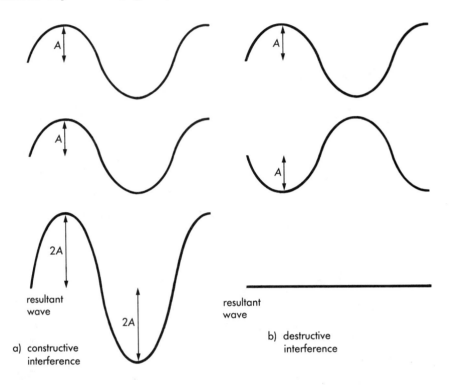

Fig. 8.1

If two sets of waves meet in such a way that crests always meet crests, and troughs always meet troughs, then the **interference** will be **constructive** and a wave of amplitude $2A$ will result. However if crests are always meeting troughs, then **destructive** interference will take place and there will be no resultant wave. If these are light waves, then as intensity is proportional to the square of the wave amplitude, constructive interference will result in brightness and destructive interference in darkness. A pattern of interference will only be observed if the positions of constructive and destructive interference stay in the same place.

In order to achieve this observable pattern the sources must be **coherent**, i.e. they must have the same frequency and if they are out of phase, the phase difference must remain constant.

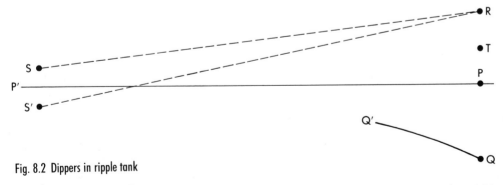

Fig. 8.2 Dippers in ripple tank

Two dippers in a ripple tank will produce an observable pattern. The sources S and S′ are in phase: that is, they produce crests at the same time and these crests, travelling at the same speed, will arrive at an equidistant point P at the same time. There will be constructive interference anywhere along the line PP′. There will also be constructive interference along QQ′, where any point along this line is one wavelength further from S than S′. Constructive interference will also occur wherever the path difference S′R – SR is a whole number of wavelengths. Similarly destructive interference will occur where the path difference is an odd number of half wavelengths such as T where S'T – ST is half a wavelength.

An ordinary lamp emits light in short bursts of energy called photons, but the relationship between the phase of one photon and the next is quite random. Hence the photons from two separate lamps will not maintain a constant phase difference. This constantly changing phase difference will keep moving the positions of maxima and minima and so no clear pattern will be observed. For an observable pattern, the two waves must somehow originate from the same source.

YOUNG'S SLITS

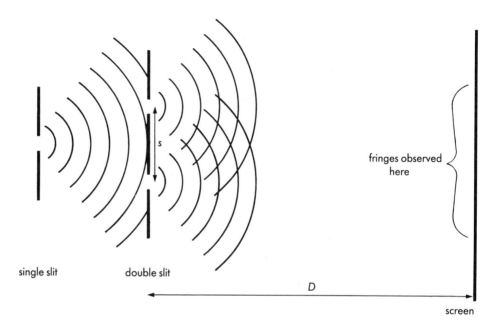

single slit   double slit

fringes observed here

D

screen

Fig. 8.3 Young's slits

The simplest way of producing two coherent waves from *one* source is simply to use two slits to divide the wavefront into two parts (Fig. 8.3). The single slit is necessary to ensure that the wave arriving at the two slits is part of the same wavefront. This single slit is not necessary if using a *laser* because light from all parts of the laser source is coherent. Note that the effect of diffraction, that is the spreading out of a wave passing through a narrow gap, is utilised at all three slits.

> This pattern is sometimes referred to as 'Young's fringes'.

Using a *monochromatic* source, a pattern of equally spaced bright and dark fringes may be observed on a screen or by looking towards the two slits through an eyepiece. By measuring the separation x of adjacent bright patches and also the distances s and D, it is possible to calculate the wavelength λ of the light using the equation:

$$\lambda = \frac{x\,s}{D} \ , \text{ provided } D \gg s.$$

> Describe this pattern in your own words.

If *white* light is used, then as all the wavelengths in the visible spectrum are present, each colour will produce equally spaced fringes, but the spacing will depend on the wavelength. The red fringes will have the greatest separation and the blue the least. This results in the fringes near the centre of the pattern being white with blue edges on the inside and red on the outside. The central fringe of the pattern is identifiable, being white because all the colours interfere constructively at the position of zero path difference. Further out the different coloured fringes begin to overlap and so merge into a uniform whitish illumination.

Another method of producing fringes is by using a mirror (Fig. 8.4). One wave goes directly to the screen and interferes with the coherent wave which has reflected off the surface of the mirror. We can treat the virtual image of S_1 in the plane mirror as the other source S_2 and then the theory is similar to Young's fringes. There is however a sudden phase change of π as the wave reflects from the mirror which is equivalent to a sudden path change of half a wavelength.

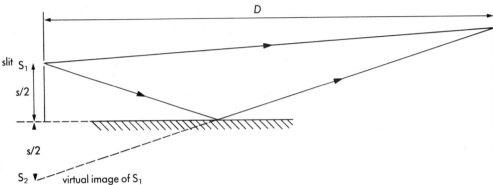

Fig. 8.4 Producing fringes using a mirror

DIFFRACTION

Diffraction occurs when a wavefront is in some way *restricted*. This restriction may be a result of the limited size of the source or receiver, or as a result of the wave being obstructed by an obstacle. The pupil of the eye and the objective lens of a telescope are both apertures of receivers which restrict the wavefront and so diffraction will affect the images they produce.

SINGLE SLIT

If the aperture is a *single slit* then experiments with a ripple tank will show the effects of diffraction as the waves spread out on passing through the gap. The narrower the slit the more the wave spreads out. To consider this diffraction pattern in more detail it is useful to apply Huygen's construction using secondary sources (Fig. 8.5).

Each point on the wavefront is considered to be a point source emitting circular wavelets. The wave amplitude in any particular direction is found by adding all the contributions made by these secondary wavelets. The resulting intensity pattern is as shown in Fig. 8.6. *Minima* of intensity are found at angles θ given by the equation $\sin \theta = n\lambda/d$, where n is a whole number. In between these minima there is some overall intensity and so a pattern is produced.

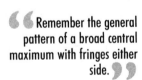

Remember the general pattern of a broad central maximum with fringes either side. **99**

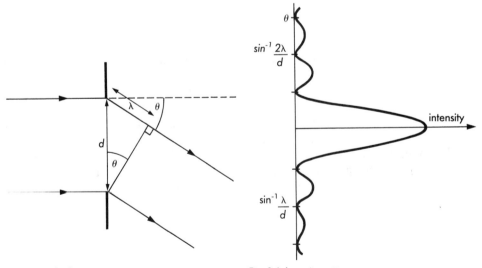

Fig. 8.5 Single slit   Fig. 8.6 Intensity pattern

CIRCULAR APERTURE

If the aperture happens to be a *circular cross-section*, such as the pupil of the eye, the diffraction patern consists of a bright central circular patch surrounded by alternate dark and bright rings (Fig. 8.7). The slightly different geometry gives the formula for the first minimum to be $\sin \theta = 1.22 \, \lambda/d$. This means that the image on the retina of a point object is not a point but a circular patch surrounded by rings. If the eye is looking at two point objects close together then their images will be close together on the retina and the circular patches will overlap. If they are very close together they may not be perceived as two separate patches and so the observer will appear to see only one object. The eye is said not to have 'resolved' the objects.

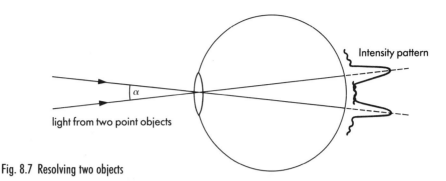

Fig. 8.7 Resolving two objects

light from two point objects

> Remember these objects will subtend *small* angles, so use approximations to calculate them.

Lord Rayleigh suggested that a useful guide would be that two objects can not be resolved if the two circular patches of their diffracted image patterns were so close that the first minimum of one overlapped the central maximum of the other. A common example of this is looking at the two headlights of a distant car. A similar situation exists for a telescope looking at the images of two distant stars close together in the sky. It should be remembered that the aperture of the *transmitting* device restricts the wavefront and so the intensity in front of a source will show the features of a broad central maximum surrounded by minima and smaller maxima.

SEVERAL SLITS

Light spreading out through the slits interferes where the diffracted waves overlap. The overall effect is one of an interference pattern of alternate maxima and minina, but the *overall* intensity of the maxima is dominated by the diffraction pattern of a single slit. The *maxima* occur when light from any slit interferes constructively with light from other slits. This will happen when the path difference between the waves passing through adjacent

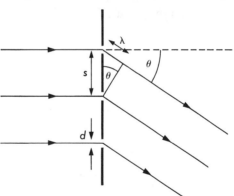

Fig. 8.8 Several slits

slits is a whole number of wavelengths, and so these maxima will occur at angles θ which are given by the equation:

$$\sin \theta = \frac{n \lambda}{s}$$

i.e their positions are governed by the separation of the slits. Remember that the first *minimum* of **diffraction** is given by

$$\sin \theta = \frac{\lambda}{d}$$

and is governed by the *width* of the slits.

The effect of adding more slits of the same width as each other and separated by the same amounts is not only to increase the overall intensity of the pattern, but also to make the maxima of interference sharper.

A diffraction grating consists of *thousands* of equal width and equally spaced parallel slits. The positions of the maxima of **interference** are still governed by the equation

$$\sin \theta = \frac{n \lambda}{s}$$

and these maxima are known as orders. When n = 1, the path difference between adjacent slits in the grating is one wavelength. This is known as the **first order image**. The *overall*

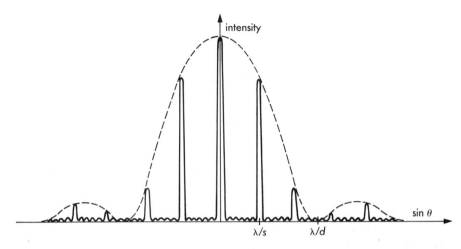

Fig. 8.9 Intensity pattern with several slits

intensity of the pattern is still dominated by the envelope of the single slit diffraction pattern. Because there are very many slits, the orders are very bright and also very sharp in that the intensity drops vary rapidly to zero on either side of the order. This is very useful if the light contains different wavelengths. The first order images will occur at different angles depending on the wavelengths, but in order to distinguish between them, the images need to be sharp so that they do not overlap.

POLARISATION

Polarisation is a phenomenon exhibited only by *transverse* waves. Electromagnetic waves are transverse in that the oscillating electric field E associated with the wave is perpendicular to the direction in which the wave is travelling. The oscillating magnetic field B is perpendicular to both the electric field and the direction of propagation, but is in phase with the electric field.

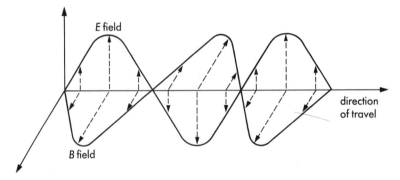

Fig. 8.10 Electromagnetic wave

Polarised waves have their electric field in one plane only, whereas in unpolarised waves there are electric fields in all planes perpendicular to the direction of travel. By the nature of their emission, waves from 3cm and 1 GHz sources are plane polarised, usually with the electric field vertical, whereas light waves from the sun or an ordinary lamp are unpolarised. Ordinary light may be polarised by scattering, or passing it through a sheet of polaroid, or partly polarised by reflection. Two beams plane polarised at right angles to each other will not interfere.

POLAROID

If light is passed through one piece of **polaroid** and then a *second* sheet of polaroid is rotated in this beam, the intensity of the light emerging from the second polaroid varies, reaching zero twice in one revolution when the polaroids are said to be crossed. A third sheet of polaroid placed between two crossed polaroids can effectively rotate the plane of polarisation of the light so that some gets through.

REFLECTION

Light **reflected** from a surface is *partially* polarised parallel to the surface. At a particular angle, known as **Brewster's angle**, the reflected light is *completely* polarised parallel to the surface. This angle p is given by the equation $\tan p = n$ (refractive index). If this equation is combined with **Snell's law** it is possible to show that, at this angle, the refracted ray is perpendicular to the reflected ray.

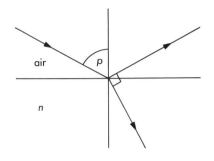

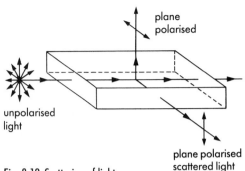

Fig. 8.11 Brewster's angle   Fig. 8.12 Scattering of light

SCATTERING

If unpolarised light is passed through cloudy water (add a drop of milk) it will be found that the light viewed from above, or the side, is plane polarised. For example, the light viewed from the side is **scattered** by the particles in the water. As the light is transverse there were no oscillations in the original beam parallel to the original direction, so there can be no oscillations in this direction in the scattered beam. The oscillations in the beam scattered to the side can only be perpendicular to the new direction, and so can only be as shown. Similar arguments apply to the beam scattered upwards.

EXAMINATION QUESTIONS

MULTIPLE CHOICE QUESTIONS

1 A two-slit arrangement and a source of monochromatic green light are used to produce interference fringes on a screen. The fringes are found to be too close together to be observed clearly. How might the separation of the fringes be increased?

  a) By decreasing the distance between the slits and the screen.
  b) By increasing the distance between the source and the slits.
  c) By increasing the distance between the two slits.
  d) By increasing the width of each slit.
  e) By replacing the light source with a monochromatic red light source.

(Oxford 1987)

2 In a Young's double slit interference arrangement the fringe spacing is x when the wavelength of the radiation is λ, the distance between the slits d and the distance between the slits and the plane of the observed fringes D. In which one of the following cases would the fringe spacing also be x?

	WAVELENGTH	DISTANCE BETWEEN SLITS	DISTANCE BETWEEN SLITS AND FRINGES
a)	2λ	$2d$	$2D$
b)	2λ	$4d$	$2D$
c)	2λ	$2d$	$4D$
d)	4λ	$2d$	$4D$
e)	4λ	$2d$	$2D$

3 The interference pattern seen on the screen in Young's two slits experiment is evidence that light:
  1) consists of photons;
  2) travels in straight lines;
  3) has wave-like properties.

  a) 1, 2, 3 correct   d) 1 only
  b) 1, 2 only   e) 3 only
  c) 2, 3 only

(London 1989)

4 A single slit is illuminated by parallel monochromatic light and a diffraction pattern is formed on a screen some distance away. Which one of the diagrams in Fig. 8.13 most nearly represents the intensity distribution across the screen?

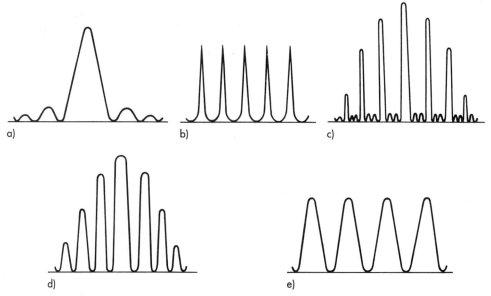

a)   b)   c)

d)   e)

Fig. 8.13

(Oxford 1988)

5 The diffraction pattern produced by a single slit may be demonstrated by illuminating a narrow slit with intense, coherent monochromatic light and observing the pattern on a screen some distance from the slit. Fig. 8.14 below shows the way in which the intensity of light in the diffraction pattern varies with distance across the screen.

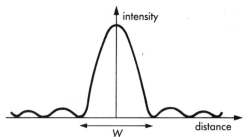

Fig. 8.14

In this diagram, the 'width' of the pattern is defined by W. Listed below are three operations which will result in a change in the width of the pattern.
1) Increasing the wavelength of the incident light.
2) Increasing the slit width.
3) Increasing the distance from slit to screen.

Which of these operations will produce an *increase* in the width of the pattern?

a) 1 only   d) 2 and 3 only
b) 2 only   e) 1, 2 and 3
c) 1 and 3 only

(NI 1988)

6 Monochromatic light of wavelength 625 nm is incident normally on a diffraction grating. A second-order diffraction image is formed in a direction at 30° to the normal to the grating. The number of lines per mm on the grating is

a) 4×10^{-1} d) 4×10^5
b) 4×10^2 e) 8×10^5
c) 8×10^2

(NI 1988)

7 When monochromatic light of wavelength 6×10^{-7} m is incident normally on a diffraction grating having 5×10^5 lines per metre, the highest order of spectra observed is

a) 3   d) 7
b) 4   e) 8
c) 6

(London 1987)

8   Fig. 8.15 shows a set of rectangular co-ordinate axes. A plane-polarised electromagnetic wave travels along the $+x$ direction. Which *one* of the following represents a possible orientation of the electric field component and the magnetic field component associated with the wave?

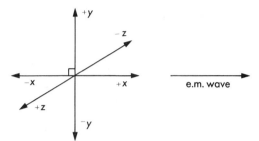

Fig. 8.15

	Electric field component	Magnetic field component
a)	$+x$	$+x$
b)	$+x$	$+y$
c)	$+y$	$-y$
d)	$-y$	$-z$
e)	$-z$	$+z$

(NI 1988)

9   The polarizer R and analyser S in Fig. 8.16 are set to cancel light from the sodium lamp L. A tube, T, of optically active solution is then introduced between R and S and

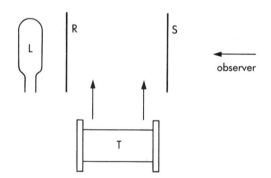

Fig. 8.16

cancellation of the beam is restored by rotating S anticlockwise by 20° as seen by an observer. The same effect could have been achieved by a similar 20° clockwise rotation of:
1) the polarizer R;
2) the tube T;
3) the lamp L.

a) 1, 2, 3 correct   d) 1 only
b) 1, 2 only   e) 3 only
c) 2, 3 only

(London 1989)

ANSWERS AND COMMENTS

Question	1	2	3	4	5	6	7	8	9
Answer	e)	b)	e)	a)	c)	d)	a)	d)	d)

1   The formula for the fringe separation x is $x = \lambda D/s$.
a) decreasing D decreases x;
b) increasing the distance between source and slits has no effect;
c) increasing s decreases x;
d) increasing the slit width has no effect on x;
e) changing from green to red increases λ so increases x.

2   Using the formula $x = \lambda D/d$, fringe separation would be:
a) $2x$ b) x c) $4x$ d) $8x$ e) $4x$

3   Interference is very much a wave effect and not evidence for the particulate nature. It relies on diffraction at the slits so is not evidence for light travelling in straight lines.

4   See Fig. 8.6.

5   The width W is determined by the first minimum of diffraction given by the equation $\sin \theta = \lambda/s$.
1) Increasing λ will increase W.
2) Increasing s will decrease W.
3) Increasing the distance from slit to screen will not change θ but the pattern will be more spread out if the screen is further away, so W will be increased.

6   $\sin 30° = 2 \times 6.25 \times 10^{-9}/s$
$$s = \frac{2 \times 6.25 \times 10^{-9}}{\sin 30°} = 2.5 \times 10^{-8} \text{ m}$$
$s = 2.5 \times 10^{-5}$ mm
no of slits per mm $= 1/s = 400000$.

7   There are 5×10^5 lines per m so,
$s = 2 \times 10^{-6}$, and $\sin \theta_n = n\lambda/s$ so $\sin \theta_n = n \times 0.3$. This will exceed 1 when $n = 4$, so 3 orders.

8   Both components must be at right angles to each other and at right angles to the direction of travel ($+x$ direction).

9   Rotating the polariser will rotate the plane of polarisation. Rotating the tube will not help as it will always rotate the plane through 20°. Light from the lamp is unpolarised so rotating the lamp will not help.

10 Fig. 8.17 shows an experimental arrangement for observing light-wave interference fringes using a double-slit method. The partially shrouded extended source S produces monochromatic light of wavelength 450 nm. The separation of the double-slits is 1.2 mm.

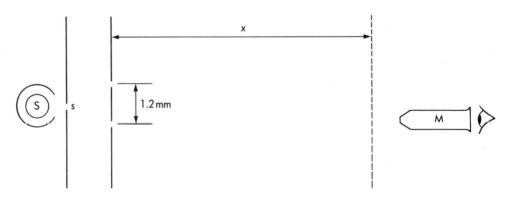

Fig. 8.17

a) Why is the single slit s needed?   (1)
b) At what distance x from the plane of the double-slit does the microscope M need to be focused in order to see these fringes with a separation of 0.10 mm?   (3)
c) Describe the changes that occur in the fringe pattern previously observed when S is replaced by:
i) a monochromatic source producing light of wavelength 600 nm;   (2)
ii) a tungsten filament white-light source.   (3)

(Oxford 1988)

11 Light from a cadmium discharge lamp can be used to determine the spacing of the lines on a plane diffraction grating. The is done by measuring the angle ϕ between the diffracted beams either side of the normal in the first order spectrum for light incident normally on the grating.

a) If the measured value of φ is 46°43′ and the red line used in the cadmium spectrum is of wavelength 644 nm, calculate the number of lines per metre on the grating.

b) Make a suitable calculation to test whether the second order spectrum of this line will be visible.

(7)

(London 1988)

OUTLINE ANSWERS

10 a) See text (p. 73).

b) $x = \dfrac{0.1 \times 10^{-3} \times 1.2 \times 10^{-3}}{450 \times 10^{-9}} = 0.26\,\text{m}.$

c) i) Fringe separation is proportional to wavelength, so using 600 nm will mean fringes further apart and a different colour.

ii) see text (p. 73).

11 a) $\sin\theta = \lambda/s$

$s = \dfrac{644 \times 10^{-9}}{\sin 46°43′} = 8.84 \times 10^{-7}\,\text{m}$

no of lines per metre $= 1/s = 11.3 \times 10^{7}$

b) $\sin\phi_2 = 2\sin\phi = 2 \times 0.72 > 1$, so not visible.

TUTOR'S QUESTION AND ANSWER

12 This question is about the measurement of the wavelength of light using the Young two-slit experiment. Fig. 8.18 shows the principle of the method. Monochromatic

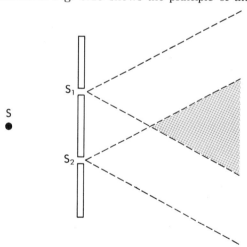

Fig. 8.18

light from source S falls on two narrow parallel slits S_1 and S_2, and diffraction causes the emerging beams to spread into the region to the right of the slits. Constructive and destructive interference then occurs where the beams overlap and interference fringes can be observed.

a) Distinguish between *constructive* and *destructive interference* in this case. (4)

b) For interference effects to be observed, the slits must act as coherent sources.

i) Explain what is meant by *coherent sources*.

ii) Explain why S_1 and S_2 act as coherent sources. (4)

c) To make measurements, a sufficient number of well-spaced fringes must be observable.

i) Use the expression for the fringe spacing to explain why well-spaced fringes will only be observed if the distance between S_1 and S_2 is small. In what other way can the spacing be increased?

ii) Explain how the number of fringes observed can be increased by decreasing the width of each slit. (4)

d) Suppose you are required to perform a two-slit experiment to determine the wavelength of the light from a given monochromatic source.

    i) Describe, with the aid of a diagram, the apparatus you would use, paying particular attention to the method of measuring the fringes and to the important dimensions of the apparatus.

    ii) Assuming that the wavelength of the light is about 6×10^{-7} m, describe in detail the fringe pattern you would expect to observe.

    iii) Describe how the measurements would be made, and show how the wavelength would be calculated.

    iv) Explain which measurement has the greatest effect on the accuracy of the result.

(13)
(AEB 1987)

ANSWER

12 a) Constructive interference occurs where the wave from S_1 is in phase with the wave from S_2. The crests in the wave from S_1 coincide with the crests in the wave from S_2 and similarly for the troughs. This will result in a wave of large amplitude corresponding to a bright fringe. Destructive interference will occur wherever the crests from one source meet the troughs from the other source. This results in a wave of small or zero amplitude and hence a dark fringe.

  b) i) Coherent sources have the same frequency and are either in phase or there is a constant phase difference.

     ii) S_1 and S_2 are coherent because they originate from the same source S. The waves spreading out from the slits must be the same frequency and be in phase.

  c) i) The expression for fringe spacing $= \lambda D/s$. λ, the wavelength of the light is very small and so s, the distance between S_1 and S_2 must be small. Increasing D, the distance from the slits to the fringes, will also increase the spacing of the fringes.

     ii) Decreasing the width of the slits increases the width of the diffraction central maximum where the fringes are observed. The fringe separation is unchanged and so there are more fringes within the central maxima where the intensity is bright enough to observe the fringes.

  d) i) The fringes are not very bright and therefore are best viewed directly and, as the fringes are close together, preferably using a magnifying eyepiece. The approximate dimensions are shown on the diagram.

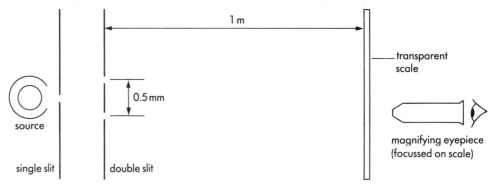

Fig. 8.19   single slit   double slit

     ii) Using fringe separation $= \lambda D/s$, we get

$$\frac{6 \times 10^{-7} \times 1}{5 \times 10^{-4}}$$

$= 1.2 \times 10^{-3}$ m. $= 1.2$ mm.

We would expect to see equally spaced bright and dark fringes with the bright fringes 1.2 mm apart. The intensity of the bright fringes would decrease as you move away from the centre of the pattern.

     iii) The distance D could be measured with a metre ruler with a mm scale. The separation of the fringes could be measured by placing a transparent mm scale in front of the magnifying eyepiece. The distance s could be measured with a travelling microscope. The wave length is then calculated using the equation $\lambda = s \times$ fringe separation$/D$.

     iv) The uncertainty in measuring the slit width would have the greatest effect on the accuracy of the result.

ELECTRO-MAGNETIC SPECTRUM AND PHYSICAL OPTICS

GETTING STARTED

Most A Level syllabuses include a reference to the properties and order of magnitude of the **electromagnetic spectrum**. The rest of this chapter deals with the topics of **reflection**, including the **concave mirror**, **refraction** and the **convex lens**, which are mentioned in only a few syllabuses. You should make yourself familiar with the requirements of the syllabus you are following.

The **electromagnetic spectrum** is the name given to a family of waves, including gamma rays, X-rays, light, microwaves and radio waves, which all travel by the same method and whose main difference is in wavelength. They are *transverse* waves, consisting of an oscillating electric field E and an oscillating magnetic field B, at right angles to each other and both at right angles to the direction in which the wave is travelling (Fig. 9.1). They do not need a medium to travel through and can all travel through a vacuum at the same *speed*, 3×10^8 m s^{-1}. They also travel through air at virtually this speed. They can exhibit the wave properties of reflection, refraction, interference and diffraction and, being tranverse, can be polarised. The frequency, f, and wavelength, λ, are related by the equation $c = f\lambda$, where $c = 3 \times 10^8$ m s^{-1}.

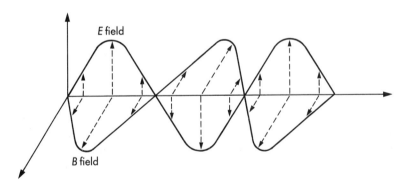

Fig. 9.1 Electromagnetic waves

ESSENTIAL PRINCIPLES

<table>
<tr><td>

**THE
ELECTRO-
MAGNETIC
SPECTRUM**

</td><td>

In Chapter 20, the wave-particle duality of electromagnetic waves is considered. In many circumstances the members of the spectrum show wave properties, but sometimes it is more convenient to consider them as particles, called **photons**, whose energy, E, is given by the equation $E = hf$, where h is the Planck constant (6.6×10^{-34} J s).

</td></tr>
</table>

NAME	WAVELENGTH IN AIR/m	METHOD OF PRODUCTION/ ORIGIN	METHOD OF DETECTION	USES
γ ray	$10^{-13} - 10^{-11}$	radioactive decay	Geiger tube	medicine, tracer, cancer treatment
X-ray	$10^{-12} - 10^{-8}$	decelerating electrons	Geiger tube	photography
U-V	$10^{-8} - 10^{-7}$	electron transitions	photocell	spectroscopy
Visible Light	$(4 - 7) \times 10^{-7}$	electron transitions	retina photographic	photography
Infra-red	$10^{-7} - 10^{-3}$	hot bodies	thermopile	heating, photography
Micro- waves	$10^{-3} - 10^{2}$	oscillators	diodes	cooking
Radio	$10^{2} - 10^{5}$	oscillators, aerials	tuned circuit	communication

Note that the ranges are only approximate and that there is some overlap. The names given to different parts of the spectrum arise from their method of production.

<table>
<tr><td>

**ELECTRO-
MAGNETIC
WAVE SPEED
MEASUREMENT**

</td><td>

The frequency, f, and wavelength, λ, are related by the equation $c = f\lambda$, where $c = 3 \times 10^{8}$ m s^{-1}.

This **speed** can be measured for visible light by sending a short pulse of light down a fibre optic and detecting the arrival of the pulse at the far end of the fibre. The pulse leaving the near end and the pulse arriving at the far end are displayed on a c.r.o. which is used with a calibrated time-base to measure the time the pulse took to travel down the length of the fibre. The speed is then calculated by dividing the distance travelled (fibre length) by the time. There are some problems with the pulse spreading out and becoming smaller (attenuating) as it travels down the fibre.

A similar experiment can be performed to measure the speed of electromagnetic waves down a coaxial cable. A sharp voltage pulse is generated at one end of a long cable and its arrival at the far end is detected. Once again a c.r.o. is used to measure the time taken for the pulse to travel the length of the cable.

</td></tr>
</table>

<table>
<tr><td>

**PROPERTIES
OF LIGHT**

</td><td>

The properties of light discussed here are often shared by other waves. If light is coming from a point source, then the **wavefronts** spreading out from the source are spherical. The direction of travel (shown by rays) of the waves is radially outwards. If the waves are *plane* then the rays are *parallel* (once again perpendicular to the waves).

</td></tr>
</table>

REFLECTION

Fig. 9.2 shows plane waves (and rays) **reflecting** from a plane surface. The left hand end of the wave hits the surface first and bounces off. The other end arrives at the surface later. The angle, i, of incidence is equal to the angle, r, of reflection.

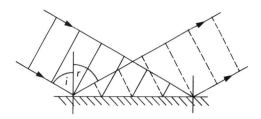

Fig. 9.2 Plane waves (and rays) reflecting from a plane surface

REFRACTION

Refraction occurs whenever the speed of a wave changes as it crosses a boundary e.g. water waves slow down when moving into a shallower region and light waves slow down on entering glass or water from air. Fig. 9.3 shows a plane wave crossing a boundary and slowing down. The left hand end reaches the boundary first and then travels slower whilst the right hand end is still travelling to the boundary. This results in refraction (a change in the direction of travel shown by the rays). The wavelength also decreases.

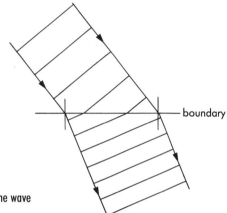

Fig. 9.3 Refraction of a plane wave

For light, the ratio of 'speed in vacuo to speed in the medium' is known as the **refractive index**, n, of the material medium. e.g.

n_{glass} is 3:2 and light travels at 2×10^8 m s^{-1} in glass.
$n_{\text{water}} = 4:3$ and the speed of light in water $= 2.25 \times 10^8$ m s^{-1}.

Glass has a higher refractive index than water and so is said to be **optically denser** than water. Light slows down and the ray bends towards the normal on entering a denser medium. Light speeds up and the ray bends away from the normal on leaving a denser medium. As the frequency of the wave cannot change, the ratio of 'wavelength in vacuo to wavelength in medium' is also equal to the refractive index.

Snell's law

Fig. 9.4 shows a ray travelling from glass to water. **Snell's law** states that the product $n \sin i$ is constant.

Hence $n_g \sin i_g = n_w \sin i_w$

Remember that $n_{\text{air}} = 1$.

Fig. 9.4 Ray travelling from glass to water

Critical angle

If light travels into a less dense medium, the ray bends away from the normal. A **critical angle** (Fig. 9.5) is reached when the ray emerges just along the boundary. Then,

$n_1 \sin c = n_2 \sin 90°$ so,

$\sin c = \dfrac{n_2}{n_1}$

Total internal reflection

At angles greater then the critical angle the ray cannot emerge and so it is **totally internally reflected** (Fig. 9.6).

Fig. 9.5 Critical angle

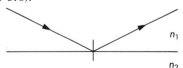

Fig. 9.6 Total internal reflection

Optic fibres

Fig. 9.7 shows light entering the **optic fibre** and then totally internally reflecting until it emerges from the far end. Such fibres are used in medicine to see inside the body and in communications to send messages.

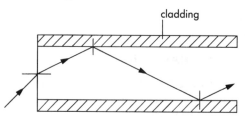

Fig. 9.7 Light entering optic fibre

CONCAVE MIRROR

FOCAL POINT

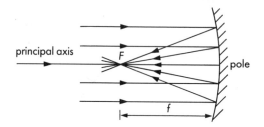

Fig. 9.8 Focal point of concave mirror

Rays *close* to and *parallel* to the principal axis reflect through one point known as the **focal point** F. The distance between this point and the *pole* of the mirror is the **focal length**, f. Fig. 9.9 shows a ray diagram constructing the image of the top of the object. Two rays diverge from O′. One travels parallel to the principal axis and reflects through the focal point and the other passes through the focal point and reflects parallel to the principal axis. The image is formed where the rays meet at I′. It is real, upside down and diminished.

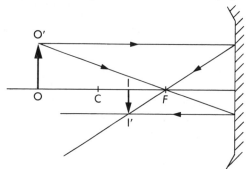

Fig. 9.9 Image of object in concave mirror

Fig. 9.10 shows what happens when the object is nearer than the focal point. The image is *virtual*, the right way up and enlarged.

The position of the image can be found using the equation: $\dfrac{1}{u} + \dfrac{1}{v} = \dfrac{1}{f}$.

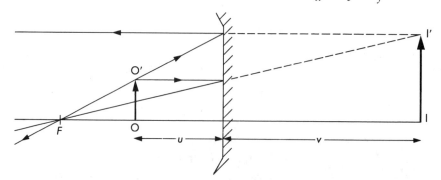

Fig. 9.10 Object nearer than focal point

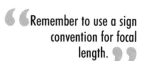
Remember to use a sign convention for focal length.

A *sign convention* must be used, e.g., the cartesian convention, where distances to the right of the mirror are positive and distances to the left negative.

The **linear magnification** $= \dfrac{\text{image size}}{\text{object size}} = \dfrac{v}{u}$

FOCAL LENGTH

CONVEX LENS

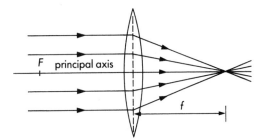

Fig. 9.11 Focal point of convex lens

Rays *close* to and *parallel* with the principal axis converge to the **focal point**. The distance from this point to the centre of the lens is the **focal length** (*f*). A lens with a shorter focal length is more powerful. The power is 1/*f*, measured in dioptres, if *f* is in m.

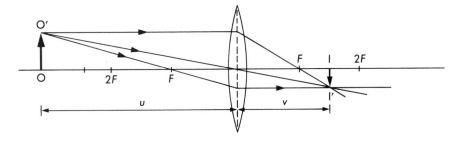

Fig. 9.12a) Construction of a real image in a convex lens

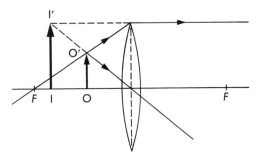

Fig. 9.12b) Construction of a virtual image

Figs. 9.12a) and b) show the construction of a) a real image and b) a virtual image. One ray goes straight through the middle of the lens and another passes through the focal point and emerges parallel to the principal axis. The equation to be used is:

$$\frac{1}{v} - \frac{1}{u} = \frac{1}{f}$$

using the cartesian sign convention. The **linear magnification** is given by:

$$\frac{v}{u}$$

ANGULAR MAGNIFICATION

Fig. 9.13 shows that the size of the image on the retina depends on the angle (α) subtended at the eye. The purpose of the telescope is to increase this angle.

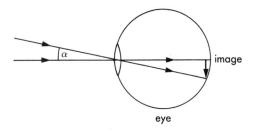

Fig. 9.13 Angle subtended at the eye

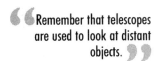
Remember that telescopes are used to look at distant objects.

ASTRONOMICAL TELESCOPE

When considering an astronomical telescope in normal adjustment (where the final image will be at infinity), the intermediate image is at the common focal point of the two lenses.

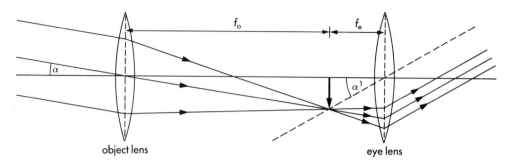

Fig. 9.14 Astronomical telescope in normal adjustment

The **angular magnification**, M is given by the angle subtended by the telescope divided by the angle subtended at the naked eye. i.e.

$$M = \frac{\alpha^1}{\alpha} = \frac{f_o}{f_e}$$

The eye ring

Fig. 9.15 shows the image of the object lens formed by the eye lens. All the light which

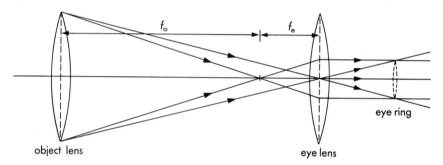

Fig. 9.15 Image of the object lens formed by the eye lens

passes through both lenses must go through this image. This is the best place to position the eye and is known as the **eye ring**.

$$M = \frac{f_o}{f_e} = \frac{\text{diameter of object lens}}{\text{diameter of eye lens}}$$

Resolving power

The ability to resolve two close objects is improved by increasing the diameter of the aperture. The fact that the objective lens is larger than the pupil of the eye means that the telescope has a better **resolving power** than the eye.

COMPOUND MICROSCOPE

<blockquote>Microscopes are used to view small objects.</blockquote>

As a small object is brought nearer and nearer to the eye, the angle it subtends at the eye increases. There is, however, a limit as to how near the object can be to the eye and yet

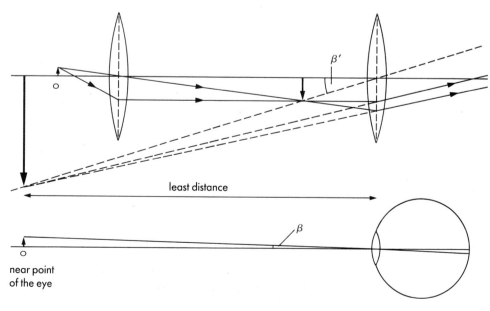

Fig. 9.16 Compound microscope

still be focussed. The distance from the eye to this near point is known as the **least distance of distinct vision**. In the microscope the final image is arranged to be at the near point in order to obtain maximum angular magnification. In this case:

$$M = \frac{\text{angle subtended by final image}}{\text{angle subtended by object at near point}} = \frac{\beta'}{\beta}$$

EXAMINATION QUESTIONS

MULTIPLE CHOICE QUESTIONS

1 What is the order in **decreasing** frequency of these electromagnetic waves?
1) ultraviolet radiation
2) radio waves
3) visible light
4) X-rays
5) infrared radiation.

a) 2, 5, 3, 1, 4   d) 4, 3, 1, 5, 2
b) 4, 3, 1, 2, 5   e) 2, 5, 1, 3, 4
c) 4, 1, 3, 5, 2

(Oxford 1988)

2 A cathode ray oscilloscope displays a transmitted radar pulse followed by the return pulse after reflection from a distant object. The pulse travels at a speed of 3.0×10^8 m s^{-1} and the oscilloscope time base is set at 0.050 ms per division. The display is shown in Fig. 9.17.

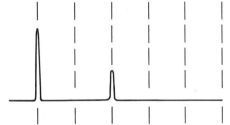

Fig. 9.17

The distance of the object from the transmitter is approximately

a) 3.0 km   d) 150 km
b) 15 km   e) 300 km
c) 30 km

(London 1988)

3 Fig. 9.18 shows a ray of light passing through a block of transparent plastic in which is trapped a spherical bubble of air. Which arrow, a), b), c), d) or e), correctly shows the direction of the light ray in the bubble?

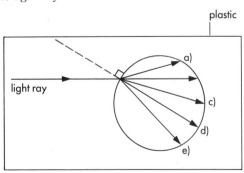

Fig. 9.18

(Oxford 1987)

4 When a parallel beam of monochromatic light is incident normally on an air/glass boundary, which of the following are correct.
1) The speed of the beam is less in the glass.
2) The wavelength of the beam is less in the glass.

3) The direction of propagation of the beam in the glass is different from that of the incident beam.

a) 1 only   d) 2 and 3 only
b) 2 only   e) 1, 2 and 3
c) 1 and 2 only

5 The speed of blue light
1) in glass is greater than the speed of red light in glass.
2) in free space is the same as the speed of red light in free space.
3) in a given medium is proportional to its wave-length measured in that medium.

a) 1, 2, 3 correct   d) 1 only
b) 1, 2 only   e) 3 only
c) 2, 3 only

(London 1988)

6 A very distant object on the principal axis of a convex lens moves towards the focal point (but does not pass it). The distance between the object and the image formed by the lens:

a) decreases continuously;
b) increases continuously;
c) remains the same;
d) increases and then decreases;
e) decreases and then increases.

(NI 1987)

7 An astronomical telescope consists of two lenses of focal length 60 cm and 5 cm. It is used to view a distant object so that the final image is at infinity. Which of the following statements is (are) correct?
1) The objective lens is the one with the greater power.
2) The angular magnification of the telescope is 12.
3) The separation of the lenses is 60 cm.

a) 2 only   d) 2 and 3 only
b) 1 and 2 only   e) 1, 2 and 3
c) 1 and 3 only

(NI 1987)

ANSWERS AND COMMENTS

Question	1	2	3	4	5	6	7
Answer	c)	b)	a)	c)	c)	e)	a)

1 In order of decreasing frequency (increasing wavelength) 4, 1, 3, 5, 2.
2 Pulse takes two divisions to return, so one divison (0.05 ms) to get there.
   Distance = speed × time
   $= 3 \times 10^8 \times 0.05 \times 10^{-3} = 15000$ m.
3 Ray is travelling from plastic to air so bends away from normal.
4 On entering glass the wave slows down, frequency stays the same, so wavelength decreases. Direction does not change as it is travelling along a normal.
5 Blue refracts more so slows down more then red. All em waves travel at same speed in vacuo. Frequency is constant so speed $\propto$ wavelength.
6 When object at infinity, image at F; when object at 2F image at 2F; when object at F image at infinity.
7 Objective has focal length 60 cm and eye lens 5 cm. The power of a lens = $1/f$, so objective has smaller power. Angular magnification = $f_o/f_e = 12$. Separation of lenses $= f_o + f_e = 65$ cm.

STRUCTURED QUESTION

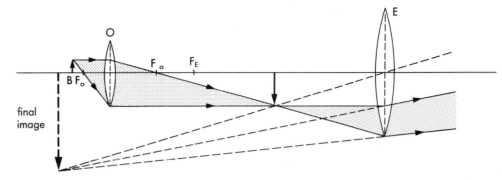

Fig. 9.19

8 The diagram shows the paths of two rays of light from the tip of an object B through the objective, O, and the eyelens, E, of a compound microscope. The final image is at the near point of an observer's eye when the eye is close to E. F_o and F'_o are the principal foci of O and F_e is one of the principal foci of E. The diagram is *not drawn to scale*.

a) Explain why

   i) the object is placed just to the left of F_o.

   ii) the eyepiece is adjusted so that the intermediate image is to the right of F_E. *(4)*

b) In this arrangement, the focal lengths of O and E are 10 mm and 60 mm respectively. If B is 12 mm from O and the final image is 300 mm from E, calculate the distance apart of O and E. *(4)*

(JMB 1987)

OUTLINE ANSWER AND COMMENT

8 a) i) The object is just outside the focus so that the intermediate image is real but considerably magnified.

   ii) The intermediate image acts as object for the eyelens and is just inside the focus to produce a virtual magnified final image.

b) Using lens formula for objective with $u = -12$ and $f = +10$:

$$\frac{1}{v} - \left(\frac{1}{-12}\right) = \frac{1}{10}$$

$v = 60$ mm.

For the eyelens $f = +60$ and $v = -300$,

$$-\frac{1}{300} - \frac{1}{u} = \frac{1}{60} \qquad \text{Hence } u = +50\,\text{mm.}$$

Distance between lenses $= 60 + 50 = 110\,\text{mm}$

(Using cartesian convention)

GETTING STARTED

This chapter covers the basic ideas needed in the study of **electric circuits** which are fundamental to any A Level course. It is essential that you clearly understand the basic concepts of **charge**, **current**, **e.m.f.**, **potential difference** and **resistance**. It is also important to know the **units** in which these quantities are measured and to know the relationships between them.

Some particles are said to be electrically **charged** in that they attract or repel other charged particles. The unit of charge is the **coulomb**. The electron and proton both have a charge of 1.6×10^{-19} coulombs, but the electron is negatively charged and the proton positively charged. Like charges attract and opposite charges repel. Electrons attract protons but repel other electrons. When charged particles move, a current flows, the **current** being equal to the charge passing per second or the rate of flow of charge. The unit of current is the **ampere** (defined in Chapter 13). 1 coulomb of charge passes by if 1 ampere flows for 1 second. Examples of currents are the flow of free electrons in a solid conductor, the flow of charged particles through a vacuum, and the flow of positive and negative ions in solution.

A solid consists of an array of atoms tightly bound together. The atoms themselves have a small nucleus, comprising protons and neutrons, surrounded by electrons. There is an electrostatic attraction between the electrons and the protons. In some solid structures all the electrons in each atom are firmly bound to the nucleus. These solids are **insulators**. In other structures one or two electrons from each atom are only loosely bound and become 'free' to move around randomly inside the lattice structure at speeds which depend on the temperature. Such materials are **conductors** and when a current flows through them, these electrons move in one direction with a drift speed superimposed on their random thermal motion.

ESSENTIAL PRINCIPLES

DRIFT VELOCITY

If the **drift velocity** of the electrons in a conductor is v then all the electrons in a section of length v will pass through the end section XX′ in one second (Fig. 10.1). If there are n electrons per unit volume and the cross sectional area of the conductor is A then there are nAv electrons in a length v. If each electron carries a charge e then the total charge on these electrons is $nAev$. The **current** I, which is the charge passing through the end section per second, is thus $nAev$.

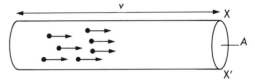

Fig. 10.1 Drift velocity of electrons in a conductor

In an intrinsic *semiconductor* at room temperature there are usually many fewer charge carriers per unit volume than in a good conductor. However, unlike a good conductor, the number of charge carriers increases as the temperature rises thus improving the conducting properties.

E.M.F AND POTENTIAL DIFFERENCE

In the simple circuit shown in Fig. 10.2 a current will flow and the bulb will light. Overall, chemical energy from the cell is being converted *into* heat and light in the bulb. If we follow 1 coulomb of charge moving round the circuit it *gains* electrical energy (from chemical energy) as it passes through the cell, and *loses* electrical energy (to heat and light) as it passes through the resistance of the bulb. The **e.m.f.**(E) of the cell (measured in volts) is the electrical potential energy (in joules) *gained* by one coulomb passing through the cell. Thus 1 volt is 1 joule/coulomb.

The **potential difference** (p.d.) across the bulb is the electrical energy *lost* (to heat and light) by one coulomb passing through the bulb. This p.d. can be measured by placing a voltmeter across the bulb.

In a circuit with several bulbs the total energy lost by one coulomb in passing through all of the bulbs is equal to the energy it gains from the cell. This means that the sum of all the p.d.s is equal to the e.m.f.:

$$E = V_1 + V_2$$

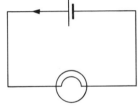

Fig. 10.2 Simple circuit

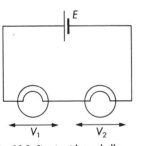

Fig. 10.3 Circuit with two bulbs

The electrical energy lost or gained *per second* is the power (in watts), and the charge passing *per second* is the current (in amperes). So 1 volt is also equal to 1 watt/ampere, and the e.m.f. = total power/current. Thus:

Total power $= EI$,

and for an individual component power, the formula is VI, where V is the p.d. across the component.

Also, Energy = Power × time = EIt or VIt

RESISTANCE

In a simple circuit with a fixed total resistance it is the e.m.f. of the power supply which determines the current flowing. The current which flows is proportional to the e.m.f. of the power supply. The constant ratio 'e.m.f.: current' is the **total resistance** (R) of the circuit (including any internal resistance in the power supply). Hence:

$$R = \frac{E}{I} \ .$$

If E is in volts and I in amps, then R is measured in ohms. For a fixed value of E, increasing the total resistance of the circuit will decrease the current.

The resistance of an individual component in a circuit is the p.d. (V) across that component divided by the current flowing through it. Here, $R = V/I$. Some components, such as *carbon resistors*, and also *wires* at constant temperature, are '**Ohmic**', in that the current flowing through them is proportional to the p.d. across them and so the resistance (V/I) is constant. The resistance of a wire is not usually constant, but increases with increasing temperature as the current increases.

❝❝ You should be able to work out that if power = VI and $V = IR$ then power = I^2R etc. ❞❞

The **temperature coefficient of resistance**, α, is defined from the relationship:

$$R_\theta = R_o \ (1 + \alpha\theta).$$

R_θ is the resistance at temperature $\theta°C$ and R_o is the resistance at $0°$ C.

Most *thermistors* have **negative temperature coefficients** (n.t.c.) and so the resistance decreases with increasing temperature. The resistance of **light dependent resistors** (LDR's) decreases as the amount of light falling on them increases.

RESISTIVITY

The resistance of a wire is proportional to its length l (quadrupling the length quadruples the resistance), and inversely proportional to the cross-sectional area A (doubling the diameter quadruples the area and quarters the resistance). The resistance also depends on a property of the material called the **resistivity**, ρ, which can be calculated according to the equation:

$$\rho = \frac{R \ A}{l} \text{ , measured in ohm m.}$$

Conductivity, σ, is the reciprocal of resistivity ($\text{ohm}^{-1} \text{ m}^{-1}$).

RESISTORS IN SERIES

If several resistors are placed in *series* so that they have the same current passing through them, then the *total p.d.* across them is equal to the sum of the individual p.d.s. across them, and the *total resistance* is the sum of all the resistances. Hence:

$$V = V_1 + V_2 + V_3, \text{ and}$$
$$R = R_1 + R_2 + R_3.$$

The *ratio of the p.d.s* across two components is equal to the *ratio of their resistances*.

$$\frac{V_1}{V_2} = \frac{R_1}{R_2}$$

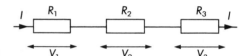

Fig. 10.4 Resistors in series

THE POTENTIAL DIVIDER

The **potential divider**, is essentially two resistors in series with the p.d.s across the resistors being proportional to their resistances. In Fig. 10.5 the bottom is 'earthed' and hence at zero potential. The potential of the top is 6 V. The potential at the 'mid-point', P, depends on the ratio of the resistors. If they are equal then the potential at P is 3V. If R_1 is $2R_2$ then the potential of P is 2V, (i.e. 2V across R_1 and 4V across R_2). The potential divider is often used in electronics with the point P connected to the input of a gate. The top resistor R_1 might be a variable resistor, such as an LDR. When light shines on the LDR its resistance falls and so the ratio of the resistances changes so that the potential of P rises. This change in the potential of P might be sufficient to 'switch' the gate so that its output changes.

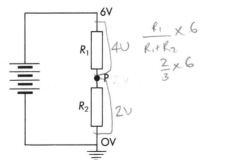

Fig. 10.5 Potential divider

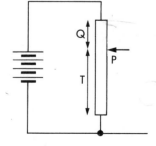

Fig. 10.6 Potentiometer

THE POTENTIOMETER

The **potentiometer** (Fig. 10.6) is essentially the same as the potential divider but using one resistance with a sliding contact to effectively divide it into two resistors. The potential at P connected to the slider depends on the ratio of the two effective resistances Q and T.

As with the potential divider, the two resistors are treated as though they are in series and so the current flowing to or from P must be negligible.

The sliding contact P (Fig. 10.7) is moved until there is no reading on the **microammeter**. The e.m.f. of cell C (there is no current flowing through cell C so the p.d. across its terminals is equal to the e.m.f.) is then equal to the p.d. between P and Q.

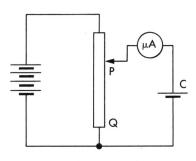

Fig. 10.7 Balanced potentiometer

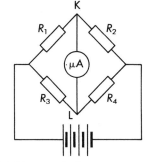

Fig. 10.8 Wheatstone bridge

WHEATSTONE BRIDGE

When the bridge (Fig. 10.8) is *balanced* there is no current through the **picoammeter**. Thus K and L are at the same potential; the current through R_1 is equal to the current through R_2 and the current through R_3 is equal to the current through R_4. Hence:

p.d. across R_1 = p.d. across R_3 so $I_1R_1 = I_3R_3$
p.d. across R_2 = p.d. across R_4 so $I_1R_2 = I_3R_4$

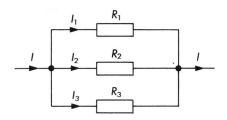

Fig. 10.9 Resistors in parallel

The total current is equal to the sum of all the currents passing through the resistors. Thus we have:

$I = I_1 + I_2 + I_3.$

The p.d. across each resistor is the same, giving:

$V = I_1R_1 = I_2R_2,$

which leads to the idea that the currents through the resistors are inversely proportional to the resistances. This gives us:

$$\frac{I_2}{I_1} = \frac{R_1}{R_2}$$

The *total* resistance is given by the equation:

$$\frac{1}{R} = \frac{1}{R_1} + \frac{1}{R_2} + \frac{1}{R_3}$$

It is possible to convert meters into *ammeters* or *voltmeters* with larger *full scale deflection* (f.s.d.) by adding resistors to the meters. In considering these calculations remember that the f.s.d. of the original meter is unaffected.

AMMETER

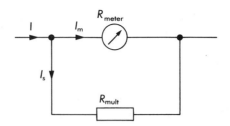

Fig. 10.10 Converting meter into ammeter

To convert a meter into an **ammeter** with a larger f.s.d. it is necessary to add a shunt resistor in parallel with the meter so that some of the current passes through the shunt. The total current is the sum of the currents through the shunt and the original meter. The p.d. across the shunt equals the p.d. across the meter.

VOLTMETER

Fig. 10.11 Converting meter into voltmeter

To convert a meter into a **voltmeter** with larger f.s.d. it is necessary to add a multiplier resistance (R_{mult}) in series. The current through the multiplier is the same as the current through the meter. The total resistance is the sum of the multiplier resistance and the resistance of the original meter.

KIRCHOFF'S LAWS

Kirchoff's laws are formal statements of ideas already discussed:

1 *The algebraic sum of the currents at a junction is zero.* No current is lost or gained at a junction. This has been used in considering parallel resistors.
2 *In a closed loop in a circuit, the algebraic sum of the e.m.f.s is equal to the algebraic sum of the products of current times resistance.* In following a coulomb around a closed loop, any energy it gains passing through cells it must lose in passing through resistors, so that it ends up at the same level of potential. Care has to be taken with signs.

Consider any closed loop, choose a corner to start and go round the loop in, say, a clockwise direction. The e.m.f.s are added together on the left hand side of the equation remembering that going from the negative to the positive terminal is considered positive and the opposite direction negative. On the right hand side of the equation add the products IR, remembering that passing through a resistor in the direction of current gives a positive product.

INTERNAL RESISTANCE

If a coulomb of charge passes through a cell, it gains electrical energy E. However if the cell has **internal resistance**, r, some (Ir) of this energy is converted to heat inside the cell. The net effect is that the coulomb gains energy according to the equation: $V = E - Ir$.

This p.d. (V) would be recorded by a voltmeter placed across the cell. (See Fig. 10.12) In some questions it is made quite clear that the cell or power supply has no internal resistance (or in the case of A.C. no internal impedance) and hence the cell provides a voltage E no matter what current is flowing. However in practical situations, and in some questions, power supplies have internal resistance. This means that when a current is flowing, the p.d. across the supply is less than the e.m.f. by an amount Ir. Note that Ir increases as I increases and therefore the p.d. across the supply will get less as the current rises. If no current is flowing (the supply is said to be on open circuit) then Ir is zero and so the p.d. across the supply equals the e.m.f. A potentiometer circuit can be set up so that a 'test' cell is on open circuit as in Fig. 10.7.

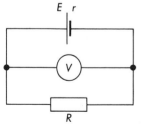

Fig. 10.12

MAXIMUM POWER THEOREM

It can be shown that a supply will deliver maximum power to an external resistor if the external resistance R is equal to the internal resistance r of the cell. This is called the **maximum power theorem**.

EXAMINATION QUESTIONS

1 The main reason for the increase in electrical resistance of a metallic conductor when its temperature is raised is the:

a) higher drift speed of the electrons;
b) increased amplitude of vibration of lattice ions;
c) increase in the cross-sectional area of the conductor;
d) increase in the length of the conductor;
e) reduction in the number of free electrons.

(London 1987)

2 A piece of wire has a resistance of 2Ω. It is then stretched, without any change in volume, temperature or resistivity, so that its diameter is reduced to half of the original value. What is the new resistance of the wire, in ohms?

a) 2   d) 16
b) 4   c) 32
c) 8

(NI 1988)

3 A battery of negligible internal resistance and e.m.f. V is connected across a circuit containing four equal resistors, as shown in Fig. 10.13. The potential difference between the points X and Y is

a) V d) $V/4$
b) $V/2$ e) $V/5$
c) $V/3$

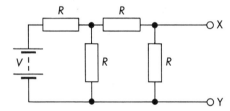

Fig. 10.13

(NI 1988)

4 Fig. 10.14 shows a battery of e.m.f. 42V and negligible internal resistance connected across two resistors of resistance 2 kΩ and 5 kΩ. A voltmeter of internal resistance 20 kΩ is used to measure the potential difference across the resistor of resistance 5 kΩ. The reading of the voltmeter, in volts, is

a) 12   d) 30
b) 14   e) 42
c) 28

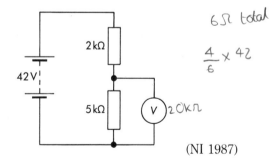

Fig. 10.14

(NI 1987)

5 Fig. 10.15 shows four resistors connected in a closed square. If the arrangement were put into a circuit it would show the least resistance if connection were made across

a) P and Q   d) S and P
b) Q and R   e) Q and S
c) R and S

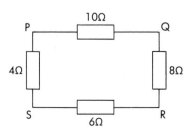

Fig. 10.15

6 In the circuit shown in Fig. 10.16 P, Q and R are identical resistors. The ratio:

$$\frac{\text{rate of production of heat in P}}{\text{rate of production of heat in Q or R}} \text{ is}$$

a) 0.25   d) 2

b) 0.5   e) 4

c) 1

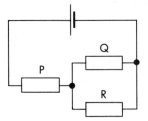

Fig. 10.16

(London 1987)

7 The e.m.f. of the battery in the circuit shown in Fig. 10.17 is 9.0 V. The reading on the high-resistance voltmeter V is 7.5 V. What is the current flowing through the battery?

a) 0.1 A   d) 1.1 A

b) 0.5 A   e) 2.0 A

c) 0.6 A

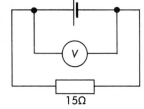

Fig. 10.17

(Oxford 1987)

8 In the circuit shown in Fig. 10.18 each cell has negligible internal resistance. The reading on the voltmeter, in V, is

a) 0   d) 3

b) 1   e) 4

c) 2

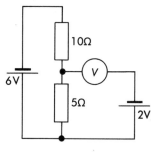

Fig. 10.18

(AEB 1988)

9 The circuit in Fig. 10.19 shows a balanced Wheatstone bridge network. Listed below are a number of changes which can be made to the circuit.

1) The battery and galvanometer are interchanged.

2) R_1 and R_3 are interchanged.

3) R_2 and R_3 are interchanged.

Which of these changes, made separately, will result in the bridge remaining balanced?

a) 1 only   c) 1 and 2 only

b) 2 only   d) 1 and 3 only

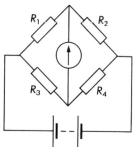

Fig. 10.19

(NI 1988)

10 In an investigation of the power delivered to a variable load of resistance R by a cell of internal resistance r the circuit shown in Fig. 10.20 is set up. Which *one* of the following statements about this experiment is correct?

a) The current in the circuit is a maximum when the load resistance R is equal to the internal resistance r of the cell.

b) The current in the circuit is a maximum when the power delivered to the load is a maximum.

c) The power delivered by the cell to the load is a minimum when the load resistance R is equal to the internal resistance r of the cell.

d) The potential difference across the terminals of the cell increases as the load resistance R increases.

e) The potential difference across the terminals of the cell is always greater than the potential difference across the load.

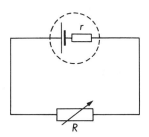

Fig. 10.20

(NI 1988)

11 A galvanometer giving a full scale deflection for a current of 10 mA and having a resistance 99 Ω is to be converted to an ammeter measuring currents up to 1.0 A. This could be done by using a resistor of resistance

a) 0.001 Ω d) 1.0 Ω

b) 0.01 Ω e) 10.0 Ω

c) 0.1 Ω

(London 1987)

12 A d.c. electric motor shown in Fig. 10.21, with a permanent field magnet, operates from a 24-V supply, and takes a current of 1.0 A. The resistance of the armature winding is 2.0 Ω. What is the mechanical power developed by the motor (neglecting friction, hysteresis, and similar losses)?

a) 288 W   d) 22 W

b) 26 W   e) 2 W

c) 24 W

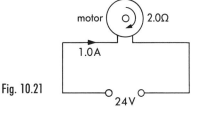

Fig. 10.21

(London 1989)

ANSWERS AND COMMENTS

Question	1	2	3	4	5	6	7	8	9	10	11	12
Answer	b)	e)	e)	c)	d)	e)	b)	a)	d)	d)	d)	d)

1 Requires recall.

2 The diameter is halved, so the area is quartered which by itself would quadruple the resistance. However the volume stays the same, so the length must quadruple, which also quadruples the resistance. The resistance increases by a factor of 16.

3 Effectively a parallel combination of R and $2R$, in series with R. Resistance of parallel combination $= 2R/3$. Effectively $2R/3$ and R in series. So p.d. across parallel combination is 2V/5. (3V/5 across R) P.d. across XY is half p.d. across parallel combination.

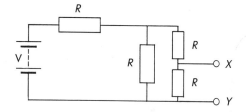

Fig. 10.22

4 The resistance of the voltmeter is not high enough compared to 5 kΩ to be ignored. The resistance of the parallel combination of 5 kΩ and 20 kΩ (voltmeter) = 4 kΩ. So p.d. across V = $\frac{4}{6}$ × 42 = 28 V.

5 Between P and Q the resistance is 10Ω in parallel with (4+6+8) 18Ω.
Between Q and R, 8Ω in parallel with 20Ω.
Between R and S, 6Ω in parallel with 22Ω.
Between S and P, 4Ω in parallel with 24Ω.
Between Q and S, 14Ω in parallel with 14Ω.
The resistance of a parallel combination is always less than the smaller resistance, so the answer is likely to be betwen S and P.
Check using parallel resistance formula.

6 The current through Q or R is half the current through P. The power dissipated in a resistor = I^2R so power dissipated in Q or R is one quarter of that dissipated in P.

7 The voltmeter is connected across the 15 ohm resistor and so the current through this resistor is 7.5/15 = 0.5 A. As the voltmeter is high resistance, negligible current will pass through it, so 0.5 A also flows through the battery. The reason why the voltmeter reads less than 9.0 V is because of internal resistance of the battery.

8 The ratio of the two resistances is 2:1 so the p.d.s will be in the same ratio if no current flows through the voltmeter. The p.d. across the 4 ohm resistor is 2V which balances the 2V e.m.f. of the battery.

9 The balance condition is that $\dfrac{R_1}{R_3} = \dfrac{R_2}{R_4}$

1) balance condition is $\dfrac{R_2}{R_1} = \dfrac{R_4}{R_3}$ which is the same

2) R_1 and R_3 are not interchangeable in the balance equation.

3) R_2 and R_3 are interchangeable in the equation.

10 a) The current is a maximum when $R = 0$.
b) & c) The power is a maximum when $R = r$.
d) As the load resistance increases the current decreases and so the 'lost volts' (Ir) gets less and the p.d. across the cell ($E - Ir$) increases.
e) The p.d. across the terminals of the cell always equals the p.d. across the load.

11 The current to be shunted = (1000 − 10) mA = 990 mA.
p.d. across meter = p.d. across shunt
$$R_{\text{shunt}} = \frac{R_{\text{meter}} I_{\text{meter}}}{I_{shunt}} = \frac{99 \times 10}{990} = 1.0 \text{ ohm.}$$

12 The power delivered by the supply = EI = 24 × 1.0 = 24 W.
The power dissipated as heat in the armarture in:
I^2R = 1 × 1 × 2 = 2 W.
Ignoring losses, mechanical power delivered to motor = 24 − 2 = 22 W.

STRUCTURED QUESTIONS

13 The diagram shows a length L of electrical conductor which has an area of cross section A. The conductor has n free electrons each of charge e per unit volume. These free electrons are drifting in the direction shown at a mean velocity v.
a) i) Deduce an expression for the quantity of free charge in the conductor.
ii) State the mean time taken for a free electron to travel the distance L.
iii) Hence deduce an expression for the current flowing the wire.
b) Given that the p.d. across the conductor is fixed, how would you expect v to vary with temperature?

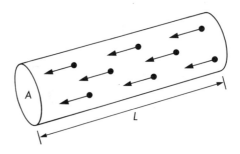

Fig. 10.23

(Southern 1987)

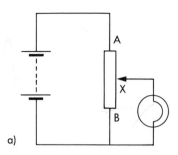
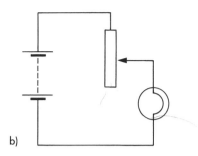

Fig. 10.24

14 a) The current flowing through a torch bulb can be controlled by a potential divider (Fig. 10.24a)) or a rheostat (Fig. 10.24b)). Explain the advantages and disadvantages of each of these methods. *(4)*

b) In a), the linear potentiometer, AB, has a total resistance of 16Ω. When the slider of the potentiometer is set at X, exactly mid-way along AB, the bulb works according to its specification of 2.0 V, 500 mW. Calculate:
  i) the resistance of the bulb under these conditions;
  ii) the current through section XB of the potentiometer;
  iii) the p.d. across the section AX of the potentiometer;
  iv) the e.m.f. of the battery if its internal (source) resistance is 6.0Ω. *(5)*

(JMB 1988)

15 Fig. 10.25 shows an arrangement by which the resistance between A and B may be varied. Explain briefly why the 1 kΩ variable resistor may be used as a means of making fine adjustments to the total resistance of the combination. *(2)*

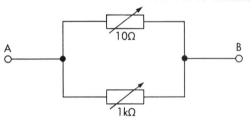

Fig. 10.25   (Cambridge 1987)

16 In the circuit shown in Fig. 10.26, a 12 V battery of negligible internal resistance is connected to a potentiometer X of the total resistance 100 Ω. Filament lamps L_1 and

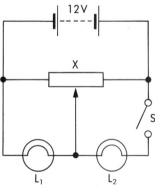

Fig. 10.26

L_2 are each marked '6 V 18 W' and are connected as shown with the sliding contact positioned so that the resistance of X is equally divided.
a) What is the significance of the markings on the lamps?
b) Calculate the resistance of each lamp when operating normally.
c) Switch S is closed. Explain whether you would expect lamp L_1 to light to its normal brightness.
d) Discuss the effect on the brightness of lamp L_1 of opening the switch. *(9)*

(AEB 1987)

17 A power supply used in a laboratory has an e.m.f. of 5000 V. When however a voltmeter of resistance 20 kΩ is connected to the terminals of the power supply a reading of only 40 V is obtained.
a) Explain this observation.

b) Calculate the current flowing in the meter and the internal resistance of the power supply.

(Southern 1987)

18   A cell has e.m.f. 1.5 V and internal resistance 0.5Ω. Calculate the power delivered when the cell is connected to an external 2.5Ω resistor. What is the value of the external resistance if the power delivered is to have a maximum value?   (6)

(Cambridge 1988)

OUTLINE ANSWERS AND COMMENTS

13   a)   i) Volume $= AL$

no. of charges $= nAL$

quantity of charge $= enAL$.

ii) mean time $= L/v$.

iii) current = charge/time $= \dfrac{enAL}{L/v} = enAv$.

b) An increase in temperature will increase the resistance of the wire and so for a fixed p.d. the current will be less. As n, A and e do not change so v will be less.

14   a) The advantage of the potential divider is that the p.d. across the bulb can be varied over the full range of the battery voltage (slider at A) down to zero volts (slider at B). With the rheostat, the maximum p.d. across the bulb is the battery voltage (slider at top), but the minimum p.d. (slider at bottom) is not zero. With the slider at the bottom the bulb is effectively in series with the total resistance of the rheostat. The disadvantage of the potential divider is that power is 'wasted' in the bottom part XB of the resistor. The smaller range of p.d.s using the rheostat means that the current through the bulb can be altered more sensitively.

b)   i) The p.d. across the bulb $= 2.0$ V, and the power $= 0.5$ W.

Using power $= V^2/R = \dfrac{(2.0)^2}{0.5} = 8.0$ ohm.

ii) Section XB of the potentiometer has resistance $16/2 = 8\Omega$ and the p.d. across it $= 2.0$V so the current $= 2/8 = 0.25$ A.

iii) There is a current of 0.25 A through section XB and a current of 0.25 A through the bulb. The current through AX is 0.5 A. The p.d. across AX $= IR = 0.5 \times 8 = 4$V.

iv) The p.d. across the battery $= 4 + 2 = 6$ V, and the current flowing $= 0.5$ A. Hence:

e.m.f. $= V + Ir = 6 + 0.5 \times 6 = 9$V.

15   Most of the current passes through the 10 ohm resistor. Adjusting the $10\,k\Omega$ resistor will change only slightly the total current flowing for a fixed p.d. across AB and hence will change only slightly the total resistance.

16   a) 6 V is the voltage which should be connected across the lamp for normal operation. Under these circumstances the electrical energy converted per second will be 18 W.

b) $R = V^2/\text{power} = 36/18 = 2$ ohms.

c) With S closed, both bulbs will be lit normally as there will be 6 V across each.

d) With S open, L_2 will be unlit. The circuit now consists of a resistance of 50Ω (half of X) in series with a parallel combination of L_1 (2Ω) and the other 50Ω of X. The resistance of this parallel combination is a little less than 2Ω, and the total resistance about $(50 + 2)\Omega$. So the p.d. across this combination (and hence across the bulb) will be small (about 2/52 of 12 V) and L_1 will be dim.

17   a) When the voltmeter is connected across the terminals a current flows through the internal resistance of the power supply. There is a large potential drop across this internal resistance and so the voltage across the terminals is much less than 5000 V.

b) Current $= \dfrac{\text{p.d. across meter}}{20\ \text{k}\Omega} = \dfrac{40}{20 \times 10^3} = 2 \times 10^{-3}$ A.

The p.d. across the internal resistance $= 5000 - 40 = 4960$ V.

The internal resistance $= \dfrac{4960}{2 \times 10^{-3}} = 2.48 \times 10^6 \Omega = 2.6$ MΩ.

18 The total resistance $= 2.5 + 0.5 = 3.0\Omega$.

The current flowing $= \dfrac{E}{R} = \dfrac{1.5}{3.0} = 0.5$ A

The power delivered $= I^2R = (0.5)^2 \times 2.5 = 0.625$ W.

To give maximum power the external resistance = internal resistance = 0.5Ω.

STUDENT'S ANSWER WITH EXAMINER COMMENTS

STUDENT'S ANSWER TO QUESTION 14

> **Needs advantage and disadvantage of each method.**

a) The potential divider gives the full range of voltages down to OV, but the rheostat never gets down to OV, so the lamp is always lit.

b) i) $R = \dfrac{V}{I}$, Power $= VI$.

$I = \dfrac{\text{Power}}{V} = \dfrac{500 \times 10^{-3}}{2} = 0.25$A

$R = \dfrac{V}{I} = \dfrac{2}{0.25\text{A}} = 8\Omega$

> **but current through AX = 0.5A**

ii) $I = \dfrac{V}{R} = \dfrac{2}{8} = 0.25$A

> **e.c.f.**

iii) AX same resistance as BX so same P.D. = 2.0V.

iv) $E = V + Ir = 4 + 0.25 \times 6$

$E = 5.5$ V

> **Current through cell = 0.5A**

Overall comment: The student has not answered the part of the question concerning the advantages and disadvantages of each method. Marks are clearly lost, possibly as a result of the candidate failing to read the question fully. There is an e.c.f. (error carried forward) to part iv) but credit will be given for the correct working in part iv). The answer is typical of a C/D candidate.

CAPACITORS

GETTING STARTED

The basic concepts of **charge** and **capacitance**, the charging and discharging of **capacitors** and the energy stored in them, are mentioned in the core syllabus and are basic to A Level. The **reed switch** is mentioned in several syllabuses; check to see if yours is one of them.

A **capacitor** (effectively two conducting plates separated by an insulating gap) is a device which can store a charge (Fig. 11.1). The p.d. (V) across a capacitor is proportional to the charge, Q, on the capacitor.

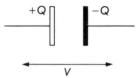

Fig. 11.1 Electrolytic capacitor

The constant ratio Q/V is called the **capacitance** of the capacitor and is measured in *farads*. Hence $Q = CV$ (Q in coulombs, V in volts). The larger the capacitance, the larger the charge it will store for a particular p.d. across the capacitor.

ESSENTIAL PRINCIPLES

**CHARGING A
CAPACITOR
THROUGH A
RESISTOR**

The p.d. (V_C) across the capacitor added to the p.d. (V_R) across the resistor gives the battery voltage E (Fig. 11.2). At $t = 0$, the capacitor is uncharged, so $V_C = 0$ and $V_R = E$.

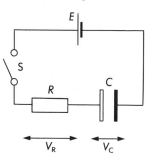

Fig. 11.2 Charging a capacitor through a resistor

As the current is given by V_R/R, so the capacitor is charging and V_C is increasing. Eventually $V_c = E$ and $V_R = 0$, so the current has stopped flowing and the capacitor is fully charged.

GRAPHS OF CURRENT AND CHARGE AGAINST TIME

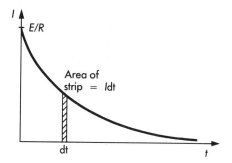

Fig. 11.3 Graph of current against time

The total *area* under the graph is given by $\int I \mathrm{d}t$, which equals the total charge which has flowed on to the capacitor. An oscilloscope placed across the resistor would display V_R (proportional to the current) against t.

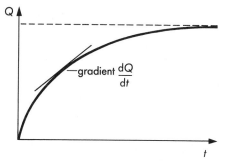

Fig. 11.4 Graph of charge against time

The *gradient* of the graph at any instant equals the current at that instant. An oscilloscope placed across the capacitor would display V_C (proportional to the charge) against t.

**DISCHARGE OF
A CAPACITOR**

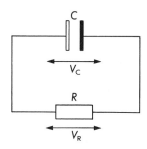

Fig. 11.5 Discharge of a capacitor

At any instant $V_R + V_C = 0$, so if after a time t the charge remaining on the capacitor is Q, and the current flowing is I, then:

$$I = -Q/RC$$

(the minus sign indicates that Q is decreasing).
Hence $dQ/dt = -Q/RC$, and

$$Q = Q_0 e^{-t/RC}$$

where Q_o is the charge on the capacitor at time $t = 0$.

GRAPHS OF CHARGE AND CURRENT AGAINST TIME

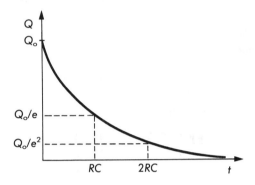

Fig. 11.6 Graph of charge against time

The *gradient* $= dQ/dt$ which is the current.

The product RC is then called the '**time constant**', (T). It is the time taken for the charge on the capacitor to decrease from Q_o to Q_o/e or $0.37Q_o$. After a time $2T$, the charge remaining $= Q_o/e^2$ or $0.14Q_o$.

In Fig. 11.7, the total *area* under curve $= \int I dt = Q_o$, the initial charge on the capacitor.

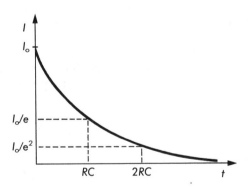

Fig. 11.7 Graph of current against time

<table>
<tr><td>**PARALLEL PLATE CAPACITOR**</td></tr>
</table>

Capacitance $C = Q/V = \epsilon_o A/d$ if air filled.

ϵ_o is the *permittivity* of free space, A the overlapping plate area and d the plate separation.

Hence $Q/A = (V/d)$,

where Q/A is the surface density of charge (the charge per unit area) on the plates and V/d is the electric field strength between the plates. If an insulator (dielectric), such as

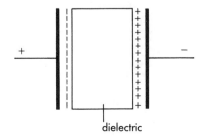

Fig. 11.8

dielectric

polythene, is placed between the plates, its molecules become polarised by the electric field, increasing the capacitance. In this situation:

$$C = \epsilon_r\epsilon_o A/d,$$

where ϵ_r is the **relative permittivity** of the dielectric.

Some questions involve changing the capacitance, say, increasing it by decreasing the separation of the plates. If the capacitor is isolated then the charge remains constant and so the p.d. decreases. If the capacitor is connected to a battery, then the p.d. will remain constant and the charge will increase.

ENERGY STORED IN CAPACITORS

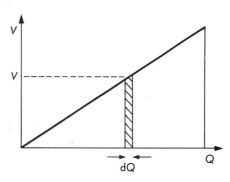

Fig. 11.9 Energy stored in a capacitor

As charge is being stored on the capacitor plates the p.d. across it is increasing in proportion. To transfer a small charge dQ when the p.d. is V requires VdQ joules of energy, which is the *area* of the strip shaded on the graph. The total energy stored in the capacitor is the *area* under the graph:

> *You should not need to remember all three equations.*

$$\tfrac{1}{2}QV = \tfrac{1}{2}CV^2 = \tfrac{1}{2}\frac{Q^2}{C}.$$

CAPACITORS IN SERIES

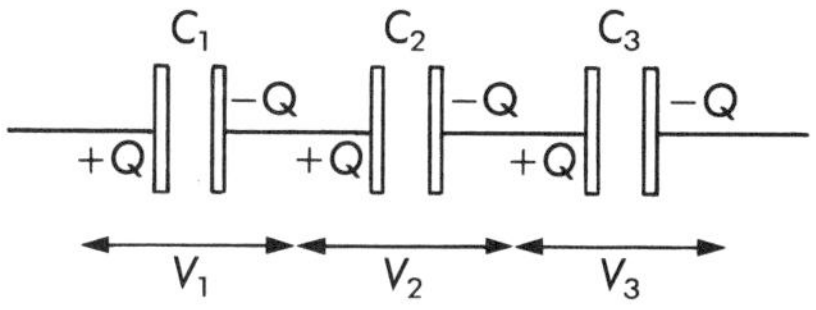

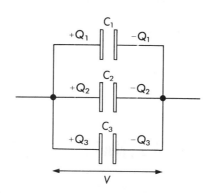

Fig. 11.10 Capacitors in series

Four points need to be noted here:

1 Each capacitor has the same charge, Q.
2 The p.d. across each capacitor is given by the equation $V = Q/C$, e.g. $V_1 = Q/C_1$.
3 The total p.d. is $V = V_1 + V_2 + V_3$.
4 They can be replaced by a single capacitor C where $\dfrac{1}{C} = \dfrac{1}{C_1} + \dfrac{1}{C_2} + \dfrac{1}{C_3}$.

CAPACITORS IN PARALLEL

Fig. 11.11 Capacitors in parallel

The two points to be noted here are:

1 The p.d. across each capacitor is the same.

2 They can be replaced by a single capacitor with the same total charge
$$Q = Q_1 + Q_2 + Q_3$$
and $C = C_1 + C_2 + C_3$.

SHARING CHARGE

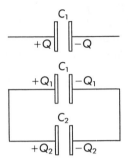

Fig. 11.12 Sharing charge

If a capacitor C_1 *shares* its charge Q with an uncharged capacitor C_2 they share this charge in the ratio of their capacitances.

> ❝ C_1 and C_2 are in parallel. ❞

$$\frac{Q_1}{C_1} = \frac{Q_2}{C_2} \text{ and } Q = Q_1 + Q_2$$

(the original charge is conserved). If $C_2 > C_1$ then $Q_2 > Q_1$ and $Q_2 \approx Q$. This means that almost all the original charge is transferred from C_1 to C_2. The p.d. across C_2 is now

$$\frac{Q_2}{C_2} \approx \frac{Q}{C_2}$$

By measuring the p.d. across C_2, the original charge on C_1 can be measured. This is the basis of the coulomb meter.

REED SWITCH

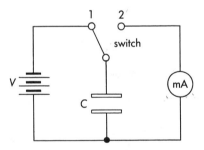

Fig. 11.13 Reed switch

When the **reed switch** is in position 1, the power supply charges the capacitor, while in position 2, the capacitor discharges through the ammeter. If this happens rapidly enough the meter will record a steady reading. For capacitance C and supply voltage V the charge Q on the capacitor each time is CV, and if the reed switches at frequency f, the capacitor will charge and discharge f times in one second. Hence the flow of charge per second, the current, is given by $I = Qf$. By measuring the current on the ammeter and knowing f, then Q and C can be measured.

EXAMINATION QUESTIONS

MULTIPLE CHOICE QUESTIONS

1 A circuit is set up as shown in Fig. 11.14 with the capacitor C initially uncharged. At time $t = 0$ the switch is closed. Which one of the graphs in Fig. 11.15 best represents the variation with t of the current I in the circuit?

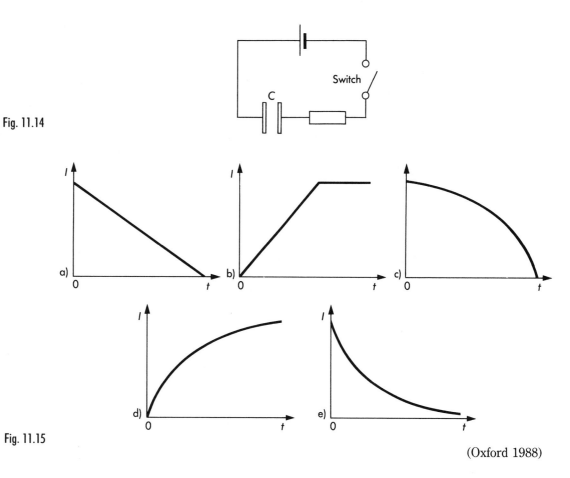

Fig. 11.14

Fig. 11.15

(Oxford 1988)

2 The potential difference between the plates of a charged parallel plate air capacitor increases if the capacitor is modified by:
1) increasing the area of the plates;
2) inserting a sheet of polythene between the plates;
3) increasing the distance between the plates.

a) 1,2,3   d) 1 only
b) 1, 2 only   e) 3 only
c) 2, 3 only

(London 1987)

3 A parallel plate capacitor is charged by connecting it to a d.c. supply. If the separation of the plates is now reduced, which of the following are correct statements?
1) the charge stored on the capacitor increases;
2) the p.d. across the capacitor increases;
3) the energy stored in the capacitor increases.

a) 1 only   d) 2 and 3 only
b) 2 only   e) 1, 2 and 3
c) 1 and 3 only

4 Three identical capacitors P, Q and S, initially uncharged, are connected to a battery as shown in Fig. 11.16. Compared with the p.d. across either Q or S, the p.d. across P is

a) one quarter   d) twice
b) one half   e) four times
c) the same

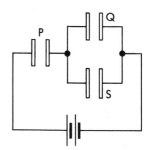

Fig. 11.16

(London 1987)

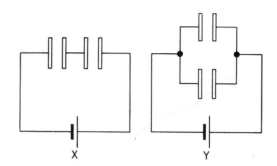

Fig. 11.17

X   Y

5 Two identical capacitors are connected to the same d.c. source first in series (circuit X) and then in parallel (circuit Y). The magnitude of the ratio:

$$\frac{\text{total energy stored by the capacitors in circuit Y}}{\text{total energy stored by the capacitors in circuit X}} \text{ is}$$

a) $\frac{1}{4}$ d) $\frac{2}{1}$

b) $\frac{1}{2}$ e) $\frac{4}{1}$

c) $\frac{1}{1}$

6 An 8-μF capacitor charged to a potential difference of 200 V and a 4-μF capacitor charged to a potential difference of 800 V are connected in parallel by joining terminals of like polarity. The potential difference across the combination will be

a) 133 V   d) 500 V

b) 300 V   e) 1000 V

c) 400 V

(London 1987)

7 A capacitor of capacitance C is discharging through a resistor. At time t, the charge on the capacitor is Q and the p.d. across it is V. At this instant the current flow is
1) dQ/dt;
2) V/C;
3) $C\,dV/dt$.

a) 1 only   d) 2 and 3 only

b) 2 only   e) 1, 2 and 3

c) 1 and 3 only

ANSWERS AND COMMENTS

Question	1	2	3	4	5	6	7
Answer	e)	e)	c)	d)	e)	c)	c)

1 The capacitor is initially uncharged and so the p.d. across it is O V. The p.d. across the resistor equals the battery voltage, and so there is a large initial current. As the capacitor charges, the p.d. across the capacitor increases and that across the resistor decreases, thus reducing the current. This is an exponential change.

2 Assuming the charge does not change, the p.d. will increase if C decreases ($V = Q/C$).
1) Increasing A increases C so V decreases.
2) Inserting a dielectric increases C and so V decreases.
3) Increasing the plate separation decreases C and so V decreases.

3 The capacitor is still connected to the power supply so the p.d. across the capacitor will remain constant.
1) Reducing the plate separation increases C so Q increases.
3) The energy = $\frac{1}{2}C V^2$ so will increase.

4 Q and S are in parallel and so have total capacitance Q + S = 2P.
The p.d. across P is twice the p.d. across Q or S.

5 Let the p.d. across the source be V. In series the total capacitance is $C/2$, so the energy is $\frac{1}{4}C V^2$. In parallel, the total capacitance is $2C$, so the energy is $\frac{1}{2}2C V^2$.

6 The charge ($Q=CV$) on the $8\mu F$ capacitor = 1600 μC.
The charge on the $4\mu F$ = 3200 μC.
When they are joined in parallel the total charge will be 4800 μC and the total capacitance will be 12 μF, so the p.d. = 400 V.

7 The current is the rate of flow of charge, given by dQ/dt. But as $Q = CV$, then

$$\frac{dQ}{dt} = \frac{d(CV)}{dt} \cdot C\,\frac{dV}{dt}$$

STRUCTURED QUESTIONS

8 Given a number of capacitors each with a capacitance of 2 μF and a maximum safe working potential difference of 10 V, how would you construct capacitors of
a) 1 μF capacitance, suitable for use up to 20 V?
b) 2 μF capacitance, suitable for use up to 20 V?   (2)

(Cambridge 1987)

9 a) Fig. 11.18 shows a typical capacitor. What do the markings on the capacitor indicate?

Fig. 11.18

b) In the circuit shown in Fig. 11.19, V is a very high resistance voltmeter and the two capacitors are initially uncharged.

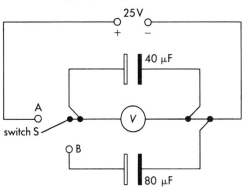

Fig. 11.19

i) When switch S is moved to position A, what will be the final steady reading on the voltmeter, and how much charge will then be stored on the 40 μF capacitor?

ii) Switch S is then moved to position B. State and explain whether the voltmeter reading will increase or decrease. Calculate the new steady voltmeter reading.   (10)

(AEB 1987)

OUTLINE ANSWERS

8 a) Two 2 μF capacitors in series have a total capacitance of 1 μF. With 20 V across both, the p.d. across each would be 10 V.
b) Adding another pair in parallel with the first pair would make a total of 2 μF.

9 a) 25 V is the maximum potential difference to be applied with the correct polarity. 5000 μF is the capacitance of the capacitor, i.e. it will store 5000 μC of charge for a p.d. of 1 V.

b) i) The final reading on the voltmeter will be 25 V and the charge will be 25 × 40 = 1000 μC.

ii) Moving the switch to position B will disconnect the supply and the 40 μF capacitor will share its charge with the 80 μF capacitor. The charge and hence the p.d. across the 40 μF will be less. The total capacitance is 120 μF, and so

$$V = \frac{1000}{120} = 8.3 \text{ V.}$$

TUTOR'S QUESTION AND ANSWER

QUESTION

10 This question is about experiments to obtain an accurate value for the relative permittivity of an insulating material such as perspex.

a) In one method, a parallel-plate air capacitor is constructed using two aluminium plates, each measuring 200 mm × 200 mm placed 1.0 mm apart in air. A very high resistance voltmeter is connected across the plates. The capacitor is first charged using a d.c. battery. A sheet of perspex is then inserted to fill the space between the plates, taking care not to discharge the capacitor.

   i) Draw a diagram of a suitable circuit, showing how the battery, the capacitor, the voltmeter and a switch are connected. *(3)*

   ii) Assuming that the relative permittivity of perspex is about 3.0, calculate an approximate value for the capacitance of the capacitor when the perspex is in place. (Permittivity of free space, $\epsilon_0 = 8.8 \times 10^{-12} \, \text{F m}^{-1}$) *(2)*

   iii) State and explain how you would expect the voltmeter reading to change when the perspex is inserted. *(3)*

   iv) Explain why the voltmeter must have a very high resistance. Assuming that one experiment will take about 30 seconds to complete, suggest a suitable value for the voltmeter resistance. Explain carefully how you arrived at your answer. *(4)*

   v) Show how you would use the voltmeter readings to calculate the relative permittivity of perspex. *(1)*

b) In another experiment to determine the relative permittivity of perspex, the capacitor in (a), with the perspex in place, is connected in the circuit shown in Fig. 11.20. The e.m.f. of the battery is 6.0 V, and the reed switch S is made to vibrate so that the capacitor is charged and discharged 400 times a second.

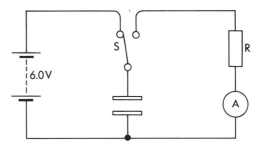

Fig. 11.20

   i) Estimate the charge transferred to the capacitor plates during each charging process, and suggest a suitable range for the ammeter placed in the discharge circuit. Justify your answer in each case. *(4)*

   ii) The resistor R is placed in the discharge circuit to protect the reed switch. State and explain how the ammeter reading may be affected if the value of R is large. *(3)*

   iii) Assuming that you have access to a supply of 1 mm perspex sheet, describe the procedure you would adopt to determine the relative permittivity of perspex. State the measurements you would make, and show how the relative permittivity would be calculated. *(5)*

(AEB 1988)

ANSWER

10 a) i)

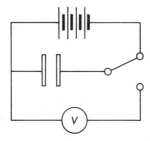

Fig. 11.21

ii) $C = \dfrac{\epsilon_o \epsilon_r A}{d} = \dfrac{3 \times 8.8 \times 10^{-12} \times 0.2 \times 0.2}{1 \times 10^{-3}} = 1 \times 10^{-9} \text{ F.}$

iii) Inserting the perspex increases the capacitance by a factor of 3, and with the charge remaining the same, $V = Q/C$ will decrease by a factor of 3.

iv) The voltmeter must have a very high resistance so that the charge which flows off the capacitor through the voltmeter in 30 seconds is negligible. The time constant (RC), the time it takes for the charge to decrease by a factor e, must be much greater than 30 seconds (say 3000 s).

So $R = \dfrac{3000}{10^{-9}} = 3 \times 10^{12} \Omega.$

v) The relative permittivity is the ratio of the voltmeter readings.

b) i) $Q = CV = 1 \times 10^{-9} \times 6 = 6 \times 10^{-9}$ C.
A charge of 6×10^{-9}C discharging 400 times a second will give a current $= 6 \times 10^{-9} \times 400 = 2.4 \times 10^{-6}$ A, so a suitable range is 5 μA.

ii) If R is too large the capacitor will not discharge completely each time and so the current will be less.

iii) The ammeter reading is proportional to the capacitance and so a reading needs to be taken with and without the perspex and the relative permittivity is the ratio of the readings.

STUDENT'S ANSWER WITH EXAMINER COMMENTS

STUDENT'S ANSWER TO QUESTION 10

> **When S is closed the battery will still be connected across the capacitor.**

> **Error; substitution of numbers before using calculator would help.**

> **Approximate value asked for**

a) i)

ii) $C = \dfrac{\epsilon_o \epsilon_r A}{d} = 1.06 \times 10^{-6}$ F

iii) The capacitance will increase and so will voltage.

iv) So that the capacitor does not discharge need $RC \gg 30$ $RC = 30$
$R = 3 \times 10^7 \Omega$ so need $R = 3 \times 10^9 \Omega.$

> **e.c.f.**

v) From ratio of readings.

> **Needs to be clear.**

b) i) $Q = CV = 6 \times 10^{-6}$ C
$I = Qf = 6 \times 10^{-6} \times 400 = 2.4 \times 10^{-3}$ A
range 10 mA

> **e.c.f.**

ii) Introducing R might reduce the ammeter reading.

> **Explain**

> **Reading of what?**

iii) Take reading without sheet.
Take reading with sheet between plates.

Relative permitivity $= \dfrac{\text{reading with}}{\text{reading without}}$

Overall comment: The candidate has made a number of slips and the reasoning is not fully explained. Overall it is typical of a D grade candidate.

e.c.f. is examiner's shorthand for 'error carried forward'. The candidate does not lose further marks.

INVERSE SQUARE LAW FIELDS

GETTING STARTED

Before studying the physics of electric, gravitational and magnetic fields it is necessary to master the basic concepts of **fields** and **potential**, and recognise the similarities between **gravitational** and **electric** fields. Magnetic fields will be dealt with in Chapter 13. A field is simply a region where a suitable object experiences a force. A **gravitational field** is a region where any mass experiences a force. The region surrounding a mass is a *gravitational field*, in which any other mass will experience a force of gravitational attraction. The **field strength** at a point is the force experienced by a mass of 1 kg, measured in N kg^{-1} (or force experienced per unit mass).

An **electric field** is any region where a charged object or particle experiences a force. The region surrounding a charge is described as an electric field in which another charge will experience a force. The **field strength** at a point is the force experienced by 1 coulomb measured in N C^{-1} (or force experienced per unit charge).

Work is done whenever an object is moved by a force and this results in an increase in the object's energy which is equal to the work done. Moving a mass against the force of gravitational attraction requires work to be done and results in an increase in the **gravitational potential energy**. The work done in moving 1 kg is described as the change in gravitational potential or **gravitational potential difference**, measured in J kg^{-1}.

Similarly moving a charge in an electric field requires work to be done and the potential energy of the charge is changed. The change in potential energy involved in moving 1 coulomb is called the **electrical potential difference**, measured in J C^{-1}.

The topics covered in this chapter are basic A Level material.

ESSENTIAL PRINCIPLES

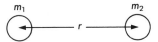

Fig. 12.1 Two 'point' masses

Any two masses m_1 and m_2 attract each other with a force F. This is given by **Newton's Law of Gravitation** according to the equation:

$$F = \frac{Gm_1m_2}{r^2} \, ,$$

> Note that the size of the force is proportional to both masses and obeys an inverse square law of distance. i.e. if r is doubled than F decreases by a factor of 4.

where r is the distance between their two centres of mass, and G is the universal constant of gravitation whose value in 6.7×10^{-11} Nm^2 kg^{-2}. Substitution in the equation shows that two 1 kg masses ($m_1 = 1$ kg, $m_2 = 1$ kg) a distance 10 cm ($r = 0.1$ m) apart, attract each other with a force of 6.7×10^{-9} N.

THE GRAVITATIONAL FIELD OF THE EARTH

The huge mass of the earth gives us our everyday experience of a gravitational field. In applying Newton's law it can be shown that, outside the earth, we can regard the mass of the earth as though it were all concentrated at its centre. Therefore distances are always measured to the centre of the earth. An object on the surface is effectively a distance equal to the radius of the earth from the mass of the earth. Hence the force that the earth exerts on a mass m on its surface is given by:

$$F = \frac{GM_e m}{R_e^2} \, ,$$

where M_e is the mass of the earth and R_e is the radius of the earth. The mass m is said to be in the gravitational field of the earth and the *strength* of the field is found by substituting $m = 1$ kg. i.e. the field strength, g, at the surface of the earth is given by:

> This equation provides useful substitution in other equations.

$$g = \frac{GM_e}{R_e^2} \, .$$

Since $M_e = 6.0 \times 10^{24}$ kg, $R_e = 6.4 \times 10^6$ m, then $g = 9.8$ N kg^{-1}, i.e. the earth pulls down on a mass of 1 kg with a force of 9.8 N.

$$\text{From } g = \frac{GM_e}{R_e^2} \text{ we can also get } g\,R_e^2 = GM_e.$$

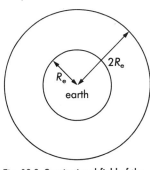

Fig. 12.2 Gravitational field of the earth

The value of the field strength g decreases as you move away from the earth, obeying an inverse square law e.g. at a distance R_e above the surface ($2R_e$ from the centre) g = 9.8/4 ≈ 2.5 N kg^{-1}.

The force exerted by the earth on a mass m is mg, which is called the weight of the mass.

From **Newton's second law of motion** ($F = ma$), the acceleration of an object is equal to the force acting on 1 kg, and so the acceleration of any mass falling freely at the earth's surface is 9.8 m s^{-2}.

FIELD INSIDE THE EARTH

Inside the earth we need only consider the mass of earth beneath us; the shell of earth further out can be shown to have no effect. If we consider the earth to be of uniform density, ρ, then at a distance R from the centre, the mass of earth beneath is given by

$$\frac{4}{3}\pi R^3 \rho.$$

The field is thus:

$$g = \frac{GM}{R^2} = \frac{4}{3}\pi \rho G R.$$

i.e. the field decreases uniformly with R below the earth's surface.

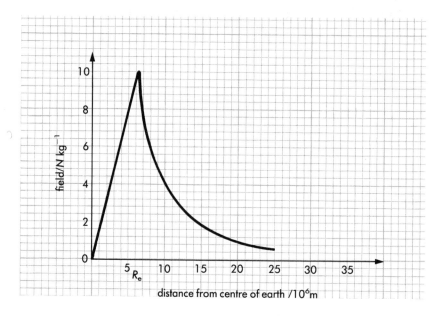

Fig. 12.3 Variation of the gravitational field of the earth

If we lift a mass from the floor on to the bench, work has to be done against the pull of the earth and some of our chemical energy is used to increase the potential energy (p.e.) of the mass. (The change in p.e. = work done). The pull of the earth obeys an inverse square law, but over such a *small* distance that we can regard the weight of the object as constant (i.e. the field is uniform). If we lift a weight mg through a height h, the work done is given by (force × distance) mgh. Doing this work has increased the potential energy of the mass by an amount mgh. If, however, a mass is lifted a *large* distance above the earth, then the pull of the earth decreases as the mass gets further away and the work done per metre gets less and less.

At a distance R from the earth's centre the force is given by:

$$\frac{GM_e m}{R^2}$$

and so the work done in moving a small distance dR (over which the force is considered constant) is found according to the equation:

$$\frac{GM_e m}{R^2} \times dR$$

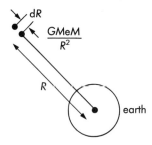

Fig. 12.4 Work done in moving mass m

The total work done is found by adding these small amounts of work:

Increase in p.e. = total work done

$$= \int_{R_1}^{R_2} \frac{GM_e m}{R^2} \, dR$$

$$= GM_e m \left(\frac{1}{R_1} - \frac{1}{R_2} \right),$$

where R_1 is the starting distance and R_2 the final distance.

The change in *gravitational potential* (as opposed to gravitational potential energy) is defined as the increase in gravitational potential energy per kg. Hence change in gravitational potential (substituting m = 1 kg) is given by:

$$\frac{GM_e}{R_1} - \frac{GM_e}{R_2}.$$

The change in gravitational potential can also be obtained from the area under the field/distance graph (Fig. 12.3).

If a 1 kg mass falls from infinity it loses energy (i.e. the gravitational potential decreases). The loss of energy can be found by:

$$\frac{GM_e}{R}.$$

As it is conventional to say that the potential at infinity is zero, then the potential V at a distance R is less than zero (i.e. it is negative)

$$V = -\frac{GM_e}{R}.$$

At the surface of the earth the potential $V = -\dfrac{GM_e}{R_e}$.

Using the values of M_e and R_e given earlier, $V = -6.3 \times 10^7 \text{ J kg}^{-1}$
$$= -63 \text{ MJ kg}^{-1}.$$

> **Note that the potential obeys an inverse law, i.e. doubling the distance halves the potential.**

RELATIONSHIP BETWEEN GRAVITATIONAL FIELD AND POTENTIAL

If we move a 1 kg mass a small distance dR in a direction away from the earth, then the work done and increase in gravitational potential is

$$dV = F \times dR,$$

where F is the field at this distance.
Rearranging this gives

$$F = -\frac{dV}{dR}$$

i.e. the field is the potential gradient (slope of potential graph).

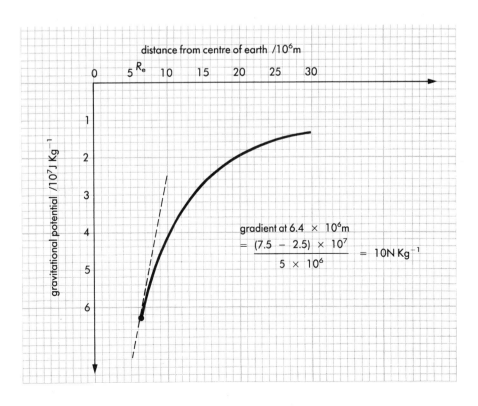

Fig. 12.5 Variation of gravitational potential of the earth

ELECTRIC FIELDS

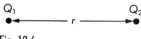

Fig. 12.6

Understanding the behaviour of gravitational fields should help you with understanding the *electric field* around a point charge, because it is also based on the inverse square law.

In Fig. 12.6 two point charges Q_1 and Q_2, a distance r apart, exert a mutual force on each other given by **Coulomb's Law**:

$$F = \frac{Q_1 Q_2}{4\pi\epsilon_o r^2}$$

which compares with **Newton's law**,

$$F = \frac{G m_1 m_2}{r^2} \,,$$

with the charges replacing the masses and the constant $\left(\dfrac{1}{4\pi\epsilon_o}\right)$ replacing the constant G. The constant ϵ_o, known as the **permittivity of free space**, has the value

$$8.8 \times 10^{-12} \text{ C}^{-2} \text{ N m}^2, \text{ and } \frac{1}{4\pi\epsilon_o} = 9 \times 10^9 \text{ C}^2 \text{N m}^{-2}.$$

It is, however, to be remembered that with electric fields, forces can be attractive or repulsive depending on the sign of the charges. Coulomb's law is easier to test in the laboratory as the force between two ordinary sized charged objects is more measurable. The strength of the electric field in the region surrounding any charged object is defined as *the force per unit charge*, and so at a distance r from a charge Q the field strength (E) is

> **This field obeys an inverse square law.**

$$E = \frac{Q}{4\pi\epsilon_o r^2} \,.$$

The *direction* of an electric field is conventionally taken to be that of the direction of the force on positive charge and so the field surrounding a point positive charge is radially outwards. If the object is a charged sphere then, if the charge is uniformly distributed around the surface, the problem may be treated as though the charge is concentrated at the centre of the sphere.

ELECTRIC POTENTIAL AND POTENTIAL ENERGY

If a charge is moved in the direction of an electric field, then work has to be done, and so electric potential energy of the charge changes. The change in electric potential or potential difference is defined as the work done per unit charge in moving the charge between two points in the field.

Using the same arguments as for gravitational potential energy, the change in electrical potential energy in moving a charge Q_1 away from a point charge Q_2 is given by:

$$\frac{Q_1 Q_2}{4\pi\epsilon_o r_1} - \frac{Q_1 Q_2}{4\pi\epsilon_o r_2}$$

where r_1 and r_2 are the initial and final distances from Q_2.

The change in potential is given by:

$$\frac{Q_2}{4\pi\epsilon_o r_1} - \frac{Q_2}{4\pi\epsilon_o r_2} \,.$$

As with gravitational potential, the zero of electrical potential is taken to be an infinite distance from the charge. If a unit of positive charge is brought towards a positive charge, then work has to be done against the force of *repulsion*, and so the electric potential is increasing. The electric potential surrounding a positive charge is thus positive, and that surrounding a negative charge is negative. The electric potential surrounding a point charge varies as the inverse of the distance from the charge.

INVERSE SQUARE LAW FIELD

FIELD LINES AND EQUIPOTENTIALS

It is conventional to represent fields by drawing lines to represent their directions. The electric field surrounding a point charge can be represented as in Fig. 12.7. The gravitational field surrounding the earth has a similar shape, but is always directed inwards.

The variation of potential in a field can be represented by drawing lines joining points

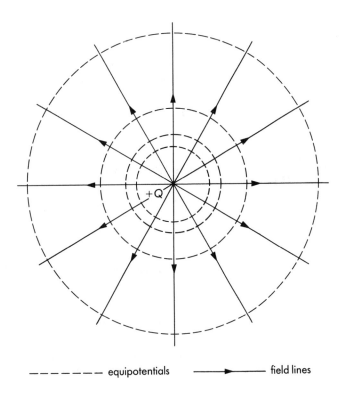

------- equipotentials   ————▶ field lines

Fig. 12.7 Electric field and potential
surrounding a point charge

which are at the same potential. These are known as **lines of equipotential**, and are
similar to contour lines joining points of equal height. If we move a charge along an
equipotential line, no work is being done, and so the lines must be perpendicular to the field
lines. As with contours, the lines are drawn with equal spacings of potential.

UNIFORM FIELD

The electric field between two parallel plates is *uniform* (the field strength is the same
anywhere between the plates), and the lines of equipotential are parallel to the plates.
Over small heights (e.g. a few km), the earth's field is approximately uniform and the
equipotentials are equally spaced horizontal lines.

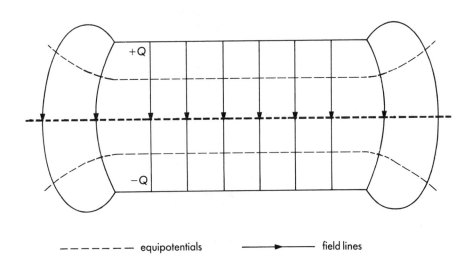

------- equipotentials   ————▶ field lines

Fig. 12.8 Uniform field between
charged parallel plates

RELATIONSHIP BETWEEN ELECTRIC FIELD AND POTENTIALS

As with gravitational fields, the electric field depends on the potential gradient. i.e.

$$E = - \frac{\mathrm{d}V}{\mathrm{d}x}.$$

Here, the magnitude of $\dfrac{\mathrm{d}V}{\mathrm{d}x}$ can be obtained from the slope of the graph of potential V against distance x.

It is to be noted that *electric potential* is a scalar quantity, and so to add two potentials we use scalar addition taking care with the signs. *Electric field strength* (or electric intensity) is a vector quantity, and to find the resultant of two fields we have to use the rules of vectorial addition taking into account the directions.

SATELLITES IN ORBIT

In any problem involving uniform motion in a circle, we need to remember that in order to confine a mass to describe a circle at a steady speed, v, then a constant force acting towards the centre of the circle is required to provide the constant centripetal acceleration towards the centre. The acceleration is given by:

$$a = \frac{v^2}{r}, \text{ or } rw^2,$$

where w is the angular velocity and r is the radius of the circle. Hence the centripetal force is:

$$F = ma = m\frac{v^2}{r} = mrw^2.$$

In the case of satellites orbiting a planet, it is the gravitational force of attraction which provides the centripetal acceleration. Hence:

$$\frac{GMm}{R^2} = \frac{mv^2}{R} = mRw^2,$$

for a satellite of mass m, in an orbit of radius R, about a planet of mass M.

The *speed* of the mass in orbit is thus determined by the radius R of the orbit, as G and M are constant. The higher the orbit, the greater the value of R, and so the smaller the value of v and w.

The *period* or time for one orbit is related to w and v by the equations:

$$T = \frac{2\pi}{w} = \frac{2\pi R}{v}.$$

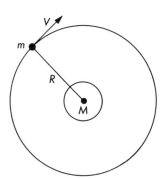

Fig. 12.9 Mass *m* in orbit about a planet of mass *M*

Hence:

$$T^2 = \frac{4\pi R^3}{GM},$$

and so the period squared is proportional to the radius cubed.

Two useful calculations can be made using the above equations.

1 The radius of orbit of a geostationary satellite around the earth. This is a satellite which remains above the same point on the earth. As the earth rotates about a north/south axis, the satellite must be above the equator rotating in the same direction and with the same angular velocity as the earth, so that the force is always towards the centre of the orbit. The important point is to substitute T = 24 hrs (in secs). You should be able to show that:
$$R = 42 \times 10^6 \text{ m}.$$

2 The radius of the moon's orbit around the earth. Using $T = 28$ days (in secs) you should be able to show:
$$R = 3.9 \times 10^8 \text{ m}.$$

POTENTIAL AND KINETIC ENERGY OF SATELLITES IN ORBIT

For a satellite of mass m travelling at speed v in an orbit of radius R about a planet of mass M. Assuming the orbit to be circular, then

$$\frac{GMm}{R^2} = \frac{mv^2}{R}$$

Thus the **kinetic energy** (K.E.) of the satellite is:

$$\tfrac{1}{2}mv^2 = \frac{GMm}{2R},$$

The **potential energy** (P.E.) is:

$$- \frac{GMm}{R} \; .$$

The **total energy** = P.E. + K.E.

$$= - \frac{GMm}{R} + \frac{GMm}{2R}$$

$$= - \frac{GMm}{2R} \; ,$$

which is negative and exactly half the P.E.

ESCAPE VELOCITY

The **escape velocity** is the speed a mass needs at the surface of a planet so that it has just sufficient K.E. to escape completely from the gravitational field of the planet.

$$\text{P.E. required to escape} \; = \frac{GMm}{R} \; ,$$

$$\text{so K.E.} \; = \tfrac{1}{2}mv^2 \; = \frac{GMm}{R} \; ,$$

$$\text{and so} \quad v \; = \sqrt{\frac{2GM}{R}} \; .$$

To escape from the earth: $R_e = 6.4 \times 10^6$ m, $M_e = 6.0 \times 10^{24}$ kg, giving $v = 11,200$ m s^{-1} = 11.2 km s^{-1}.

EXAMINATION QUESTIONS

MULTIPLE CHOICE QUESTIONS

1 Two identical lead spheres of radius r are in contact and attract each other with a gravitational force F (see Fig. 12.10 a)). What would be the gravitational force of attraction between two similar lead spheres of radius $2r$ (see Fig. 12.10 b))?

a) $\tfrac{1}{4}F$ d) $8F$
b) $\tfrac{1}{2}F$ e) $16F$
c) $2F$

a)

2r

Fig. 12.10   b)

(Oxford 1988)

2 The Earth may be considered as a uniform sphere of mass M and radius r. Which one of the following equations correctly relates the gravitational constant G and the acceleration of free fall g at the surface of the Earth?

a) $G = \dfrac{gM}{r^2}$ d) $G = \dfrac{M}{gr^2}$

b) $G = \dfrac{gr^2}{M}$ e) $G = gMr^2$

c) $G = \dfrac{r^2}{gM}$

(Oxford 1988)

3 A spacecraft of mass m is launched from the surface of the Earth, reaching an orbit at a distance above the surface equal to the Earth's radius R. If the gravitational constant is G, the acceleration of free fall at the Earth's surface is g, and the mass of the Earth is M, the gravitational potential energy gained by the spacecraft during this operation is

a) zero   d) GMm/R
b) mgR e) GM/R
c) $GMm/2R$

(NI 1988)

4 Near the surface of a certain planet, the gravitational field may be considered to be uniform. The gravitational potential difference between a point on the surface and a point 2.0 m above it is $5.0\,\mathrm{J\,kg^{-1}}$. The work done, in joules, in lifting a mass of 0.50 kg from the surface to a height of 4.0 m is

a) 2.0   d) 5.0
b) 2.5   e) 10.0
c) 4.0

(NI 1987)

5 The planet Saturn revolves around the Sun in a circular orbit of radius R_s and period of rotation T_s. The planet Uranus revolves around the Sun in a circular orbit of radius $2R_s$ and period of rotation T_u. The ratio T_u/T_s is

a) $2^{1/2}$ d) $2^{3/2}$
b) $2^{2/3}$ e) 2^2
c) 2

(NI 1987)

6 An artificial satellite moves in a circular orbit about the Earth. The following statements relate to the period and the energy of the satellite in this orbit. (By convention, the potential energy of an object at an infinite distance from the Earth is taken as zero.)
1) The orbital period of the satellite must be 24 hours.
2) The gravitational potential energy of the satellite in its orbit is a negative quantity.
3) The total energy of the satellite in its orbit is a negative quantity.

Which of these statements is (are) correct?

a) 1 only   d) 2 and 3 only
b) 2 only   e) 1, 2 and 3
c) 1 and 2 only

(NI 1987)

7 Which ONE of the following statements relating to Fig. 12.11 is *incorrect*?

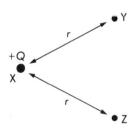

Fig. 12.11

a) The magnitude of the electric field intensity at Y is equal to the magnitude of the electric field intensity at Z.
b) The potentials at Y and Z are equal.
c) The potential at Y is positive.
d) No work is done in taking a charge from Y to Z.
e) The electric field intensity at Z acts along ZX in the direction from Z to X.

(NI 1987)

8 Fig. 12.12 shows how the electric potential varies along a straight line in a given

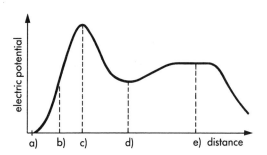

Fig. 12.12

electrical field. At which one of the points a), b), c), d) or e) is the magnitude of the electric field strength a maximum?

9 A negatively charged particle is transferred between the plates of a large parallel-plate capacitor. The particle moves from the point P, the centre of the negatively charged plate, to Q, the centre of the positively charged plate, as shown in Fig. 12.13. Which *one* of the graphs in Fig. 12.14 best shows the way in which the magnitude of the electric force F on the particle varies with distance along the line PQ?

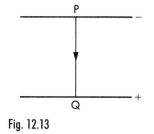

Fig. 12.13

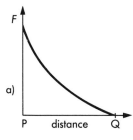
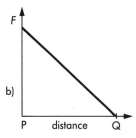
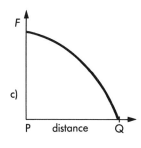

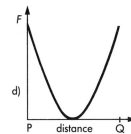
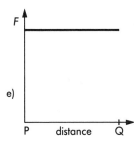

Fig. 12.14

(NI 1988)

10 A thin isolated, spherical conducting sphere of radius r carries a charge $+Q$. Which one of the graphs in Fig. 12.15 correctly illustrates how the electric field strength E varies with distance x from the centre of the sphere?

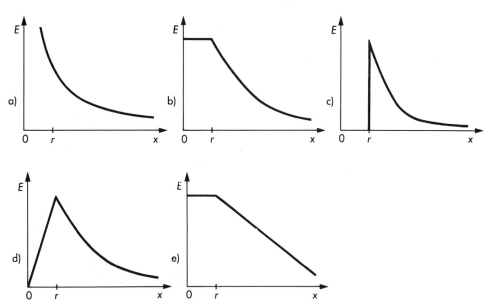

Fig. 12.15

(Oxford 1987)

11   Fig. 12.16 shows two charged spheres, X and Y, of masses $2m$ and m respectively, which are just prevented from falling under gravity by the application of a p.d. between the two parallel metal plates. If the plates are moved closer together:

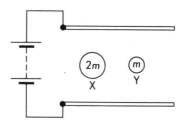

Fig. 12.16

a) X and Y will both remain stationary;
b) X and Y will both begin to move upwards with the same acceleration;
c) X and Y will both begin to move downwards with the same acceleration;
d) X will begin to accelerate upwards faster than Y;
e) X will begin to accelerate downwards faster than Y.

(London 1989)

ANSWERS AND COMMENTS

Question	1	2	3	4	5	6	7	8	9	10	11
Answer	e)	b)	c)	d)	d)	d)	e)	b)	e)	c)	b)

1   Using $F = \dfrac{Gm_1m_2}{r^2}$ when the radii = $2r$, both the masses are 8m so the top line increases by a factor of 64, but the bottom line increases by a factor of 4. The overall increase is by a factor of 16.

2   See text p. 115.

3   The distance from the earth's centre changes from R to $2R$ so the change in potential energy is
$$\frac{GmM}{R} - \frac{GmM}{2R} = \frac{GmM}{2R}.$$

4   The work done is equal to the change in potential multiplied by the mass. The change in potential = 2×5.0, so the work done is:
$(2 \times 5.0) \times 0.5 = 5$ J.

5   T^2 is proportional to R^3 so:
$$\frac{T_u^2}{T_s^2} = \frac{R_u^3}{R_s^3} \text{, and } \frac{R_u^2}{R_s} = 2 \text{, so } \frac{T_u}{T_s} = 2^{3/2}.$$

6   1) The period of the satellite depends on the height of the orbit.
2) It will need energy to lift the satellite to an infinite distance.
3) The total energy is the sum of the K.E. and the P.E.
$$= -\frac{GMm}{2R}.$$

7   Y and Z are the same distances from Q and so are at the same potential and in the same field. The potential around a positive charge is positive. The field at Z acts away from X.

8   The field is equal to the negative potential gradient and so the magnitude of the field is greatest where the magnitude of the gradient of the graph is greatest.

9   The field between the plates is uniform and so the force experienced by a charge is constant.

10   There is no field inside the sphere, and outside the field obeys an inverse square law.

11   As they are in equilibrium, the electric force on $2m$ is twice that on m to balance their weights, and so the charge on $2m$ *is twice that on m*. When the plates are moved closer together, the field increases, but the force on $2m$ *will always be twice that on m*.

STRUCTURED QUESTIONS

12 Taking the radius of the earth to be 6000 km:
a) Calculate the ratio of the gravitational field strength at a height of 144 km above the earth's surface to that at the earth's surface.
b) Calculate the change in the kinetic energy of a mass of 100 kg in falling freely from 144 km to 72 km above the earth's surface.
c) Would the answer to b) be different if the object initially had a tangential velocity? (9)

(Welsh 1987)

13 a) What do you understand by the term *gravitational field*; define *gravitational field strength*.

Show that the radius R of a satellite's orbit about a planet of mass M is related to its period as follows:

$$R^3 = \frac{GM}{4\pi^2} T^2$$

where G is the universal gravitational constant. (8)

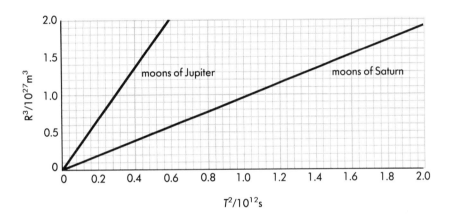

Fig. 12.17

b) Figure 12.17 shows two graphs of R^3 against T^2; one is for the moons of Jupiter and the other is for the moons of Saturn. R is the mean distance of a moon from a planet's centre and T is its period. The orbits are assumed to be circular. The mass of Jupiter is 1.90×10^{27} kg.
i) Why are the lines straight?
ii) Find a value for the mass of Saturn.
iii) Find a value for the universal gravitational constant G. (8)

(London 1987)

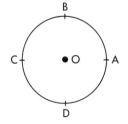

Fig. 12.18

14 In Fig. 12.18 O is the centre of a circle of radius 3 m. COA and BOD are diameters which are at right angles to each other. Charges of 6 nC.–2 nC. 3 nC and 4 nC are placed at A, B, C and D respectively.
Find:
i) the electric potential at O.
ii) the electric intensity at O.

$$\left[\frac{1}{4\pi\epsilon_0} = 9 \times 10^9 \, \text{F}^{-1}\,\text{m} \right]$$ (8)

(Welsh 1988)

15 a) Define the terms i) electric field strength, ii) electric potential, both at a point in an electric field.
b) An electric field is established between two parallel plates as shown in Fig. 12.19. The plates are 50 cm apart and a p.d. of 1000 V is applied between them. A point charge of value + 1.0 μC is held at point A. It is moved first to B then to C and finally back to A. The distances are shown in the diagram.

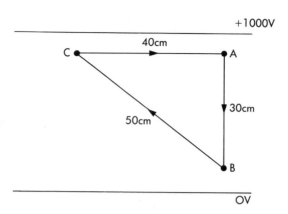

Fig. 12.19

Calculate:

    i) the force experienced by the charge at A;
    ii) the force experienced by the charge at B;
    iii) the energy involved in moving the charge from A to B;
    iv) the energy required to move the charge from C to A;
    v) the net energy needed to move the charge along the route $ABCA$.   *(8)*

  c) In an attempt to measure the capacitance C of a large capacitor, a student charges it to a p.d. of 20 V and then discharges it through a series combination of resitor R and sensitive meter. A graph of current against time is produced from readings obtained (Fig. 12.20).

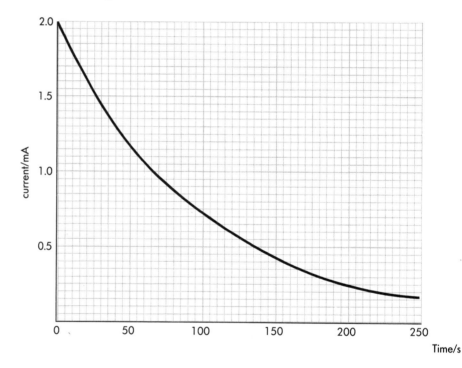

Fig. 12.20

    i) Draw a suitable circuit diagram for the experiment.
    ii) From the graph obtain values for C and R explaining your procedure carefully.   *(8)*

(Southern 1987

OUTLINE ANSWERS AND COMMENTS

12   a) Field strength obeys an inverse square law, so the ratio of the field strength 144 km above the surface to that at the surface

$$= \frac{R_E^2}{(R_E + 144^2)} = \left(\frac{6000}{6144}\right)^2 = 0.95.$$

  b) Increase in K.E. = loss in P.E. $= mGM_E\left(\dfrac{1}{6072} - \dfrac{1}{6144}\right)$

but $GM_E = gR_E{}^2$

so change in K.E. $= mgR_E{}^2 \left(\dfrac{1}{6072} - \dfrac{1}{6144} \right)$

$$= 6.8 \times 10^7 \text{ J.}$$

c) The change in K.E. would be the same, as it equals the change in P.E. which depends only on the change in height.

13 a) Gravitational field is a region where a mass experiences a force. Field strength is the force per unit mass (see text for proof of equation).
   b) i) The lines are straight because R^2 is proportional to T^3.
      ii) Taking a common value of $T(0.6 \times 10^{12}$ s$)$, M is proportional to R^3, and

$$\frac{M_s}{M_J} = \frac{R_s{}^3}{R_J{}^3}$$

$$M_s = 1.9 \times 10^{27} \times \frac{(0.55 \times 10^{27})^3}{(2 \times 10^{27})^3} = 3.9 \times 10^{25} \text{ kg.}$$

   iii) The gradient of the lines $= \dfrac{GM}{4\pi^2}$

The gradient of the Jupiter line $= \dfrac{2 \times 10^{27}}{0.6 \times 10^{12}} = 3.3 \times 10^{15} = \dfrac{GM}{4\pi^2}$

$$G = \frac{3.3 \times 10^{15} \times 4 \times \pi^2}{1.9 \times 10^{27}} = 6.9 \times 10^{-11} \text{ N m}^2 \text{ kg}^{-2}.$$

14 i) The potential at a distance r from a charge $Q = \dfrac{Q}{4\pi\epsilon_o r}$

The potential at O is the algebraic sum of the potentials

$$= (6 + (-2) + 3 + 4) \times 10^{-9} \times \frac{9 \times 10^9}{3} = 33 \text{ V.}$$

ii) The field strength at a distance r from a charge $Q = \dfrac{Q}{4\pi\epsilon_o r^2}$ e.g. field strength

due to 6 nC $= 6 \times 10^{-9} \times \dfrac{9 \times 10^9}{3^2} = 6 \text{ NC}^{-1}.$

The directions need to be taken into account.
The resultant field $= (6^2 + 3^2) = 6.71 \text{ NC}^{-1}$ at angle $\theta = 60°.$

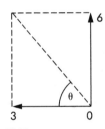

3   0

Fig. 12.21

15 a) Field strength is the force experienced by a charge of $+1$ C. Potential is the work done in bringing a charge of $+1$ C from infinity to that point.
   b) The uniform field $= V/d = 1000/0.5 = 2000 \text{ N C}^{-1}$
      i) & ii) The force experienced by 1.0 μC anywhere in the field
$$= 2000 \times 1 \times 10^{-6} = 2 \times 10^{-3} \text{ N.}$$
      iii) Energy change $=$ work done
$$= \text{force} \times \text{distance moved in direction of force}$$
$$= 2 \times 10^{-3} \times 0.3 = 6 \times 10^{-4} \text{ J.}$$
      iv) Energy change $= 0.$
      v) The net energy change is zero because the route ends up back at A at the same potential.
   c) i) See Fig. 12.22
      ii) The initial current $= 20/R \quad = 2 \times 10^{-3}$ A (from graph)
$$\text{Hence } R = 10000\Omega$$
The time constant (RC) is the time taken for the current to fall to $1/e$ of its initial value, i.e.
$$\frac{2 \times 10^{-3}}{e} = 0.73 \times 10^{-3} \text{ A}$$
From the graph $RC = 100$ s. $C = 100/R = 0.01$ F.

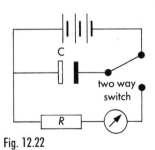

Fig. 12.22

TUTOR'S QUESTION AND ANSWER

QUESTION

16 A point mass m is at a distance r from the centre of the Earth. Write down an expression, in terms of m, r, the Earth's mass m_E and the gravitational constant G, for the gravitational potential energy V of the mass. (Consider only values of r greater than the Earth's radius.) (2)

Certain meteorites (tektites) found on Earth have a composition identical with that of lunar granite. It is thought that they may be debris from a volcanic eruption on the Moon. Fig. 12.23 which is not to scale, shows how the gravitational potential

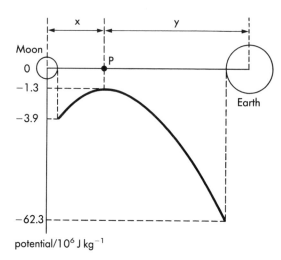

Fig. 12.23   potential/10^6 J kg^{-1}

between the surface of the Moon and the surface of the Earth varies along the line of centres. At the point P the gravitational potential is a maximum.

a) By considering the separate contributions of Earth and Moon to the gravitational potential, explain qualitatively why the graph has a maximum, and why the curve is asymmetrical. (3)

b) State how the resultant gravitational force on the tektite at any point between the Moon and the Earth could be deduced from Fig. 12.23 (2)

c) When a tektite is at P the gravitational forces on it due to Moon and Earth are F_M and F_E respectively. State the relation which applies between F_M and F_E. Hence find the value of x/y, where x and y are the distances of P from the centre of the Moon and the centre of the Earth respectively. (4)

d) If a tektite is to reach the Earth, it must be projected from the volcano on the Moon with a certain minimum speed v_0. Making use of appropriate values from Fig. 12.23 find this speed. Explain your reasoning. (4)

e) Discuss very briefly whether a tektite will reach the Earth's surface with a speed less than, equal to or greater than the speed of projection. (Neglect atmospheric resistance.) (2)

(Mass of Moon $=$ 7.4×10^{22} kg;
mass of Earth $=$ 6.0×10^{24} kg.)

(Cambridge 1987)

ANSWER

16 $V = -\dfrac{Gmm_E}{r}$.

a) If a 1 kg mass is taken from the surface of the moon to the earth, the potential will initially increase as work has to be done against the stronger attractive force of the moon. However at P, the mass will experience no overall attraction and beyond P, the potential will fall as work is done by the greater attractive force of the earth. The curve is assymmetrical because the much larger mass of the earth means that the point of zero overall force is nearer the moon.

b) The force at any point is the gradient of the curve of potential against distance.

c) In magnitude $F_E = F_M$. Hence $\dfrac{GM_E}{y^2} = \dfrac{GM_M}{x^2}$

$$x/y = \sqrt{\frac{Mm}{M_E}} = \sqrt{\frac{7.4 \times 10^{22}}{6.0 \times 10^{24}}} = 0.11$$

d) To reach the earth the tektite must be given enough energy to climb the potential hill from the surface of the moon to P.
Kinetic energy needed $= m \times (-1.3 - (-3.9)) \times 10^6 = \frac{1}{2}mv^2$,

Hence $v = \sqrt{(2 \times 2.6 \times 10^6)} = 2{,}300 \text{ ms}^{-1}$.

e) In falling from P the tektite will gain more energy $(62.3 - 1.3) \times 10^6 \text{ J kg}^{-1}$ than it lost in climbing to P. It will arrive at the surface of the earth with a greater speed.

STUDENT'S ANSWER WITH EXAMINER COMMENTS

STUDENT'S ANSWER TO QUESTION 15 a) AND b)

a) Field strength is force per coulomb.

b) Potential is work per coulomb to bring a charge to that point.

i) Force = field × charge $= \dfrac{V}{d} \times q = \dfrac{1000}{0.5} \times 1 \times 10^{-6} = 2 \times 10^{-3}$ N.

ii) Same.

iii) Energy = force × distance $= 2 \times 10^{-3} \times 0.3 = 6 \times 10^{-4}$ J.

iv) Energy $= 2 \times 10^{-3} \times 0.4 = 8 \times 10^{-4}$ J.

v) Total $= 2 \times 10^{-3} \times 1.2 = 2.4 \times 10^{-3}$ J.

> Distance must be in the direction of field.

Overall comments: Descriptive parts of the question are abbreviated which could lead to the loss of marks. In the last two parts of the question the candidate has misunderstood the crucial feature of the electric field i.e. that the work done in moving the charge is independent of the route through the field. Overall the answer is typical of a C/D grade candidate.

GETTING STARTED

This chapter deals with **magnetic fields**. The region surrounding a charge is an **electric field** in which other charges experience an **electrostatic force**. When charged particles *move*, they create a magnetic field in the surrounding region, i.e. a region in which other moving charges or magnets will experience a force. Hence there is a magnetic field in the region surrounding a wire carrying a current of moving electrons. These fields are represented by drawing lines to show the direction of the force at various points in the field. It is agreed by convention that the *direction* of the field is that of the force on a North pole placed at that point in the field. The *strength* of a magnetic field is defined in terms of the force it exerts on a current carrying conductor placed in the field. Two current carrying wires placed side by side exert forces on each other. This effect is used in the definition of the **ampere**. These basic ideas are considered in all A Level courses.

ESSENTIAL PRINCIPLES

MAGNETIC FIELDS

When a current flows through a wire, a **magnetic field** is created around the wire. The shape of the field lines makes a set of concentric cylinders centred on the wire (Fig. 13.1).

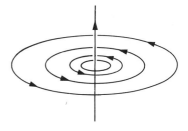

Fig. 13.1 Magnetic field of current flowing through straight wire

Note the direction of the arrows on the field lines and the direction of the conventional current in the wire.

The strength B of the field at a distance r from a wire carrying a current I is given by the equation:

$$B = \frac{\mu_o I}{2\pi r} \; ,$$

where μ_o is called the **permeability of a vacuum**. (See p. 132 for the value of μ_o).

> As the distance doubles, the field halves.

Note that the field decreases as r increases (as you move further from the wire). This variation is represented in Fig. 13.1 by drawing the lines further apart where the field is weaker. Fig. 13.2 a) shows the shape of the field associated with a flat coil and Fig. 13.2 b)

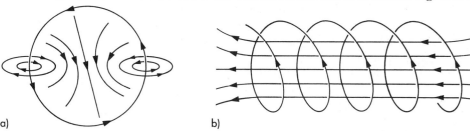

Fig. 13.2a) Field of flat coil

Fig. 13.2b) Field within long coil (solenoid)

a)   b)

shows the field inside a long coil (solenoid). The *flux density* inside the middle region of the solenoid is uniform and is given by the equation:

> Note that the field at the middle of the solenoid depends on the number of turns per unit length (*N/L*).

$$B = \frac{\mu_o N I}{L} \; ,$$

where I is the current N is the number of turns and L is the length. The field inside the solenoid decreases towards the ends to about half the value in the middle. The flux density is increased by a factor μ_r (relative permeability) if the coil is filled with iron.

STRENGTH OF A MAGNETIC FIELD

This is measured in terms of a vector quantity, B, called the **magnetic flux density**. If a wire carrying a current is placed in a magnetic field, then the wire will experience a force which depends on the magnetic flux density at the wire. This effect can be used to measure the B value of the magnetic field.

The B value of a magnetic field is defined as the force per unit length per unit current. Thus if a wire of length L, carrying a current I, placed at right angles to a uniform field B, experiences a force F, then the flux density will be:

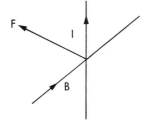

Fig. 13.3 Fleming's left-hand rule

$$B = \frac{F}{I L}$$

measured in $N\,A^{-1}\,m^{-1}$ or tesla (T). The direction of the force is perpendicular to both the field B and the current I (use **Fleming's Left Hand rule**). Hold the thumb and first two fingers of the left hand at right angles to each other, and point the First finger in the direction of Field, the seCond finger in the direction of the Current, and the thuMb will point in the direction of the force (Motion).

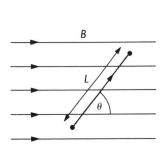

Fig. 13.4 Wire at angle θ to field B Fig. 13.5 Couple on a coil in field B

If a wire of length L carrying a current I is placed at an angle θ to a field B, then it will experience a force given by $BIL\sin\theta$.

If a rectangular coil of N turns with a current I is placed in a field B, then two sides of length L of the coil will experience a force $NBIL$ in opposite directions as shown in Fig. 13.5. Hence the coil will experience a couple $BILa\sin\alpha$. The turning effect produced by this couple is used in the d.c. motor and the moving coil galvanometer.

FORCES BETWEEN CURRENT CARRYING CONDUCTORS

If two current carrying conductors are placed side by side, then they will each be in the field of the other and so experience a force perpendicular to both their own current and the other's field. You should be able to show this means that when the currents are in the same direction, the two wires experience a force of attraction towards each other, and if the currents are in the opposite direction, a force of repulsion occurs. This force is the basis for the following definition of the ampere.

> Remember, when the currents are in the same direction the force is attractive.

The **ampere** is that constant current which, flowing in two infinitely long, straight parallel conductors of negligible cross-section, placed in a vacuum 1 metre apart, produces a force between them of 2×10^{-7} newton per metre length.

> This definition need not be memorised.

The value 2×10^{-7} N m^{-1} is not a measurement but a definition and from this follows the value of μ.

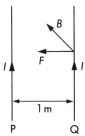

Fig. 13.6 Force between two parallel current-carrying wires

The field B, due to the current in wire P, is given by $\dfrac{\mu_o I}{2\pi r}$,

and so with $I = 1$ A and $r = 1$ m, $B = \dfrac{\mu_o}{2\pi}$.

The force F on length L of wire Q $= BIL$,

and so with $L = 1$ m, $I = 1$ A and $B = \dfrac{\mu_o}{2\pi}$, $F = \dfrac{\mu_o}{2\pi}$,

But by definition $F = 2 \times 10^{-7}$ N, so $\mu_o = 4\pi \times 10^{-7}$ H m^{-1}.

FORCES ON CHARGES MOVING THROUGH FIELDS

A field of flux density B will exert a force BIL on a wire of length L carrying a current I at right angles to the field. If the current is a stream of electrons of charge e travelling at speed v through a wire of area A with n electrons per unit volume, then in a length L there will be nAL electrons. The force on these electrons will be BIL, where $I = nAev$. Hence the force on each electron will be:

$$\frac{BnAenL}{nAL} = Bev$$

The force will be perpendicular to both the field and to the direction of travel of the electrons.

A force Bqv will also be exerted on a particle of charge q moving at speed v at right angles to a magnetic field B. If the field is uniform, the particle experiences a constant force whose direction remains perpendicular to the particle's direction of motion, and so it describes a circle of radius r where:

$$Bqv = \frac{mv^2}{r}.$$

> **The derived equation for r is very useful.**

Hence the radius of the circle is given by

$$r = \frac{mv}{Bq}.$$

Note that the radius of the circle is proportional to m and to v, but inversely proportional to B and q. This effect is used in the cathode ray tube, mass spectrometer and cyclotrons. For some syllabuses it would be worth studying the detail of a mass spectrometer.

THE HALL EFFECT

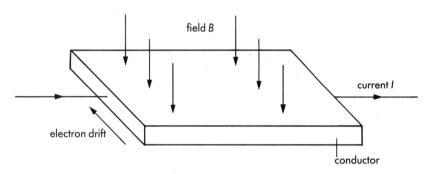

Fig. 13.7 The Hall effect

> **Not in all syllabuses.**

When a conductor carrying a current is placed in a magnetic field B, the electrons experience a force perpendicular to their direction of motion, and so they drift towards one side of the conductor. This drift of negative charge to one side, leaving the other side positively charged creates an electric field E which opposes the drift. The drift will cease when the force on the electrons due to the electric field balances the force due to the magnetic field. i.e.

$$Ee = Bev.$$

If the electric field is uniform, then $E = V/d$, where V is the potential difference across the width d. Hence:

$$V = Bvd.$$

This potential difference is known as the **Hall voltage**, which can be measured by placing a sensitive voltmeter across the sides of the conductor.

For a particular current the charge carriers are moving at a greater speed v in a semi-conductor than a conductor because of the smaller charge density n. Hence for the same value of B, the Hall voltage V is greater in a semi-conductor of the same width d.

MEASURING OR INVESTIGATING MAGNETIC FIELDS

The concepts considered in this chapter give two different methods for measuring flux density.

THE CURRENT BALANCE

In this method, a known current is passed down one side of a balanced wire frame which is then placed in the horizontal magnetic field. The field exerts a vertical force on this side of the frame which is then rebalanced by placing a counter weight on the frame. The force BIL is then equated to this weight, and so B can be found after measuring the length of the frame in the field. It is only suitable for steady fields.

THE HALL PROBE

This device utilises the *Hall effect*. A current is passed through a small slice of semiconductor which is then placed perpendicular to the magnetic field. The Hall voltage, which develops across the sides of the slice and is proportional to the field, can be measured with a voltmeter. The device needs to be calibrated with a known field to obtain absolute values.

A third method using a search coil is described in the next chapter.

EXAMINATION QUESTIONS

MULTIPLE CHOICE QUESTIONS

1   The flux density is determined at different points along the axis, both inside and outside, of a long solenoid carrying a constant current. A graph is plotted of the flux density. B, against the distance, x, from a point on the axis outside the solenoid. Which of the positions a), b), c), d) or e) marks the end of the solenoid?

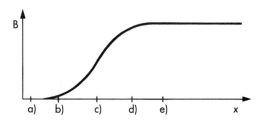

Fig. 13.8

(London 1989)

2   The definition of the ampere states that the force per unit length between two infinitely long parallel straight thin wires separated in a vacuum by a distance of 1.0 m is $2.0 \times 10^{-7}\,\mathrm{N\,m^{-1}}$ when each wire carries a current of 1.0A. If two wires are 1.5 m apart in a vacuum and each carries a current of 3.0 A the force per unit length is therefore

a) $2.7 \times 10^{-7}\,\mathrm{N\,m^{-1}}$;   d) $12 \times 10^{-7}\,\mathrm{N\,m^{-1}}$;
b) $4 \times 10^{-7}\,\mathrm{N\,m^{-1}}$;   e) $27 \times 10^{-7}\,\mathrm{N\,m^{-1}}$.
c) $9 \times 10^{-7}\,\mathrm{N\,m^{-1}}$;

(London 1987)

3   Two long thin metal wires P and Q are separated by 0.05 m in vacuum and carry currents of 2.0 A and 4.0 A respectively, flowing in the same direction, as shown in Fig. 13.9. P is fixed, but Q is free to move. What force must be applied per metre of Q to keep it in the same position?

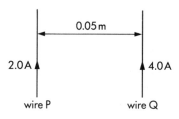

Fig. 13.9

a) 1.6×10^{-5} N towards P
b) 1.6×10^{-5} N away from P
c) 3.2×10^{-5} N towards P
d) 3.2×10^{-5} N away from P
e) 3.2×10^{-5} N perpendicular to the plane of P and Q

(Oxford 1988)

4   Fig. 13.10 shows a plan view of four long straight current-carrying wires. The wires

P●   ●Q

●X

Fig. 13.10   S●   ●R

are parallel to each other and are perpendicular to the plane of the page, passing through the points P, Q, R, S at the corners of a square. X is the intersection of the diagonals of the square.

The magnetic flux density at the point X is zero. In order for this to be the case, which of the following conditions *must* hold?
1 The current in Q must be in the same direction as that in S.
2 The currents in all four wires must be of the same magnitude.
3 The currents in all four wires must be in the same direction.

a) 1 only   d) 1 and 2 only
b) 2 only   e) 2 and 3 only
c) 3 only

(NI 1987)

5 A proton travelling in a direction perpendicular to a uniform magnetic field follows a circular path of radius r. An alpha-particle moving at the same speed under the same conditions would follow a path of radius

a) $\frac{1}{4}r$ d) $2r$
b) $\frac{1}{2}r$ e) $4r$
c) r

(Oxford 1987)

6 On which of the following particles is (are) magnetic forces exerted when in a uniform magnetic field?
1 A neutron moving at right angles to the direction of the field.
2 A stationary electron.
3 A proton moving along the direction of the field.

a) None of these   d) 2 and 3 only
b) 1 only   e) 1, 2 and 3
c) 3 only

(NI 1987)

7 An electron travelling at a constant speed passes into a uniform magnetic field in such a direction that it describes a circular path of radius r. If the flux density of the field were halved and the speed of the electron doubled, the new radius would be

a) $\dfrac{r}{4}$ d) $2r$
             e) $4r$
b) $\dfrac{r}{2}$
c) r_1

(London 1989)

8 When a current passes through a rectangular coil mounted with its plane parallel to a uniform magnetic field it produces a couple tending to turn the coil. The moment of the couple produced by a given current can be increased by:
1 increasing the area of the coil;
2 increasing the number of turns on the coil;
3 decreasing the strength of the magnetic field in which the coil is situated.

a) 1, 2, 3 correct   d) 1 only
b) 1, 2 only   e) 3 only
c) 2, 3 only

(London 1989)

ANSWERS AND COMMENTS

Question	1	2	3	4	5	6	7	8
Answer	c)	d)	d)	d)	d)	a)	e)	b)

1 The field at the end of the solenoid is half that of the uniform field in the middle.

2 The increased current will increase the field by a factor of 3 and the force (*BIL*) on the wire by a factor of 9. However the increased distance will reduce the field by 1.5, so overall the change is by a factor of 9/1.5 = 6.

3 The field of P at Q $= \dfrac{\mu_o I_p}{2\pi r} = 8 \times 10^{-6}$ T.

The force per metre on Q $= BI_Q = 3.2 \times 10^{-5}$ N. The force exerted by P on Q is towards P, so the balancing force must be in the opposite direction. You could also use the definition of the ampere as a starting point.

4 The flux density, or field, from each wire is circular. The fields from Q and S must cancel and the fields from R and P must cancel.
1) The fields from Q and S are in opposite directions.
2) The cancelling fields are the same strengths.
3) Currents in Q and S must be in same direction and the currents in R and P must be in the same direction but not necessarily in the same direction as those in Q and S. Note that there isn't an answer 1, 2, 3.

5 The radius of the path is given by $r = \dfrac{mv}{Bq}$. *m* for the alpha particle is 4 times *m* for the proton but *q* for the alpha particle is twice that of the proton so the overall increase in *r* (*B* and *v* unchanged) is by a factor of 2.

6 1) The neutron is uncharged so experiences no magnetic force.
2) The electron experiences no force because it is stationary.
3) The proton experiences no force because it is moving along the field direction.

7 The radius is given by $r = \dfrac{mv}{Bq}$. Halving *B* and doubling *v* will quadruple *r*.

8 If the length of the sides is *L*, (see Fig. 13.5) then each side experiences a force *BIL*. The couple on each turn of wire is therefore *BILa*. On *N* turns the couple is *NBILa*.
1) *aL* represents the area, so increasing the area increases the moment.

STRUCTURED QUESTIONS

9 a) Sketch the magnetic field pattern due to the current in a long straight wire. Your diagram should show the directions of the field and the current.

b) Fig. 13.11, shows two long parallel wires, P and Q, placed 0.15 m apart in air. Wire P carries a current of 8.0 A, and wire Q carries a current of 4.0 A in the same direction. At which distance from wire P will the resultant magnetic field be zero? Justify your answer.

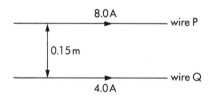

Fig. 13.11

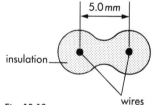

Fig. 13.12

c) The twin core cable shown in Fig. 13.12, is used to supply a current of 0.25 A to a lamp. The wires are thin and the distance between their centres is 5.0 mm. Calculate the force per metre between the wires and state its direction (Permeability of the insulating material $= 1.3 \times 10^{-6}$ H m^{-1}).

(AEB 1988)

10 Write down the equation defining *magnetic flux density* in terms of *F* the force it produces on a long, straight conductor of length *L* carrying a current *I* at an angle θ to the field. Draw a clear diagram to illustrate the direction of the force relative to the current and magnetic field. (4)

A small square coil of *N* turns has sides of length *L* and is mounted so that it can pivot freely about a horizontal axis PQ, parallel to one pair of sides of the coil, through its centre (see Fig. 13.13). The coil is situated between the poles of a magnet which produces a uniform magnetic field of flux density *B*. The coil is maintained in a vertical plane by moving a rider of mass *M* along a horizontal beam attached to the coil. When a current *I* flows through the coil, equilibrium is restored by placing the rider a

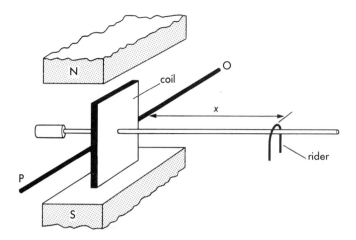

Fig. 13.13

distance x along the beam from the coil. Starting from the definition of magnetic flux density, show that B is given by the expression:

$$B = \frac{Mgx}{IL^2N}. \qquad (5)$$

If the current is supplied by a battery of constant e.m.f. and negligible internal resistance, discuss the effect on x if the coil is replaced by one wound with similar wire but having:

a) sides of length L with $2N$ turns;
b) N turns with sides of length $L/2$. $\qquad (8)$

(Cambridge 1987)

OUTLINE ANSWERS AND COMMENTS

9 a) See Fig. 13.1.
  b) The field due to each wire is proportional to I/r.
     As the current in P is twice the current in Q, the fields will be the same magnitude twice as far from P. i.e. at 0.1 m from P and 0.05 m from Q. The fields will be in opposite directions and so cancel.

  c) The field at one wire due to the current in the other $= \dfrac{\mu I}{2\pi r}$

$$= \frac{1.3 \times 10^{-6} \times 0.25}{2\pi \times 5 \times 10^{-3}}$$
$$= 1.03 \times 10^{-5} \text{ T}.$$

  The force on each wire $= BIL$, so the force per metre $= BI$
     $= 1.03 \times 10^{-5} \times 0.25 = 2.59 \times 10^{-6}$ N.
  The currents in the two wires are in opposite direction and so the force is one of repulsion between the wires.

10 See text (p. 132).
  Each turn of the horizontal sides of the coil experiences a force $= BIL$ i.e. a total force $= NBIL$.
  The force on the bottom side is in the opposite direction to the force on the top side and so a couple is produced of moment $= NBIL \times L$. This anti-clockwise is balanced by the clockwise moment produced by the rider $= Mgx$. Thus:

$$NBIL^2 = Mgx, \text{ and } B = \frac{Mgx}{I L^2 N}$$

  a) N is doubled, L stays the same but I halves because the wire making the coil is twice as long and so has twice the resistance. The effect is that x is unchanged.
  b) N stays the same, L is halved and I is doubled because the resistance is halved. Overall this means that the left hand side increased by a factor of 2, so x must increase by the same factor to keep the balance.

TUTOR'S QUESTION AND ANSWER

QUESTION

11 What do you understand by a *magnetic field*?

The apparatus shown in Fig. 13.14 is used to compare the masses of ions of different isotopes of the same element. In one experiment magnesium ions of mass M and charge e from a hot source J were accelerated by a potential difference V and passed through a slit K with speed v.

i) Show that

$$v = \sqrt{\frac{2eV}{M}} \ . \tag{1}$$

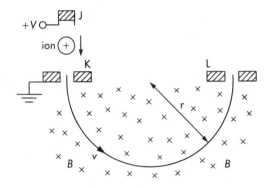

Fig. 13.14

Once through the slit K, the ions move with constant speed v at right angles to a uniform magnetic field of intensity B and along a circular path of radius r.

ii) Show that

$$r = \frac{Mv}{Be} \tag{2}$$

and that

$$M = \frac{eB^2 r^2}{2} \left(\frac{1}{V} \right) \tag{3}$$

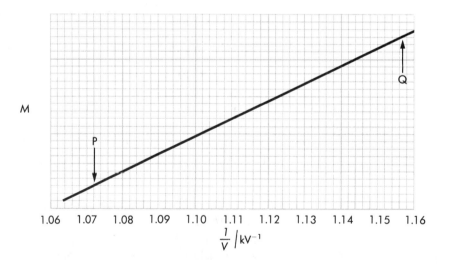

Fig. 13.15

Fig. 13.15 is a graph which shows the values of $1/V$ for which magnesium ions of different masses M are detected at L.

iii) The isotope corresponding to the point marked P has atomic mass (M) 39.8×10^{-27} kg. Calculate a value for the gradient of the graph. (Hint: what does equation (3) tell you about this straight line graph?)

iv) Find the atomic mass of the isotope corresponding to the point marked Q.

(8)

(London 1987)

ANSWER

11   i) K.E. gained = loss in electrical P.E.

$$\tfrac{1}{2} Mv^2 = eV$$

$$\therefore v = \sqrt{\frac{2eV}{M}}$$

$$F = \frac{Mv^2}{r} = Bev \qquad \therefore r = \frac{Mv}{Be}$$

Squaring and substituting $r^2 = \dfrac{M^2v^2}{Be^2} = \dfrac{2M^2eV}{MB^2e^2}$

$$\therefore M = \frac{eB^2r^2}{2V}$$

Equation 3) tells you that the straight line goes through the origin, and so the gradient $= \dfrac{39.8 \times 10^{-27}}{1.072 \times 10^{-3}} = 3.71 \times 10^{-23}$ kg V.

Mass of isotope at Q $= 3.71 \times 10^{-23} \times 1.156 \times 10^{-3}$
$= 4.29 \times 10^{-26}$ kg.

STUDENT'S ANSWER WITH EXAMINER COMMENTS

STUDENT'S ANSWER TO QUESTION 10

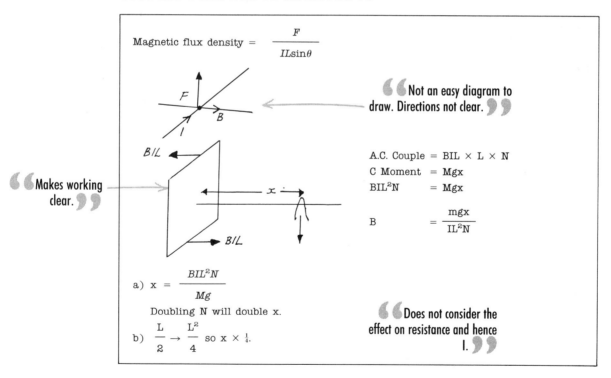

Magnetic flux density $= \dfrac{F}{ILsin\theta}$

❝Not an easy diagram to draw. Directions not clear.❞

❝Makes working clear.❞

A.C. Couple $= BIL \times L \times N$
C Moment $= Mgx$
$BIL^2N = Mgx$

$B = \dfrac{mgx}{IL^2N}$

a) $x = \dfrac{BIL^2N}{Mg}$

Doubling N will double x.

b) $\dfrac{L}{2} \rightarrow \dfrac{L^2}{4}$ so x × ¼.

❝Does not consider the effect on resistance and hence I.❞

Overall comments: The answer is typical of a C grade candidate. Some of the equations and working are correct but rather lack explanation. At the end of the question the candidate falls into the trap of ignoring the effect of resistance. Nevertheless some marks would be awarded for computing the effects which are considered.

14

ELECTRO-MAGNETIC INDUCTION

GETTING STARTED

The following basic ideas summarise the essential concepts needed for this chapter.

In a **cell** chemical energy is converted into electrical energy to provide the **e.m.f.** to drive the electrons round the circuit. It is possible to generate an e.m.f. in a circuit without a cell by changing the magnetic flux linked with the circuit. **Magnetic flux** $\phi = BA$, measured in **weber** (*Wb*), is where B is the **flux density** perpendicular to area A. There are different ways of changing the flux linked with a circuit. This can be achieved by moving a conductor through a magnetic field, moving a magnetic field passed a conductor or by changing the strength of the magnetic field linked with the circuit. An e.m.f. generated by changing the flux linked with a circuit is said to be induced.

The **first law of electromagnetic induction** states that the induced e.m.f. is equal to the rate of change of flux linkage, where **flux linkage** Φ is equal to flux ϕ multiplied by number of turns N. Thus

$$\Phi = \phi N, \text{ so } V = \frac{d\Phi}{dt} = \frac{d}{dt}(NBA).$$

Note that the flux linked with a circuit has to *change* to induce an e.m.f. (i.e. an e.m.f. can be induced by changing N, B or A).

The **second law** states that the induced e.m.f. is always in such a direction as to oppose the change which caused it.

ESSENTIAL PRINCIPLES

THE FIRST LAW

If a conductor of length L is moving through a magnetic field B at speed v (Fig. 14.1), then the free electrons in the conductor are being carried along through the field, and so they experience a force Bev which pushes them to one end of the conductor. This migration of negative charge creates an electric field (in some ways similar to the *Hall effect*), and so an e.m.f. (V) is induced between the ends of the conductor. The migration stops when $Ee = Bev$ and $E = V/L$. Hence an e.m.f. BvL is induced, which equals the flux cut through in one second.

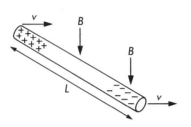
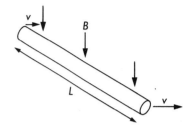

Fig. 14.1 Wire length L travelling at speed v through field B

Fig. 14.2 Migration of electrons

This change of magnetic flux linkage was achieved by *moving* the conductor through a field. It is also possible to induce an e.m.f. in a stationary conductor by *changing* the *flux* linked with it. An e.m.f. can be induced in a stationary coil by increasing or decreasing the field linked with the coil or using an alternating field. If a graph of the field is plotted against

> **An e.m.f. can also be induced by moving the coil out of the field.**

time, the rate of change $\left(\dfrac{\mathrm{d}B}{\mathrm{d}t}\right)$ is given by the slope. For a sinusoidal change, the slope is greatest when the field passes through zero. Hence the induced e.m.f. will be greatest when the field is passing through zero but changing fastest. The induced e.m.f. will be zero when the field is a maximum, but the slope is zero. i.e. the induced e.m.f. and the field are 90° out of phase.

The induced e.m.f. is always equal to $\dfrac{\mathrm{d}\Phi}{\mathrm{d}t}$, and the induced *current* is equal to the induced e.m.f. divided by the resistance of the circuit. The flux in a coil can be greatly increased by wrapping the coil on an iron core.

THE SECOND LAW

The **second law (Lenz's)** of electromagnetic induction states that the induced e.m.f. must be in such a *direction* as to *oppose* the change which is causing the induced e.m.f. This law is a consequence of the **law of conservation of energy**, since if a change induced an

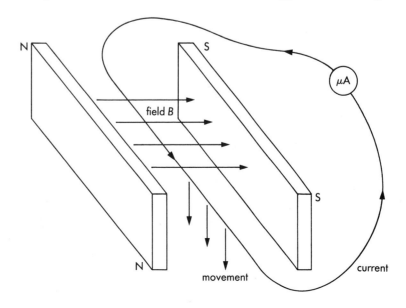

Fig. 14.3 Inducing an e.m.f. in a straight wire

e.m.f. in a circuit and this e.m.f. actually assisted the change then, once started, the system would self-generate energy.

Moving a wire through a magnetic field will induce an e.m.f. in the wire. If the wire forms part of a complete circuit then a current will flow (Fig. 14.3). The direction of this current can be remembered using Fleming's right hand rule, where the *first* finger points in the direction of the magnetic *field*, the *thumb* points in the direction of *motion* of the wire and *second* finger will give the direction of the induced *current*. The wire is then a current carrying conductor in a magnetic field and as a result will experience a force in the opposite direction to motion.

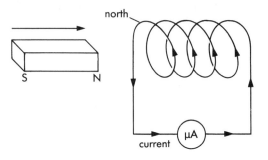

Fig. 14.4 Inducing an emf in a coil

Another example of electromagnetic induction can be shown by jabbing a bar magnet into a coil (Fig. 14.4). If the north pole of the magnet is pushed into the coil then, when the induced current flows, this end of the coil becomes a north pole, to try to repel the incoming magnet.

A.C. GENERATOR OR DYNAMO

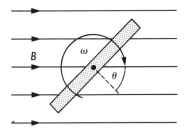

Fig. 14.5 Coil rotating in field *B* at angular velocity *w*

Here, flux linkage $\Phi = NBA\cos\theta$, where N is the number of turns and A the area of the coil.

> This e.m.f. is induced by *turning* the coil in a steady field.

The induced e.m.f. $= d\dfrac{\Phi}{dt} = \dfrac{d}{dt}(NBA\cos\theta) = (NBA\dfrac{d}{dt}(\cos wt)) = NBAw\sin wt.$

The maximum value ($NBAw$) occurs when the plane of the coil is perpendicular to the field.

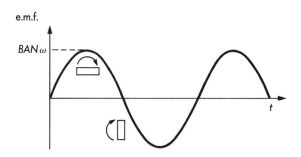

Fig. 14.6 Induced e.m.f. in a rotating coil showing positions of the coil

MUTUAL INDUCTANCE

In a transformer an e.m.f. is generated in a *secondary* coil because it is wound on a core in which the flux is continually changing due to an alternating current in a *primary* coil. The effect whereby an e.m.f. is induced in one coil as a result of it being linked with the changing flux created by another coil is known as **mutual inductance**. If the current in the first coil is changing at a rate $\dfrac{dI}{dt}$, then the e.m.f. induced in the second coil $= -M\dfrac{dI}{dt}$, where M is known as the mutual inductance, measured in henries. The negative sign indicates the direction of the induced e.m.f.

SELF INDUCTANCE

An e.m.f. can also be induced in a coil because the current in the coil itself is changing, so changing the flux linked with the coil. Such an e.m.f. is said to be **self induced**, and if the rate of change of current is $\dfrac{dI}{dt}$ then the e.m.f. is given by

$$- L\frac{dI}{dt} ,$$ where L is the self inductance.

This self induced e.m.f. must, by Lenz's law, oppose the changing current causing it and is said therefore to be a back e.m.f., and hence the negative sign.

The unit of self inductance is the **henry**. The self inductance of an iron cored coil is much greater than a similar air cored inductor, since the permeability of iron is much greater than that of air.

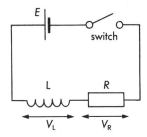

Fig. 14.7

If a d.c. supply is connected across an inductor of inductance L, the initial current is zero, but the current is growing at a rate $dI/dt = E/L$. There is bound to be some resistance in the circuit, and as the current grows there will be a p.d. across this resistance ($V = IR$). The p.d. across the inductor will then be less ($V_L + V_R = E$), and the current will grow at a slower rate $\left(\dfrac{dI}{dt} = \dfrac{V_L}{L}\right)$. Eventually the current will be such that the p.d. across the resistor will equal E and the current will stop growing.

> **If there is a lamp in the circuit it will take a short while to light.**

Fig. 14.8 Graph of current against time

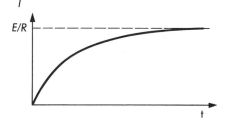

THE TRANSFORMER

These ideas of self and mutual induction are essential to the operation of the **transformer**, the purpose of which is to either increase or decrease an alternating e.m.f. It consists of

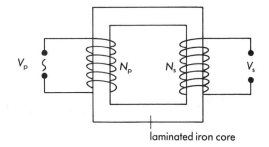

Fig. 14.9 Transformer

two coils wound on the same iron core. An alternating e.m.f. applied to the primary generates an alternating flux in the core, and this induces an alternating e.m.f. in the secondary.

In the **primary** $V_p = N_p\dfrac{d\phi}{dt}$, and in the **secondary** $V_s = N_s\dfrac{d\phi}{dt}$, and so

$$\frac{V_s}{N_s} = \frac{V_p}{N_p}$$

If the transformer is nearly 100% efficient, then the power dissipated in the secondary will be very nearly equal to the power dissipated in the primary. Hence $V_s I_s = V_p I_p$.

A step-up transformer is designed so that the output voltage V_s is greater than the input voltage V_p. Hence the secondary turns N_s is greater than the primary turns N_p, and secondary current I_s is less than the primary current I_p.

The reasons for efficiency in the transformer being less than 100% are:

i) heat generated in the coils, which can be reduced by using thicker wire;

ii) heat generated by eddy currents flowing in the core. These eddy currents can be reduced making the core of laminated strips of iron separated by insulating strips.

iii) hysteresis losses in reversing the magnetism in the core.

THE SEARCH COIL

MEASURING OR INVESTIGATING MAGNETIC FIELDS

This relies on an e.m.f. being induced in a small coil of a few thousand turns, and can therefore only be used for alternating fields. The coil is placed *perpendicular* to the field being investigated, and as the coil has a fixed area and number of turns, the induced e.m.f.

is proportional to the rate of change of B, i.e. $\left(\dfrac{dB}{dt}\right)$. At a fixed frequency the peak induced e.m.f. depends on the strength of the field and so if the coil is connected to an oscilloscope, the height of the trace is proportional to the field. For *absolute* measurements the **search coil** needs to be calibrated.

MAGNETIC CIRCUITS

The flux 'circulating' in the centre of the toroid in Fig. 14.10 is $= BA = \mu_o NIA/L$ where N is the number of turns, I, the current, A the area and L the length. μ_o is the permeability of free space. If the toroid has an iron core then the flux is greater, given by $\mu_r \mu_o NIA/L$, where μ_r is the relative permeability of iron.

This **magnetic circuit** is sometimes compared to an electric circuit.

- The 'flow' of flux in the magnetic circuit is compared to current in the electric circuit.

- The current turns NI which drive the flux is compared to the e.m.f. E.

- In the electric circuit, the e.m.f./current = resistance.

❝ Line up the comparisons. ❞

- In the magnetic circuit the NI/flux is called the **reluctance**.

- Hence reluctance $= \dfrac{L}{\mu_o \mu_r A}$ and resistance $= \dfrac{L}{\sigma A}$.

- Thus $\mu_o \mu_r$ compares to the electrical conductivity.

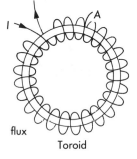

Fig. 14.10   flux

Toroid

EXAMINATION QUESTIONS

MULTIPLE CHOICE QUESTIONS

1   Fig. 14.11a) shows a copper ring which is moving at constant speed towards and over a bar magnet. Which ONE of the graphs in Fig. 14.11b) best represents the way in which the induced current I in the ring varies with time t?

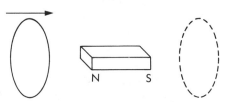

Fig. 14.11a)

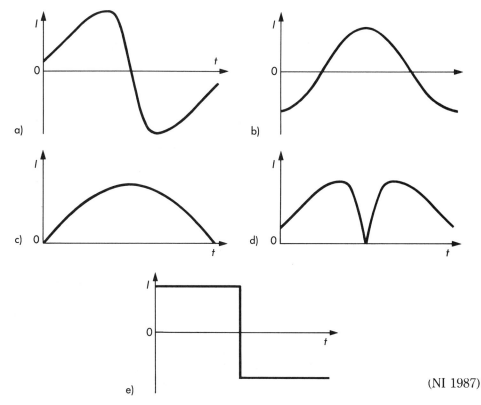

Fig. 14.11b)

e)

(NI 1987)

2   The axle of a railway carriage is 1.5 m long and it cuts the vertical component of the Earth's magnetic field of flux density 4×10^{-5} T as it travels north at a speed of 10 m s^{-1}. The e.m.f. generated between the ends of the axle is

a) 0.60 mV   d) 0.0027 mV
b) 0.27 mV   e) 0.0006 mV
c) 0.06 mV

(London 1988)

3   The current through a coil changes at the rate of 2 A s^{-1} for a time of 5 s. If the total flux change through the coil is 10 mWb, the self-inductance, in mH, of the coil is

a) 0.5   d) 5.0
b) 1.0   e) 0.4
c) 2.0

(AEB 1987)

4   With the arrangement shown in Fig. 14.12, the aluminium ring is thrown upwards when the switch S is closed. This is because:
1 it becomes magnetised
2 a charge is induced in it
3 a current is induced in it.

a) 1, 2, 3 correct   d) 1 only
b) 1, 2 only   e) 3 only
c) 2, 3 only

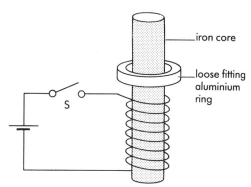

iron core

loose fitting aluminium ring

S

Fig. 14.12

(London 1987)

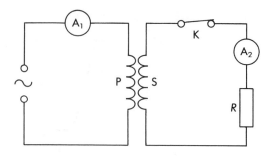

Fig. 14.13

5 The insulated coils P and S are close to one another. P is connected to an alternating supply and to an a.c. ammeter A_1. S is connected to an a.c. ammeter A_2 via a switch K and a resistor R. Which of the following statements is **NOT** correct?

a) There is a reading on A_2 when K is closed.
b) Coil P produces an alternating magnetic field.
c) Increasing the number of turns on S increases the voltage produced across S.
d) Moving the coils further apart reduces the magnitude of the voltage produced across S.
e) If switch K is opened the steady reading on A_1 will increase.

(London 1989)

6 The diagram shows a simple arrangement for investigating the e.m.f. induced in the coil Q by mutual induction with the coil P. A cell is connected across X_1X_2 and a

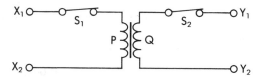

Fig. 14.14

sensitive centre-zero voltmeter across Y_1Y_2. In which of the following cases will **NO** induced e.m.f. be observed across Y_1Y_2?

a) A magnet is plunged into coil P.
b) Coil P is moved rapidly away from coil Q.
c) Switch S_1 is opened.
d) Switch S_1 is closed again.
e) Switch S_2 is opened.

(London 1989)

7 The core of a transformer is laminated to reduce energy losses. For maximum reduction in the losses the laminations should be:
1) of low electrical resistivity
2) as thin as possible
3) insulated from each other.

a) 1, 2, 3 correct   d) 1 only
b) 1, 2 only   e) 3 only
c) 2, 3 only

(London 1987)

8 The circuit shown in Fig. 14.15a) is used to demonstrate electromagnetic induction. S is a power source which provides a current I in coil P which varies with time as shown in Fig. 14.15b). Coil Q is connected to a cathode ray oscilloscope. Which one of the diagrams a) to e) could show the trace observed on the screen of the cathode ray oscilloscope? (All diagrams have the same time scale.)

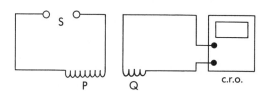

Fig. 14.15a)

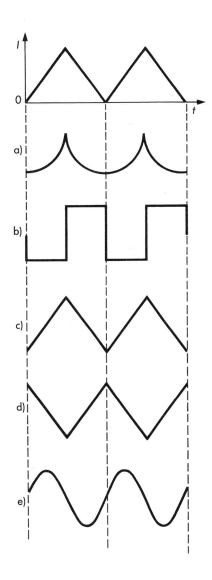

Fig. 14.15b)

(NI 1986)

9 In Fig. 14.16 the transformer has a turns ratio of approximately 1:4. If electrical energy is converted to heat in the windings and the core at the rate of 4 watts, what is the current in the secondary.

a) 0.1A   d) 0.6A
b) 0.4A   e) 0.8A
c) 0.5A

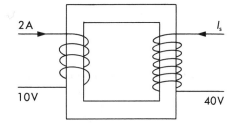

Fig. 14.16

(Scottish 1985)

ANSWERS AND COMMENTS

Question	1	2	3	4	5	6	7	8	9
Answer	a)	e)	b)	e)	e)	e)	c)	b)	b)

1 As the ring approaches an e.m.f. will be induced in the ring which will increase as the coil gets nearer (flux stronger) and whose direction will repel the N pole. As the coil leaves the other end the e.m.f. will fall and the direction will be opposite (to attract the S). This leaves us with answer a).

2 Use $V = BvL$, where $L = 1.5$ m, $B = 4 \times 10^{-5}$T, $v = 10$ m s^{-1}.
$V = 6 \times 10^{-4}$ V $= 0.0006$ mV.

3 The induced voltage = rate of change of flux = $10/5 = 2$mV.
Using $V = -L\ dI/dt$, $L = 2/2 = 1$ m H.

4 The ring is made of aluminium and does not become magnetised. A current is induced in the ring due to the changing flux in the core.

5 a) When K is closed there will be a reading on A$_2$ because a voltage is induced in S because it is linked with the changing flux of P.
   b) Alternating current in P produces alternating magnetic field.
   c) Increasing number of turns increases the flux linkage and so the induced voltage.
   d) Moving coils apart reduces the flux linkage and so reduces voltage.
   e) Other responses are clearly correct so this must be incorrect! In fact, opening K reduces the reading on A$_2$. When K is closed the a.c. power supply has to provide the energy dissipated in resistor R.

6 a) Plunging a magnet into P will change the flux linked with Q and so induce an e.m.f. in Q.
   b) This will reduce the flux linked.
   c) When S$_1$ is opened the flux suddenly decreases.
   d) When S$_1$ is closed the flux suddenly increases.

7 The core is laminated to prevent eddy currents flowing through it, so the resistance needs to be high.

8 The oscilloscope trace shows the voltage induced in the coil Q, which depends on the rate of change of current in P. This is obtained from the slope of the I against t graph. Where there is a constant slope the trace will have a constant value.

9 The power delivered to the primary is $V_pI_p = 10 \times 2 = 20$ W. Of this, 4 W is dissipated as heat in the windings and the core, and 16 W is generated in the secondary. Hence $V_sI_s = 16$, so $I_s = 16/40 = 0.4$A.

STRUCTURED QUESTIONS

10 A circular coil C of 20 turns and area 1 cm^2 is mounted centrally inside a long solenoid of 10^4 turns per metre so that its plane is at right angles to the axis of the solenoid. C is connected in series with a resistor and a galvanometer, the total resistance of this circuit being 10 Ω. The current in the solenoid is increased uniformly from 0 to 12 A in 4 s. [The magnetic flux density within a long solenoid of n turns per metre carrying a current I is given by B = μ_onI, where $\mu_o = 4\pi \times 10^{-7}$ H m^{-1}.]
   a) Calculate the maximum flux through C. (5)
   b) Calculate the reading on the galvanometer. (5)
   c) Find the total charge which circulates in the circuit containing C. (4)
   d) Find the total energy dissipated in the circuit containing C. (4)
   e) Where does the power in d) come from? (2)
   f) Draw a diagram to show how the direction of the current in C is related to that in the solenoid. (2)
   g) How could a reading on the galvanometer be produced when I is constant? (3)
   (Welsh 1987)

11 a) Define *magnetic flux density* and *magnetic flux*. (5)
   b) A large flat coil is connected in series with an ammeter and a 50 Hz sinusoidal alternating supply whose r.m.s. output can be varied. At the centre of this coil is situated a much smaller coil which is connected to the Y-plates of a cathode-ray oscilloscope (c.r.o.). The planes of the two coils are coincident (see Fig. 14.17).

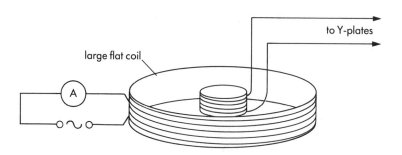

Fig. 14.17

i) Draw sketch graphs, one in each case, to show the variation with time of 1) the magnetic flux, and 2) the induced e.m.f., in the small coil. Give physical explanations for the shapes of your graphs. *(6)*

Hence, describe how you could use this apparatus to demonstrate how the magnetic flux density at the centre of a large flat coil varies with the number of turns on the coil. *(6)*

ii) Explain how the trace on the screen of the cathode-ray oscilloscope would be affected if the angle between the planes of the two coils were slowly to increase from zero to 90° whilst maintaining a constant r.m.s. current in the large coil. *(5)*

(Cambridge 1988)

OUTLINE ANSWERS AND COMMENTS

10 a) Max flux $= B_{max}A = \mu_o n I_{max}A$
$= 4 \times \pi \times 10^{-7} \times 10^4 \times 12 \times 10^{-4} = 1.5 \times 10^{-5}$ *Wb.*

b) Induced voltage = flux linkage change/time
$= 20 \times 1.5 \times 10^{-5}/4 = 7.5 \times 10^{-5}$ V $= 75$ μV.

c) Current $= V/R = 7.5 \times 10^{-5}/10 = 7.5 \times 10^{-6}$ A $= 7.5$ μA.
Steady current flows for 4 seconds, so charge $= 7.5 \times 10^{-6} \times 4 = 30 \times 10^{-6}$ C $= 30$ μC.

d) Total energy dissipated $= I^2Rt = (7.5 \times 10^{-6})^2 \times 10 \times 4 = 2.25 \times 10^{-9}$ W.

e) Power comes from whatever is changing the current in solenoid.

f) Current in coil in opposite direction to solenoid.

g) By rotating the coil so that flux linked with it changes.

11

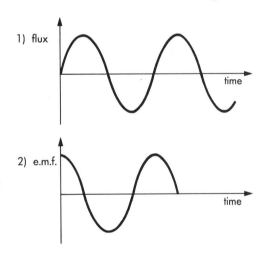

Fig. 14.18

b) i) The magnetic flux is proportional to the current in the large flat coil and so is sinusoidal in shape.
The e.m.f. induced in the small coil depends on the rate of change of this flux and depends on the slope of the flux graph. The induced e.m.f. is a maximum where the slope is a maximum etc. The maximum induced e.m.f. is proportional to the flux at the centre of the large coil. If the number of turns is doubled, the flux will double and so will the maximum e.m.f.

ii) If the small coil is rotated through 90° the flux linked with it will decrease and so the trace showing the e.m.f. will also decrease to zero.

TUTOR'S QUESTION AND ANSWER

QUESTION

12 a) An electron of charge $- e$ moves with velocity v. A uniform magnetic field of flux density B is applied perpendicular to the direction of v. Write down an expression for the force F acting on the electron, and show the relative directions of F, v and B on a labelled sketch. *(2)*

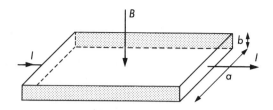

Fig. 14.19

A steady current I passes through a metal bar of rectangular cross-section, as shown in Fig. 14.19. A uniform magnetic field of flux density B acts normal to the upper face of the bar. Give a simple explanation of why a potential difference (the Hall potential difference) appears between the shaded faces of the bar, and deduce the polarity of this potential difference. Show that the magnitude of the Hall potential difference is $\dfrac{IB}{enb}$, where n is the number of free electrons per unit volume in the bar and b is the depth of the bar. (7)

Experiments to demonstrate the Hall effect normally make use of a semiconductor specimen, instead of the metal bar described above. Why is this? (2)

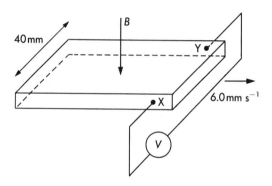

Fig. 14.20

b) A long metal bar, 40 mm wide, is pulled along a horizontal table at a uniform velocity of 6.0 mm s^{-1}, as shown in Fig. 14.20. Stationary brushes X and Y make electrical contact with the sides of the bar. When a uniform magnetic field of flux density B is directed downwards, normal to the table, it is found that there is a potential difference of 5.0 μV between the brushes X and Y.
i) Explain how this potential difference is set up. (2)
ii) Find the flux density B of the magnetic field. (4)

(Cambridge 1988)

ANSWER

12 a) The force acting on the electron is $F = Bev$.

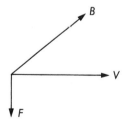

Fig. 14.21

The current consists of electrons moving to the left. These moving electrons experience a force towards the back edge of the bar. The electrons migrate towards the back leaving the front edge positive. An electric field E is created by this redistribution of charge which stops when $Ee = Bev$ and $E = V/a$, where V is the Hall potential difference. Hence $V = Bva$.
Also the current $I = nAev$ but $A = ab$ so $I = nabev$ and $v = I/nabe$

$$\text{Thus } V = \frac{BIa}{nabe} = \frac{BI}{enb}$$

For semiconductors n is smaller and so if I, B and b are the same V is larger and easier to measure.

b) i) As the bar moves the electrons are carried along through the B field and so experience a force which makes them move to the front of the bar, leaving the back positive. Hence $Ee = Bev$ where $E = V/w$.

ii) $V = Bvw$ and $B = V/wv = \dfrac{5 \times 10^{-6}}{40 \times 10^{-3} \times 6 \times 10^{-3}} = 0.02$ T.

STUDENT'S ANSWER WITH EXAMINER COMMENTS

STUDENT'S ANSWER TO QUESTION 10

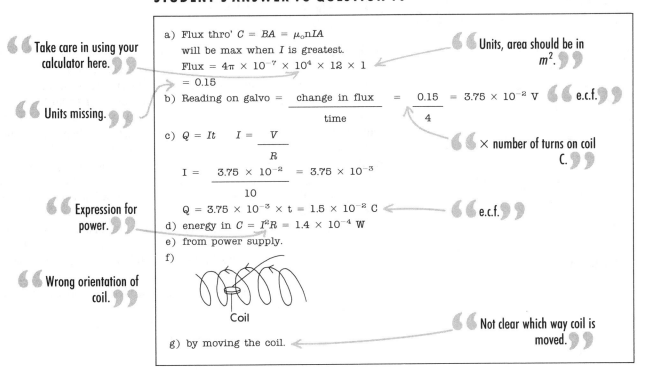

Take care in using your calculator here.

a) Flux thro' $C = BA = \mu_o nIA$
   will be max when I is greatest.
   Flux $= 4\pi \times 10^{-7} \times 10^4 \times 12 \times 1$
   $= 0.15$

Units, area should be in m^2.

Units missing.

b) Reading on galvo $= \dfrac{\text{change in flux}}{\text{time}} = \dfrac{0.15}{4} = 3.75 \times 10^{-2}$ V **e.c.f.**

× number of turns on coil C.

c) $Q = It \qquad I = \dfrac{V}{R}$

$I = \dfrac{3.75 \times 10^{-2}}{10} = 3.75 \times 10^{-3}$

Expression for power.

$Q = 3.75 \times 10^{-3} \times t = 1.5 \times 10^{-2}$ C **e.c.f.**

d) energy in $C = I^2R = 1.4 \times 10^{-4}$ W
e) from power supply.
f)

Wrong orientation of coil.

Coil

Not clear which way coil is moved.

g) by moving the coil.

Overall comments: Some basic errors and substitution in equations without understanding or paying attention to detail, typical of D grade candidate.

ALTERNATING CURRENT THEORY

GETTING STARTED

Alternating current theory is commonly regarded as a difficult subject. To understand it properly it is necessary to have a thorough grounding in **circular motion, oscillations** and **resonance**, and in basic work in **electrical circuit theory**. The subject links both of these topics. You should start by revising your work on circular motion and Simple Harmonic Motion (SHM) (Chapters 5 and 6) and then making sure you understand the basic vocabulary of the subject, e.g. **peak** and **root mean square (r.m.s.)** values. The effect of alternating p.d.'s on individual components must also be understood before you can cope with combinations of components, the hardest of which will usually be **L-C-R series circuits**.

Whilst it is possible to recall and use various formulae for working out the kinds of a.c. problems which may be set, it is much more sensible to learn the rudiments of **'phasor'** theory, i.e. the use of vector diagrams, even if phasors are not explicitly demanded in your syllabus. There is then much less to memorise. In this chapter we have simply summarised the basic ideas. Alternating current theory is important in two areas of engineering, the **transmission of electrical energy** and in **signal communication** (telephones, radio, etc.).

ESSENTIAL PRINCIPLES

POWER TRANSMISSION

Alternating current is much preferred to direct current for the transmission of **electrical power**. This is because it can be transformed. The loss due to transmission line heating is I^2R where I is the current and R the resistance of the transmission cables. So it is better to transmit electricity, where possible, at very high voltages and small currents. Power is generated at relatively low voltages which are 'stepped down' for transmission purposes and finally 'stepped up' again for domestic consumption using **transformers**, which have no moving parts, and small energy losses.

The e.m.f. of an a.c. power supply varies sinusoidally (Fig. 15.1) according to the equation $E = E_o\sin\omega t$ where $\omega = 2\pi/T = 2\pi f$.

ω is the angular frequency, f the frequency and T the period as in SHM theory. One complete alternation of the supply is called a **cycle**.

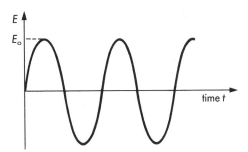

Fig. 15.1 Alternating current of a sinusoidal form

COMMUNICA-TIONS

A.c. theory also has an application in **telecommunications**. Here, waveforms other than sinusoidal ones are encountered, as in Fig. 15.2 and 15.3. By means of a technique called **Fourier analysis**, each of these can be analysed into a series of simultaneous sinusoidal waveforms of different frequencies. The beauty of this is that the theory for sinusoidal signals can then be employed.

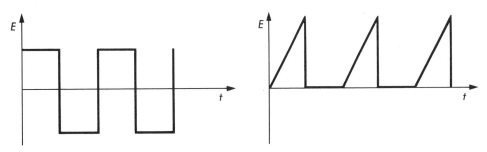

Fig. 15.2 Square wave a.c.

Fig. 15.3 Ramp and space a.c.

ROOT MEAN SQUARE VALUES (R.M.S.) OF SINE AND SQUARE WAVES

The r.m.s. value of an *a.c. current* is:
i) the square root of the mean value of the square of the current, or
ii) that steady d.c. current which would convert electrical energy to internal energy (heat) and light in a resistance at the same rate as the a.c.

The r.m.s. current for a *sinusoidal* a.c. is given by:

$$I_{\text{r.m.s.}} = \frac{I_o}{2} = 0.707\,I_o$$

(where I_o is the peak value).

This is because the average value of $\sin^2\omega t$ is 0.5.

Similar relationships hold for voltages. The r.m.s. value is the one usually quoted. In the U.K., for example the mains is supplied at 240 V (r.m.s.) which is equivalent to a peak value of 339 V.

The r.m.s. for a *square wave* that has value $\pm I_o$ is simply I_o. This is because the square of both I_o and $-I_o$ is I_o^2, and the root of this is I_o. So the average value of I_o^2 is constant.

PHASE

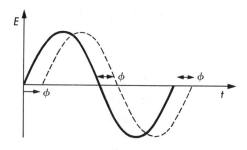

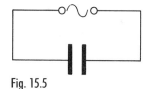

Fig. 15.4 Phase difference between two alternating currents

In a.c., a voltage and the corresponding current may not be in step, or '**in phase**' with each other. In the example shown (Fig. 15.4) the waveform denoted by the broken line lags behind the other waveform. It reaches its peak slightly later in time than the waveform shown by the continuous line. ϕ is the **phase lag**, sometimes measured in radians and sometimes in degrees. Remember that 1 complete cycle is 360° or 2π radians.

A.C. AND A PURE RESISTANCE

The current and voltage are in phase.

The p.d. across the load resistor is equal to the e.m.f. of the supply. So with an e.m.f. given by $E = E_0\sin\omega t$, we have a p.d. given by $V = V_0\sin\omega t$ and $V_0 = E_0$. The current is given by: $I = I_0\sin\omega t$,
where $I_0 = V_0/R$, V_0 being the peak value of the p.d.

The power delivered is: $P = \dfrac{V_0 I_0}{2} = V_{r.m.s.}I_{r.m.s.} = I^2_{r.m.s.}\ R$

A.C. AND A PURE CAPACITANCE

Here the current leads the voltage by 90° ($\pi/2$).

In this arrangement the e.m.f of the supply equals the p.d. across the capacitor. For the *capacitor*, the formula $Q = CV$ holds, and as $I = dQ/dt$, so $I = C\ dV/dt$. Then, if the variation of voltage is given by $V = V_0\sin\omega t$, we have $I = C\omega V_0 \cos\omega t = C\omega V_0 (\sin\omega t + \pi/2)$.

Hence we can write I in the form $I = I_0\cos\omega t$, and in terms of magnitudes $I_0 = V_0/X$ where X is the '**reactance**'. Reactance is measured in ohms, like resistance, as it is a ratio of voltage/current.

Here, $X = 1/\omega C$ or $X = 1/2\pi fC$.

No power is delivered to the capacitor. In this circuit, charge 'sloshes' in and out of the capacitor in a regular charge one-way-round, discharge, charge the-other-way round, discharge cycle. But as the electricity does not flow through a resistance, no conversion of electrical energy to heat or light takes place. Another way of considering it is to plot V and I curves and note that over one cycle the net value of VI is zero.

Fig. 15.5

A.C. AND A PURE INDUCTANCE

In this arrangement there is a forward e.m.f. from the supply $E = E_0\sin\omega t$, and a back e.m.f. generated by the **inductance** L, equal to $-L\ dI/dt$. The net e.m.f. in the circuit is zero so that:

$E + (-L\ dI/dt) = 0$.
So $E = L\ dI/dt$, or, $dI/dt = E/L$.

Integrating, we get:

$$\int dI = \int E/L\ dt = \int \frac{E_0}{L}\sin\omega t\ dt.$$

Hence $I = -\dfrac{E_0}{L\omega}\cos\omega t = \dfrac{E_0}{L\omega}\sin(\omega t - \pi/2)$,

i.e. the current lags behind the voltage by 90° ($\pi/2$). As before we can write X for the reactance, and here:

$X = \omega L.$

No power is delivered to the inductor. As with the capacitor circuit the net value of voltage × current over one cycle is zero. The following points are worth noting:

a) Reactances can also be expressed in terms of r.m.s. values:

$$X = \frac{V_o}{I_o} = \frac{V_{r.m.s.}}{I_{r.m.s.}} .$$

b) The reactance of both capacitors and inductors is frequency dependent.

At low frequencies a capacitor has a large reactance and lets only a small current pass, but at high frequencies it has only a small reactance. The opposite is true of inductors.

In circuits containing resistance and reactance, voltage and current will generally be out of phase by an angle which is NOT $\pm$ 90° (= $\pm$ $\pi/2$). In this case $Z = E_o/I_o = E_{r.m.s.}/I_{r.m.s.}$, where E is the e.m.f. of the source. Z is called the **impedance**, and again as a ratio of voltage/current, is measured in ohms. Note that the ratio can either be in terms of peak values or r.m.s. values.

> A useful mnemonic to remember phase angles is CIVIL: I ahead of V for C; I after V for L.

USING PHASORS TO ADD TWO VOLTAGES TOGETHER

PHASORS

Chapter 5 showed how the projection of a rotating point on to an axis produced a sinusoidal quantity. So the projection of a rotating vector along say the y-axis can represent a varying a.c. voltage $v = v_o\sin\omega t$. Such a rotating vector is called a **phasor**. To add two voltages together, the phasors are added using the parallelogram rule for vectors (see Chapter 3) taking account of the phase angle between them. The resultant is the phasor which represents the addition of the two out-of-phase voltages.

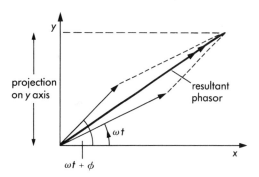

Fig. 15.6 Adding two phasors using the parallelogram rule

Although the methods has been described in terms of *peak* values of voltage, the addition process can be done with r.m.s. values, provided it is remembered that the computed value is an r.m.s. value. This is because on a vector diagram the effect is simply to scale the lengths of all vectors down by a factor of $\dfrac{1}{\sqrt{2}}$. In the subsequent examples, whenever voltages and currents are referred to, it is the r.m.s. values that are considered. The method can also be used to add currents which are not in phase. However, numerical examples set at A Level will be no more complicated than series circuits, requiring only voltage addition, (but note Multiple Choice Question 6).

SERIES CIRCUIT RULES USING PHASORS

In solving *series circuits*, there are two key points to consider in working out voltages and currents:

a) at any instant the current is the same in each circuit component (because they are in series).
b) the sum of the p.d.s. at any instant is equal to the source e.m.f. at that instant.

The following rules should then be adopted:

1 First draw the current vector, horizontally (for convenience).
2 Draw the vector representing voltage across a resistance in phase with the current vector, (i.e. along the direction of the current vector).
3 Draw in the other voltage vectors at right angles remembering the mnemonic CIVIL.

4 Find the resultant voltage vector.

5 Compare the magnitude of this with the magnitude of the current vector in order to find the circuit impedance Z.

6 Compare its direction with the horizontal in order to establish the phase angle between current and voltage.

CR CIRCUIT

The voltage $V_R(= IR)$ is in phase with the current vector and is drawn horizontally (Fig. 15.7). With the capacitor, the current leads the voltage by 90°, and so its voltage vector V_C is drawn downwards (Fig. 15.8). In magnitude, $V_C = IX$, where $X = 1/\omega C$.

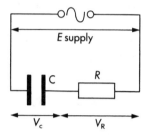

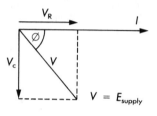

Fig. 15.7   **Fig. 15.8**

The resultant p.d. (V) which is equal to the e.m.f. (E) of the source is given by the vector resultant of V_R and V_C.

In magnitude: $E^2 = V_R{}^2 + V_C{}^2$
$$= I^2(R^2 + 1/\omega^2 C^2)$$

or $E = IZ$, where Z is the impedance and given by:
$$Z = \sqrt{R^2 + 1/\omega^2 C^2}$$

Phase: $\tan \phi = \dfrac{V_C}{V_R} = \dfrac{I}{\omega C} \cdot \dfrac{1}{IR}$

so $\tan \phi = \dfrac{1}{\omega R C}$

RL CIRCUIT

For the inductance the applied voltage leads the current by 90°, so its voltage vector V_L is drawn upwards (Fig. 15.9).

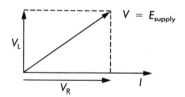

Fig. 15.9

In magnitude $V_L = IX$ where $X = \omega L$. The resultant p.d. (V_L) equal to E, is then drawn in. Doing the same analysis as before we obtain:

$$E^2 = V_R{}^2 + V_L{}^2$$
$$= I^2(R^2 + \omega^2 L^2)$$
or $E = IZ$

where Z is the impedance and is given by:

$$Z = \sqrt{R^2 + \omega^2 L^2}$$

$\tan \phi = \dfrac{V_L}{V_R} = \dfrac{\omega L}{R}$.

LCR CIRCUIT

Note that in practice there may only be a coil and a capacitor. A real coil will always have

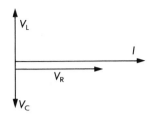

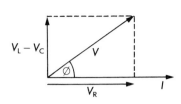

Fig. 15.10

Fig. 15.11

some resistance and R is then the resistance of the coil. The phasor diagram is as shown in Fig. 15.10 with V_L leading I by 90° and V_C lagging it by 90°. $V_L - V_C$ can then be drawn (in Fig. 15.11 it is assumed that V_L is greater than V_C). The calculation is then as before:

$$E^2 = V_R{}^2 + (V_L - V_C)^2$$
$$= I^2(R^2 + (\omega L - \frac{1}{\omega C})^2)$$

or $E = IZ$ where

$$Z = \sqrt{R^2 + (\omega L - \frac{1}{\omega C})^2}$$

and $\tan \phi = \dfrac{V_L - V_C}{V_R}$.

RESONANCE

The LCR series circuit provides an electrical example of resonance. The impedance Z has a minimum value when $V_L = V_C$ and the current is a maximum.

i.e. when $\omega L = 1/\omega C$ giving $\omega = \sqrt{1/LC}$

or $f = \dfrac{1}{2\pi} \sqrt{\dfrac{1}{LC}}$.

Thus if the supply frequency, f, is varied through this value the current will go through a maximum when $f = \dfrac{1}{2\pi\sqrt{LC}}$

PARALLEL RESONANCE

Another circuit that gives resonance is an LC *parallel* circuit (Fig. 15.12). To analyse this with phasors, you need to know that because the components are in parallel it is the voltage which is now common and not the current. So in drawing a phasor diagram you start by drawing the voltage vector and then add the current vectors (Fig. 15.13).

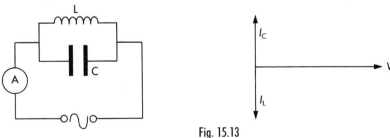

Fig. 15.12

Fig. 15.13

When $1/\omega C = \omega L$ the two currents I_L and I_C have the same magnitude but are in antiphase. This occurs at the frequency $f = 1/2\pi \sqrt{(LC)}$ and the supply current is a minimum. The voltage V is then large; for the same current at other frequencies it would be much smaller due to Z being smaller. The curve of Z against frequency is as shown in Fig. 15.14. As resistance is introduced into the circuit the curve becomes less sharp. (See Multiple Choice Question 6 for the type of exercise that may be set on this circuit.)

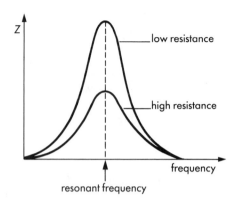

Fig. 15.14

ALTERNATING CURRENT AS A SOURCE OF D.C.

Many domestic appliances use electronic circuits which require a low voltage d.c. power supply. It is therefore necessary to use a step-down transformer and to rectify the d.c. supply. Transformers are considered in the chapter on electromagnetic induction.

RECTIFICATION

The simplest way to rectify an a.c. is to use a single silicon diode (Fig. 15.15). Current only flows when A is positive with respect to B as shown. This is called **half-wave rectification**. More commonly a **bridge rectifier circuit** is used (Fig. 15.16). If A is positive with respect to B, current flows by the route Q-Load-R, and if B is positive with respect to A by the route S-Load-P. The wave form now include every half-cycle and this is called **whole wave rectification**.

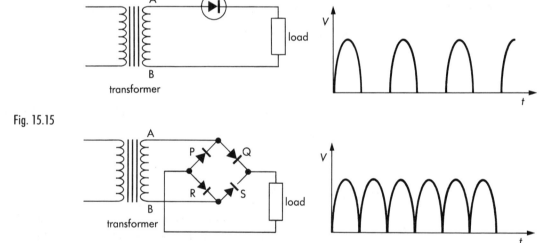

Fig. 15.15

Fig. 15.16

The current is now rectified but is not smoothed. A large capacitor across the output terminals of the bridge rectifier helps to keep the voltage 'topped up' when the rectified supply falls to zero. The current is then smoothed. Note that the ripple voltage is twice the mains frequency (Fig. 15.17).

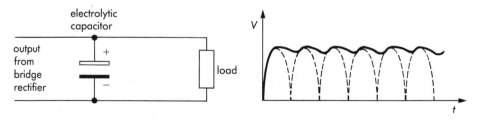

Fig. 15.17

These circuits can also be used for converting d.c. and moving coil meters into a.c. meters.

EXAMINATION QUESTIONS

MULTIPLE CHOICE QUESTIONS

1 Fig. 15.18 shows four identical diodes and a resistor connected to an a.c. supply. Between which two points will the voltage waveform be of the same shape and phase as that between the points K and L?

a) K and M   d) N and M
b) N and L   e) M and L
c) K and N

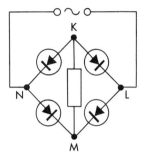

Fig. 15.18

(London 1988)

2 A series circuit consists of a pure inductor L, a pure capacitor C and a pure resistor R. When an alternating p.d. of frequency f is applied, a current of r.m.s. value i flows in the circuit. Which one of the following statements is *not* true?

a) The p.d. across L leads the current in L by $\pi/2$.
b) The current in C leads the current in L.
c) The current in C leads the p.d. across C by $\pi/2$.
d) The p.d. across R $= iR$.
e) For maximum i, $2\pi fL = 1/(2\pi fC)$.

(AEB 1988)

3 Alternating currents of sinusoidal and square waveforms (shown in Fig. 15.19) pass in turn through a resistor. The power dissipated is the same in each case. Given that

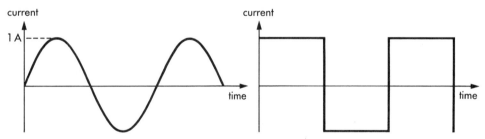

Fig. 15.19

the peak value of the sinusoidal current is 1 A, the peak value, in A, of the square waveform is

a) 2   d) $1/\sqrt{2}$
b) 2   e) $1/2$
c) 1

(AEB 1988)

4 An alternating current of r.m.s. value I flows through a resistor of resistance R and an inductor of reactance X. Which one of the following expressions gives the power dissipated?

a) $I^2(R+X)$ d) I^2R
b) $I^2 \sqrt{R^2 + X^2}$ e) I^2X
c) 0

5 Fig. 15.20 below shows a resistor R of resistance 4 Ω, an inductor L, and a capacitor C connected in series. At a certain frequency the reactances of the inductor and

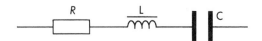

Fig. 15.20

capacitor are 3 Ω and 6 Ω respectively. At this frequency the total impedance of the series combination, in ohms, is

a) 1 d) $\sqrt{97}$
b) 5 e) 13
c) 7

(NI 1987)

6 Fig. 15.21 shows a circuit containing a resistor R_1 and a capacitor C in parallel with a resistor R_2 and inductor L. The parallel combination is connected to an a.c. supply of

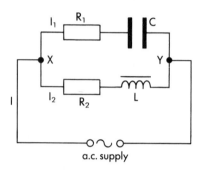

Fig. 15.21

variable frequency. The frequency of the supply is adjusted until the current I and the potential difference V between X and Y are in phase with each other; this is the condition for resonance. Under these conditions, which of the following statements is (are) true?

1 The currents I_1 and I_2 in the two branches of the parallel circuit are in phase with each other.
2 The impedance between points X and Y is a *minimum* at the resonance frequency.
3 The current I is a *minimum* at the resonance frequency.

a) 3 only d) 2 and 3 only
b) 1 and 2 only e) 1, 2 and 3
c) 1 and 3 only

(NI 1987)

7 The supply frequency to a full-wave rectifier circuit is 50 Hz. The output voltage to a load resistor is smoothed using a single capacitor. The frequency of the ripple across the load, in hertz, is

a) 25 d) 100
b) 50 e) 200
c) $100/\sqrt{2}$

(NI 1987)

ANSWERS AND COMMENTS

Question	1	2	3	4	5	6	7
Answer	d)	2)	d)	d)	b)	a)	d)

1 Think about the half-cycle during which the diode between KL conducts. The current passes through the resistor and must come from the point M. The only route is through NM.
2 This is a good test of your knowledge. Because it is a series circuit the current is the same for all circuit elements.
3 First note that the square wave has the same heating effect as a steady d.c. current of the same *magnitude*. The sinusoidal wave has the heating effect of a d.c. current of magnitude $1/\sqrt{2}$ (its r.m.s. value).
4 A 'trick' question. No power is dissipated in a pure inductance and so only the current in the resistance needs to be considered.
5 Think of the phasor diagram when a current of 1A flows. $V_L = 1 \times 3 = 3V$, $V_C = 1 \times 6 = 6V$ and $V_R = 1 \times 4 = 4V$. The phasor diagram is shown in Fig. 15.22 with a resultant V of $\sqrt{3^2 + 4^2} = 5V$. Hence Z is 5 Ω.

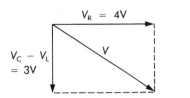

$$V = \sqrt{3^2 + 4^2}$$
$$= 5V$$

Fig. 15.22

6 See Fig. 15.13; I_C and I_L are in antiphase so 1) is false and so is 2): the impedance is at a maximum (see Fig. 15.14).

7 See Fig. 15.17. The peaks occur every *half*-cycle. Note the various distractors.

STRUCTURED QUESTIONS

8 Prove that an alternating current *through* a capacitor leads the alternating voltage applied to it by $\pi/2$ radians, and derive the expression for the capacitative reactance X_C in terms of f (the frequency) and C (the capacitance).

(Welsh 1985 Part question)

9 a) A sinusoidally varying voltage supply has a *root mean square* value of 12 V. Explain what the term root mean square means and calculate the amplitude of the supply.

b) With the aid of a circuit diagram, show how the supply in a) could be rectified to give a reasonably smooth source of direct current. Show how several cycles of this supply would appear as an oscilloscope trace.

c) Fig. 15.23 shows a sinusoidally alternating 12 V r.m.s., 50 Hz supply connected to a series combination of a 300 Ω resistor and a 1.0 H inductor. The supply and the inductor both have negligible resistance. Draw a phasor diagram for this circuit and use it to calculate:
   i) the current flowing in the circuit, and
   ii) the voltage across the inductor.
   Explain why the net power dissipated in the inductor is zero.

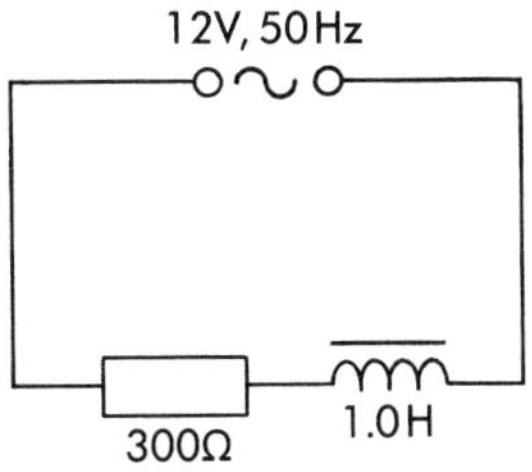

d) Fig. 15.24 is a circuit diagram of a simple two-way loudspeaker consisting of a treble speaker, a bass speaker, a capacitor and an inductor. Suggest how this system works.

Fig. 15.23

12V, 50Hz

300Ω   1.0H

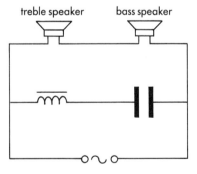

treble speaker   bass speaker

Fig. 15.24

(Southern 1988)

10 The graphs show the variation of output voltage with time for two alternating supplies A and B. The supplies are connected in turn to a pure resistor of resistance 3.0 Ω.

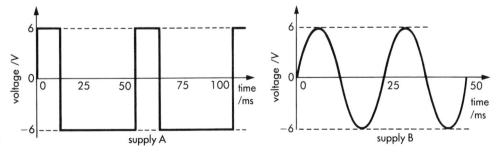

Fig. 15.25

supply A   supply B

a) Calculate:
   i) the frequency of each supply;
   ii) the power dissipated in the resistor in each case.

b) With supply B connected, the pure resistor is replaced by another 3.0 Ω resistor, the inductance of which is not negligible. Account briefly for the reduced power dissipation.

(AEB 1988)

OUTLINE ANSWERS AND COMMENTS

8 The required theory is described in the text.

Let $V = V_o \sin \omega t$ and use $Q = VC$. Differentiate to get $I = \dfrac{dQ}{dt} = \dfrac{CdV}{dt}$. You

should get $I = \omega C V_o \cos \omega t$ which can be written

$\omega C V \sin \left(\omega t + \dfrac{\pi}{2} \right)$

$$X_C = \dfrac{1}{\omega C} = \dfrac{1}{2\pi f C}$$

9 a) R.M.S. is explained in the text.

$$V_{RMS} = \dfrac{V_{peak}}{\sqrt{2}}, \text{ so the amplitude } = \sqrt{2} \times 12$$
$$= 16.97 \text{ V}$$

b) Again this is explained in the text.

c) To solve this one it is necessary to have vectors representing r.m.s. values. Let the r.m.s. current be I. Then the voltages across the resistor and inductors respectively are IR and $I\omega L$.

The vector diagram in Fig. 15.26 then follows using the rules outlined in the text.

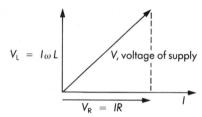

Fig. 15.26

   i) $V^2 = I^2 \omega^2 L^2 + I^2 R^2$
     giving $144 = I^2 (4\pi^2 \times 50^2 + 300^2)$
               $= I^2 (98,696 + 90,000)$
     so $I = 0.0276$ A.

   ii) The voltage across the inductor $= I\omega L$.
       $= 2\pi \times 50 \times 1 \times 0.0276 = 8.68$ V. (r.m.s. value).
     The graphs of current and voltage through the inductor are:

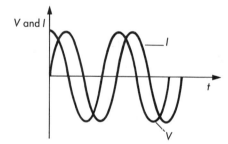

Fig. 15.27

     Over 1 cycle the power = average of $V \times I = 0$.

d) We can regard the two speakers as wired across a potential divider circuit formed by the capacitor and the inductor. At low frequencies X_L is low and X_C large. The larger of the two voltages V_C and V_L will be V_C and hence there will be a comparatively large output from the bass speaker. At high frequencies X_L is high and X_C low, and the treble speaker will dominate.

10 a) i) $T_A = 50$ ms so $f_A = 20$ Hz
       $T_B = 25$ ms so $f_B = 40$ Hz.

   ii) Supply A delivers the same power as a d.c. supply of 6 V. So power dissipated
       $= V^2/R = 12$ W.

     Supply B has an r.m.s. voltage of $\dfrac{6}{\sqrt{2}}$ V,

     so power $= \left(\dfrac{6}{\sqrt{2}} \right)^2 \times \dfrac{1}{3} = 6$ W.

b) The circuit now behaves like that of a resistance of 3 Ω in series with an inductance of reactance X_L. The supply voltage is given by
$$V^2 = (IR)^2 + (IX_L)^2$$
where $R = 3 \ \Omega$.
so $(IR)^2 = V^2 - (IX_L)^2$
or IR, the p.d. across the resistor $= \sqrt{V^2 - (IX_L)^2}$
and hence is less than V.

A smaller voltage across the resistor implies less power dissipated, as the inductance dissipates no power.

TUTOR'S QUESTION AND ANSWER

11 a) i) Explain the meaning of the term *reactance* as used in a.c. circuit theory.

ii) A simple a.c. generator with output of the form $E=E_o\sin\omega t$ may be used as a power supply for circuits containing electrical components. Sketch three labelled graphs which illustrate the variation of reactance X with ω, for each of the following components: a resistor, a capacitor and an inductor (all assumed to be ideal).

b) A real inductor which has resistance R and inductance L is connected in series with a current meter to an a.c. supply. The voltage and frequency of this supply are both variable, and may be altered in such a way that the current flow in the circuit remains constant at a known r.m.s. value. If corresponding values of voltage and frequency, which give this constant reading, are tabulated, show how they may be presented in the form of a linear graph from which the value of L may be deduced. Sketch the graph, and explain how L may be obtained from it. (The effect of the current meter may be neglected.)

c) An air-cored inductor of resistance R and inductance L is connected in series with a pure capacitor of capacitance C.

i) Sketch a labelled graph showing how the impedance of the L-C-R combination is frequency dependent for a range of frequencies which includes the resonant frequency.

ii) Describe how the graph you have drawn in answer to c) i) would alter if the inductor were replaced by a similar one, of equal inductance but wound with much finer wire. How would the graph further alter if an iron core were now placed in the inductor wound with fine wire?

iii) An L-C-R combination is connected to a sinusoidally-alternating supply. How does the phase relationship between the current in the circuit and the supply voltage change as the frequency is increased through the resonant frequency? Illustrate your answer using a phasor diagram.

d) A sinusoidally-alternating voltage supply is connected to a half-wave rectifier, the output of which is displayed on a cathode ray oscilloscope (c.r.o.). The vertical height of each peak of the trace is 3.0 cm on the screen. The horizontal distance between two adjacent peaks of the trace is 4.0 cm. The setting of the amplifier sensitivity control is 50 V cm^{-1} and the time-base control setting is 10 ms cm^{-1}. Calculate the r.m.s. value of the rectified voltage, and the frequency of the unrectified supply. This voltage is measured across a 50 Ω load resistor. What power is dissipated in the load?

The controls of the c.r.o. are now altered so that, for the same input signal, the vertical height of the trace is doubled and the horizontal distance between adjacent peaks is halved. What are the new settings of the amplifier sensitivity and the time-base control?

(NI 1986)

11 a) i) is considered in the text.

a) ii)

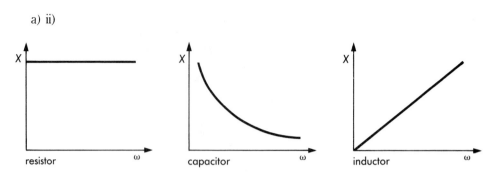

Fig. 15.28

b) V, the voltage developed across L, is 90° out of phase with V the voltage across R, and so the phasor diagram is as shown.

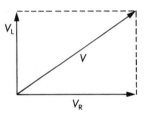

Fig. 15.29

$V^2 = V_L^2 + V_R^2$
$V_L = IX_L$, where X_L is the reactance of the inductor and equal to $2\pi fL$ and I is the current. Also $V_R = IR$.

so $V = I\sqrt{R^2 + 4\pi^2f^2L^2}$
$V^2 = I^2(R^2 + 4\pi^2f^2L^2)$

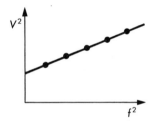

Fig. 15.30

If V^2 is plotted as ordinate against f^2 as abscissa, a linear graph of the form shown results. The gradient G is measured.
$G = 4\pi^2L^2I^2$
giving $L = \sqrt{G}/2\pi I$
where I is the known current.

c) i) $Z = \sqrt{R^2 + \left(\omega L - \dfrac{1}{\omega C}\right)^2}$

$= \sqrt{R^2 + \left(2\pi fL - \dfrac{1}{2\pi fC}\right)^2}$

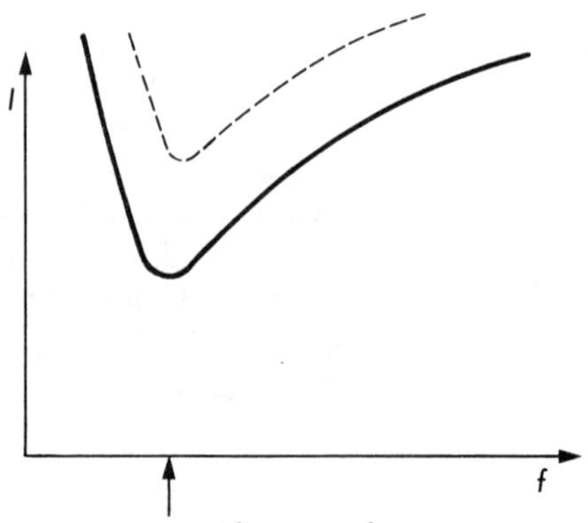

Fig. 15.31

resonant frequency f_o

ii) Using finer wire keeps L the same but increases R. The curve shape becomes like the dotted one. If an iron core were introduced L would be increased. This would reduce the resonant frequency f and shift the new curve to the left.

iii) There are three cases to consider:
$$X_L < X_C, \quad X_L = X_C \quad \text{and} \quad X_L > X_C,$$
where X_C is the reactance of the capacitor. The first case corresponds to $f > f_o$, the second to $f = f_o$ (resonance) and the third to $f < f_o$.

The phasor diagrams in the three cases are shown in Figs. 15.32 and 15.33.

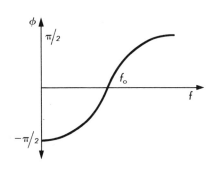

Fig. 15.32

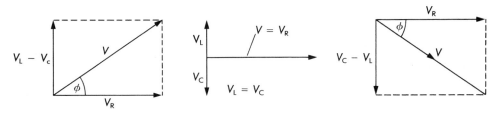

Fig. 15.33

The graph shows how the phase ϕ changes with frequency.

Fig. 15.34

d)

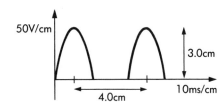

For one of the half cycles actually present
$$V_{\text{r.m.s.}} = 150/\sqrt{2} = 106.08 \text{ V}$$
So the mean square voltage is 11252 V^2.
With one half cycle present and the other missing.

$$\text{the mean square voltage} = \frac{11252 + 0}{2},$$
$$= 5626 \text{ V}^2$$

giving $V = 75.0$ V.
The time period of the unrectified supply = 40 ms.

So the frequency $= \dfrac{1}{40 \text{ms}} = 25$ Hz.

Power dissipated in the load $= \dfrac{V^2_{\text{r.m.s.}}}{R} = \dfrac{75^2}{50} = 112.5$ W.

With the vertical height doubled, the sensitivity must be doubled, giving 25 V cm^{-1}, and with the horizontal distance between adjacent peaks halved there must be twice as much time per distance across the screen, giving 20 ms cm^{-1}.

STUDENT'S ANSWER WITH EXAMINER COMMENTS

STUDENT'S ANSWER TO QUESTION 10 c)

"Diagram not clearly labelled. Vector representing p.d. across inductor is in wrong direction."

$V^2 = I^2\omega^2L^2 + I^2R^2$

giving $144 = I^2 (4\pi^2 50^2 + 300^2)$

$\quad\quad\quad = (98,696 + 90,000) I^2$

so $I^2 = 7.63 \times 10^{-4}$

$\quad I = 0.02762484.$

"No units. Too many significant figures."

$V_L = 2\pi fLI$

"Too many significant figures. Needs to explain clearly that this is the r.m.s. value of voltage."

$\quad\quad = 2\pi \times 50 \times 1 \times 0.02762484$

$\quad\quad = 8.6786$ Volts

"A weak answer. A good deal more explanation is needed."

Net power dissipated is zero because the inductance has reactance not resistance.

Overall comments: The candidate clearly understands a.c. theory and has only made a few errors in the setting out of the calculation. The descriptive part of the answer is poor. Typical of a grade C candidate.

ELECTRONICS

GETTING STARTED

Syllabus constructors have had a lot of mixed feelings about how much electronics, if any, should be in an A Level Physics course. They have also worried about the kind of electronics, whether it should be the **systems approach**, treating the electronics as a set of interconnecting 'black-boxes' knowledge of whose internal structure is unnecessary, or whether it should be a **component approach** focussing on individual circuit items such as the transistor. One board (ULSEB), has recently removed all its electronics from the main syllabus to an 'option'.

What is not in dispute is the importance of electronics in everyday life, from video-recorders to railway signalling equipment. In most applications similar components are used and the basic set of operations performed is quite limited: amplification, logic functions, counting, coding, decoding, etc. You will probably have already done some electronics at GCSE Level. A good starting point therefore would be your old notes, or Chapter 8 and 16 of the *Longman Physics GCSE Revise Guide*. For the physicist, a knowledge of the elements of electronics is important primarily in instrumentation. To know how to make a simple amplifier is useful if the output signal in an electrical experiment is too small. Knowledge of how counting and logic circuits is essential for work which involves 'interfacing' into commercial 'off-the-shelf' devices can be useful. This chapter has been laid out in two parts following those Boards which have retained electronics in the core. The first part is about **digital** logic and the second about the operational-amplifier on which all the **analogue** electronics has been focussed.

ESSENTIAL PRINCIPLES

In electronics it is usual to draw circuits in the form shown (Fig. 16.1) with all the components powered where necessary from two or more voltage 'rails' drawn horizontally on the page. Here the upper rail is called the high-voltage or 'high' rail, even though it may be as little as +5V and the other rail is the 0 volts or 'low' rail. An example of such a circuit is that shown in Multiple Choice Question 5. Sometimes the low rail is called 'ground', particularly if it is connected to earth or the chassis of some equipment.

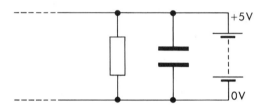

Fig. 16.1 Circuit diagram convention in electronics

DIGITAL LOGIC

Digital Logic is concerned with electronic systems where input voltages are supplied to logic components either at a 'high' voltage state or a 'low' state. The output voltages of the system are also 'high' or 'low'. For positive logic, the high voltage state is represented algebraically by 1 and the low voltage state by 0.

Circuit construction is carried out by connecting together logic gates located on integrated circuits (ICs). Typically these might be TTL (Transistor-Transistor Logic e.g. 7400 series) devices or CMOS (Complementary Metal Oxide Semiconductor, e.g. 4000B Series) devices. In TTL logic levels are 0V and 5V, in CMOS 0V and from 3 to 15 volts. Experimental details of any particular set of devices including these logic levels will not be required in most examinations. Indeed, in the logic problems in digital electronics it is quite usual to leave out both the power supply rails and circuit diagrams altogether. See, for example, Fig. 16.2 where all that is shown is the input and output connections of particular logic 'gates'. The simpler logic gates will have already been encountered at GCSE and so they are summarised under the following seven headings.

NOT GATE OR INVERTER

This is the simplest with one input and one output. Its circuit symbols in British and American form are shown in Fig. 16.2. Its input-output characteristics are summarised in the truth table (Table 16.1).

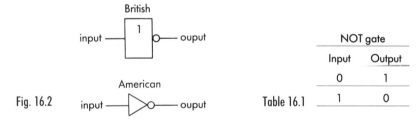

Fig. 16.2

NOT gate	
Input	Output
0	1
1	0

Table 16.1

2-INPUT OR GATE

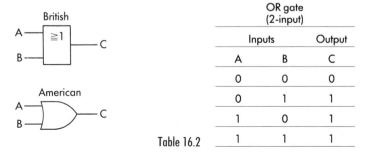

Fig. 16.3

OR gate (2-input)		
Inputs		Output
A	B	C
0	0	0
0	1	1
1	0	1
1	1	1

Table 16.2

2-INPUT NOR GATE

This is an OR gate followed by a NOT gate.

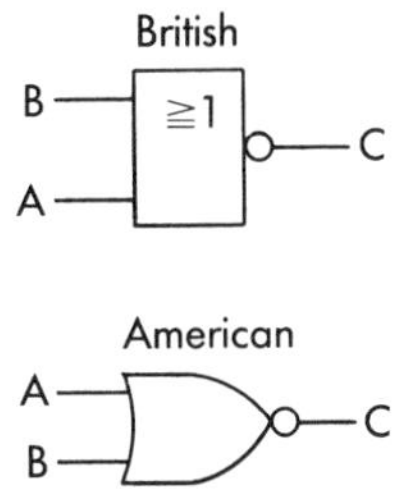
British
B
≥1
C
A
American
A
C
B

Fig. 16.4

Table 16.3

NOR gate (2-input)		
Inputs		Output
A	B	C
0	0	1
0	1	0
1	0	0
1	1	0

2-INPUT AND GATE

The output is high if, and only if, both inputs are high.

"The output is high only if A and B are both high."

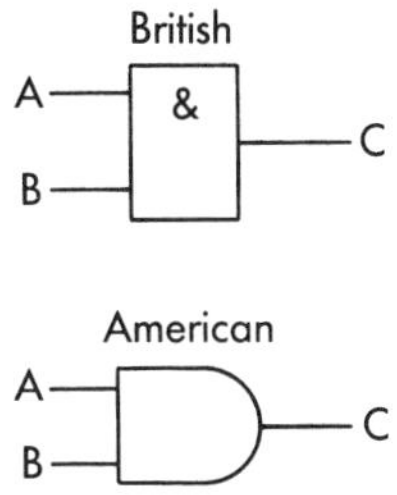
British
A
&
C
B
American
A
C
B

Fig. 16.5

Table 16.4

AND gate (2-input)		
Inputs		Output
A	B	C
0	0	0
0	1	0
1	0	0
1	1	1

2-INPUT NAND GATE

This is an AND gate followed by a NOT gate.

"Again get the truth table by writing the AND truth table and inverting it."

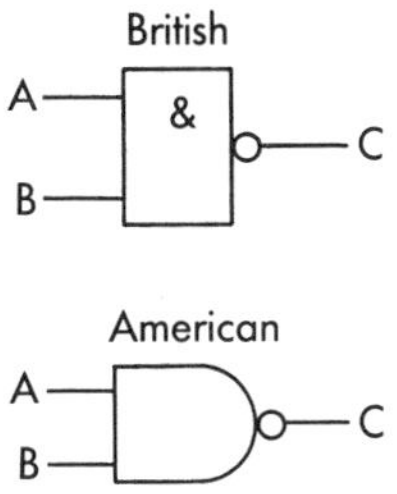
British
A
&
C
B
American
A
C
B

Fig. 16.6

Table 16.5

NAND gate (2-input)		
Inputs		Output
A	B	C
0	0	1
0	1	1
1	0	1
1	1	0

Two other gates probably not previously encountered are the

2-input Exclusive-OR (EXOR) gate and the
2-input Exclusive-NOR (EXNOR) gate.

2-INPUT EXCLUSIVE-OR (EXOR) GATE

The output is high if one or other of the inputs is high but not if both are high. This is sometimes called a **difference gate** because the output is high when the inputs are different.

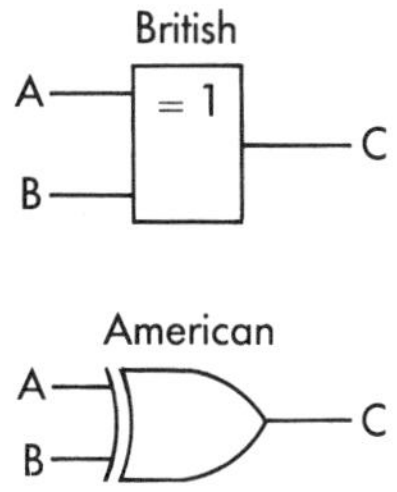
British
A
= 1
C
B
American
A
C
B

Fig. 16.7

Table 16.6

Exclusive-OR gate		
Inputs		Output
A	B	C
0	0	0
0	1	1
1	0	1
1	1	0

2-INPUT EXCLUSIVE-NOR (EXNOR) GATE

This is simply the previous gate followed by a NOT gate. This is sometimes called a **parity gate**. The output is high only when both inputs are the same.

TRUTH TABLE PROBLEMS

The simplest kind of problem at A Level (see Multiple Choice Questions 1 to 5) is one where you have to construct a **truth table** for a series of interconnecting gates in sequence. To do this, simply set out a grid so that each input and output is listed, and work through from left to right. Remember to check whether the gate has any kind of inverting function (e.g. NOR rather than OR). Note the 'blob' on the symbols which indicate this function.

Some boards take digital logic a little further in their core syllabuses. We shall just consider the half-adder, the bistable, the astable and the JK-flip-flop.

HALF-ADDER

The **half-adder** is used for electronic arithmetic and performs addition of binary arithmetic. It has to deal with four cases:

sum	carry
(EXOR)	(AND)

$$0 + 0 = 0 \quad\quad 0$$
$$0 + 1 = 1 \quad\quad 0$$
$$1 + 0 = 1 \quad\quad 0$$
$$1 + 1 = 0 \quad\quad 1$$

In the last case the 0 is called the 'sum' and the 1 is the 'carry', i.e. it is carried over to the next column on the right.

As with all logic circuits there are several combinations of logic gates which would perform the required operation. The simplest is that shown using an EXOR and an AND gate (see Fig. 16.8).

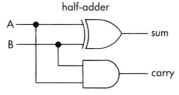

half-adder

Fig. 16.8

THE BISTABLE

The **bistable** is sometimes the set-reset (SR) flip-flop. It can be constructed from two NAND gates and two NOT gates. Note how the outputs of the NAND gates are

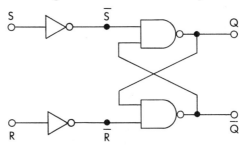

Fig. 16.9

cross-connected to their inputs. This is called **feedback**. The output depends upon the output as well as the input. As the name suggests, a bistable can exist in one of two stable states. These are:

   i) $Q = 1$ $\bar{Q} = 0$ the so-called 1 stable state, the flip-flop being said to be 'set', and
   ii) the $Q = 0$ $\bar{Q} = 1$ state, the flip-flop being said to be 'reset'.

The behaviour of the circuit can be worked out by going through the sequence of input conditions shown in the truth table (Table 16.7).

S	R	$\bar{S}$	$\bar{R}$	Q	$\bar{Q}$
1	0	0	1	1	0
0	0	1	1	1	0
0	1	1	0	0	1
0	0	1	1	0	1

Table 16.7

For example if $S = 1$ and $R = 0$ then $\bar{S} = 0$ and $\bar{R} = 1$. Q must be 1, since one of the inputs, that from $\bar{S}$ is 0. Both inputs to the bottom NAND gate are 1 and so $\bar{Q} = 0$.

Note that when $S = R = 0$, Q can be either 0 or 1 depending upon what the state of the bistable was before this input condition existed. Note also that this type of bistable has an indeterminate state when $S = R = 1$, and this situation is best avoided.

The most important property of the bistable is that it 'remembers' the state it was last in. If S is made high *momentarily* then $Q = 1$ and *remains* at 1 until either S or R are made high again.

ASTABLE

Pulses are useful in electronic circuits for timing purposes. The first requirement is a device which will produce a continuous train of pulses. Such a circuit is called an **astable multivibrator** or just an astable for short, and is made by coupling two logic switches with resistors and capacitors. The simplest way of making an astable uses two NOT gates as shown in Fig. 16.10.

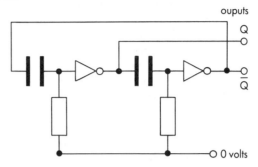

Fig. 16.10

When the circuit is first connected it may not initially oscillate and produce a train of pulses. In this case it needs to be started by momentarily shorting across one of the capacitors.

JK FLIP-FLOP

Unlike the bistable described on page 170, the data inputs J and K are allowed to both be high simultaneously and this makes it more useful. And also unlike the previous circuit it has a third input called a clock (CK) into which is fed a pulse from a clock circuit, i.e. a square wave pulsing circuit of the kind just described, the pulse going from logic 0 to 1 and then back to 0 again.

In a typical JK flip-flop, e.g. a 7474 dual type positive edge JK flip-flop, 0 will take on the value of the J input at the time when the clock is rising from logic 0 to 1 (positive edge triggering). It will do this provided J = 0 and K = 1, or J = 1 and K = 0. If the two data inputs J and K are both at logic 0, Q will not change. If the two data inputs are at logic 1, Q 'toggles' between 0 and 1 each time the clock rises from logic 0 to logic 1.

The circuit and the truth table are shown in Fig. 16.11 and Table 16.8 respectively.

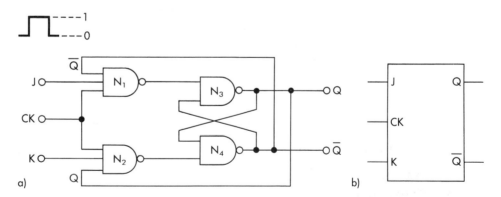

Fig. 16.11

Table 16.8

Inputs		Outputs before clock pulse		Outputs after clock pulse		
J	K	Q	$\overline{Q}$	Q	$\overline{Q}$	
0	0	1	0	1	0	No change in
0	0	0	1	0	1	outputs
1	0	1	0	1	0	Stays at or sets to
1	0	0	1	1	0	Q = 1 and $\overline{Q}$ = 0
0	1	1	0	0	1	Stays at or resets to
0	1	0	1	0	1	Q = 0 and $\overline{Q}$ = 1
1	1	1	0	0	1	
1	1	0	1	1	0	Toggles

Note that N_1 and N_2 are three input NAND gates. These have an output of 1 unless all three inputs are 1.

You should note that there are other types of flip-flop which follow negative edge triggering, i.e. there is a change of state as the clock falls from 1 to 0.

Note that Q = 1 occurs only once every two pulses, i.e. the output has half the frequency of the input. The flip-flop is therefore a frequency divider circuit and could be used in an electronic organ for dividing the frequency of a master oscillator in order to produce a note one octave lower. It also forms the basic component of a binary counter. Fig. 16.12 shows several flip-flops connected together. Suppose all the JK inputs are connected to logic state 1 and the flip-flops are all initially set to Q = 1. The graphs show what happens when a train of pulses is sent to the CK of A. For example after the 4th input pulse, and before the fifth, Q at C is 1 and all other outputs are 0. The outputs in order DCBA are therefore 0100 which is the number 4 in binary.

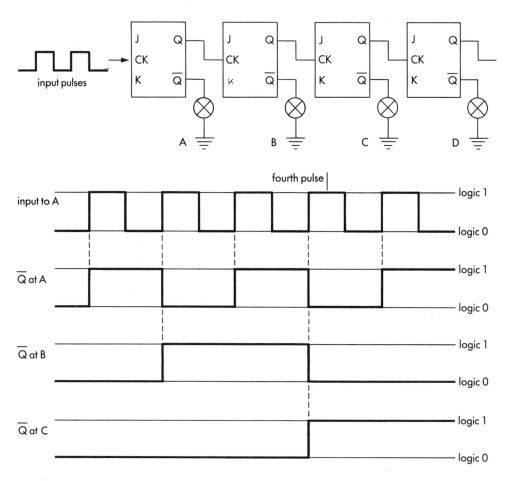

Fig. 16.12

Analogue electronics is the branch of electronics dealing with inputs and outputs which can vary over a range of voltages and are not just at one of two fixed levels. A Level syllabuses have focussed heavily on the operational amplifier integrated circuit (IC) because of its versatility.

THE OPERATIONAL AMPLIFIER

The **operational amplifier** (op. amp.) is a silicon chip with a number of terminals, including those for its power supply and for input and output signals. It has the following properties:

a) It is a very high voltage gain A which is typically $\approx 10^5$ for d.c. work (with a.c. signals A diminishes with frequency).

b) It has very high input resistance, typically 10^{11} Ω. This means it draws insignificant amounts of current from a source of input, and can therefore be used to amplify signals from very feeble sources, e.g. a thermocouple.

c) It has low output resistance (typically 100 Ω). In normal circuit work this would be considered a sizeable resistance, but by the standards of electronics it is very small, and

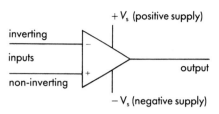

Fig. 16.13

means that the op. amp. is not itself likely to be what limits the power supplied to an output circuit.

The circuit symbol is as shown in Fig. 16.13.

Unlike the logic circuits the op. amp. is usually used with three voltage rails. These are two rails with voltages between $\pm$ 5 V and $\pm$ 15 V above and below the third which is a 'zero' reference voltage or 'ground rail'. On circuit diagrams the connections to the first two rails which power the IC are often omitted for clarity.

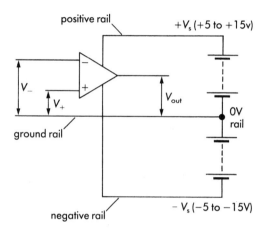

Fig. 16.14

DIFFERENTIAL AMPLIFIER

The operational amplifier has two inputs, the so-called '+' or **non-inverting input** and the '−' or **inverting input**. The device works by sensing the voltage difference between these two terminals and amplifying it. For this reason it is sometimes called a **differential amplifier**. Thus if V_+ and V_- are the voltages at the two inputs:

$$V_{out} = A\ (V_+ - V_-),$$

where A is the gain mentioned earlier and V_{out} the output voltage.

The inverting input is so called because if V_+ is held constant an increase $\triangle V$ in V_- makes V_{out} *fall* by an amount $A\triangle V$. Similarly V_+ is called the non-inverting input because if V_- is held constant and V_+ increases by $\triangle V$ the output *increases* by $A\triangle V$.

Because the output cannot rise above $+V_s$ or fall below $-V_s$ the I.C. is only linear for a certain narrow range of input voltages.

Because $V_{out} = A(V_+ - V_-)$, and A is so large, as soon as $(V_+ - V_-)$ exceeds about 60 μV the device 'saturates' at a maximum output voltage, usually slightly less than V_s.

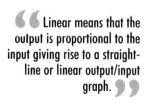

Linear means that the output is proportional to the input giving rise to a straight-line or linear output/input graph.

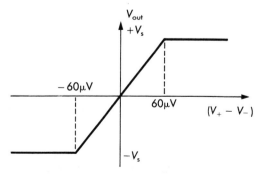

Fig. 16.15

Note also that $V_+ - V_- = \dfrac{V_{out}}{A}$ .So with $V_{out} \approx 10$ V and A large $V_+ - V_-$ is very small. In other words the difference between V_+ and V_- is negligible unless the op. amp. is saturated.

USE OF NEGATIVE FEEDBACK TO CONTROL THE GAIN

To control the gain external resistors have to be added to the I.C. Consider the circuit shown in Fig. 16.16. With the non-inverting terminal connected to the 0 V rail, the amplifier action is determined solely by the inverting terminal. Note that in this and in subsequent diagrams power supply rails have not been drawn. Secondly, experiment shows that unless the input voltage V_{in} is relatively large, the output voltage V_{out} does not reach one of the power rail voltages $\pm V_s$, but is proportional to minus the input voltage $(-V_{in})$. Thirdly, such a circuit is an example of **negative feedback**. This is because as V_{in} drives the input in one direction the current through the feedback resistance generates a potential in the opposite sense, thus reducing the effect of V_{in}.

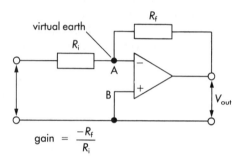

Fig. 16.16

Let the voltage at A with respect to ground be V_A. Then

$$V_{out} = AV_A.$$

But because $A \approx 10^5$, V_A must be almost zero. As before, V_+ and V_- are almost at the same potential, the amplifier being unsaturated. In this particular case because V_A is almost zero it is sometimes called a **virtual earth**.

Because of the enormous input resistance of the op. amp. almost none of the current through R_i passes through the op. amp. and so the current i in R_f equals that in R_i.

Applying Ohm's Law to R_i and R_f and assuming $V_A = 0$

we obtain $\dfrac{V_{in}}{V_{out}} = \dfrac{-iR_i}{iR_f} = \dfrac{-R_i}{R_f}$

and so the gain $= -R_f/R_i$.

The minus sign indicates that the output *inverts* the input.

An alternative circuit generates a non-inverting amplifier. Here the gain $= \dfrac{R_f + R_i}{R_i}$

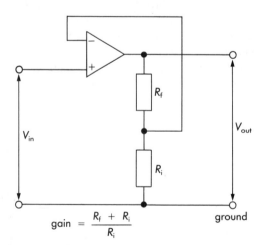

Fig. 16.17

THE OP. AMP. AS A VOLTAGE COMPARATOR

Consider the op. amp. with two inputs and no feedback in Fig. 16.18. As already explained, because of the large gain A, the operational amplifier saturates. If $V_+ > V_-$, V_{out} becomes $+ V_s$, the positive supply voltage. When $V_+ < V_-$, V_{out} 'flips' to $-V_s$. Only if V_+ is within about 60 μV of V_- will the output be anything other than $\pm V_s$. Thus the op. amp.

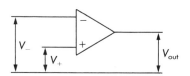

Fig. 16.18

effectively behaves as a digital two state device, comparing the two voltages. Regarding $+V_s$ as logic state 1 and $-V_s$ as logic state 0, and the non-inverting and inverting inputs as inputs A and B, the system can be described by the statement below:

IF A > B THEN OUTPUT = 1
IF B < A THEN OUTPUT = 0.

POSITIVE FEEDBACK AND ELECTRICAL OSCILLATIONS

By using **positive feedback**, i.e. feedback where the output enhances the input, the op. amp. can be used to produce a free-running oscillator. The simplest circuit to understand

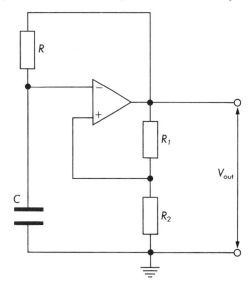

Fig. 16.19

and the easiest to set up is the **relaxation oscillator** which produces a square wave output (Fig. 16.19). It has the following properties:

a) The circuit has two possible output states.
b) Except at cross-over points the op. amp. operates as a differential amplifier with a saturated output which is either positive or negative.
c) The resistors R_1 and R_2 act as a voltage divider to determine the point at which cross-over occurs.
d) The switching frequency is determined by the time constant RC.

Consider the following simple example.

If the capacitor is initially uncharged the voltage at the inverting terminal, V_-, is zero. V_{out} may be either positive or negative. If positive, a fraction of its voltage will be fed back to the non-inverting terminal holding this positive. Because of the high gain of the op. amp. the effect of this will be to hold V_{out} in a saturated state at $+V_s$. Equally V_{out} may be negative. The same argument then holds and V_{out} will be held at $-V_s$ by this positive feedback loop.

Suppose the output voltage is initially $+V_s$. Then the behaviour with time is as shown in Fig. 16.20.

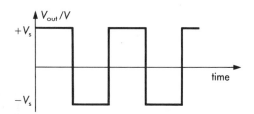

Fig. 16.20

With V_{out} at $+V_s$ volts the capacitor steadily charges through R. As it does V_- rises until at the moment when it reaches (and just exceeds) the steady value at V_+, $(V_+ - V_-)$ goes negative, and so the amplifier switches into its negative saturated state. Because V_{out} is negative V_+ must also be negative, reinforcing this. The capacitor then begins to discharge through R, and continues to do so until it has become negatively charged and reaches (and just gets lower than) the (negative) steady value at V_+. The op. amp. then switches to the positive saturated state.

Changing the capacitor C will change the cycle time of the oscillator. This is because this depends upon the time constant for discharging the capacitor. Doubling the value of the capacitance will double the cycle time. Changing the ratio of R_1 and R_2 will also change the cycle time. This is because the ratio sets the magnitude of the voltage of V_-, above and below zero at which the system changes state. As R, gets smaller with respect to R_2 this voltage gets smaller and so the cycle time will get shorter.

EXAMINATION QUESTIONS

MULTIPLE CHOICE QUESTIONS

1

	X	Y	Z
a	0	0	1
b	1	0	1
c	0	1	0
d	0	1	0
e	0	0	0

Fig. 16.21   Table 16.9

The logic circuit shown in the diagram contains two NOR gates and a NAND gate, the inputs being 1 (= high) and 0 (= low) as shown. Which line gives the correct outputs X, Y and Z?

In questions **2** to **4** below you will see diagrams of three logic circuits. Each has inputs X and Y, and the output of each is connected to a lamp. The lamp is switched ON when the output of the circuit is in logic state 1, and is switched OFF when the output is in logic state 0. In the circuits in questions **3** and **4** the inputs marked U are not connected, and these inputs are permanently in logic state 1.

Listed below are five possible combinations of logic signals to the inputs X and Y in the circuits. These combinations are lettered a to e.

a) $X = 0, Y = 0$ only
b) $X = 0, Y = 1$ only
c) $X = 1, Y = 0$ only
d) $X = 1, Y = 1$ only
e) $X = 0, Y = 1$ and $X = 1, Y = 0$ only

Consider the circuits shown in questions **2** to **4** which follow, and in each case select ONE combination of logic signals from the list above which will switch ON the lamp.

2

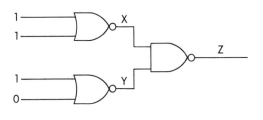

Fig. 16.22

3

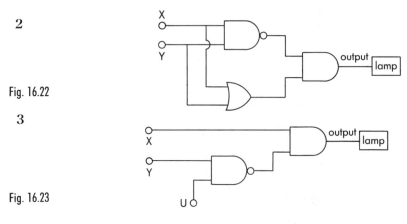

Fig. 16.23

4

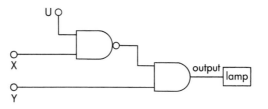

Fig. 16.24   (NI 1987)

For questions **5** and **6** select your answer using the following code:

a)	b)	c)	d)	e)
1, 2, 3 correct	1, 2 only correct	2, 3 only correct	1 only correct	3 only correct

5

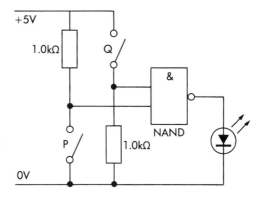

Fig. 16.25

The light emitting diode (l.e.d.) in the circuit shown in Fig. 16.25 will be on provided:
1 switches P and Q are both open;
2 switches P and Q are both closed;
3 switch P is closed and switch Q is open.

(London 1987)*

6

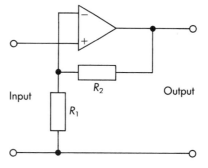

Fig. 16.26

Which of the following statements is (are) true for the circuit in Fig. 16.26?
1) The feedback is negative.
2) The voltage gain is R_2/R_1.
3) A.C. signals will be amplified but d.c. signals will not.

(London 1987 Specimen paper)*

7   The operational amplifier shown in Fig. 16.27 has an open loop gain of 10,000. When the switch S is closed V_{out} will have a value of about

a) 10 volts   d) 0.50 volts
b) −10 volts   e) 0.56 volts
c) 20 volts

* London board candidates should note that these have been provided for illustration and that from 1990 London has removed electronics from its core syllabus.

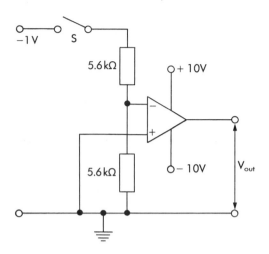

Fig. 16.27

ANSWERS AND COMMENTS

Question	1	2	3	4	5	6	7
Answer	a)	e)	c)	b)	a)	d)	a)

1 – 4 In Question **1**, work forward step by step from left to right, but with the others work from right to left. In **2** note that there are two possibilities. Both inputs to the AND gate must be high, and so one input to the OR gate must be high and one input to the NAND must be low. Answers b) and c) would be wrong because each excludes the other possibility. Note also that **3** and **4** are essentially the same questions but with X and Y interchanged.

5   Here you need to understand how the switch/resistor circuits work. With P open the bottom NAND input is high. With it closed it is low and a p.d. of 5V is applied to the lefthand 1kΩ resistor, which is used to avoid short-circuiting the supply.

6   A factual recall question.

7   The potential divider chain delivers $-0.5V$ to the inverting terminal. Hence the output is positive and the amplifier is saturated.

8   a) What do you understand by a *logic gate*?

   b) Fig. 16.28 illustrates a circuit which has inputs I_1 and I_2 and output S.

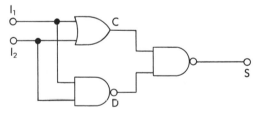

Fig. 16.28

   i) Identify the logic gates shown in Fig. 16.28 and write out their respective truth tables.

   ii) Copy out and complete the truth table shown below for the circuit.

I_1	I_2	C	D	S
0	0			
0	1			
1	0			
1	1			

Table 16.10

   iii) Describe in words the logic function of the circuit.

   c) An electric motor is to be controlled by three switches P, Q and R. The motor is to be running (logic state 1) when switches P and Q are in the same state. Whenever P and Q are in different states, the motor is to be controlled by switch R, such that the motor is running when R is in logic state 1.

i) Write out a truth table for the control circuit.

ii) Hence, using the circuit of Fig. 16.28 or otherwise, design a circuit which could be used to control the motor.

(Cambridge 1988 Part question)

9 a) Draw operational amplifier circuits (each with a gain of 10) for:
   i) an inverting amplifier;
   ii) a non-inverting voltage amplifier.

b) An a.c. voltage amplifier (based on a single operational amplifier) is set up in such a way that its amplification A can be varied. A signal generator producing a sinusoidal signal of variable frequency f is connected to the amplifier input.
Draw sketch-graphs to illustrate the *frequency response* of the amplifier (that is, how A varies with f) within the frequency range 0 to 10^6 Hz.

c) An operational amplifier oscillator circuit is set up as shown in Fig. 16.29. The output voltage at X oscillates between ± 15 V. At time $t=0$, the output voltage has just changed from -15 V to $+15$ V.

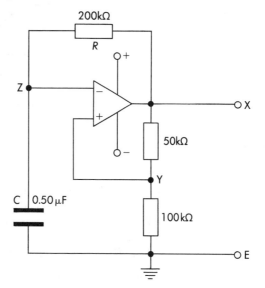

Fig. 16.29

Calculate:
   i) the voltage at point Y at $t=0$.
   ii) the current that flows through the resistor R at this moment.
   iii) the time-constant of the resistor R and the capacitor C.

d) Draw diagrams to show the traces that would be observed on the screen of a cathode-ray oscilloscope whose input terminals were connected in succession (with the same time-base setting) between:
   i) X and E;
   ii) Z and E;
   iii) X and Z.

(Oxford 1988)

OUTLINE ANSWERS AND COMMENTS

8 a) and b i) are considered in the text.

b) ii) The truth table is shown in Table 16.11.

I_1	I_2	C	D	S
0	0	0	1	1
0	1	1	1	0
1	0	1	1	0
1	1	1	0	1

Table 16.11

iii) i.e. EXNOR or parity gate.

c)

P	Q	R	Motor
0	0	0	0
0	0	1	1
0	1	0	0
0	1	1	0
1	0	0	0
1	0	1	0
1	1	0	0
1	1	1	1

Table 16.12

The circuit may be the same as in Fig. 16.28, but with P and Q replacing I_1 and I_2, and with S and R inputs to an AND gate, the output of which drives the motor.

9 a) i) See Fig. 16.16. R_f should be 100kΩ and R_i 10kΩ.
       ii) See Fig. 16.17. R_i should be 10kΩ and R_f 90kΩ.

   b)

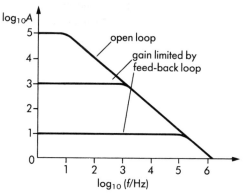

Fig. 16.30

It is best to sketch a log/log graph. With an open-loop amplifier the gain diminishes steadily with frequency. If the low frequency gain is restricted by the use of feedback then it remains at a reduced level until a frequency is reached where it is limited by the intrinsic gain of the I.C.

   c) This is the relaxation oscillator described in the text (Fig. 16.19), with $R = 200kΩ$, R_1 50kΩ and R_2 100kΩ.

   i) 10V   ii) $I = V/R = \dfrac{(15 - (-5))V}{200kΩ} = 0.1$ mA

   iii) $\tau = RC = 0.5 \times 10^{-6} \times 200 \times 10^3 = 0.1$ s.

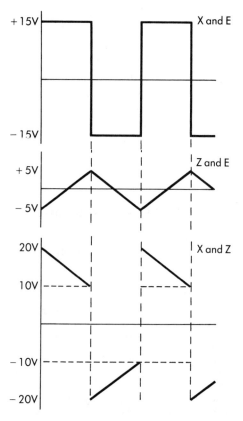

Fig. 16.31

TUTOR'S QUESTION AND ANSWER

10

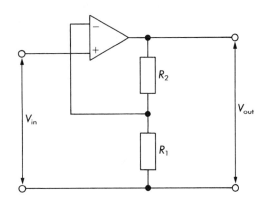

Fig. 16.32

i) This question is about the non-inverting amplifier shown above in Fig. 16.32. Explain what is meant by negative feedback and describe how it is achieved in the circuit shown. State one advantage of using negative feedback in an amplifier.

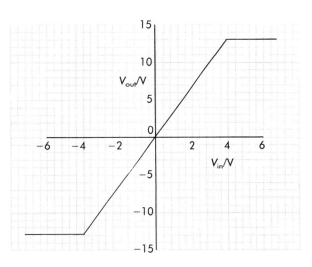

Fig. 16.33

ii) Fig. 16.33 shows how the output voltage varies with the input voltage for this amplifier. Use this graph to calculate the voltage gain of the amplifier. What value of the ration (R_2/R_1) is required to produce this gain?
What are the maximum and minimum values of the input voltage such that an input signal could be amplified without distortion?
A 3.9-V r.m.s. sinusoidal voltage of frequency 500 Hz is fed into the input of the amplifier. Sketch a graph showing how the output voltage varies with the time. Mark scales on both the time and voltage axes.

(London 1989 Part question)

10 i) Negative feedback is a term applied to an amplifier in electronics, when a fraction of the output voltage is applied to the input of the amplifier so as to *reduce* the resultant output voltage from what it would otherwise be, or, put in other words, to reduce the gain of the amplifier. In the circuit shown, the voltage gain G is given by $G = V_{out}/V_{in}$. If a rising voltage is applied to V_{in}, V_{out} will also increase and the potential divider chain will apply a voltage $\dfrac{R_1}{R_1 + R_2}$. V_{out} to the inverting terminal of the amplifier. Because this is a *rising* voltage applied to the *inverting* terminal the effect is to reduce the output voltage. In fact unless the amplifier saturates the voltage difference between the two inputs is very small so that

$$V_{in} \approx \frac{R_1}{R_1 + R_2}. \ V_{out} \text{ giving G} = \frac{R_1 + R_2}{R_1}.$$

One advantage of using negative feedback is that the gain is controlled by the resistors in the feedback circuit and not by the integrated circuit forming the amplifier. If the i.c. were to fail and had to be replaced, the overall gain would remain unchanged even though the intrinsic gain of the new i.c. might differ substantially from that of the original.

$G = $ slope of graph

$$= \frac{13}{4} = 3.25$$

Hence $\dfrac{R_1 + R_2}{R_1} = \dfrac{13}{4}$ giving $4R_2 = 9R_1$ or $\dfrac{R_2}{R_1} = 2.25$.

The graph shows that V_{in} must lie between $-4V$ and $+4V$ if a signal is to be amplified without distortion. So the maximum and minimum values of an input signal are $+4V$ and $-4V$.

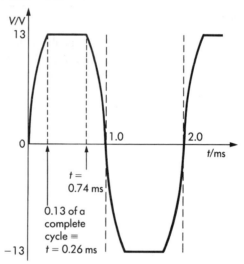

Fig. 16.34

Note that the input voltage is 3.9 V r.m.s. and so peaks at $\sqrt{2} \times 3.9V$ or 5.52V. But the amplifier saturates at $+4V$. This occurs at arcs in $\left(\dfrac{4}{5.52}\right)$ which is 46° or 0.13 of a complete cycle. Hence the graph 'clips' at $t=0.26$ms, etc. An answer with this degree of detail is within the capability of an A-grade candidate, but it was not necessary for full marks.

STUDENT'S ANSWER WITH EXAMINER COMMENTS

STUDENT'S ANSWER TO QUESTION 10

> Negative feedback is when the output is fed back to the input to reduce the output. In the circuit shown V_- and V_+ are at the same potential and hence
>
> $$\frac{V_{out}}{V_{in}} = \frac{R_1 + R_2}{R_1}$$
>
> The non-inverting input is a virtual earth.
> Negative feedback is an advantage because it avoids temperature effects in the amplifier.
>
> Voltage gain $= \dfrac{10}{3.2} = 3.1$.

66 Vague: needs further clarification. **99**

66 Analysis is correct but doesn't answer the question asked. **99**

66 Not true. Student has confused this with an inverting amplifier. Unlike that case although $V_+ \approx V_-$ neither are at ground potential. **99**

66 These need to be explained. **99**

66 Needs further explanation for a mark. **99**

66 Ratio is incorrect. **99**

66 Labelling is incorrect. This should be -13. **99**

66 The candidate has not understood r.m.s. voltage and assumed the peak input voltage is 3.9 V. **99**

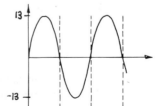

Overall comments: This is typical of a D grade candidate.

GETTING STARTED

Very recent changes in syllabuses have substantially reduced the topics which might be included in a study of **matter**. Until recently, topics in the theory of liquids such as viscosity, surface tension, and surface physics, were commonly studied, as was crystal structure in the theory of solids. Some syllabuses included the behaviour of vapours, Andrew's experiments, etc. But with recent pruning, only one or two syllabuses (AEB and JMB) are likely to include these topics, and then only in a peripheral way. In the common core, matter is largely restricted to the mechanical properties of solids and the properties and kinetic theory of gases.

So you should start with the **properties of solids**, including topics such as **plasticity** and **elasticity**. Here both the macroscopic or experimental properties should be known together with some appropriate understanding of a **microscopic** (i.e. a molecular or atomic) model. You should be able to give a broad description of the differences between **crystalline, glassy, amorphous** and **polymeric** solids. You should also be able to apply your knowledge of force and energy to an understanding of solids.

The **kinetic theory of gases** is an example of a *model* in theoretical Physics, and you should understand a simplified version of it and know how it provides an explanation of the gas laws. There are a number of formulae with which you should be familiar. Make sure you understand them and the various constants which appear in them. At the end of this topic you should have some understanding of why real gases at low pressures approximate closely to an ideal gas, and why they are used as a standard in thermometry.

GCSE Physics focusses on a general understanding of the differences between solids, liquids and gases, and some idea of the differences between their molecular structures. You should begin by revising these topics. The other topics of the chapter are hardly touched upon in GCSE, but they are ones to which other branches of Physics, principally mechanics, contribute significantly.

ESSENTIAL PRINCIPLES

**PROPERTIES
OF SOLIDS**

You should be familiar with the following terms which apply to the behaviour of solids under forces of tension and compression.

- **Stress** = F/A, where F is the force acting on unit cross-sectional area A. (The unit is $N\,m^{-2}$ or the Pascal, Pa.) Stress can be either *tensile*, as when the solid is stretched, or *compressive*, if it is compressed.

- **Breaking stress** is the greatest force per unit area that a material can withstand without fracture.

" A-level boards will only ask quantitative questions about the treatment of deformations in one dimension, i.e. bulk and shear changes are generally not considered. "

- **Strain** = e/l where e is the extension and l the original length. Because it is a ratio of distances it is dimensionless.

- **Strong** means the material can stand a large applied stress before breaking.

- **Stiff** means a large force is needed to bend the material.

- **Ductile** means the material can be easily rolled or pressed or drawn into wires.

- **Brittle** means the material cracks easily, and the broken pieces fit together showing no plastic deformation.

- **Malleable** means the material can be hammered into shape.
  Other terms such as *plastic, elastic, hysteresis*, etc. are explained in the text below.

**FORCE-
EXTENSION
AND
STRESS-STRAIN
GRAPHS**

The behaviour of a material in the form of a wire can be described in terms of either a **force-extension** or a **stress-strain graph**. The advantage of the latter is that it is characteristic of the material, so that direct comparisons between the stress-strain graphs for different materials can be made when the dimensions of the specimens are different, e.g. a steel rod can be compared with a copper wire.

MEASUREMENT OF STRESS-STRAIN CHARACTERISTICS

Any apparatus used must enable the experimenter to steadily increase the force/stress whilst simultaneously allowing accurate *measurement* of the extension/strain. In the school laboratory, a metal is usually measured in the form of a thin wire suspended from a rigid support. A tensile force/stress is applied by loading with weights. The extension/strain is measured by means of a vernier scale attached to a control wire; this automatically allows for temperature compensation. In industry purpose-built testing rigs are used with forces applied hydraulically, and strains are measured electronically using strain gauges.
The graph in Fig. 17.1 shows a typical set of results.

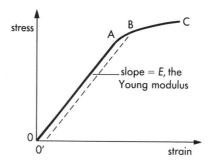

Fig. 17.1 Elastic deformation caused by stress

OA represents **elastic deformation**. Here strain is directly proportional to stress.
Tensile Stress/Tensile Strain = E, the **Young modulus**, and is the gradient of a stress-strain graph.
As Stress = F/A, we obtain $F = EAe/l$ or $E = Fl/Ae$.
B identifies the **Yield Point**. If the material is stressed beyond this point it starts to behave **plastically**. If the stress is removed, it relaxes to a point $0'$ having acquired a permanent extension or 'set' represented by $00'$.

BEHAVIOUR OF NON-METAL SAMPLES

The types of graph for non-metals vary considerably.

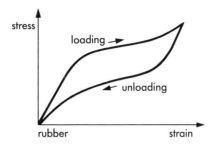

Fig. 17.2 Rubber

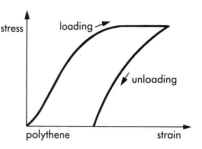

Fig. 17.3 Polythene

For both Fig. 17.2 and Fig. 17.3, the curve obtained on unloading is different from that on loading. This is called **hysteresis**. Rubber regains its original length and is **elastic**. Polythene becomes permanently stretched and so is **plastic**.

ENERGY

The energy W stored in a stretched wire is given by:

$$W = \tfrac{1}{2}kx^2,$$

where k is the Hooke constant and x the extension.

This formula comes from the definition: 'Work done = force × distance moved'. So the area under a force/extension graph gives the work done in loading the wire (Fig. 17.4).

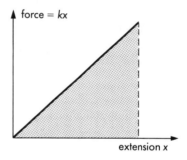

Fig. 17.4 Force/extension graph

Thus:

$$W = \tfrac{1}{2}Fe.$$

Division by the volume of the wire Al gives the energy per unit volume:

$$\frac{\tfrac{1}{2}Fe}{Al} = \tfrac{1}{2} \times \frac{F}{A} \times \frac{e}{l} = \tfrac{1}{2}\,(\text{stress}) \times (\text{strain})$$

MICROSCOPIC UNDERSTANDING

Figs. 17.5 and 17.6 show the variation of force and potential energy respectively against separation for a single pair of atoms or molecules.

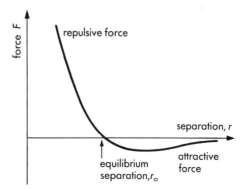

Fig. 17.5 Graph of force against separation

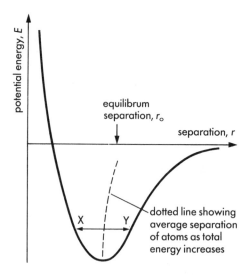

Fig. 17.6 Graph of potential energy against separation

a) The equilibrium separation is r_0, the force being zero. For $r > r_0$, the force is attractive and energy must be supplied to increase the separation.

b) For $r < r_0$, the force is repulsive and energy has to be supplied to decrease the separation.

c) So at $r = r_0$ the potential energy is a minimum corresponding to zero force. In general $F = -\dfrac{\mathrm{d}E}{\mathrm{d}r}$, i.e. the force is the slope of the potential/energy graph.

d) Energy is needed to completely separate the atoms.

e) When atoms are oscillating as they do in a solid, the potential energy varies with separation as shown by the curve between X and Y. As the temperature increases, the atoms have more energy and the amplitude of the oscillations is greater. The average separation is shown by the dotted line which shows that solids expand on heating.

TYPES OF SOLID

CRYSTALLINE SOLIDS

These are solids where the atoms, ions or molecules are found in a regular repeating structure called a lattice. Crystals are usually 3-dimensional, but 2-dimensional ones exist such as graphite and those used in liquid crystal displays in electronics. Examples of crystal structure are shown, somewhat schematically, in Figs 17.7 to 17.9.

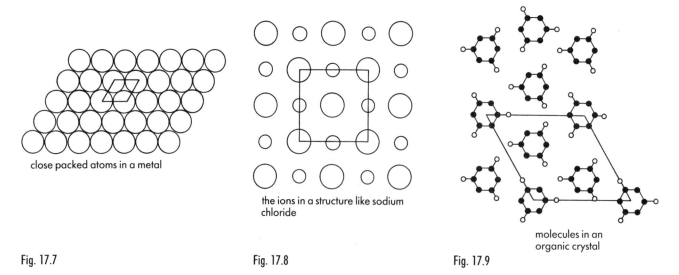

close packed atoms in a metal

the ions in a structure like sodium chloride

molecules in an organic crystal

Fig. 17.7   Fig. 17.8   Fig. 17.9

The heavy line indicates the unit cell or the basic repeat unit. Bonding may be of several types which may generally be of more importance in Chemistry at A Level than in Physics. **Ionic** bonding is caused by electrostatic attraction between ions of opposite charge. The bond is non-directional. **Covalent** bonding is a quantum-mechanical effect which results from atoms sharing electrons, and is a directional bond. **Metallic** bonding is an even more complicated quantum-mechanical effect, resulting from interactions between the 'sea' of conduction electrons and the lattice of ions. **Van der Waals** bonding is due to molecules behaving as electric dipoles which can weakly attract one another.

Many solids, including most metals, are actually crystalline, but with the crystal structure only apparent at a microscopic level. A piece of copper, for example, consists of a large number of microcrystals, each much smaller than a millimetre in length.

AMORPHOUS OR GLASSY MATERIALS

Substances of this kind do not have the same degree of order as is found with the crystalline form. Fig. 17.10 shows the typical structure of glass. The rigidity of a crystal structure is missing, and there is a viscosity which steadily decreases with temperature. However, when the viscosity gets very large at very low temperatures, the glass can become elastic and brittle.

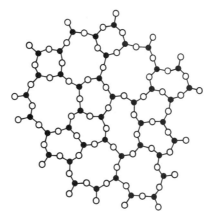

Fig. 17.10 Structure of glass

POLYMERIC MATERIALS

A **polymer** is a long chain consisting of hundreds or thousands of identical units. Each unit is basically itself a small molecule, and the chain is formed when these molecules link together. The distance between units is fixed, but the chain can be bent and can curl up. Chains can slide past each other as the forces between them are weak. In some polymers the chains are tangled. An everyday example is rubber, where on being strained, the individual polymer chains straighten out and slide past parallel chains. As a result there is a much larger deformation before breaking than in a crystal. However once the chains are fully stretched out it becomes difficult to stretch the substance further, and it then breaks.

THE GASEOUS STATE

The gaseous state of matter is the state in which the molecules are no longer in close contact with each other but move separately throughout the space available to them. Strictly speaking the term *gas* should only be used when above the substance's **critical temperature**. This is the temperature above which the gas cannot be liquified by compression alone. The term **vapour** is used below this temperature. Below the critical temperature, liquefaction can occur by simply compressing the gas. When a closed vessel contains a vapour in equilibrium with its liquid, the vapour is called a **saturated vapour**; otherwise it is **unsaturated**.

At very high temperatures, the collisions between molecules become so energetic that ionisation takes place. The gas is then called a **plasma**.

THE GAS LAW

The **Gas Laws** provide a good description of both gases and unsaturated vapours. The laws are:

■ **Boyle's Law**
   For a fixed mass of gas at constant temperature, pressure is inversely proportional to volume i.e.

$$p \propto \frac{1}{V} ,$$

or pV = constant

or $p_1V_1 = p_2V_2$.

- **Charles' Law**
  For a fixed mass of gas at constant pressure, the volume increases by $\dfrac{1}{273}$ rd of its volume at 0°C for each degree C rise in temperature *or*, as an equivalent statement, the volume is directly proportional to the absolute temperature i.e.

$$V/T = \text{constant, or} \frac{V_1}{T_1} = \frac{V_2}{T_2}\ .$$

- **The Pressure Law**
  For a fixed amount of gas at constant volume, the pressure increases by $\dfrac{1}{273}$ rd of the pressure at 0°C for each degree C rise in temperature, *or*, as in equivalent statement, the pressure is directly proportional to the absolute temperature.
  These three laws are combined in the **general gas equation**:

$$pV = nRT,$$

where p is in Pa, V in m³, n is the number of moles of gas present, and R is the molar gas constant.

Note that a mole of a gas is defined as the amount of a gas containing as many molecules as there are carbon atoms in 12 grams of carbon 12. R is $8.31\ \text{J mol}^{-1}\ \text{K}^{-1}$.

IDEAL GAS AND THE KINETIC THEORY MODEL

An **ideal gas** perfectly obeys the general gas equation. In constructing a theoretical model, the main assumptions that are made are:

i) the gas is largely empty space in which a very large number of molecules are moving about in random directions at high speed, colliding with each other and the walls of the container;

ii) the intermolecular forces are negligible except during collisions;

iii) the volume occupied by the molecules is negligible compared with the volume of the gas;

iv) there is no loss of energy in the collision process, i.e. the collisions are 'elastic'.

DERIVATION OF THE $p = \frac{1}{3}\rho<c^2>$ FORMULA

Look up your text-book for a derivation. In the A Level examination, a very simplified treatment will suffice, such as considering the gas particles as spheres moving in a rectangular box with the statistics treated by dividing them into three groups, one third travelling in each of the three dimensions of space.

Note the meaning of $<c^2>$. The **root mean square** (r.m.s.) **speed** of the gas molecules is the square root of the mean value of the molecular speeds i.e.

$$\text{r.m.s. speed} = \sqrt{<c^2>}$$

$$= \left(\sqrt{\frac{(c_1{}^2 + c_2{}^2 + \ldots + c_N{}^2)}{N}} \right.$$

where $c_1, c_2, \ldots c_N$ are the individual molecular speeds.

The formula $p = \frac{1}{3}\rho<c^2>$ can be written:

$$p = \frac{1}{3}\ \frac{Nm<c^2>}{V}\ ,\qquad \text{where } N \text{ is the number of molecules, } m \text{ the mass of each mole-cule, and } V \text{ the volume.}$$

When one mole is considered this becomes:

$$pV = \tfrac{1}{3}\ N_A m\ <c^2>.$$

Here N_A is the **Avogadro constant**, 6.02×10^{23} particles mol.$^{-1}$

MEANING OF TEMPERATURE AND HEAT CAPACITY

Rearranging the expression for pV:

$$pV = \tfrac{2}{3}N_A(\tfrac{1}{2}m<c^2>).$$

$\tfrac{1}{2}m<c^2>$ is the *mean kinetic energy* of a gas molecule, and this is also equal to its mean total energy as it has no potential energy. The experimental result embodied in the general gas equation is $pV = RT$ for one mole. Combining these two equations gives:

$$RT = \tfrac{2}{3}(N_A \times \tfrac{1}{2}m <c^2>)$$
$$= \tfrac{2}{3}(\text{total energy of 1 mole of the gas}),$$

and hence a meaning to temperature, T, and heat capacity.

Rearranging, we get:

Total energy of 1 mole of the gas $= \tfrac{3}{2}RT.$

Thus the energy required to raise the temperature of 1 mole of the gas by $1K = \tfrac{3}{2}R$, i.e. its molar heat capacity at constant volume, c_V, (for a monatomic gas).

Also, dividing $RT = \tfrac{2}{3}(N_A \times \tfrac{1}{2}m<c^2>)$ by N_A gives

$$\frac{RT}{N_A} = kT = \tfrac{2}{3}(\text{mean energy of a molecule}),$$

where $k = R/N_A$ is the **Boltzmann constant** $(= 1.38 \times 10^{-23}\,\text{J K}^{-1}).$

Thus $\tfrac{1}{2}m<c^2> = \tfrac{3}{2}kT,$

showing that the temperature T is proportional to the mean kinetic energy of a gas molecule.

DISTRIBUTION OF MOLECULAR SPEEDS IN A GAS

The theory so far, and the use of the root mean square speed $\sqrt{<c^2>}$ is only approximate. A more accurate treatment results in the graph of Fig. 17.11 which shows the general way in which the molecular velocities are distributed and the effect of an increase in temperature.

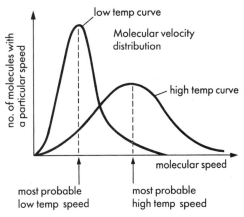

Fig. 17.11 Molecular velocity distribution

Neither the derivation nor the explicit formula for the curves are required at A Level, but you should note the following features:
i) the molecular speeds range from zero to infinity;
ii) the speed for which the curve is a maximum is the most probable speed, i.e. the most likely speed found in an experimental measurement.

EXPERIMENTAL EVIDENCE

Experimental evidence in support of the kinetic theory of gases is provided by the phenomena of *diffusion* and *Brownian motion*.

Diffusion is the phenomenon in which a quantity of one gas introduced into another will gradually spread out until it is evenly spread throughout the containing vessel. The process takes some time because of the random collisions of the molecules with each other. Measurements of the speed of diffusion, and the differences between the behaviour of gases of different molecular weights at the same temperature are in agreement with theoretical predictions made with kinetic theory.

Brownian motion is the name given to the microscopic movements of smoke particles in air. These can be observed when a sample of smoke is illuminated and observed with a microscope. The movements are random and are caused by the random bombardments of the smoke particles by the much smaller, lighter, and faster moving invisible air molecules.

EXAMINATION QUESTIONS

MULTIPLE CHOICE QUESTIONS

1 One mole of a monatomic ideal gas is at temperature T. If the molar gas constant is R, what is the total kinetic energy of the molecules of the gas?

a) $\frac{1}{3}RT$ d) RT
b) $\frac{1}{2}RT$ e) $\frac{3}{2}RT$
c) $\frac{2}{3}RT$

(Oxford 1988)

2 A fixed mass of an ideal gas at pressure P is cooled at constant volume until the pressure becomes $\dfrac{P}{2}$. What will be the r.m.s. speed of the molecules if their r.m.s. speed was originally c?

a) $\dfrac{c}{2}$ d) $2c$
       e) $c/4$
b) $\dfrac{c}{\sqrt{2}}$

c) $c\sqrt{2}$

(JMB 1988)

3 1 g of hydrogen (relative molecular mass 2) is enclosed in a certain volume and exerts a pressure of 16 kPa. The same mass of oxygen (relative molecular mass 32) contained in the same volume at the same temperature would exert a pressure of:

a) 1 kPa d) 64 kPa
b) 4 kPa e) 256 kPa
c) 16 kPa

(London 1987)

4 During an experiment involving a fixed mass of gas, the kelvin temperature is trebled and the volume is doubled. Due to these changes the pressure is:

a) $\frac{1}{6}$ of its original value   d) $1\frac{2}{3}$ times its original value
b) $\frac{2}{3}$ of its original value   e) 6 times its original value
c) $1\frac{1}{2}$ times its original value

(Scottish 1985)

5 Which of the following changes would lead to the greatest increase in the pressure of a gas in a container?

a) Doubling the number of molecules in the gas.
b) Doubling the r.m.s. speed of the molecules.
c) Doubling the Kelvin temperature of the gas.
d) Doubling the volume of the container.
e) Doubling the mass of the gas in the container.

(Scottish 1986)

6 A sample of material was stretched and then allowed to contract. A stress-strain graph was obtained as shown. Which one of the following may be deduced from Fig. 17.12?

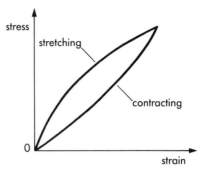

Fig. 17.12

a) More work is done in stretching than is recovered in contracting.
b) The Young modulus for the material is a constant.
c) The temperature of the material falls as it is stretched.
d) The material is permanently deformed.
e) All the work done in stretching the material is converted into potential energy.

(AEB 1987)

7 The graph in Fig. 17.13 shows how the force exerted by one molecule, positioned at O, on a similar molecule varies with the distance the molecules are apart. Which of the following gives the approximate separation between the molecules when the material is in the solid state and when it is in the gas state?

	Solid state	Gas state
a)	OP	OQ
b)	OP	OR
c)	OP	OS
d)	OQ	OR
e)	OQ	OS

Fig. 17.13

(Scottish 1985)

Answer questions **8** and **9** using the following code

a) 1, 2, 3 correct   d) 1 only
b) 1 and 2 only   e) 3 only
c) 2 and 3 only

8 The behaviour of vulcanised rubber when subjected to an extending force is shown in Fig. 17.14. When the force is removed, the stress-strain curve does not retrace its original path OPQ but follows the curve QRO. Which of the following is (are) correct?

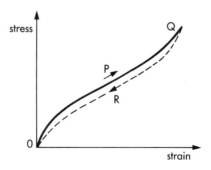

Fig. 17.14

1) When a load is applied and then removed energy is dissipated in the rubber.
2) If the Young modulus is defined for such a case as the slope of the stress-strain curve at a point, then the Young modulus for rubber increases with stress throughout the range covered by the diagram.
3) After application and removal of the extending force the rubber will have acquired a permanent set.

(London 1987)

9 Which of the following statements about glassy substances is (are) correct?

   1) At low temperature plastic behaviour is apparent at the end of long time intervals only.
   2) The positions of the molecules within the substances do not form a geometrical pattern.
   3) Such substances do not have identifiable melting points.

(London 1987)

ANSWERS AND COMMENTS

Question	1	2	3	4	5	6	7	8	9
Answer	e)	b)	a)	c)	b)	a)	e)	d)	a)

1 A question requiring recall of knowledge.

2 $<c^2>$ is proportional to T and so is p. Hence a halving of pressure occurs with a halving of absolute temperature.

3 Here it is the dependence on the number of molecules present which is the key factor. If there is the same mass of oxygen, there will be only 1/16th of the number of molecules and only 1/16th of the number of molecular bombardments per second and hence only 1/16th of the previous pressure. Don't make the mistake of applying the formula $p = \frac{1}{3}\rho<c^2>$ and assuming that because the gas density is the same, the pressure is unchanged. This is because $<c^2>$ is reduced when oxygen replaces hydrogen.

4 Requires use of $pV = nRT$. Rearranging we get $p \propto T/V$, and hence
$$\frac{p_2}{p_1} = \frac{T_2 V_1}{T_1 V_2}$$ where the index 1 refers to the earlier quantity and 2 to the latter.

5 a), c) and e) double the pressure, but b) quadruples it because of $p = \frac{1}{3}\rho<c^2>$.

6 b), d) and e) are false. Of the other two alternatives a) is the only one which can be made on the basis of the graph.

7 Note how the y-axis is inverted from the more usual form, (e.g. Fig. 17.5). The question is similar to Question **12**, part b).

8 Note that statement 2) is incorrect because the slope of the graph, equal to the Young modulus, increases, decreases and then increases again.

9 Recall again.

STRUCTURED QUESTIONS

10 A long rod is stretched by the application of a tensile force, F; define a) stress, b), strain, for such a case. Prove that the work done in the stretching is the area under the Force-Extension curve in Fig. 17.15 a) and b).

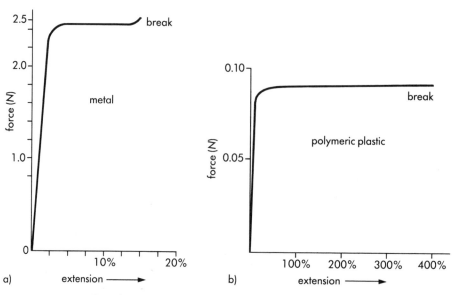

Fig. 17.15

(force/extension) curves: extension is % of original length

Fig. 17.15 gives Force-Extension curves for two identically shaped rods of a polymeric plastic and of a metal.
i) Compare the breaking stresses of the two materials.
ii) Compare the work done in breaking them.
iii) Explain your results in terms of the molecular structure of such materials.

(Welsh 1985)

11 Fig. 17.16 shows how the potential energy $\phi(r)$ of a pair of molecules varies with molecular separation r.

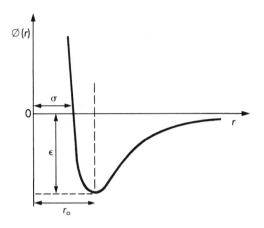

Fig. 17.16

a) Explain what the symbols i) ϵ, ii) r_0, iii) σ represent.
b) Given that a solid melts when the average thermal energy of a pair of molecules is $\epsilon/10$, divide the figure into appropriate regions labelled 'solid,' 'liquid',' 'gas'.

(Welsh 1987)

12 a) Find the volume occupied by one mole of an ideal gas at a temperature of 290 K and a pressure of 1.0×10^5 Pa.
b) The diameter of a molecule of this gas is 2.5×10^{-10} m. What fraction of the volume you have calculated in a) above do the molecules occupy?
Take the gas content as 8.31 J mol^{-1} K^{-1} and the Avogadro number as 6.02×10^{23}.

(Cambridge 1987)

13 The kinetic theory of gases sets out to explain the properties of gases in terms of the random motion of particles. Explain *qualitatively* how this theory accounts for:
i) the pressure exerted by a gas on the walls of its container.
ii) why this pressure increases if the volume of the container gets smaller while the temperature of the gas stays constant, and
iii) why the pressure increases if the temperature rises while the volume stays constant.
The kinetic theory leads to the relation:
$p = \frac{1}{3}\rho\langle c^2\rangle.$ 　　　　　　　　　　　　　　　　　　　　　(1)
The general gas equation is often written:

$$pV = \frac{m}{M} RT = nRT.$$ 　　　　　　　　(2)

Explain the symbols n and $\langle c^2\rangle$.
Show how, by means of *one* assumption, the second equation can be derived from the first. State this assumption.
All molecules in a mixture of gases at one temperature have, on average, the same kinetic energy. How does this principle account for Brownian motion?

(London 1987 Part question)

OUTLINE ANSWERS AND COMMENTS

10 a) Stress $= \dfrac{\text{applied tensile force}}{\text{cross-sectional area of sample}}$

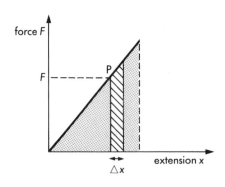

Fig. 17.17

b) Strain $=$ $\dfrac{\text{change in length of a sample}}{\text{its original length}}$

Consider point P of the force/extension graph. Suppose at this point the force is F. If the wire is extended by a further small amount $\triangle x$ the work done is $F\triangle x$, equal, to first approximation, to the shaded area. Clearly if all the stages of stretching are considered a series of strips under the curve would be accumulated, each corresponding to the work done in a particular stage. Hence the area under the graph is equal to the work done. Let the original length of each sample be l and the original area of cross section be A.

i) In the case of the metal the final length is about $1.16\, l$. If the volume of the sample remains the same then the area of cross section becomes $\dfrac{A}{1.16}$, so the breaking stress is $\dfrac{2.5 \times 1.16}{A}$

$= \dfrac{2.90}{A}$ Pa.

For the polymeric plastic the final length is $5l$. Therefore the final cross sectional area is $\dfrac{A}{5}$, and the breaking stress is

$\dfrac{0.9 \times 5}{A} = \dfrac{4.50}{A}$ Pa.

So more stress is needed by the plastic, by a factor of 1.55.

ii) For the metal the break occurs at $0.16l$, so the area under the curve (work done) is approximately $2.5 \times 0.16l = 0.40l$ J.

For the polymeric plastic we obtain $0.9 \times 4l = 3.6l$ J.

Thus more work is done in the case of the polymer by a factor of 9.

Thus the explanation needs to consider that whilst the breaking stresses are about the same, considerably more work is done in breaking the polymeric plastic. A really good answer would need to point to the comparative ease of stretching a metal, due to the movement of dislocations. And for the polymer there would need to be reference to the breaking of cross-linkages.

> **Note the need to make allowance for the change in cross-sectional area.**

11 a) ϵ represents the energy needed to completely separate the molecules from the equilibrium separation which is r_0. σ represents the distance at which one molecule starts to experience the 'hard sphere' repulsive force of the other. So σ represents the distance apart of the two centres, or two molecular radii.

b)

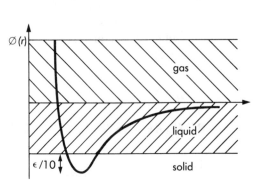

Fig. 17.18

12 a) Using $pV = nRT$,
we have $p = 1 \times 10^5$ Pa, $n = 1$, $R = 8.31$ J mol^{-1} K^{-1} and $T = 290$ K
giving $V = 0.0241$ m^3.

b) 1 mole contains 6.02×10^{23} particles
Volume of 1 molecule $= \frac{4}{3}\pi r^3 = 8.18 \times 10^{-30}$ m^3,
so total volume $= 4.92 \times 10^{-6}$ m^3,
and required fraction $= 2.04 \times 10^{-4}$ or 1/4893.

13 In the first part of the question candidates are simply expected to rehearse the appropriate elements of the kinetic theory model.

i) The molecules bounce off the walls of the container elastically. As they do so their components of momentum normal to the wall are reversed, i.e. there is a change in momentum normal to the wall. With a very large number of particles moving randomly this amounts to a continuous rate of change of momentum. Newton's 2nd law says that there will be a force equal to the rate of change of momentum. It is this force which is the origin of the pressure of the gas.

ii) If the volume of the container is reduced the number of particles per unit volume is increased. This increases the rate at which unit area of the walls is bombarded, and hence increases the pressure.

iii) Kinetic theory associates an increase of temperature with an increase in the internal energy of the gas, i.e. in an increase in the kinetic energy of the particles. With the particles moving at a higher speed there is an increase in the change in momentum on collision with the walls and more collisions per second. Hence both the force exerted and the pressure are increased. n and $<c^2>$ are explained in the text.

In equation 1: $\rho = \dfrac{m}{V}$

so 1 becomes $\rho = \frac{1}{3}\dfrac{m}{V}<c^2>$. Call this equation (3)

Assuming that $\frac{3}{2}RT = $ the kinetic energy of 1 mole
we have $\frac{3}{2}RT = \frac{1}{2}M<c^2>$.
(Note M is the molar mass, and m the mass of gas).
Hence $<c^2> = 3RT/M$, and hence, by substitution in (3), the result.

In Brownian motion the smoke particles move in equilibrium with the gas particles. The average kinetic energy of a smoke particle is equal to the average kinetic energy of a gas molecule. So the smoke particles move randomly, as do the molecules, but with smaller speeds on account of their much larger masses.

TUTOR'S QUESTION AND ANSWER

QUESTION

14 a) Give the meanings of the terms *tensile stress* and *Young modulus*. Define the quantity which relates these terms.

b) When measuring the Young modulus of a material it is common to use a specimen which is i) very long, and ii) very thin. Give the reasons for this.
Describe how you would measure accurately the extension of such a wire under an applied load.

c)

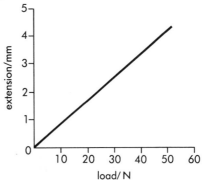

Fig. 17.19

Fig. 17.19 shows how the extension of a wire varies with the load applied to it. The wire used has a length 3.00 m and a diameter 5.0×10^{-4} m.

i) Calculate the tensile stress produced by a load of 50 N.
ii) Find the energy stored in the wire when this load is acting.
iii) Calculate the reduction in gravitational potential energy of a 5.0 kg mass used to provide the load.
iv) Suggest why the answers to ii) and iii) above are different.
v) Calculate the Young modulus for the metal of the wire.

(Southern 1987)

ANSWER

14 a) See text (p.184).

b) The formula $F = EA \dfrac{e}{l}$ applies, where F is the applied force, E the Young modulus, A the cross sectional area, e the extension and l the original length. Rearranging, $e = \dfrac{Fl}{EA}$. As the measured quantity and dependent variable of the experiment is e, it follows that the larger e can be made for a given force F, (the independent variable) the better. The formula shows that e is proportional to l and inversely proportional to A. Hence a very long and very thin specimen will have comparatively large values of e.

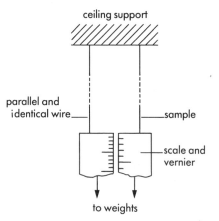

Fig. 17.20

To measure the extension accurately I would hang the wire sample from a ceiling support. I would also hang a parallel identical wire close to it (the control) and clamp a mm scale to the sample and a corresponding vernier scale to the parallel wire. The control wire should be lightly loaded so that it is taut and therefore straight. On loading the sample I would be able to compare the extension with that of the control wire. If there were a temperature change both wires would expand by the same amount with no effect on the scale.

i) Force, $F = 50$ N.
Cross sectional area $A = \pi \dfrac{d^2}{4}$, where d is the wire diameter.

Hence $A = \pi \times \dfrac{(5 \times 10^{-4} \text{m})^2}{4} = 1.96 \times 10^{-7} \text{ m}^2$

Stress $= F/A = 2.54 \times 10^8$ Pa.
ii) Extension $= 4$ mm
Energy stored $= \frac{1}{2}$ force $\times$ extension
$\frac{1}{2} \times 50 \times 0.004$ J $= 0.1$ J
iii) With a 5 kg mass, and taking g as 10 N kg^{-1}, the reduction in potential energy
$= mgh$
$= 5 \times 10 \times 0.004$
$= 0.2$ J
iv) Loading the wire is like loading a spring. If the load were attached to a spring it would fall downwards, move past the equilibrium position and then oscillate

about that position until the excess energy was dissipated by air friction or by damping forces in the spring itself. The same is true of the wire.

$$\text{v)} \quad E = \frac{Fl}{Ae} = \frac{50 \times 3}{1.96 \times 10^{-7} \times 0.004} = 1.91 \times 10^{11} \text{ Pa}$$

STUDENT'S ANSWER WITH EXAMINER COMMENTS

STUDENT'S ANSWER TO QUESTION 14 c)

i) $\text{Stress} = \dfrac{\text{load}}{\text{Area}} = \dfrac{50\text{N}}{\pi \times (2.5 \times 10^{-4})^2}$

$$= 254647909 \ \frac{\text{N}}{\text{m}^2}$$

> The calculation is correct but too many significant figures are quoted: a result of bad practice with a calculator. Be guided by the number quoted in the question. The load is quoted to 2 significant figures and the diameter also. Two would therefore be appropriate in the answer. This error is common, although not in this extreme form. Note also that N/m^2 could be simplified to Pa.

ii) Energy stored $= \frac{1}{2}$ (stress) (strain)

$$\text{strain} = \frac{4\,\text{mm}}{3\,\text{m}} = 1.3333 \times 10^{-3}$$

$$\text{Energy} = \tfrac{1}{2}\,(254647909)\,(1.3333 \times 10^{-3})$$

$$= 16978.2 \text{ J}$$

> Here the wrong formula is used. The formula (Stress)/(Strain) is the formula for the energy *per unit volume*. The student should have recognised this error by noticing that the units are those of stress (i.e. pascals), strain being dimensionless. The units required are joules.

> This is just a small point, but it should have been clear from the wording of the question that g is to be taken as 10.

iii) Loss of p.e. $= 50 \times 9.81 \times 0.004$

$$= 0.1962 \text{ J}$$

iv) This is because the wire heats up on being loaded.

> A desperate and unconvincing attempt to slide over the discrepancy. Examiners don't trick candidates and this huge discrepancy should have caused the candidate to check his working.

v) Young's Modulus $= \text{Stress/strain}$

$$= \frac{254647909}{1.33 \times 10^{-3}}$$

$$= 1.9 \times 10^{11} \ \frac{\text{N}}{\text{m}}$$

> Much better use of significant figures.

> The index 2 has been left off the m. This may be only a hurried slip but it will be penalised. The examiner will assume the units are misunderstood.

Overall comments: There are quite a number of common errors here, all of which could have been avoided. It is typical of a C/D candidate.

GETTING STARTED

In everyday life motion is usually obtained by a cycle of events which starts with the combustion of fuel. The conversion of 'heat' to 'work' in this way is crucial to our civilisation, and is the reason why a study of heat is central to Physics.

In Chapter 17 the related topic of **kinetic theory** was studied. Here we begin by considering topics of a more practical and experimental nature. **Calorimetry** and an understanding of **specific heat** and **latent heat** are frequently expected in GCSE study. You should start by revising these topics, and then move on to temperature scales including the scale based upon the properties of an ideal gas. **Thermodynamics** should be studied at least as far as the **First Law** of thermodynamics. A.E.B. and Nuffield require some understanding of **entropy** and the **Second Law**. Some knowledge of entropy is useful even if not explicitly required in your syllabus.

Thermal conduction is a small but important topic regularly examined in all syllabuses. Physically it is an example of a 'transport phenomenon' and is related to electrical conduction and diffusion. **Radiation** is only examined in detail by some boards. As with entropy, it is briefly included here because of the usefulness of the ideas.

Some boards, but not all, frequently set questions on the principles of the experimental measurements of specific heats of solids and liquids and of the specific heat of vaporisation, and so this is also covered.

ESSENTIAL PRINCIPLES

TEMPERATURE SCALES

Before the invention of thermometers and **temperature scales** people were only able to record how hot or cold it was by their subjective impressions or by the effect on certain critical material phenomena. For example, in a particularly bad winter in Norfolk in the eighteenth century, a diarist noted that it was cold enough for the urine in his bedroom chamber pot to freeze. Thermometers and temperature scales were invented so that numbers could be assigned to particular degrees of hotness (or coldness). All systems use two fixed points. Before 1954 the fixed points were the ice point (labelled 0°C on the Celsius scale) and the steam point (labelled 100°C). A particular material property which changes with temperature is then used to give numerical values to temperatures. It should be noted that the expression 'temperature scale' as used here refers to the particular material property (**themometric property**) used, e.g. the expansion of mercury. It should *not* be confused with the scale *notation* e.g. Celsius, Kelvin, etc.

At 0°C, the value X_0 of the material property X, is found and plotted at the point P (Fig. 18.1). At 100°C the value X_{100} is found and plotted at Q. At another temperature t°C, X_t is

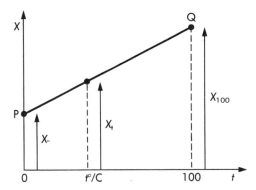

Fig. 18.1

measured. A straight line graph is drawn through P and Q, and the temperature t°C read off. Notice how the straight line graph locks the temperature scale on to the change in the material property between the fixed points.

An inspection of the diagram gives the formula:

$$\frac{t°/C}{100} = \frac{X_t - X_0}{X_{100} - X_0}$$

Check your textbook for experimental details of mercury-in-glass, gas pressure, platinum resistance, and thermocouple (i.e. e.m.f.), thermometers, where this formula is used. In the case of the two electrical methods you should memorise the electrical circuits used. You need to be aware of the use of temperature switching circuits in electronics (see Chapter 16). You should also recognise clearly that because different physical properties vary differently with temperature, only at the two fixed points will temperatures measured on different types of thermometer agree.

USE OF THE TRIPLE POINT OF WATER

Since 1954 the two fixed points have been the absolute zero of temperature: 0 K, and the **triple point of water** (the temperature at which ice, liquid water, and water vapour coexist) 273.16 K (nearly 0.01°C).

Then $T = 273.16\, X_T/X_{tr}$,

where T is the temperature on the Kelvin scale, X_T the value of the material property at this temperature, and X_{tr} the value at the triple point of water.

ABSOLUTE TEMPERATURE SCALE

Kelvin proposed that there should be an **absolute scale of temperature** based upon the behaviour of gases at low pressure. Gases like this obey the general gas equation, $pV = nRT$ (see Chapter 17) and are like ideal gases. This makes the scale effectively independent of the properties of any particular material (gas) and therefore can be used as a standard. If the pressure of the gas is measured at constant volume, then:

$$T = 273.16 \, p_T/p_{tr},$$

where p_T is the pressure at a temperature T and p_{tr} the pressure at the triple point. Alternatively if only the mass of gas is held constant, i.e. the volume can vary, the formula used is:

$$T = 273.16 \, \frac{(pV)_T}{(pV)_{tr}}.$$

This absolute scale is also known by other names: absolute thermodynamic scale; gas scale, ideal gas scale. You should be familiar with all of these names.

Conversion from the Kelvin to the Celsius notation is obtained using:

$$t/°C = \frac{T}{K} - 273.15.$$

You should look up your text-book for details of an experimental arrangement for the constant volume gas thermometer.

CALORIMETRY

Calorimetry will not be explicitly tested at A Level except in Multiple Choice Questions. However, it should be understood and will be tested implicitly in other questions. You need to be aware of the following terms.

TERMINOLOGY

- **Thermal Capacity** (C): the quantity of heat required to raise the temperature of a body by 1 degree.

- **Specific heat capacity** (c): the heat capacity per unit mass, i.e. per kg.

    So $C = mc$, and $Q = mc\triangle\theta$,

    where Q is the heat or thermal energy supplied and $mc\triangle\theta$ the increase in internal energy, and where $\triangle\theta$ is the change in temperature.

    Hence if $\dfrac{d\theta}{dt}$ is the rate of temperature rise, $\dfrac{dQ}{dt}$ the rate of supply of thermal energy, is given by:

    $$\frac{dQ}{dt} = mc \frac{d\theta}{dt}$$

    For gases, molar heat capacities may be used.

- **Molar heat capacity of a gas at constant volume** (C_V): the quantity of thermal energy required to produce a 1 degree rise in temperature of a gas when the volume is kept constant.

- **Molar heat capacity of a gas at constant pressure** (C_p): the quantity of thermal energy required to produce a 1 degree rise in temperature of a gas when the pressure is kept constant.

- **Specific latent heat of fusion** (l_m): the quantity of thermal energy required to change unit mass of a substance from solid to liquid without change of temperature.

- **Specific latent heat of vaporisation** (l_v): the quantity of thermal energy required to change unit mass of a substance from liquid to vapour without change of temperature.

Note that for these last two, the London board uses the term *enthalpy change* and *specific enthalpy change*. An **enthalpy** change is a change which takes place at constant pressure.

EXPERIMENTAL METHODS IN CALORIMETRY

Most methods for determining the specific heats of solids or liquids or the latent heat of

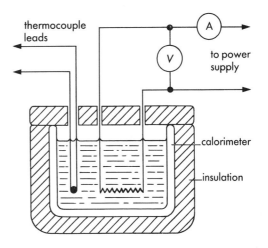

Fig. 18.2 Circuit for measuring the specific heat capacity of a liquid

vaporisation are electrical. A typical circuit used for measuring the specific heat capacity of a liquid is shown in Fig. 18.2. It uses an insulated calorimeter.

The liquid is heated for a time, t, using the heating element. The temperature increase should be measured with a thermocouple thermometer as this will have a very low thermal capacity. The thermal capacity, C, of the calorimeter needs to be known. The specific heat capacity, c, of the liquid is then found from:

$$IVt = mc\triangle\theta + c\triangle\theta,$$

where I is the current, V the potential difference, t the time, m the mass of liquid under test and $\triangle\theta$ the temperature rise.

Some correction for heat loss is needed for accurate work. You will not be asked for details of this at A Level. The simplest way of avoiding a heat loss correction is to begin heating with the calorimeter and liquid at a temperature $\dfrac{\triangle\theta}{2}$ *below* room temperature and to heat to $\dfrac{\triangle\theta}{2}$ *above* it. The heat gained from the background in the first half of the heating cycle is then equal to the heat lost in the second half.

The specific heat c_s of an insoluble solid of mass m_s can be found using the same apparatus by adding a small sample of the solid to the liquid.

Then $IVt = (mc + m_s c_s)\triangle\theta + C\Delta\theta$

The usual apparatus for measuring the latent heat of vaporisation of a liquid, l_v, is shown in Fig. 18.24 (Multiple Choice Question 3). The heater is run at a rate which causes vaporisation of the liquid. The amount of vaporisation can be measured by weighing the liquid before and after the experiment. The experiment is then repeated, but with increased current and voltage, and run for the same amount of time. In this way the heat losses are the same, as the temperature of the apparatus is the same in both cases. For the first run:

$$V_1 I_1 t = m_1 l_v + Q,$$

where Q is the heat lost from the apparatus, and m_1 the mass of liquid evaporated. For the second run:

$$V_2 I_2 t = m_2 l_v + Q,$$
$$\text{giving } l_v = \frac{(V_2 I_2 - V_1 I_1)\, t}{m_2 - m_1}.$$

TERMINOLOGY

THERMO-DYNAMICS

- **Thermodynamics**: the branch of physics concerned with processes in which heat flows in or out of a 'system', whilst work is done on or by the 'system'.

- **Thermodynamic System**: a fixed mass of matter used for the energy conversion processes. A simple example is the gas in the cylinder of a petrol engine.

- **Heat (Q)**: energy which is transferred by conduction, convection, or radiation from one body to another, because one body is at a higher temperature than the other.

- **Work** (*W*): energy which is transferred from one system to another by a force moving through a distance. e.g. when the gas in the cylinder of a car engine expands as a result of petrol combustion a force is generated, and work is transferred out of the system (the gas) as the force moves (downwards) through the cylinder.
- **Internal Energy** (*U*): the total energy possessed by the system. You should be clear about the definitions and the careful use of this vocabulary. Students sometimes think of a hot body as having 'heat inside it'. Let us remind you again that a hot body has internal energy and its internal energy increases when it is supplied with heat (see also Chapter 4). Also note that only *changes* in internal energy are measurable in practice.

FIRST LAW OF THERMO-DYNAMICS

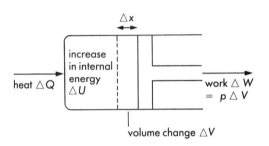

Fig. 18.3

> At A Level it is very important to note that for an ideal gas *U* depends only on the temperature of the gas.

The **first law** is really a statement of the principle of the conservation of energy and states that when an amount of heat $\triangle Q$ is applied to, say a gas (but equally to any system) the effect is to increase the internal energy of the gas by an amount $\triangle U$ and generate external work of an amount $\triangle W$ so that $\triangle Q = \triangle U + \triangle W$.

Sign convention

The **sign convention** adopted here is:

- $\triangle Q$ is positive if heat is supplied to the gas and negative if heat is transferred from it.
- $\triangle W$ is positive if the gas expands to do external work and negative if it is compressed, i.e. if work is done on it.

> Watch out for the sign convention used in your particular syllabus.

In an **adiabatic** change, no heat enters or leaves the system, i.e. $\triangle Q = 0$, and so $- \triangle U = \triangle W$. This means that any external work is performed at the expense of the internal energy. But note that some boards employ a variation on this sign convention.

APPLICATION TO GAS ENGINES

Questions about gas engines, meaning petrol, diesel, and steam engines are sometimes asked at A Level. Engines are usually considered by examination of their p,V curves on a so-called '**indicator diagram.**'

Consider the piston shown in the previous diagram (Fig. 18.3). When the gas expands:

$$\triangle W = F \triangle x.$$

If the pressure is constant we can write:

$F = pA,$ where A is the cylinder area.
Thus $\triangle W = pA \triangle x = p \triangle V,$
$\triangle V$ being the volume change of the gas.

If the pressure changes, then using the notation of the calculus for an infinitesimal change $dW = p dV$. On an indicator diagram the work done is shown (Fig. 18.4) by the hatched area under the curve and equals $\int_{V_1}^{V_2} p \, dV$.

Engines don't just operate with one stroke but work in repetitive cycles. One such cycle is shown in Fig. 18.5, with the net work done being the shaded area.

If questions on this topic are set in your syllabus you may need to know how the two *molar specific heats* defined earlier are related. C_p, the **molar specific heat capacity at constant pressure** is greater than C_V, the **molar specific heat capacity at constant volume**, because when the volume changes, some of the heat is converted into

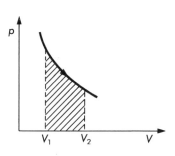

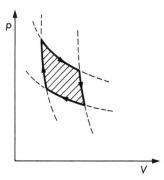

Fig. 18.4 Work done shown on an indicator diagram   Fig. 18.5 Nett work done in a cycle

mechanical energy when the gas expands. It can be shown that: $C_p = C_V + R$. In a *monatomic gas*, kinetic theory gives:

$$C_V = 3R/2,$$
and so $C_p = 5R/2$.

$\dfrac{C_p}{C_V}$ is usually written as γ, the ratio of molar specific heats.

PARTICULAR TYPES OF p, V CHANGE

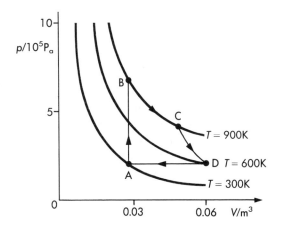

Fig. 18.6 Indicator diagram for engine with four different types of p, V change

Fig. 18.6 shows the indicator diagram for an imaginary engine with four different types of p, V change.

- A → B represents a heating of the gas at constant volume. Because V does not change no work is done (the area under the curve is zero).
  So $\triangle Q = \triangle U$,
  which means that the gas gains internal energy by taking in heat.

- B → C represents an **isothermal** (constant temperature) expansion during which the gas absorbs more heat. There is no change in U, the internal energy of the gas, as there is no change in the temperature. Here work is done by the gas.

- C → D represents a rapid further expansion of the gas during which there is insufficient time for heat to leave the gas. As a result the work done by the gas is equal to the loss in internal energy. The curve CD is described by the formula:

  $pV^\gamma = $ constant, where γ is the ratio of molar specific heats.

- Finally D → A represents an **isobaric** (constant pressure) change. In this change the gas loses heat energy. Some of the heat energy comes from the work done on it to compress it and some from the drop in temperature, and therefore the reduction in internal energy.
  Notice that for the cycle taken as a whole $\triangle U = 0$.

CALCULATIONS

The boards will limit use of formulae to situations where the changes are isobaric (as in

D → A above). For such a change:

$$\triangle U = n\,C_p\,(T_2 - T_1),$$

where n is the number of moles and $\triangle W = p(V_2 - V_1)$. Note especially this last formula. Because p is constant, the area under a pV graph is simply $p(V_2 - V_1)$.

Worked example

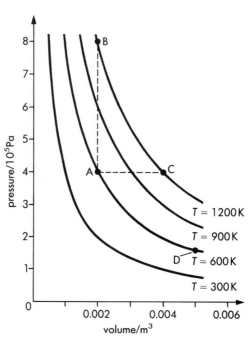

The graph shows data concerning the pressure, volume and temperature of a fixed mass of gas.

a) Use the ideal gas equation to find the number of moles of gas.

b) The gas has a heat capacity of 3.33 JK^{-1} at constant volume and 4.66 JK^{-1} at constant pressure. Calculate the quantity of heat required to take the gas:
   i) from A to B along AB.
   ii) from A to C along AC.

c) The internal energy of the gas at A is 2000J. Find the internal energy at B and at C.

d) How much work is done by the gas if an expansion at constant pressure takes place from A to C?

e) Find the internal energy of the gas at D.

Answers

a) $pV = nRt$ giving $n = PV/RT$
   Using values from point B
   $$p = 8 \times 10^5\,\text{Pa}$$
   $$V = 0.002\,\text{m}^3$$
   $$T = 1200\text{K}$$
   and $R = 8.31\,\text{J}\,\text{mol}^{-1}\,\text{K}^{-1}$
   giving $n = 0.160$ moles.

b) i) $\triangle W = 0$ and $\triangle Q = \triangle U$
   $$\triangle Q = nC_v\triangle T$$
   Note that nC_v is just the heat capacity

of the gas at constant volume and so is 3.33 JK^{-1}
giving $\triangle Q =$
3.33 × (1200 − 600) = 1998J.
   ii) Isobaric change
   $$\triangle Q = nC_p\triangle T$$
   where nC_p is just the heat capacity of the gas at constant pressure
   so $\triangle Q = 4.66\,(1200 - 600)$
   $$= 2796\,\text{J}$$
   As an alternative way of doing the calculation you can recognise that the internal energy of the gas at C is the same as at B. Using the first law
   $$\triangle Q = \triangle U + p\triangle V$$
   $\triangle U$ is the same as going from A to B, i.e. 1998 J
   and $p\triangle V = p(V_2 - V_1)$
   $$= 4 \times 10^5 \times$$
   $$(0.004 - 0.002)\,\text{J}$$
   $$= 800\,\text{J}$$
   $\triangle Q = 1998 + 800 = 2798\,\text{J}$

c) $\triangle U = 2000 + \triangle Q(\text{A} \rightarrow \text{B})$
   $$= 2000 + 1998\,\text{J}$$
   $$= 3998\,\text{J}.$$

d) This has already been done above, i.e. 800 J.

e) 2000 J: the same as at A.

SECOND LAW OF THERMO- DYNAMICS

HEAT ENGINES

Applied to engines, the **second law** states that whilst it is always possible to turn work into heat, it is not possible for an engine working in a cycle to completely turn heat into work.

For the purpose of the second law, an engine is idealised in Fig. 18.7 as a device in which heat is taken from a heat source at a high temperature T_1, in which some of the heat is converted into work, and out of which the remaining heat is transferred to a heat 'sink' at a low temperature, T_2. For example, in a power station steam turbine water is heated to steam at a high temperature in the boiler. In the turbine the steam does work by expanding and cooling, but it cools only to a certain temperature and is then discarded. As in the earlier hypothetical engine the process is cyclic and $\triangle U = 0$.

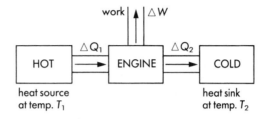

Fig. 18.7

By the first law:

$$\triangle Q_1 - \triangle Q_2 = \triangle W.$$

The efficiency of the engine as a converter from heat to work is:

$$\frac{\triangle W}{\triangle Q_1} = \frac{\triangle Q_1 - \triangle Q_2}{\triangle Q_1}.$$

In order to do calculations using the second law, it has been useful to define a property called **entropy**. When an amount of heat $\triangle Q$ is supplied into an engine at a temperature T there is an increase in entropy, $\triangle S$, given by

$$\triangle S = \frac{\triangle Q}{T}.$$

Note that the unit of entropy is JK^{-1}.

The second law of thermodynamics is then usually described by saying that in the cyclic process of an engine:

$$\triangle S \geqslant 0.$$

When an engine is working at the upper limit of its theoretical efficiency, $\triangle S = 0$, $\triangle S$ being taken over the whole cycle.

As $\triangle S = \dfrac{\triangle Q_1}{T_1} - \dfrac{\triangle Q_2}{T_2}$ for the whole cycle, then

$\triangle Q$ must be proportional to T, so that

$$\frac{\triangle Q_1}{T_1} = \frac{\triangle Q_2}{T_2}$$

Using this result the formula for efficiency becomes:

$$\frac{\triangle W}{\triangle Q_1} = \frac{T_1 - T_2}{T_1}.$$

So the higher the temperature of the heat source and the lower the temperature of the heat sink, the greater the upper limit on efficiency.

REFRIGERATORS AND HEAT PUMPS

Refrigerators are heat engines in reverse. By the action of the work done in a motor, heat is drawn from the interior of a refrigerator and dumped outside at a higher temperature via a heat exchanger. In a heat-pump, heat is pumped from cold air or water, say, in the garden of a house, and transferred at higher temperature to the interior. Thus Q, the supplied heat, exceeds the work paid for in running the motor.

ENTROPY AND STATISTICAL PHYSICS

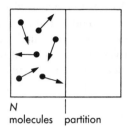

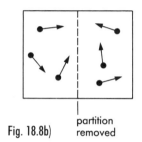

N
molecules   partition

Fig. 18.8a)

Fig. 18.8b)   partition removed

The thermal phenomena, described in this chapter, are **macroscopic** phenomena which are a result of the *microscopic* motions of the large numbers of molecules that make up matter. The 'one-way' processes involved, that is heat always flowing *down* a thermal gradient, i.e. from a high temperature region to one at low temperature, the possibility of only converting some heat into work in a heat engine, but of always being able to convert work into heat, etc., are described by introducing the concept of **entropy**, S. But entropy is itself a macroscopic quantity which needs to be understood in terms of the chance nature of the microscopic motions of the molecules.

CHANCE

Consider an ideal gas of N molecules all contained in the left-hand side of Fig. 18.8a). Once the partition is removed, the molecules can move to anywhere in the whole box. The probability of any molecule being where it started, i.e. in the left-hand side of the box is $\frac{1}{2}$. The probability of all them being in the left-hand side is $(\frac{1}{2})^N = 1/2^N$, an exceedingly small number. Another way of thinking about this is to consider the change in the ways of arranging the molecules. Once the partition is removed we would have the rare possibility of all the molecules being in the left-hand side, all but one in the left-hand side, all but two in the left-hand side, and so on. Doubling the space open to them increases the ways of rearranging them from 1 to 2^N, assuming they are distinguishable. The link between the microscopic and the macroscopic is given by the equation for entropy change:

$$\triangle S = k \ln (W'/W),$$

where W′ = new number of ways of arranging the molecules, W the old number of ways, and k is the Boltzmann constant.

ENTROPY, ENERGY AND TEMPERATURE

Some understanding of the role of chance in thermal equilibrium can be achieved by using the Einstein model of a solid. Each atom is considered to have a set of equally spaced energy levels, the difference between each level being called a quantum of energy ϵ. So an atom may only have energies of value 0, ϵ, 2ϵ, 3ϵ, 4ϵ, . . . etc., and we can number the corresponding energy levels $n = 0, 1, 2, 3, 4, . . .$ etc. Because of random interactions between atoms, the energy can be constantly redistributed between them. Four ways of distributing 4 quanta, each of energy ϵ among 3 atoms are shown in Fig. 18.9. We would write *all* these combinations out as follows:

400, 040, 004, 310, 301, 130, 031, 103, 013, 220, 202, 022, 211, 121, 112.

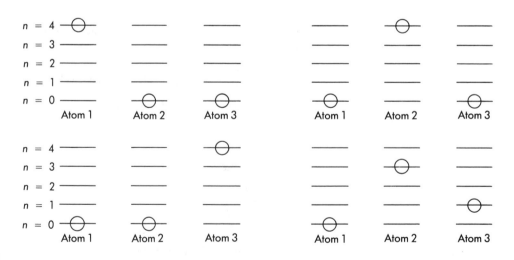

Fig. 18.9

Note that the combination of 3ϵ in one atom, 1ϵ in another and 0 in the third occurs more frequently than any other. With large amounts of energy and large numbers of atoms this pattern, i.e. of one combination occurring more frequently than any others, is even more pronounced. This combination is, of course, the equilibrium distribution. It can be represented by the histogram as shown in Fig. 18.10.

Here, Y is the number of atoms holding n quanta of energy. The graph is for 305 quanta distributed among 102 atoms. The histogram shows an exponential decrease, i.e. a constant ratio, f, between adjacent bars.

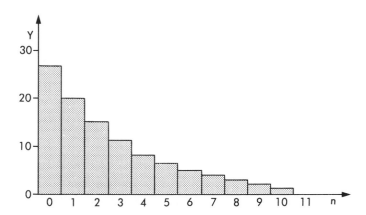

Fig. 18.10 Histogram of number of atoms (Y) against quanta of energy (n)

If f = the number of atoms with n quanta, then the number of atoms with (n−1) quanta

$$= \frac{Q}{Q + N},$$

where Q is the total number of quanta and N the total number of atoms (if both Q and N are large). At low temperatures Q is small, making f very small. At the other extreme, at very high temperatures, Q is much larger than N, and f is close to 1.

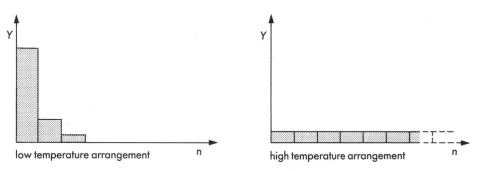

low temperature arrangement

high temperature arrangement

Fig. 18.11   Fig. 18.12

Further work in probability gives the result: f = W'/W, where W' is the number of ways of distributing Q quanta among N atoms, and W the number of ways of distributing (Q+1) quanta among N atoms.

The above results allows the derivation of further results linking energy, entropy and temperature. We shall simply summarise them here. The entropy change associated with the addition of one quantum ϵ is:

> These formulae allow us to consider the effects of chance and change without having to do probability calculations each time.

$\triangle S = \epsilon / T.$
$\ln f = - \epsilon / kT$ or $f = e^{-\epsilon/kT},$

Here, $f = e^{-\epsilon/kT}$ is often referred to as the Boltzmann factor.

THE BOLTZMANN FACTOR

The arguments of the Einstein model generalise to other forms of matter where the energy levels are not equispaced.

Evaporation

This takes place when a sizeable number of the molecules of a liquid acquire by random processes enough energy to escape. The **Boltzmann factor** $f = e^{-\epsilon/kT}$ is a good guide to the temperature dependence of the process. Evaporation is of course related to vapour pressure, and here a similar formula describes the temperature dependence of vapour pressure. If E is the energy needed to eject a molecule from the liquid, then $E = H/N$, where H is the number of joules per mole needed to vapourise a liquid and N is the Avogadro number. The fraction of molecules in the vapour is indicated by the vapour pressure, p, and so:

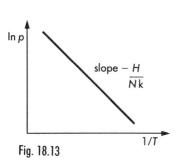

Fig. 18.13

$p \propto e^{-H/NkT}$, or $\ln p = $ constant $ - H/NkT$

Two other examples are:

i) The current in a thermistor, or other semiconductor where the current I is given by

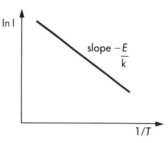

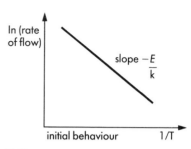

Fig. 18.14   Fig. 18.15

$I \propto e^{-E/kT}$ or $\ln I =$ constant $- E/kT$. Here, E is the energy needed to 'free' an electron into a conducting state (see Fig. 18.14).

ii) Viscosity in liquids. Here:

flow rate $\propto e^{-E/kT}$, where E is the energy needed to push aside neighbouring molecules.

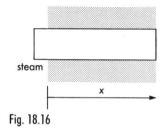

THERMAL CONDUCTIVITY

Fig. 18.16 shows a perfectly lagged metal bar connected to a chamber through which steam can be passed. The graph in Fig. 18.17 shows the temperature θ as a function of the distance x along the bar a short time after steam is passed. The rate at which heat passes down the bar $\dfrac{dQ}{dt}$ is proportional to the magnitude of the slope of the temperature/distance curve, known as the **temperature gradient**. This gives us:

$$\frac{dQ}{dt} \propto \frac{-d\theta}{dx} .$$

Fig. 18.16

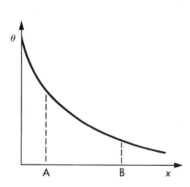

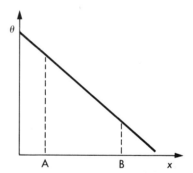

Fig. 18.17   Fig. 18.18

Note the minus sign, a result of heat always flowing from a hot body to a cold body. Note, too, that some authors and textbooks avoid the use of terms like 'heat flow' preferring instead 'transfer of thermal energy'. The rate of flow of heat at A is much greater than at B. This is obvious and implies a net flow of heat into the region between A and B. Eventually as heat is conducted into the bar a steady state is reached as shown in Fig. 18.18 where the rate of flow of heat is the same at all points along the bar. All the heat entering at one end is ultimately conducted through the bar. The rate of flow of heat is proportional to the area of cross-section A, and depends upon the material of the bar. The equation:

$$\frac{dQ}{dt} = -kA \frac{d\theta}{dx} ,$$

describes the phenomenon. k is the **coefficient of thermal conductivity** with the unusual units of W m^{-1}K^{-1}.

In a steady state situation, for a perfectly lagged bar:

$$\frac{dQ}{dt} = kA \frac{(\theta_1 - \theta_2)}{l} ,$$

where l is the length of the bar and θ_1 and θ_2 the temperatures of the ends.

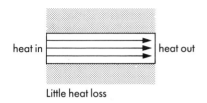

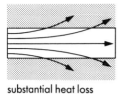

Little heat loss   substantial heat loss

Fig. 18.19   Fig. 18.20

The steady state case of a perfectly lagged bar is one in which all the heat entering at one end leaves from the other. In experiments to measure the thermal conductivity of a *good* conductor, this formula is in fact used. The bar (Fig. 18.19) is well lagged and it is assumed that the rate of transfer of heat along it is very much greater than the heat lost from the sides. Perfect lagging is difficult to achieve and in reality there will be a steady loss of heat along the bar (Fig. 18.20).

HEAT FLOW ACROSS A MATERIAL BOUNDARY

This is commonly asked at A Level, in the special case of lagged steady state conditions. As a result the temperature gradient $\dfrac{d\theta}{dx}$ changes abruptly at the interface.

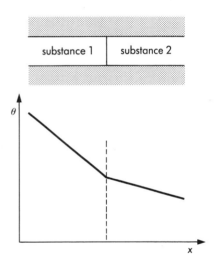

Fig. 18.21

The key concept is that the rate of flow of heat, $\dfrac{dQ}{dt}$, on either side of the boundary is the same. Hence the relationship between the temperature gradients is

$$k_1 \frac{d\theta_1}{dx} = k_2 \frac{d\theta_2}{dx}$$ (Question 11 gives an example).

In the calculation of heat lost through a material such as a piece of brick or the wall of a house, U is written for the quantity $\dfrac{k}{l}$, and is called the 'U-value' or the **thermal resistance**. The steady state equation:

$$\frac{dQ}{dt} = kA \frac{(\theta_1 - \theta_2)}{l} \quad \text{becomes} \quad \frac{dQ}{dt} = UA(\theta_1 - \theta_2).$$

This formula can be used for a whole structure, such as a wall made of lots of separate layers, e.g. brick, plaster and an air cavity. The 'U-value' has units $Wm^{-2}K^{-1}$.

MEASUREMENT OF k

Only some boards will ask for details of experimental methods, but you should be aware of the need for a long sample of small cross-sectional area for good conductors and a thin sample of large cross sectional area for bad ones. The reasons are that in the first case without a long sample an appreciable temperature difference cannot be obtained, and in the second case without a large cross-sectional area and a minute thickness little heat will be conducted. A very thin sample of large cross-sectional area is needed in the latter case to ensure that the rate of heat transferred axially through the material is large compared with the heat lost through its edge so that the formula $\dfrac{dQ}{dt} = kA \dfrac{(\theta_1 - \theta_2)}{l}$ can be used.

THERMAL CONDUCTION AND ELECTRICAL CONDUCTION

As a transport phenomenon, **thermal conduction** is described by the equation:

$$\frac{dQ}{dt} = kA \frac{(\theta_1 - \theta_2)}{l}$$

It can be compared with electrical conduction. In the electrical case, the familiar **Ohmic equation** is: $I = V/R$. V is the potential difference between the ends of the wire, and can be written:

$\phi_2 - \phi_1$, where ϕ_1 and ϕ_2 are the potentials at the ends.

$R = \rho l/A$, where ρ is the resistivity and $I = dq/dt$ where q represents the charge. With these substitutions Ohm's Law becomes:

$$\frac{dq}{dt} = \frac{1}{\rho} A \frac{(\phi_2 - \phi_1)}{l} .$$

Often this is written in the form:

$$\frac{dq}{dt} = \sigma A \frac{(\phi_2 - \phi_1)}{l} ,$$

where σ is defined as $\dfrac{1}{\rho}$, the electrical conductivity. The similarity with thermal conductivity is then obvious.

RADIATION

Thermal radiation is electromagnetic radiation (see also Chapter 9). All bodies absorb and emit radiation. For example, the earth absorbs radiation from the sun. It also emits radiation into space and remains in equilibrium at a temperature where the rate at which it gains energy is equal to the rate at which it loses it.

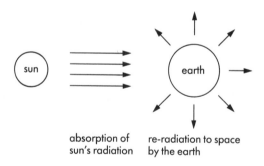

Fig. 18.22

absorption of sun's radiation | re-radiation to space by the earth

EMISSION OF RADIATION

The total energy radiated from a surface is described by **Stefan's Law**:

$$P = \sigma e A T^4,$$

where P is the radiated power in watts, A the area (m^2), T the temperature in Kelvins, σ the Stefan constant, and e a material constant called the emissivity. e varies from 0 to 1. It is 1 for a so-called black-body, i.e. one which is a perfect absorber and emitter of radiation (note that both properties go hand in hand).

The net power radiated from a black body at a temperature T_o but simultaneously absorbing radiation at a temperature T is: $\sigma A(T^4 - T_o^4)$. Black body radiation covers *all* wavelengths (frequencies). The amount of energy associated with a particular frequency varies as the graph in Fig. 18.23 shows. The energy distribution curve itself is dependent on the temperature of the body from which it is radiated.

Note that the peak of a black body radiation shifts to shorter wavelengths as the temperature rises.

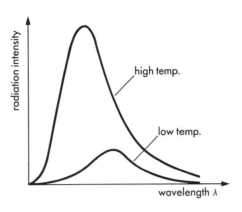

Fig. 18.23

EXAMINATION QUESTIONS

MULTIPLE CHOICE QUESTIONS

1   Why do a thermo-electric thermometer and a gas thermometer give the same reading at the ice point?

a) Zero on the Celsius scale of temperature is defined as the ice point.
b) Ice always melts at the same temperature provided the pressure is one atmosphere.
c) The relationship between the two scales is linear.
d) It is a natural law that thermometers read zero at the ice point.
e) Only pure melting ice is used.

(AEB 1987 Specimen Paper)

2   The temperature of a hot liquid, in a container of negligible heat capacity, falls at a rate of 2 K per minute just before it begins to solidify. The temperature then remains steady for 20 min by which time the liquid has all solidified. The quantity

$$\frac{\text{specific heat capacity of liquid}}{\text{specific latent heat of fusion}} \text{ is equal to}$$

a) $1/40 \text{ K}^{-1}$ d) 10 K^{-1}
b) $1/10 \text{ K}^{-1}$ e) 40 K^{-1}
c) 1 K^{-1}

(London 1988)

3   The apparatus shown in Fig. 18.24 is used to determine the specific latent heat of vaporisation of a liquid. It is found that the rate of vapour production is doubled when

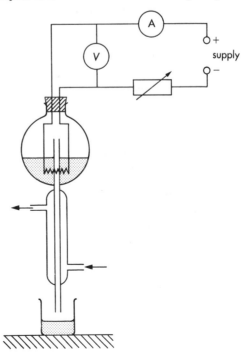

Fig. 18.24

the heater power is increased from 60 W to 100 W. What is the rate of heat loss to the surroundings (assuming that this rate remains constant)?

a) 10 W   d) 40 W
b) 20 W   e) 50 W
c) 30 W

(Oxford 1987)

4 The water for a shower is heated as it flows past an electric element. what is the flow rate of the water when the heater supplies 7 kW and warms the water from 15°C to 45°C?

(Assume that 1 litre of water has a mass of 1 kg and that the specific heat capacity of water is 4200 J kg^{-1} K^{-1}).

a) $\dfrac{1}{18}$ litres per minute   d) $\dfrac{20}{3}$ litres per minute

b) $\dfrac{20}{9}$ litres per minute   e) 200 litres per minute.

c) $\dfrac{10}{3}$ litres per minute

(London 1987)

5 A gas in a cylinder provided with a smoothly-fitting piston goes from an initial state I to a final state F, as shown in Fig. 18.25. This change can be brought about in different ways, for example by the two steps *r* and *s*, or by a single step *t*. The following statements relate to the application of the first law of thermodynamics to the system.

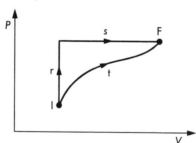

Fig. 18.25

1 No work is done on or by the gas in step *r*.
2 Heat is added to the gas in step *s*.
3 The change in internal energy of the gas is the same, no matter which path is taken between I and F.

Which of these statements is (are) true?

a) 1 only   d) 2 and 3 only
b) 3 only   e) 1, 2 and 3
c) 1 and 2 only

(NI 1987)

6 A metal bar PQ encloses a section XY of another material (see Fig. 18.26). The ends of the bar are maintained at different temperatures. The temperature difference across XY is independent of:

a) the temperature difference between P and Q;
b) the metal that–the bar is made of;
c) the length of XY;
d) the material of XY;
e) the position of XY along PQ.

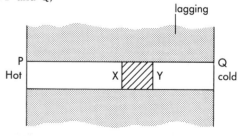

Fig. 18.26

(Oxford 1987)

For questions **7**, **8** and **9** use the following code:

a) 1, 2 and 3 correct
b) 1 and 2 only
c) 2 and 3 only
d) 1 only
e) 3 only

7 The equation $\dfrac{dQ}{dt} = -kA\,\dfrac{d\theta}{dx}$, giving the rate of heat transfer through a conductor has an electrical equivalent based on Ohm's law. When making the comparison which of the following is (are) correct?

1 $\dfrac{dQ}{dt}$ is analogous to the current.

2 $\dfrac{d\theta}{dx}$ is analogous to the potential gradient.

3 k is analogous to the resistivity.

(AEB 1987)

8 Which of the following quantities have the unit $J\,K^{-1}$?
1) Entropy.
2) The Boltzmann constant.
3) Specific heat capacity.

9 A heat engine operates between a heat source at temperature T_1 and a heat sink at temperature T_2. The efficiency of the engine would be increased by:
1) Doubling T_1 while keeping T_2 constant.
2) Doubling T_2 while keeping T_1 constant.
3) Doubling both T_1 and T_2.

(AEB 1987)

ANSWERS AND COMMENTS

Question	1	2	3	4	5	6	7	8	9
Answer	a)	a)	b)	c)	e)	e)	b)	b)	d)

1 A test of your understanding of the definition of the zero of temperature.

2 Let c be the specific heat capacity. In numerical terms the heat lost per kg in 1 minute whilst the temperature is falling is $c\triangle\theta$, in this case $2c$ joules. So in 20 minutes there would be a loss of heat of $20 \times 2c = 80c$ joules. But this must be equal to c_1 the latent heat. Hence:

$$\frac{c}{c_1} = \frac{2c}{80c} = \frac{1}{40}$$

3 With this one, as with the previous one, it is risky to try doing the exercise in your head. The algebra needed is fairly straightforward. The solution is similar to that of structured question **10**. Let x be the initial power supplied to the vapour and R be the rate of heat loss.
Then $x + R = 60$
$2x + R = 100$
Solution of these simultaneous equations gives $R = 20$ W.

4 Let x be the number of litres (kg) of water per *minute*. Then energy supplied per second = mass per sec × specific heat × temperature rise

$$= \frac{x}{60} \times 4200 \times (45 - 15) = 2100\,x\ \text{W}$$

But this is 7000 W, hence $x = \dfrac{10}{3}$ litres min^{-1}.

5 1 and 2 are answered by considering $\int p\,dV$ in both cases. 3 is true because F lies on a different isotherm (pV = constant graph) from I and the internal energy of an (ideal) gas is only a function of T.

6

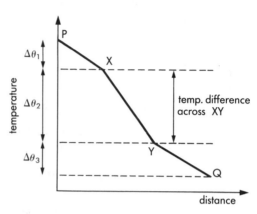

Fig. 18.27

From Fig. 18.27, it should be clear that because the graph consists of three connecting linear sections, the gradients of which are fixed, answer e) is correct.

7   3 is false: k is actually analogous to the electrical conductivity.

8   3 is false: specific heat capacity has the units $J\ kg^{-1}\ K^{-1}$.

9   Both 2 and 3 are false.

STRUCTURED QUESTIONS

10   a) Define specific heat capacity and specific latent heat of vaporisation.

b) Describe an electrical method for the determination of the specific latent heat of vaporisation of a liquid with a boiling point of about 100°C.

c) In an experiment to determine the rate at which the human body loses energy, a man is placed inside a chamber around which water is pumped as shown in Fig. 18.28. When the rate of flow of water is 4.0 kg h^{-1} and the inlet temperature is 23°C, it is found that the outlet temperature reaches a steady value of 31.0°C.

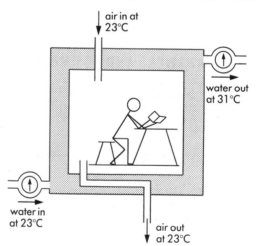

Fig. 18.28

In the second experiment, two men occupy the chamber. If the flow rate is increased to 11.0 kg h^{-1} and the inlet temperature is again 23.0°C, the outlet temperature again reaches a steady value of 31.0°C.

Assuming that each of the men loses energy at the same rate, calculate

i) the rate of loss of energy, in W, from the human body.

ii) the rate at which energy is lost from the chamber by means other than the flow of water.

(Assume that the specific heat capacity of water = 4200 J kg^{-1}K^{-1})

(AEB 1985)

11   The *incomplete* diagram (Fig. 18.29) shows how the temperature changes across a double glazed window unit. Each pane of glass is 4 mm thick and the air gap is 8 mm. The temperature of the innermost surface of the glass is 20°C and of the outermost surface is 4°C.

Copy the diagram on to graph paper and complete it to show how the temperature falls across the air gap and the outer pane of glass.

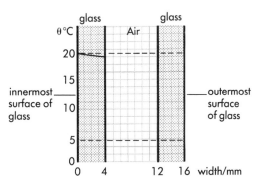

Fig. 18.29

Use the diagram to calculate the average temperature gradient across the whole unit. If the power transfer per unit area is 120 W m^{-2}, what is the 'equivalent' thermal conductivity of the unit as a whole?

(London 1989)

12 a) State **one** situation in which a constant-volume gas thermometer would be used (in preference to other types of thermometer). Give a reason for your choice.
 b) State, with a reason, the type of thermometer you would choose for each of the following:
   i) locating the hottest point in a Bunsen burner flame;
   ii) recording the mean temperature of the gases emerging from the exhaust pipe of a car.
 c) State **three** ways in which the behaviour of a thermistor differs from that of a platinum coil when used in a resistance thermometer.

(Oxford 1988)

13 The decay of charge on a capacitor and the decay of the activity of a radioactive sample are examples of *exponential changes*.
 Exponential relationships also occur in other branches of physics such as in the distribution of quanta of energy among atoms in an ideal (Einstein) solid.
 Write an essay about exponential changes and relationships in science, including the above examples to illustrate your answer. Include, in addition, *one other* example, from any branch of science, which involves an exponential change or relationship.
 Your answer should contain
 a) brief descriptions of any relevant experiments, and
 b) relevant formulae and numerical examples wherever possible.

(O and C (Nuffield) 1986)

OUTLINE ANSWERS

10 Parts a) and b) of the question are considered in the text.
 c) First, note that no heat is lost by the air as it leaves the chamber at the temperature at which it entered. Let us assume that the rate of loss of energy by means other than the flow of water is the same in both cases and equal to R watts. In the first experiment, the rate at which the water gains heat is:
 mass of water per second × temperature rise × specific heat capacity
 $$= \frac{4.0 \times 8.0 \times 4200}{3600} = 37.3 \text{ W}.$$
 So the total rate of loss of heat $W = R + 37.3$
  giving $W - R = 37.3$.
 In the second experiment, $\dfrac{11 \times 8 \times 4200}{3600} = 102.6$ W,
  giving $2W - R = 102.6$.
 Subtracting the first equation from the second we obtain:
  $W = 65.3$ W and $R = 28$ W

11 The completed diagram should look like Fig 18.27 but with $\triangle\theta_1 = \triangle\theta_3$
 Average temperature gradient $= -\left(\dfrac{20 - 4}{16 \times 10^{-3}}\right)$ K m^{-1}
  $= -10^3$ K m^{-1}

With unit area we have
$$120 = k \times 10^3$$
or $k = 0.12$ W m^{-1} K^{-1}

12 a) The gas thermometer is needed in order to calibrate other thermometers. This is because it gives readings on the ideal gas (thermodynamic) scale.

b) i) A thermocouple would be used (the small heat capacity would be useful).

    ii) A mercury-in-glass thermometer could be used (the heat capacity would promote an averaging effect).

c) A thermistor differs from a platinum coil in that:

    i) the resistance (usually) decreases with an increase in temperature;

    ii) the resistance varies non-linearly with temperature;

    iii) the useful temperature range is smaller.

13 This question shows the style of this kind of Nuffield long question, and shows the kind of question that might be set on thermodynamics, here, specifically the Boltzmann factor. Note that in current Nuffield teaching, the term 'Einstein' is not used.

TUTOR'S QUESTION AND ANSWER

QUESTION

14 a) A fixed mass of an ideal gas is compressed under adiabatic conditions.

    i) Explain what is meant by the phrase *under adiabatic conditions*, and describe experimental conditions which approximate to adiabatic.

    ii) Explain why such an adiabatic compression will always result in an increase in temperature.

    iii) Describe and explain the change, if any, in the entropy of the gas.

b) Distinguish carefully between *a heat engine* and *a heat pump*.

c) A prototype engine, intended for use in a small car, is tested by measuring the pressure of the gas in one cylinder as the volume is changed by the movement of the piston. The graph shows the variation of pressure against volume for one complete cycle when the engine is running at its maximum design speed of 3000 revolutions per minute.

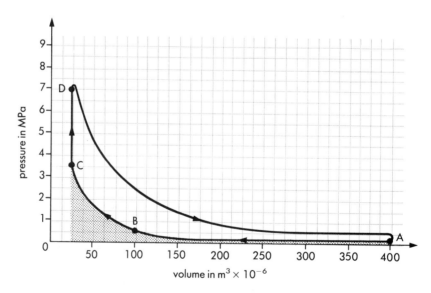

Fig. 18.30

During the first part of the cycle, air in the cylinder is compressed (A to C on the graph). There follows a further increase in pressure (C to D) before the gas expands back to its original volume (D to A). The cycle is then repeated.

    i) Use the values of pressure and volume at B and C to provide evidence that the compression of the air is adiabatic. Assume that the ratio of the principal specific heat capacities of air, γ, is 1.4.

    ii) What is represented by the shaded area between the compression curve and the volume axis?

iii) Assuming that the temperature of the air at B is 570 K, calculate the temperature at C.

iv) At C, fuel with an ignition temperature of 700 K is injected into the cylinder. Suggest an explanation for the increase in pressure at constant volume which results.

v) Use the graph to show that the net work done by one cylinder of the engine during one cycle is approximately 450 J. Use this value to calculate the power output of the engine, assuming that the cycle is completed 3000 times per minute and that the engine has four cylinders.

(AEB 1987)

ANSWER

14 a) i) Under adiabatic conditions means that during compression no heat is able to escape from the gas. This could be approximated by surrounding the gas container with insulating material to reduce heat loss, and compressing the gas very rapidly so that the time for heat transfer is minimal.

ii) In compression work is done *on* the gas. This energy goes into the gas, increasing its internal energy. As the internal energy of a gas increases with temperature so the temperature must always rise.

iii) The change in entropy is given by $\int \dfrac{dq}{T}$ where q is the heat lost from the gas and T the temperature. But because no heat is lost there is no entropy change.

b) See text (p.205).

c) i) If the change is adiabatic pV^{γ} = constant where p is the pressure and V the volume.

At B $pV^{\gamma} = 0.5 \times 10^6 \,(100 \times 10^{-6})^{1.4}$
$= 1.26$

and at C $pV^{\gamma} = 3.5 \times 10^6 \times (25 \times 10^{-6})^{1.4}$
$= 1.26$.

Hence there is evidence that the change is adiabatic.

ii) The shaded area of the graph represents the work done *on* the gas in compressing it.

iii) We can apply the general gas equation in the form $\dfrac{pV}{T}$ = constant

giving $T_2 = \dfrac{p_2 V_2 T_1}{p_1 V_1}$

$= \dfrac{3.5 \times 10^6 \times 25 \times 10^{-6} \times 570}{0.5 \times 10^6 \times 100 \times 10^{-6}}$

$= 997.5$ K.

iv) The pressure increases at constant volume because the fuel instantly ignites and burns causing a rapid temperature rise in a very short time.

v) The net work done by 1 cylinder is equal to the area enclosed by ABCD. Using the graph, the area under AD $\approx$ 92 squares and the shaded area $\approx$ 27 small squares. Hence the area enclosed $\approx$ 92 $-$ 27 = 65 squares

1 square $= 0.5 \times 10^6$ Pa $\times 12.5 \times 10^{-6}$ m^3
$= 6.25$ J

Hence net work done $\approx$ 410 J.

Work done by 4 cylinders in 1 minute $= 3000 \times 450 \times 4$ J
$= 5.40 \times 10^6$ J

Power $=$ work done per second $= 9.00 \times 10^4$ J s^{-1}
$= 90$ kW

> No more accuracy than this will be needed. It would not be necessary to use the integral calculus.

STUDENT'S ANSWER WITH EXAMINER COMMENTS

STUDENT'S ANSWER TO QUESTION 11

> A slight transcribing error on the graph.

> Candidate has different temperature gradients for the two glass plates.

> Outer and inner are mixed up.

> The temperature gradient is negative and the sign has been omitted.

Temperature gradient at outer glass face

$$= \frac{20 - 18.5}{4} = \frac{1.5}{4} \quad \frac{°C}{mm}$$

$$= 0.38 \ °C/mm$$

> These units are allowable; but K is much preferred for a temperature difference.

Temperature gradient for air $= \dfrac{18.5 - 5}{8} = \dfrac{13.5}{8} = 1.69 \ °C/mm$

Temp. gradient at inner glass $= \dfrac{5 - 4}{4} = 0.25 \ °C/mm$

So average temp. gradient $= 0.77 \ °C/mm = 0.77 \times 10^3 \ °C/mm$

$$= 770 \ °C/m.$$

$$\frac{dQ}{dt} = kA \ \frac{(\theta_2 - \theta_1)}{x}$$

So $120 = k \ A \times 770$

and so $k = \dfrac{120}{770 \ A} = \dfrac{0.16}{A} \ W \ m^{-1}K^{-1}$

> The main and common fault with this question is illustrated here; three separate temperature gradients are calculated and then the average calculated.

> The second common mistake is also illustrated; the candidate has not understood that the 120 refers to a *power per unit area*. The area of cross section is therefore unity. The final answer still therefore contains A. The units are however correct.

Overall comments: This is typical of a grade C candidate. This is because in spite of the errors the student has demonstrated a knowledge of temperature gradient and the thermal conductivity equation.

ELECTRON, PHOTON AND ENERGY LEVELS

GETTING STARTED

Light is sometimes considered as a **wave** and sometimes as a **particle**. When considering **interference** and **diffraction** we treated light as though it travelled as a **transverse electromagnetic wave**. In this chapter we explain the **photoelectric effect** by considering light arriving at a metal surface as energy packets called **photons**. We also consider the particulate nature of light when the **electrons** in an atom change energy levels and emit **photons**. Each photon carries an energy hf where h is the Planck Constant and f is the frequency. This dual behaviour is called **wave-particle duality**.

We usually consider the electrons travelling in a cathode ray tube to be particles of mass m and charge e. However electrons also exhibit *wave* properties when they are diffracted by a graphite target. The electron also exhibits wave-particle duality.

ESSENTIAL PRINCIPLES

THERMIONIC EMISSION

An electron is normally held in a metal by attractive forces from the 'sea' of positive ions, and needs to be given energy in order to escape. For a particular metal there is a minimum amount of energy, known as the **work function**, needed to release electrons. This energy can be supplied by heating the metal (e.g. by passing an electric current through it), so that the free electrons near the surface gain sufficient energy to escape. This phenomenon is **thermionic emission** and is used in vacuum tubes where a filament is heated to release electrons. These electrons are then accelerated by an electric field between the filament and a positive anode. If the potential difference between the filament and anode is V, then an electron will have lost electrical energy eV and gained kinetic energy $\frac{1}{2}mv^2$, where v is the speed at which the electrons are travelling when they reach the anode. Hence $\frac{1}{2}mv^2 = eV$.

1 **electronvolt** (eV) is defined as the energy gained by 1 electron accelerated by 1 volt. As the charge on the electron is 1.6×10^{-19} J the energy gained by 1 electron accelerated by 1 volt is also 1.6×10^{-19} J. So 1 eV = 1.6×10^{-19} J.

ELECTRIC DEFLECTION

The treatment of this problem is similar to that of a projectile travelling in a uniform vertical gravitational field where the horizontal velocity remains constant and the vertical motion is subject to a constant downwards acceleration resulting in a parabolic path.

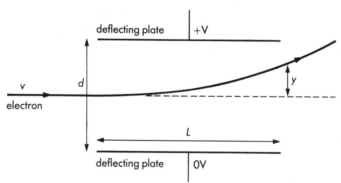

Fig. 19.1 Deflection of electron by electric field

The electron travelling at speed v arrives at the end of the deflecting plates travelling horizontally. Whilst the electron is between the plates, it is in a *uniform* electric field which exerts a *constant* force perpendicular to the plates. The field $= \dfrac{V}{d}$ where V is the p.d. across the plates and therefore the electron experiences a constant vertical *force* $= \dfrac{eV}{d}$, and a constant vertical *acceleration* $= \dfrac{eV}{md}$, whilst it passes between the plates. If it spends a time t between the plates, then it will experience a vertical *deflection* equal to:

$$\frac{1}{2} \frac{eVt^2}{m\,d}.$$

> **⟨⟨ No need to remember equations but you do need to understand each step. ⟩⟩**

As there is no *horizontal* force acting on the electron its horizontal speed v is unchanged and so it spends a time $t = \dfrac{L}{v}$ between the plates of length L.

DEFLECTION BY MAGNETIC FIELDS

An electron travelling perpendicular to a uniform magnetic field B will experience a constant force perpendicular to both its direction of travel and the magnetic field.

As the force is always perpendicular to the direction of travel there is no acceleration in the direction of travel. The electron therefore moves at constant speed v, but experiences a constant acceleration perpendicular to the direction of travel. The electron therefore describes a circular path of radius r at constant speed. The acceleration towards the centre of the circle is:

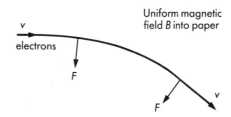

Fig. 19.2 Magnetic deflection of
moving electron

$$\frac{v^2}{r} \quad \therefore Bev = \frac{mv^2}{r} \quad \therefore r = \frac{mv}{Be}.$$

In some experiments the electron is subjected to both electric and magnetic fields whose directions are arranged so that the forces they exert on the electrons are equal and opposite, and so the electron is undeflected. In these circumstances: $Bev = Ee$.

Using these techniques it is possible to measure the specific charge (charge per unit mass) on the electron.

MILLIKAN'S EXPERIMENT

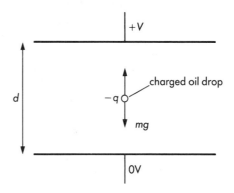

Fig. 19.3 Millikan's experiment

This experiment involves the determination of the charge on the electron. Charged oil drops are held stationary in a uniform electric field between two parallel plates. If the drop is stationary, then the upward force due to the electric field balances the weight of the drop. Thus:

$Eq = mg$, where $E = V/d$.

Millikan then allowed the drop to fall and determined the mass of the drop from measurements of its terminal velocity. He found the charge on the drops to be multiples of a smallest value of 1.6×10^{-9} C which he assumed to be the smallest charge.

CATHODE RAY OSCILLOSCOPE

In the **cathode ray oscilloscope**, the electron beam passes through two pairs of deflection plates, a horizontal pair (the Y plates) producing a vertical field for deflection in the Y direction, and a vertical pair (the X plates) of plates to produce deflections in the X direction. In normal use a 'time-base' voltage is applied to the X plates.

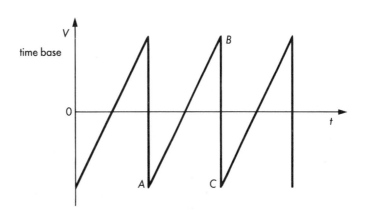

Fig. 19.4 Cathode ray oscilloscope 'time base' voltage variation with time

The steadily rising section AB increases the voltage between the plates, and so an electron spot moves steadily across the screen from left to right until the voltage suddenly changes back (section BC) to its original value, which makes the electron rapidly fly back to the left-hand side of the screen. The time base is usually calibrated in s/cm so that the time it takes the beam to travel 1 cm across (to the right) the screen is known. The voltage waveform under investigation is then applied to the Y plates and so deflects the beam vertically. Thus the graph displayed on the screen plots input voltage on the Y axis against time on the X axis. By using the time base calibration it is possible to measure the time for one complete cycle of the input voltage. The frequency, or number of cycles per second, is the reciprocal of the time for one cycle. For instance, if a microphone is connected to the Y input of the oscilloscope, the frequency of a note can be measured from the time for one cycle of the trace. An oscilloscope is a very high resistance voltmeter and so is placed in parallel with a component to measure the p.d. across it. In order to display the current in a circuit the oscilloscope is placed across a small resistance in series in the circuit. The oscilloscope thus displays the p.d. across the resistor which is proportional to the current. It can be used for both a.c. and d.c. measurements.

> The oscilloscope time base must be in calibrated position.

THE PHOTOELECTRIC EFFECT

When light is shone on some metal surfaces, electrons are released from the surface. The energy of the light arrives in packets known as *photons*. If the light is of frequency f the *energy* of each photon is hf (h is the **Planck constant**). A free electron near the surface of the metal receiving all of the energy of a photon may gain sufficient energy to escape. If the energy hf of the incoming photons is less than the *work function* ϕ of the metal, then electrons will not be released. However, increasing the frequency or using a metal with a lower work function where $hf > \phi$ will cause electrons to be emitted. The emitted electrons have a *range* of kinetic energies up to a maximum. The photons each deliver the same amount of energy hf to the electrons which lose differing amounts of energy while escaping. Those electrons which lose the least energy (the work function) will escape with the most kinetic energy.

In general $\quad hf = \tfrac{1}{2}mv^2_{max} + \phi$

MEASURING THE PLANCK CONSTANT

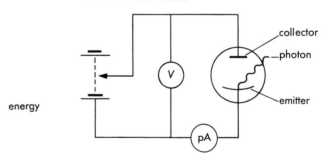

Fig. 19.5 Measuring the Planck constant

The photoelectrons are released into a vacuum and an electric field is applied to decelerate and stop them. If this p.d. is increased, fewer electrons will be able to get across to the collector until even the most energetic electrons are stopped. The flow of electrons between emitter and collector is detected by a picoammeter in series with the photocell. When this meter reads zero, the maximum stopping potential V_{max} is recorded. Then

$$\tfrac{1}{2}(mv^2)_{max} = eV_{max}.$$

The voltmeter must be of very high resistance so that it draws negligible current from the photocell. Substituting gives:

$$hf = eV_{max} + \phi.$$

Usually ϕ is not known, and so either two readings are taken giving:

$$hf_1 = eV_{1max} + \phi$$
$$hf_2 = eV_{2max} + \phi$$

subtracting $\quad h(f_1 - f_2) = e(V_{1max} - V_{2max}),$

or a set of readings are taken and a graph is drawn (Fig. 19.6). The range of frequencies can be achieved using white light and a set of filters.

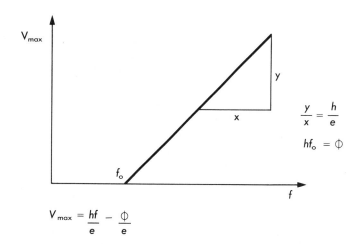

$$\frac{y}{x} = \frac{h}{e}$$

$$hf_o = \Phi$$

$$V_{max} = \frac{hf}{e} - \frac{\Phi}{e}$$

Fig. 19.6 Graph of V_{max} against f

Planck's constant can be found from the gradient, and the threshold frequency f_o is the smallest frequency which will release electrons from the metal ($hf_o = \Phi$). Increasing the intensity of the light will not affect V_{max} because the photons still have the same energy, but there will be more photons arriving per second and so there will be more electrons released per second.

ENERGY LEVELS

The model of the atom we have considered consists of electrons surrounding the nucleus. The laws of quantum mechanics allow these electrons to have only discrete amounts of energy, leading to the idea of energy levels. It is conventional to call the energy of a free electron zero, and so an electron trapped in an atom and needing to increase its energy to become free will have negative energy. The electrons in the atom fill the lowest energy levels and the atom is said to be in its **ground state**. If an atom receives sufficient energy perhaps from a colliding electron, then an electron in the highest filled level (the outer level) will jump up to another level. The atom is said to be **excited**, but this situation is unstable and the electron will quickly fall back to the ground state. The electron thus loses energy equal to the *difference* between the two levels and this is emitted as a photon of electromagnetic radiation.

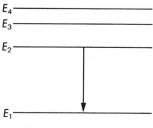

Fig. 19.7 Energy levels

If an electron falls from a level of energy E_2 to a level of energy E_1 then the frequency of the emitted radiation is given by:

$$hf = E_2 - E_1.$$

For hydrogen, the energy of the levels is given by:

$$\frac{21.8 \times 10^{-19}}{n^2}$$ J where n is the number of the level. Observation of the hydrogen

spectrum reveals three series of lines. The **Lyman series** can be explained considering transitions down to level 1, the **Balmer series** transitions to level 2 and the **Paschen series** to level 3.

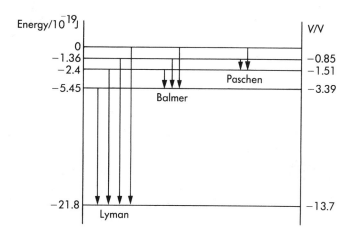

Fig. 19.8 Lyman, Balmer and
Paschen series

As the energies of the levels depend on the atomic structure, so the energy differences will also depend on the particular atom. Hence an excited gas will emit frequencies which are characteristic of the atoms of that gas. The wavelengths corresponding to these frequencies can be analysed with a diffraction grating to give the typical emission *line* spectra.

If white light is passed through a gas, then the photons within the white light which have exactly the right energy will be *absorbed* by the atoms of the gas, so that the electrons jump to a higher energy level. These excited atoms will quickly emit photons of the same energy as the electrons fall back to their original levels, but the emitted photons will not all travel in the direction of the incident light. Hence the analysed spectrum will show typical dark lines of absorption in the continuous white light spectrum.

IONISATION ENERGY AND POTENTIAL

The energy needed to lift an electron from the ground state until it is just free of the atom is known as the **ionisation energy** e.g. 21.8×10^{-9} J for hydrogen.

If this energy is provided by bombarding the atom with an electron, then the ionisation energy is provided by the k.e. of the electron. If this k.e. is provided by using a p.d. to accelerate the electron through a vacuum, then the voltage required is called the **ionisation potential**. For hydrogen $eV = 21.8 \times 10^{-19}$, so V = 13.6 V.

X-RAYS

> In only a few syllabuses.

In an **X-ray** tube, very high voltages are used to accelerate electrons through a vacuum to high speeds. X-rays are produced, by two distinct processes when the electrons hit a metal target (possibly tungsten).

i) The electrons suddenly lose energy when they collide with the target nuclei. A large percentage of the energy is converted into heat, but some is converted into X-ray photons. Each electron gains the same energy from being accelerated by the tube voltage, but varying fractions of this energy are converted into photons. As usual the energy of the photon created $= hf$. The maximum frequency (minimum wavelength) will be produced when all of the energy gained by an electron is converted into a photon. A continuous range of smaller frequencies (greater wavelengths) is created by smaller fractions of the electrons energies being converted into photons. This continuous X-ray spectrum is typical of the tube voltage but independent of the target material.

ii) The electron gives some of its energy to an electron in a target atom. The electron in the atom jumps up to a higher level and X-rays are emitted as the electron falls back to the lower level. The energy hf of the photons produced is equal to the energy level difference. The energy of an X-ray photon is very large, and so the energy levels involved must have a large separation. The frequencies (and wavelengths) emitted have discrete values which are typical of the target material. This gives rise to the peaks in Fig. 19.9.

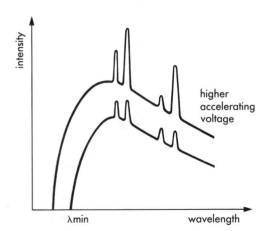

Fig. 19.9 Typical X-ray spectrum showing peaks and continuous spectrum

ELECTRON DIFFRACTION

In the preceding work in this chapter the electron has been treated as a particle. However it also displays *wave* characteristics in that it exhibits diffraction when a beam of electrons is passed through a graphite target in a vacuum tube. Diffraction rings are formed on the phosphorescent screen of the tube. Increasing the accelerating voltage of the tube makes the electrons travel faster increasing both their momenta and their kinetic energy. This

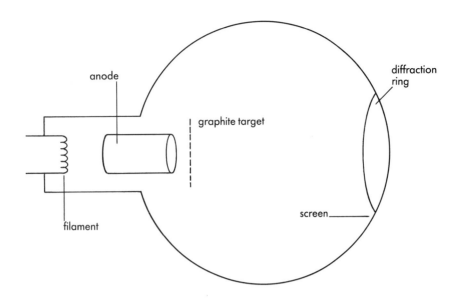

Fig. 19.10 Beam of electrons passed through graphite target in vacuum tube

results in a decrease in the size of the diffraction ring which corresponds to a decrease in wavelength.

The **de Broglie relation** explains this effect. A particle travelling with momentum mv has a wavelength given by:

$$mv = \frac{h}{\lambda}$$

For example, if $v = 5 \times 10^6$ m s^{-1}, $m = 9.1 \times 10^{-31}$ kg and $h = 6.6 \times 10^{-34}$ Js, then:

$$\lambda =. \frac{h}{mv} = 1.5 \times 10^{-10} \text{ m.}$$

An electron which has a greater momentum has a smaller wavelength. A greater momentum naturally means a greater kinetic energy.

> A useful way of expressing the relationship between momentum and k.e.

$$\text{k.e.} = \tfrac{1}{2} mv^2 = \frac{(mv)^2}{2m} = \frac{(\text{momentum})^2}{2m}$$

The following treatment of electron waves in atoms is considered in the Nuffield Course.

An electron trapped within a hydrogen atom is considered to form a standing wave (see Fig. 19.11). In a rather crude version, a one loop standing wave fits into the

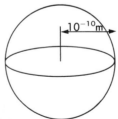

Fig. 19.11 One loop standing wave in atom

diameter of the atom. If the radius of the atom is 10^{-10}m then the diameter is 2×10^{-10}m and the wavelength of the standing wave is 4×10^{-10}m. Using

$$mv = \frac{h}{\lambda} \quad \text{and k.e.} = \frac{(\text{momentum})^2}{2m}$$

the corresponding k.e. $= 1.5 \times 10^{-18}$ J.

The p.e. of an electron at a distance of 10^{-10}m from a proton is given by

$$\frac{- e^2}{4\pi\epsilon_o \times 10^{-10}} = - 2.3 \times 10^{-18} \text{ J.}$$

So with a hydrogen atom of this size, the p.e. and k.e. are similar. If the atom were 10 times smaller, the wavelength would be 10 times less, the momentum 10 times more and the k.e. 100 times more. The p.e. would only be 10 times more and so the electron would have too much k.e. and would break out of this box.

A better model is to have the electron trapped by 1/r shaped potential well. The curve in Fig. 19.12 represents the variation of potential energy of the electron at a

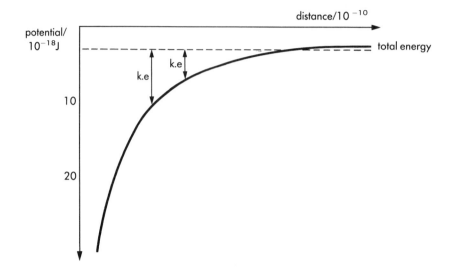

Fig. 19.12 Variations of potential energy of an electron at a distance from the proton

distance r from the proton. The dotted line represents the total energy of the electron. The k.e. = total energy − p.e. Two values of k.e. are shown on the diagram and indicate that the k.e. of the electron must increase as the electron approaches the proton. Hence the momentum increases and so the wavelength of the standing wave must decrease.

A standing wave of continuously varying wavelength can be demonstrated by swinging a heavy chain. The speed v of the transverse progressive wave down the chain is given by $\sqrt{T/m}$, where T is the tension and m is the mass per unit length. m is the same all the way down the chain but T increases towards the top where it supports more and more of the chain's weight. The frequency must be the same all the way along and so the wavelength (v/f) increases towards the top.

Fig. 19.13 Varying wavelength of standing wave from swinging heavy chain

The varying wavelength of the standing wave is shown by the nodes being nearer together, and also the curvature increasing as the wavelength decreases. The electron standing wave within the atom must therefore have this shape.

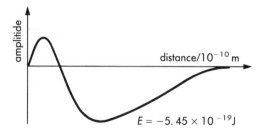

Fig. 19.14 Electron two loop standing wave within the atom

The amplitude is an indication of the probability of finding the electron. This is greatest at 5×10^{-10}m which is the 'radius' of the atom. Note that there is a chance of finding the electron where the total energy is less than the p.e. and so the k.e. is negative.

EXAMINATION QUESTIONS

**MULTIPLE
CHOICE
QUESTIONS**

1   Fig. 19.15 below shows a charged particle moving into and through the uniform vertical electric field between two horizontal metal plates. Initially, before the particle enters the field, it is travelling horizontally with velocity v. It is deflected vertically by a distance y_1 as it moves in the field. When the initial velocity of the particle is doubled, the vertical deflection is y_2. The ratio y_2/y_1 is

a) $\frac{1}{4}$ d) 2

b) $\frac{1}{2}$ e) 4

c) 1

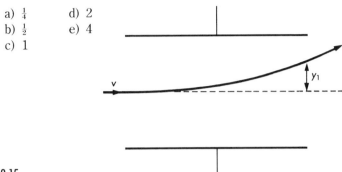

Fig. 19.15

(NI 1987)

2   A cathode ray oscilloscope is set to display 4 complete cycles of a sine wave input of frequency 50 Hz. The input to the Y-plates remains unchanged, but the frequency with which the electron beam crosses the screen from side to side is doubled by adjusting the time base. which of the following is correct?

a) 2 complete cycles are now displayed.

b) 4 complete cycles are now displayed.

c) 8 complete cycles are now displayed.

d) The frequency displayed is doubled.

e) The frequency displayed is halved.

(London 1989)

3   A charged oil-drop P, with an excess of two electron charges, is held stationary between two parallel horizontal plates by a potential difference of 150 V (see Fig. 19.16a)). A second oil-drop P′, of mass twice that of the first, is held stationary between the same plates by a potential difference of 200 V (see Fig. 19.16b)). How many excess electron charges does P′ carry?

a) 2   d) 6

b) 3   e) 8.

c) 4

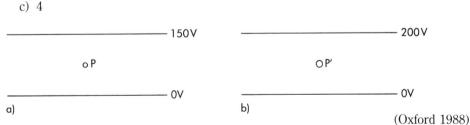

Fig. 19.16   a)   b)

(Oxford 1988)

4   Monochromatic radiation falls on a clean zinc plate. Which of the following is (are) correct?

1) If the wavelength of the radiation is sufficiently short, electrons will be emitted.

2) For a given incident wavelength, any electrons emitted will all have the same energy.

3) If electrons are emitted, their number is independent of the intensity of the radiation.

a) 1, 2, 3 correct   d) 1 only

b) 1, 2 only   e) 3 only

c) 2, 3 only

(London 1987)

5 Monochromatic light of varying intensity I is incident on a clean metal surface in a vacuum. Which of the graphs, a), b), c), d) or e), best shows the variation with I of the maximum kinetic energy E_k of the photoelectrons emitted.

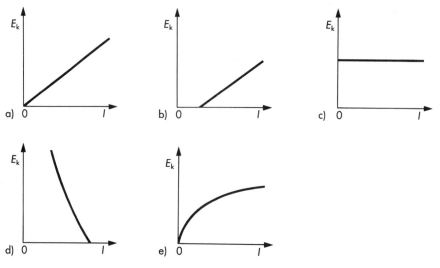

Fig. 19.17

(Oxford 1987)

6 A 3.0 mW demonstration helium-neon laser emits monochromatic light of wavelength 630 nm. What is the approximate number of photons emitted per second? Take the Planck constant h to be 6.6×10^{-34} J s, and the speed of light in vacuum c to be 3.0×10^{8} m s^{-1}.

a) 10^{10} d) 10^{19}
b) 10^{13} e) 10^{22}
c) 10^{16}

(Oxford 1988)

7 A simple model of the electronic energy levels in an atom has only three levels, X, Y and Z. A transition from level X to level Z produces radiation of wavelength 280 nm; a transition from level Y to level Z produces radiation of wavelength 200 nm. A student makes the following deductions about the energy level scheme
1) Level Y has a greater energy than levels X or Z.
2) Level X has a greater energy than levels Y or Z.
3) The wavelength of radiation emitted or absorbed in a transition between levels X and Y is 80 nm.

Which of these deductions is (are) correct?

a) None of these   d) 1 and 3 only
b) 1 only   e) 2 and 3 only
c) 2 only

(NI 1987)

8 In one model of the hydrogen atom, the energy levels W_n are given by the formula $W_n = -Rn^2$ where n is an integer and R is a constant. To produce radiation which arises from the transition $n = 3 \rightarrow n = 2$, an atom in its ground state must receive a minimum energy equal to

a) $R/9$ d) $3R/4$
b) $5R/36$ e) $8R/9$
c) $R/4$

(London 1987)

9 Which one of the spectra in Fig. 19.18b), a), b), c), d) or e), is produced by the electron energy-level transitions shown in Fig. 19.18a)? Note that the energy levels in a) and the frequencies in b) are on a linear scale.

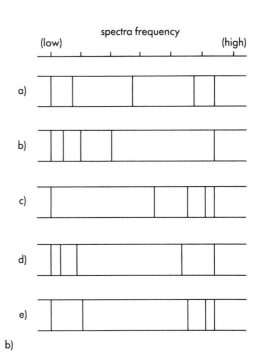

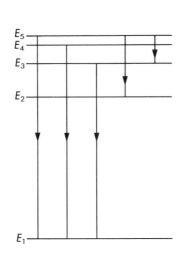

a)   b)

Fig. 19.18

(Oxford 1988)

10 What is the linear momentum of a photon of ultraviolet radiation of frequency 15×10^{14} Hz? Take the speed of light c to be 3.0×10^8 m s^{-1}, and the Planck constant h to be 6.6×10^{-34} J s.

a) 1.3×10^{-24} N s   d) 3.3×10^{-33} N s
b) 3.3×10^{-27} N s   e) 1.3×10^{-34} N s
c) 1.3×10^{-30} N s

(Oxford 1988)

ANSWERS AND COMMENTS

Question	1	2	3	4	5	6	7	8	9	10
Answer	a)	a)	b)	d)	c)	c)	b)	e)	d)	b)

1 The vertical deflection, y, is given by at^2 where a is the vertical acceleration and t is the time taken between the plates. If the initial velocity is doubled t will halve but a will be unchanged so y is quartered.

2 The frequency of the time base is doubled so that it takes less time to cross the screen and fewer cycles will be shown.

3 The field between the plates = $150/d$ where d is the plate separation. Force on drop

$$= \frac{150}{d} \times 2e = mg.$$

Similarly in diagram b) $\dfrac{200}{d} \times ne = 2mg.$

Dividing $\dfrac{200 \times n}{150 \times 2} = 2, \therefore n = \dfrac{4 \times 150}{200} = 3.$

4 1) If wavelength sufficiently short then frequency is greater than the threshold.
2) The incident photons will have the same energy but the emitted electrons will not.
3) The greater the intensity the greater the number of photons arriving per second.

5 Increasing the intensity increases the number of photons but not their energy. So k.e. of electrons is independent of I.

6 The frequency of the photons = $\dfrac{c}{\lambda} = \dfrac{3 \times 10^8}{630 \times 10^{-9}} = 4.76 \times 10^{14}$ Hz.

Energy of each photon is $hf = 6.6 \times 10^{-34} \times 4.76 \times 10^{14} = 3.14 \times 10^{-19}$ J

$$\text{The number of photons emitted per second} = \frac{\text{energy emitted per second}}{\text{energy of each photon}}$$

$$= \frac{3 \times 10^{-3}}{3.14 \times 10^{-19}} = 9.55 \times 10^{15}$$

7 A transition from level X or Y to Z produces radiation so X and Y are higher than Z. The transition from Y to Z produces a smaller wavelength corresponding to a higher frequency and so larger energy level difference i.e. Y higher than X. A transition between X and Y will produce a photon whose frequency corresponds to the frequency difference but not the wavelength difference.

8 The energy of level 3 is $-R/9$ and that of 2 is $-R/4$. To produce the required radiation the atom must receive at least enough energy to jump up from 1 to 3.

i.e. $\dfrac{-R}{9} - \dfrac{(-R)}{1} = 8R/9$.

9 There are three high energy transitions giving three high frequency, low wavelength photons and similary two low frequency, high wavelength.

10 $\lambda = \dfrac{c}{f} = \dfrac{3 \times 10^8}{15 \times 10^{14}} = 2 \times 10^{-7}$ m.

Momentum $= \dfrac{h}{\lambda} = \dfrac{6.6 \times 10^{-34}}{2 \times 10^{-7}} = 3.3 \times 10^{-27}$ Ns.

STRUCTURED QUESTIONS

11 The table shows the results of experiments in photoelectricity which gave the stopping potential V_s for photoelectrons from caesium when irradiated in turn by light of two different frequencies f.

$f/10^{15}$ Hz	0.75	0.50
V_s/V	1.22	0.19

Find, from the data, values for
a) the Planck constant and
b) the work function of caesium. (7)
    $(e = 1.6 \times 10^{-19}\,\text{C})$ (Welsh 1988)

12 A 10 W sodium lamp radiates entirely with wavelength 590 nm.
a) Assuming its efficiency is 10%, calculate the number of photons produced each second by the lamp.
b) If all the light produced is incident on metallic caesium and the photoelectric current is 48 nA, what fraction of the photons produces electrons? (8)
    $(h = 6.6 \times 10^{-34}\,\text{J s}; \quad c = 3 \times 10^8\,\text{m s}^{-1}; \quad e = 1.6 \times 10^{-19}\,\text{C})$
    (Welsh 1988)

13 A hydrogen atom emits light of wavelength 121.5 nm and 102.5 nm when it returns to its ground state from its first and second excited states respectively. Calculate:
a) the corresponding photon energies, and
b) the wavelength of light emitted when the atom passes from the second excited state to the first.
(Speed of light, $c = 3.00 \times 10^8\,\text{m s}^{-1}$; the Planck constant, $h = 6.63 \times 10^{-34}\,\text{J s}$.) (6)
    (London 1987)

14 X-rays are electromagnetic waves in the frequency range 10^{17} Hz-10^{21} Hz.
i) when a fast-moving electron is brought to a halt, X-rays may be produced. If all the kinetic energy of an electron travelling at $2.3 \times 10^7\,\text{m s}^{-1}$ is transformed into 1 photon of X-radiation, calculate the frequency of the X-radiation.
(The Planck constant $= 6.6 \times 10^{-34}\,\text{J s}$, mass of electron $= 9.1 \times 10^{-31}$ kg.)
ii) Why is it possible that X-rays may be produced at the screen of a cathode ray tube?
iii) X-rays can also be produced when an atom reverts from an excited state to its ground state. What value of the transition energy between these states would produce X-radiation of frequency 2.0×10^{17} Hz?

iv) The X-radiation produced by this transition is part of a line spectrum. Explain what is meant by a line spectrum.   (12)

(London 1988)

OUTLINE ANSWERS AND COMMENTS

11   a) Subtracting $hf_1 = eV_1 + \phi$ from $hf_2 = eV_2 + \phi$

$$h(f_2 - f_1) = eV_2 - eV_1 \quad h = e\,\frac{(V_2 - V_1)}{f_2 - f_1} = \frac{1.6 \times 10^{-19}(1.22 - 0.19)}{0.75 \times 0.5}$$

$$= 6.6 \times 10^{34}\ \text{Js}.$$

   b) Substituting $\phi = hf_2 - eV_2 = 3 \times 10^{-19}\ \text{J}$.

12   a) The frequency $= \dfrac{c}{\lambda} = \dfrac{3 \times 10^8}{590 \times 10^{-9}} = 5.08 \times 10^{14}\ \text{Hz}$.

Energy of each photon $= hf = 6.6 \times 10^{-34} \times 5.08 \times 10^{14}$
$= 3.3 \times 10^{-19}\ \text{J}$.

The lamp emits 10% of 10W as light i.e. 1W which is 1 J s^{-1}.

No. of photons emitted per second $= \dfrac{1}{3.3 \times 10^{-19}} = 3 \times 10^{18}$

   b) The current $= 48\text{nA} = 48 \times 10^{-9}\ \text{Cs}^{-1}$

This represents $\dfrac{48 \times 10^{-9}}{1.6 \times 10^{-19}} = 3 \times 10^{11}$ electrons per second.

Fraction of photons producing electrons $= \dfrac{3 \times 10^{11}}{3 \times 10^{18}} = 1$ in 10^7.

13   The frequencies are 2.47×10^{15} and 2.93×10^{15} Hz.
The corresponding photon energies are 1.64×10^{-18} and 1.94×10^{-18} J.
These represent the energies of the first and second levels above ground level, and so the difference represents the energy of the photon released when the atom passes between these levels.
Energy of photon $= (1.94 - 1.64) \times 10^{-18} = 3 \times 10^{-19}\ \text{J}$.
The wavelength $= \dfrac{3 \times 10^8 \times 6.63 \times 10^{-34}}{3 \times 10^{-19}} = 6.63 \times 10^{-7}\ \text{m}$.

14   i) $\frac{1}{2}mv^2 = hf$, hence $f = \dfrac{9.1 \times 10^{-31} \times (2.3 \times 10^7)^2}{2 \times 6.6 \times 10^{-34}} = 3.65 \times 10^{17}\ \text{Hz}$.

   ii) Fast moving electrons are stopped in a single collision at the screen of a cathode ray tube.

   iii) Energy $= hf = 6.6 \times 10^{-34} \times 2.0 \times 10^{17} = 1.32 \times 10^{-16}\ \text{J}$.

   iv) A spectrum of discrete rather then continuous wavelengths.

TUTOR'S QUESTION AND ANSWER

QUESTION

15   a) The Einstein photo-electric equation may be written in the form $hf = \frac{1}{2}mv^2 + W$. Explain the physical meaning of the three terms in this expression.   (6)

A metal surface is illuminated with light of varying frequencies and electrons are emitted. The maximum energy of the emitted electrons is measured and the following results obtained:

Frequency/Hz $\times 10^{14}$	10.00	9.0	8.0	7.0	6.0
Maximum energy/eV	2.04	1.60	1.21	0.78	0.26

By plotting a suitable graph, use this data to determine a value for the Planck constant, h. ($1\ eV \equiv 1.6 \times 10^{-19}$ J.)

What would be the maximum speed of the electrons emitted when the surface is illuminated by light of wavelength 350 nm.
(Speed of light in a vacuum, $c = 3 \times 10^8$ m s^{-1}
Mass of an electron $= 9.1 \times 10^{-31}$ kg) *(11)*

b)

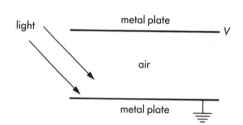

light   metal plate   V

air

metal plate

Fig. 19.19

Fig. 19.19 shows schematically how the following experiment might be performed. If the potential of the upper plate, V, was set at -2 V and radiation of frequency 8.0×10^{14} Hz was used, what fraction of the distance between the plates would the electrons of maximum velocity cover? Explain your answer.
In what ways is this situation analogous to that of a ball being thrown vertically upwards? In particular to what quantities in the case of the ball do the charge of the electron and the potential V correspond?

(6)
(London Specimen Paper)

ANSWER

15 hf is the energy of the incident photon.
$\frac{1}{2}mv^2$ is the maximum kinetic energy with which an electron is released. W (work function) is the least amount of energy needed for an electron to escape from the metal surface. The graph of frequency against $\frac{1}{2}mv^2$ has a gradient $1/h$ (see Fig. 19.20).

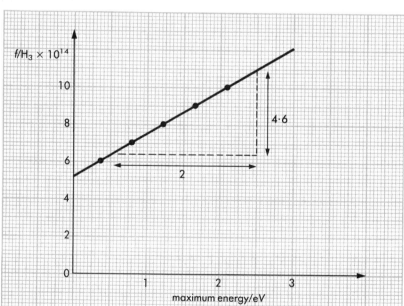

Fig. 19.20

So $1/h = \dfrac{4.6 \times 10^{14}}{2 \times 1.6 \times 10^{-19}}$, and $h = 6.9 \times 10^{-34}$ Js.

Frequency $= c/\lambda = \dfrac{3 \times 10^8}{3.5 \times 10^{-7}} = 8.6 \times 10^{14}$ Hz.

Reading from the graph, the maximum energy $= 1.5$ eV.
$\frac{1}{2}mv^2 = 1.5 \times 1.6 \times 10^{-19}$

Hence $v = \sqrt{\dfrac{(2 \times 1.5 \times 1.6 \times 10^{-19}}{9.1 \times 10^{-31}}}$

$= 7.3 \times 10^5$ m s^{-1}

b) A frequency of 8.0×10^{14} Hz corresponds to a maximum energy of 1.21 eV. A potential of 1.21 V is needed to stop such an electron and as there is a uniform potential gradient of 2 V across the plates, the electrons will stop 1.21/2 = 3/5 of the distance between the plates. A ball being thrown upwards experiences a constant downward force as does the electron. The electric field exerts a force on the charge. The gravitational field exerts a force on the mass. The potential is the energy lost per coulomb which corresponds to the energy lost per kg (change in gravitational potential).

STUDENT'S ANSWER WITH EXAMINER COMMENTS

STUDENT'S ANSWER TO QUESTION 15

"Needs to mention photon."

"A little explanation would help."

a) hf is the energy of the incident light.

b) $\frac{1}{2}mv^2$ is the kinetic energy of the ejected electron.   "Maximum."

c) W is the work function of the metal.

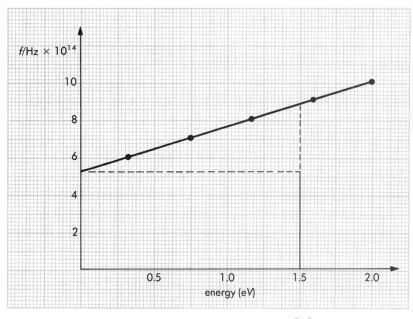

$hf = \text{energy} + W.$

$y = mx + c.$

$\text{slope} = \dfrac{1}{h} = \dfrac{\boxed{8.4} - 5.4}{1.5}$ from graph   "Misreading from graph."

$= 2.0.$

$h = \frac{1}{2} = 0.5 \ eV/Hz.$ "10^{14} missing."

$= 0.5 \times 1.6 \times 10^{-19} \ J/Hz$

"Significant figures." $= \boxed{8} \times 10^{-20} \ J \ hz^{-1}$ "Js preferable."

"Missed part of question."   b) From results table max energy = 1.21 eV ✓

$\qquad\qquad\qquad\qquad\quad$ max voltage = 1.21

$\text{fraction} = \dfrac{1.21}{2} = 0.605$ ✓

charge corresponds to mass. ✓

V to force ✗

Examiner comments: The answer gives the impression of the work of a student who understands the physics but has not left himself time to check through what he has written. As a result, instead of being of A grade standard, the cumulative loss of marks would lead to a grade C standard.

GETTING STARTED

Radioactive decay is the spontaneous emission of particles from the nuclei of certain elements. You should make sure that you are familiar with the following concepts:

- The identity of alpha, beta and gamma radiations and how their emission from the nucleus is explained.
- The random aspect of the decay.
- The terms *activity, decay constant* and *half-life*, and their interrelation.
- The ionising effects and penetrating powers of the emitted radiation; the hazards caused and relevant safety precautions.
- The principles of methods for detecting and deflecting the emitted radiation.
- The general outline of the Rutherford scattering experiment and the model of the atom predicted from the results.
- The structure of the nucleus and the ideas of the strong force, binding energy and mass defect.
- A knowledge of the basic principles of fission and fusion.

ESSENTIAL PRINCIPLES

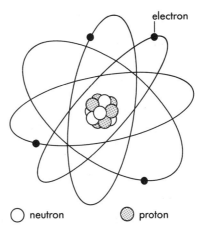

electron

neutron   proton

Fig. 20.1 Nuclear model of the atom

THE NUCLEAR MODEL OF THE ATOM

Fig. 20.1 shows a model with a massive **nucleus**, though very small in actual size, surrounded by orbiting electrons. The diameter of the nucleus is about 10^{-14} m and that of the atom about 10^{-10} m.

- The nucleus contains protons and neutrons (collectively called **nucleons**). The total number of neutrons and protons is known as the **nucleon number** A.
- The electron has a rest mass of 9.1×10^{-31} kg and a negative charge of 1.6×10^{-19} C.
- The proton has a mass about 1800 times that of the electron and a positive charge of 1.6×10^{-19} C. (i.e. $+1$ electron charge).
- The neutron has a similar mass (just slightly less) to the proton but is uncharged.
- The number of protons (the **proton number** Z) determines which element the atom is.
- In a neutral atom there are as many orbiting electrons as there are protons in the nucleus and so the atom is uncharged.
- **Ionisation** is the process whereby an atom somhow loses or gains an electron to become a positive or negative ion.
- **Isotopes** are atoms or ions of the same element but with different numbers of nucleons. i.e. the same number of protons but different number of neutrons. An isotope of element X with proton number **Z** and nucleon number A is represented by $^{A}_{Z}\text{X}$.
- A radioactive source is a collection of such atoms whose nuclei have the property of randomly but spontaneously emitting radiation.

THREE MAIN TYPES OF RADIATION

ALPHA RADIATION

This is a particle, comprising two protons and two neutrons. Hence it has a mass about 8000 times that of the electron and a charge of $+3.2 \times 10^{-19}$ C.

BETA RADIATION

There are in fact two β particles the $\beta-$ and the $\beta+$. The $\beta-$ is the beta particle normally referred to in questions and it is an electron. Electrons do not in fact exist in the nucleus, but the beta particle is created and ejected from the nucleus when a neutron changes into a proton. The $\beta+$ particle (a positron, same mass as electron, same charge as proton) is created and ejected when a proton changes into a neutron.

GAMMA RADIATION

This is a photon of electromagnetic radiation sometimes ejected by nuclei following either a beta or an alpha emission, when the nucleus adjusts its energy levels. It has no mass and no charge.

IONISATION AND RANGE

An alpha particle is a charged particle emitted with considerable energy (a few *MeV*). Alphas from one source are all ejected with the same energy. When the particle passes near to a gas atom it may attract the outer electrons and ionise the gas atom. Each ionisation requires energy and so the alpha continually loses kinetic energy. Eventually it slows down so much that it can no longer ionise. It then picks up two electrons to become a Helium atom. The average distance the alpha particles travel before this happens is known as the *range*, which depends on the energy with which it is emitted. Alphas typically have a range of a few cm in air. Alphas from one source all have the same range.

Beta particles also ionise any surrounding gas, but unlike alphas however they are emitted with a range of energies because their ejection from a nucleus is accompanied by another particle called the anti-neutrino with which they share their energy. The maximum energy with which betas are emitted is also a few *MeV*, but they produce less ionisation per cm and so travel further. Typically their *maximum* range in air is 30 cm.

Gamma particles are not charged and can travel considerable distances in air before giving up all their energy to an atom which ejects a very energetic electron.

DEFLECTION OF PARTICLES

> **Use Fleming's left hand rule to find the direction of this force.**

Alpha and beta particles are both *charged* and so will be deflected by both electric and magnetic fields, as are other charged particles. In an *electric* field E they will experience a force Eq in the direction of the field, where q is the charge (remember the charge on the beta is negative).

In a *magnetic* field of flux density B they will experience a force which cause them to describe circles of radius $r = \dfrac{mv}{Bq}$, where m is the mass of the particle, q is its charge and v its speed.

The effects of fields on charged particles are discussed in Chapter 14.

METHODS OF DETECTING PARTICLES

IONISATION CHAMBER

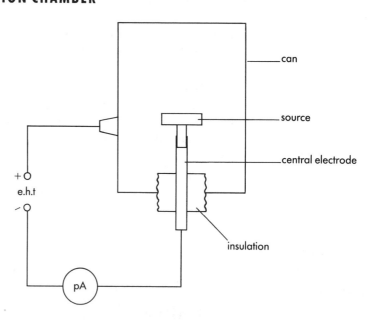

Fig. 20.2 Ionisation chamber

The particle enters the **ionisation chamber** and ionises the air inside. The e.h.t. supply, connected between the can and the central electrode, creates an electric field which accelerates the positive ions towards the centre and the negative ions (electrons) towards the can. This flow of charge constitutes an **ionisation current** which is measured by the picoammeter placed in series with the chamber. The e.h.t. voltage is increased until the ionisation current is a maximum. Thus all the ions produced are reaching the electrodes and none are recombining. This gives us:

current = charge produced per second

= number of ion pairs produced per second × the charge on each ion

$I = ne$ where e = 1.6×10^{-19} C.

If I is measured, n (the number of ion pairs produced per second by the source) can be calculated.

The ionisation chamber is suitable for detecting alphas as they produce a large number of ions in a short distance. Betas and gammas do not produce a large enough ionisation current to be detected by this method.

THE GEIGER TUBE

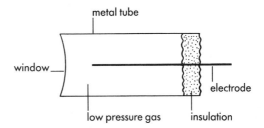

Fig. 20.3 Geiger tube

In some ways, this is similar to the ionisation chamber with an electric field to accelerate the ion pairs produced by the incoming particles (see Fig. 20.3). However, the **Geiger tube** contains a gas at low pressure so that the accelerated electrons can gain sufficient energy before they next collide with a gas atom to cause further ionisation. This effect amplifies the number of electrons arriving at the central electrode, and this 'avalanche' of charge is sufficient to be detected by a pulse counting circuit. The more massive, slower moving positive ions cause some problems, creating a short 'dead time' when the tube is not able to detect particles.

> **Remember to subtract the background count.**

The circuit *counts* the number of particles *entering the tube* per second. It is suitable for betas and gammas, but to count alphas the tube needs a specially thin window to allow in the alphas.

CLOUD CHAMBERS

Conditions inside a **cloud chamber** are arranged so that small liquid droplets form around the ions produced by radioactive particles. Viewed from above and illuminated from the side, the reflections from these droplets appear as a thin cloud called a *track*.

The tracks of alphas are straight because little deflects the massive particles, and the tracks are dense because of the profuse ionisation caused by them. The tracks of betas are less dense and also less straight. A gamma track occurs where the particle gives up all its energy to eject an energetic electron from an atom. This energetic electron produces a short 'beta' track in mid-air away from the source.

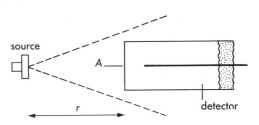

Fig. 20.4 Measurement of activity

PARTICLE COUNTING

The number of counts per second recorded by the detector gives the number of particles entering the area A per second. If N particles leave the source per second in a *forward* direction then, in travelling a distance r, they will have spread over the surface area $2\pi r^2$ of a hemisphere of radius r. The *fraction* passing through area A is therefore given by: $\dfrac{A}{2\pi r^2}$. The distance r must clearly be less than the range of the particles in air.

> **Remember with an inverse square law the value *quarters* if the distance *doubles*, etc.**

This assumes that all the particles emitted in the direction of the detector actually reach it. If this is the case, then the count rate will obey an inverse square law i.e. the count will quarter if the distance doubles. This will apply to alphas over a distance less than their range and to gammas over a long distance.

USES, HAZARDS AND SAFETY

One of the main uses of radioactivity is in medicine, where a small amount of radioactive material can be injected into the body for use as a tracer. A detector placed outside the body can be used to diagnose various ailments. The source needs to be a gamma source, so that it can penetrate the skin, and have a short half-life.

The hazards of radioactive material are caused by the effects on the body cells of the ionisation caused by the ejected particles. Alphas are the least penetrating and cannot get through the skin, but cause the most ionisation if ingested. Gammas are the most penetrating. The two points to be considered for safety are the penetrating power and half-life. Surrounding the material with lead or concrete will reduce the number of particles escaping. Keeping a safe distance is also sensible. The longer the half-life the longer the material will emit radiation.

DECAY, RANDOMNESS AND HALF-LIFE

A radioactive source is said to be **decaying** because its nuclei are ejecting particles and so are becoming nuclei of different elements.

The emission of an alpha particle reduces the proton number Z by 2 and the nucleon number A by 4. The emission of a beta particle has no effect on A but increases Z by 1. The emission of gamma radiation has no effect on A or Z.

The decay process is **random** in that each atom of a particular source has a fixed chance of decaying in one second. This chance is known as the **decay constant**, λ. There is no way of knowing which particular atoms will decay in any one second, but if there are a very large number of atoms, one can predict how many will on average decay in one second. It can be compared with when you throw a very large number of dice and there is no way of knowing which particular dice will turn up as 'threes'; but you can predict that on average, one sixth of them will be 'threes', because each die has the same fixed one sixth chance of being a 'three'. As with the dice, the number which decay in the next second will be less because there were fewer to start with.

The number dN decaying in a time dt is given by $dN = -\lambda N \, dT$, hence:

$$\frac{dN}{dt} = -\lambda N,$$

$$\text{where } \lambda \text{ is the fraction} = \frac{\text{number of disintegrations per second} \left(\dfrac{dN}{dt} \right)}{\text{number of atoms present } (N)}$$

$\dfrac{dN}{dt}$ is clearly the rate of emission of particles and is known as the **activity** of the source.

The negative sign arises because N is decreasing. An activity of 1 disintegration per second is 1 Bq (becquerel).

Hence the activity depends on N. The more atoms there are the greater the activity and rate of decay. The activity also depends on λ. The greater the chance an individual atom will decay in one second, the greater the overall rate of decay. You can verify that the relation $N = N_o e^{-\lambda t}$ can be obtained by integration from:

$$\int_{N_o}^{N} \frac{dN}{N} = \int_{o}^{t} -\lambda \, dt.$$

N_o is the number of atoms at the beginning i.e. at $t=0$, and N is the number of atoms remaining at time t later.

After a time of one *half-life* $t_{\frac{1}{2}}$, the number of atoms remaining is $N_o/2$ (the activity has also halved), and so:

$$\frac{N_o}{2} = N_o \, e^{-\lambda t_{\frac{1}{2}}}; \text{ hence}$$

$$t_{\frac{1}{2}} = \frac{ln2}{\lambda} \, .$$

A large λ means a short half-life because at any particular time there is a large rate of decay for a given number of atoms. After one half-life, both the number of atoms and the activity have halved. After two half-lives they have both quartered, and so on. Remember that the half-life of a nuclide is the *average* time it takes for half its atoms to decay.

POWER AVAILABLE FROM A RADIOACTIVE SOURCE

If the energy of an emitted particle is E, then the *rate* of emission of energy (power) is

$$E \; \frac{\mathrm{d}N}{\mathrm{d}t}$$ (energy of each particle multiplied by the number of particles emitted per second).

RADIOACTIVE SERIES

The first member of a series decays into a daughter product, but this in turn will probably itself decay until a stable non-decaying isotope is produced. The list of all the members of the family is called a radioactive series. Some time after the production of the original source all the members of the series will be in *equilibrium*, i.e. they will be being produced from their parent at the same rate at which they are decaying, i.e. $N_1\lambda_1 = N_2\lambda_2 = N_3\lambda_3$ . . . ., where N_1, N_2, ... are the equilibrium numbers of atoms of each member of the series.

An example of a series is:

$$\overset{\alpha}{} \qquad \overset{\beta}{} \qquad \overset{\beta}{} \qquad \overset{\alpha}{} \qquad \overset{\alpha}{} \qquad \overset{\alpha}{}$$
$$^{232}_{90}\mathrm{Th} \rightarrow {}^{228}_{88}\mathrm{Ra} \rightarrow {}^{228}_{89}\mathrm{Ac} \rightarrow {}^{228}_{90}\mathrm{Th} \rightarrow {}^{224}_{88}\mathrm{Ra} \rightarrow {}^{220}_{80}\mathrm{Rn} \rightarrow {}^{216}_{84}\mathrm{Po}$$

Note the effects on Z and A of the emission of alphas and betas. Note also that ^{232}Th and ^{228}Th are *isotopes*. To measure the half-life of a member of a series it has to be isolated from its parent so that it is decaying, but not being produced at the same time. Half-life is usually measured by finding the time it takes for the activity to halve.

RUTHERFORD'S EXPERIMENT

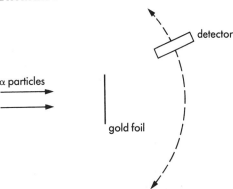

Fig. 20.5 Rutherford's experiment

In this experiment, performed by Geiger and Marsden, alpha particles were fired at a thin sheet of gold foil. Most of the alphas went straight through implying that most of the foil was empty space, but about 1 in 8000 alphas were deflected through angles greater than 90°.

At the time the results were surprising, but Rutherford put forward the explanation that the atoms of gold had *small massive* centres called *nuclei*, with a *positive charge*. Surrounding the nucleus were electrons orbiting a long way from the nucleus. Thus if a positive alpha came near the nucleus, it was repelled by the positive nucleus and so deflected. It would suffer a greater deflection the nearer it was to hitting the nucleus. Most of the alphas passed between the nuclei and were hardly affected.

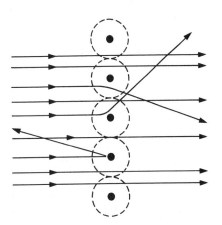

Fig. 20.6 Deflection and passage of
α particles through gold nuclei

THE NUCLEUS

This is a collection of protons and neutrons. There will be an electrostatic force of repulsion between all the protons. There must therefore be another force holding the nucleus together. This is known as the 'strong' force which is an attractive force existing between all nucleons. The strong force is very short range and only affects the nearest neighbouring nucleons; but the electrostatic force (an inverse square law) extends across the whole nucleus and beyond. If the nucleus has a small number of protons then about the same number of neutrons is sufficient to hold the nucleus together. As the proton number increases, the number of neutrons has to exceed the number of protons.

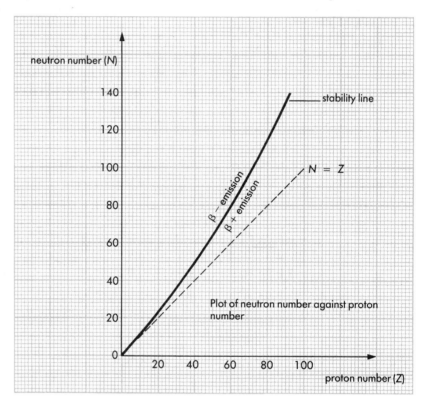

Fig. 20.7 Plot of neutron number against proton number

Fig. 20.7 shows a plot of nucleon number against proton number. The elements on the proton rich side of the dotted line tend to emit $\beta+$ particles and those on the neutron rich side tend to emit $\beta-$. Large numbers of nucleons can lead to instability, and the constant interchange of particles in the nucleus can lead to the formation of an alpha particle, which is repelled by the rest of the nucleus and ejected.

NUCLEAR FISSION

Accurate experiments performed with mass spectrometers show that the mass of a nucleus is less than the combined masses of all the separate nucleons. This difference is known as the **mass defect**. Such masses are measured in a.m.u. (u) where $1\ u = 1.66 \times 10^{-27}$ kg. Applying Einstein's equation $E = m\,c^2$ concerning the equivalence of mass and energy, the energy of the nucleons in the nucleus is less than if they are all separate (energy is required to separate the nucleons). The difference is known as the **binding energy**.

The graph in Fig. 20.8 of binding energy *per nucleon* shows a maximum at a nucleon number of about 80. If a nucleus of large mass splits (**fissions**) into two nuclei of smaller mass, then bearing in mind that the total number of nucleons remains constant, the total energy in the nuclei is less, and the energy difference is released as kinetic energy of the fragments. In ^{235}U, spontaneous fission does not occur, but fission can be caused by bombarding it with thermal (low energy) neutrons.

$$^{235}\text{U} + {}^1\text{n} \rightarrow\ X + Y + k\,{}^1\text{n}$$

X and Y represent the fission fragments whose proton and nucleon numbers are not the same values for each fission; k is the number of neutrons released in the process. k is not always the same, but the total numbers of protons and nucleons must be the same on both sides of the equation. k is usually 2 or 3 with an average value of 2.47. These neutrons can be used to produce further fissions, so producing a chain reaction which will run out of control unless the number of neutrons produced is kept under control. In fact the neutrons

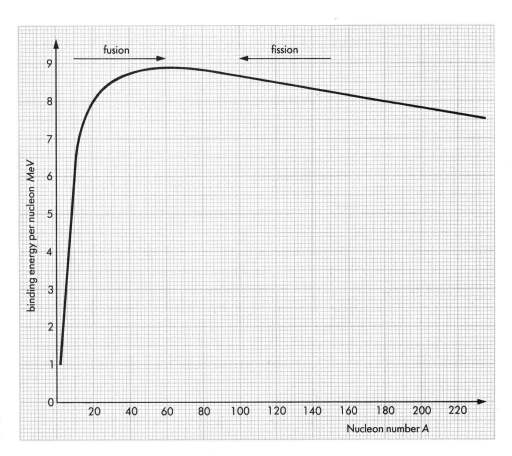

Fig. 20.8 Graph of binding energy
per nucleon against nucleon number

produced in a fission reaction have considerable energies and are known as 'fast' neutrons which do not fission ^{235}U. The neutrons have to be slowed down to thermal energies by allowing them to bounce around amongst the atoms of a **moderator** such as deuterium. To control the reaction, some of the neutrons are deliberately absorbed by boron **control rods**, which can be moved in and out of the reactor core. The situation is further complicated by the fact that natural uranium contains only 0.7% of the isotope ^{235}U, the rest being ^{238}U, which can fission with fast neutrons.

You may need to know more detail of a reactor.

FUSION

Energy can also be produced by the **fusion** of two nuclei of small mass to produce a more massive nucleus. e.g. $^{2}_{1}\text{H} + ^{2}_{1}\text{H} \rightarrow ^{3}_{2}\text{He} + ^{1}_{0}\text{n}$.

This reaction takes place in the sun. The graph in Fig. 20.8 shows how this is possible. The difficulty arises in providing the very high temperatures needed to give the two positive nuclei sufficient kinetic energy to overcome their electrostatic repulsion. At such high temperatures atoms become ionised creating a plasma which is difficult to control.

EXAMINATION QUESTIONS

MULTIPLE CHOICE QUESTIONS

1 Radioactive lead $^{210}_{82}$Pb decays by a series of disintegrations to the stable isotope $^{206}_{82}$ Pb. In order to achieve this the sequence of decays might be
a) α, α, β⁻ 　　　　d) β⁻, β⁻, β⁻, β⁻
b) β⁻, β⁻, α 　　　　e) α, β⁻, α, β⁻
c) α, α, α, α
(London 1989)

2 Isotopes of an element have the same
1) neutron number.
2) chemical properties.
3) nucleon number.

a) 1, 2, 3 correct 　　d) 1 only
b) 1, 2 only 　　　　e) 2 only
c) 2, 3 only

3 A sample of a certain radioactive nuclide has a half-life of 8.0 s. The time, in seconds, required for seven-eighths of the sample to decay is

a) 1.0   d) 24.0
b) 7.0   e) 56.0
c) 16.0

(NI 1987)

4 An isotope has a half-life of 10 years. This implies that at the end of
1) 1 year, 0.90 of the isotope remains.
2) 5 years, 0.75 of the isotope remains.
3) 20 years, 0.25 of the isotope remains.

a) 1, 2, 3 correct   d) 1 only
b) 1, 2 only   e) 3 only
c) 2, 3 only

(London 1987)

5 The phosphorus isotope $^{30}_{15}$P decays to a silicon isotope by the emission of a positron, a particle equal in mass to that of a $\beta(-)$ particle but of opposite charge. The correct symbol for the silicon isotope is

a) $^{31}_{15}$ Si   d) $^{30}_{16}$ Si
b) $^{31}_{14}$ Si   e) $^{29}_{15}$ Si
c) $^{30}_{14}$ Si

(Oxford 1987)

6 The number of disintegrations per second in a sample of a radioactive nuclide depends on the:
1) number of atoms in one mole of atoms of the nuclide.
2) number of atoms in the sample.
3) half-life of the nuclide.

a) 1, 2, 3 correct   d) 1 only
b) 1, 2 only   e) 3 only
c) 2, 3 only

(London 1989)

7 When an alpha particle approaches a heavy nucleus X, it may behave in various ways depending on its initial direction of travel. Fig. 20.9 shows various paths, P, Q, R, S and T. Which one of the following statements is correct?

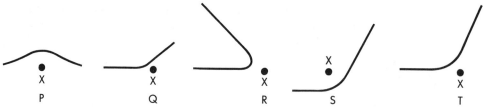

Fig. 20.9   P   Q   R   S   T

a) All of these are possible.
b) Neither P nor R is possible.
c) Both R and T are possible.
d) Both Q and S are possible.
e) None of these are possible.

(AEB 1987)

8 A sample of radioactive material contains n atoms with half-life $t_{\frac{1}{2}}$. Which one of the following gives the decay-rate of the sample?

a) $\dfrac{n}{t_{\frac{1}{2}}}$ d) $n\ln t_{\frac{1}{2}}$

b) $e^{-nt_{\frac{1}{2}}}$ e) $n\left(\dfrac{\ln 2}{t_{\frac{1}{2}}}\right)$

c) $ne^{-t_{\frac{1}{2}}}$

(Oxford 1988)

9   The atomic mass of $^{14}_{7}$N is 14.003074 u. The sum of the atomic masses of $^{1}_{1}$H and $^{13}_{6}$C is 14.011179 u. It would be reasonable to suppose that the nuclear reaction $^{1}_{1}$H + $^{13}_{6}$C → $^{14}_{7}$N:

a) could only happen if energy is supplied;
b) could never take place;
c) could only occur in conditions of zero gravity (that is, of 'weightlessness');
d) must involve the emission of a further atomic particle;
e) will result in the production of energy.

(Oxford 1988)

10   What is the function of a *moderator* in a fission reactor?

a) To cool the reactor core.
b) To slow down the neutrons released during fission.
c) To absorb excess neutrons.
d) To shield the operators from radioactivity.
e) To contain the fission products produced in the reactor.

(NI 1988)

ANSWERS AND COMMENTS

Question	1	2	3	4	5	6	7	8	9	10
Answer	b)	e)	d)	e)	c)	c)	c)	e)	e)	b)

1   βs have no effect on the nucleon number which changes from 210 to 206 by the emission of 1α, but this reduces proton number by 2, so 2β^{-} are emitted as well to make final proton number 82.

2   1) incorrect   2) correct   3) incorrect.

3   After 3 half-lives $\frac{1}{8}$ remains so $\frac{7}{8}$ decays. $3 \times 8 = 24$s.

4   Fraction f remaining given by $\dfrac{N}{N_{o}} = e^{-\lambda t} = e^{-\ln. t/t_{\frac{1}{2}}}$

   Substituting $t = 1$ year $f = 0.933$, 5 years,
   $f = 0.707$ and 20 years is two half-lives
   $\therefore f = \frac{1}{4}$.

5   The emission of a positron means nucleon number does not change but proton number decreases by 1.

6    $\dfrac{dN}{dt} = -\lambda N$. N is number of atoms in sample, λ depends on $t_{\frac{1}{2}}$.

7   P and S show attraction so not possible. R and T are possible. Q shows repulsion but not symmetry. (Also there is no answer R and T and S.)

8    $\dfrac{dn}{dt} = -\lambda n$ $\lambda = \dfrac{\ln 2}{t_{\frac{1}{2}}}$ $\dfrac{dn}{dt} = \dfrac{-(\ln 2)n}{t_{\frac{1}{2}}}$

9   The values given show that the mass decreases and so energy is less and excess is released.

10   See text (p. 241).

STRUCTURED QUESTIONS

11   a) Define the *decay constant* of a radioactive material and show how it is related to the *half-life* of the material.

   b) A gamma ray emitter, which may be considered to be a point source radiating uniformly in all directions, is situated 50 cm away from a gamma ray detector which has an effective area of 6.0 cm^{2}. The recorded count rate at a given time is 320 s^{-1}.

   i) Estimate a value for the activity of the source at this time.
   ii) Given that the half-life is 30 seconds, calculate a value for the number of radioactive atoms present in the sample 120 seconds before the measurement was made.

(10)

(AEB 1988)

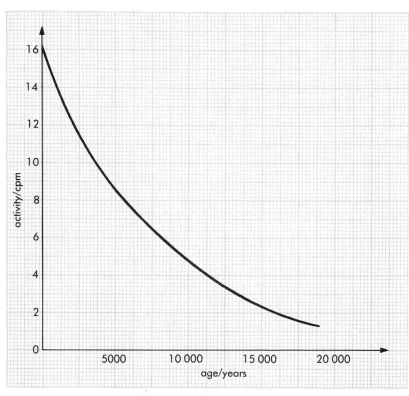

Fig. 20.10

12 a) The radioactive isotope $^{228}_{90}$ Th emits an alpha particle to become the isotope $^{a}_{b}$ Ra. Explain the meanings of the superscript and subscript numbers 228 and 90 and state the values of a and b.

b) The graph of Fig. 20.10 shows how the activity in counts per minute (cpm) of 1.00 g of processed carbon decreases as it ages.

i) State the half-life of the radioactive isotope present in the carbon.

ii) 0.50 g of similarly processed carbon taken from some ancient charcoal gave a measured activity of 5.0 cpm. Estimate the age of the charcoal. (8)

(Southern 1988)

13 A sample of radioactive caesium-137 has an activity of 1.5×10^{14} Bq and is used to provide power for a generator. The half-life of caesium-137 is 30 years and each radioactive decay emits a β-particle of average energy 0.5 MeV.

a) Calculate the initial maximum theoretical power output (in watts) of the generator.

b) Calculate the power output after 10 years.

(e = 1.6×10^{-19} C) (8)

(Welsh 1987)

OUTLINE ANSWERS AND COMMENTS

11 a) See text (p. 238).

b) i) See Fig. 20.4.

The count rate records the number entering the detector which is a fraction of those emitted. This fraction is also the ratio of area of detector to area over which particles are spread:

$$\text{Fraction} = \frac{320}{N} = \frac{6.0}{4\pi 50^2}$$

$$N = \frac{320 \times 4\pi \times 50^2}{6}$$

$$N = 1.68 \times 10^6 \text{ Bq}$$

ii) 120 secs is 4 half-lives, during which count rate decreases by factor 16 s estimated count = $16 \times 1.68 \times 10^6 = 2.68 \times 10^7$

$$\lambda = \frac{\ln 2}{t_{\frac{1}{2}}} = \frac{\ln 2}{30} = 0.023 \text{ so number of atoms } N = \frac{dN/dt}{\lambda} = \frac{2.68 \times 10}{0.023}$$

$$N = 1.16 \times 10^9$$

12 a) 228 = nucleon number, 90 = proton number, a = 224, b = 88.
    b) i) Activity decreases from 16 to 8 in 5075 years. Half-life = 5075 years.
       ii) 1 g gives account rate of 10.0 cpm after 3700 years
         0.5 g would give count rate of 5.0 cpm after this time.
         So estimated age = 3800 years.

13 $1 \text{ eV} = 1.6 \times 10^{-19} \text{ J}$ $1 \text{ MeV} = 1.6 \times 10^{-13} \text{ J}$

    a) Power = rate of emission of energy = $\dfrac{dN}{dt} \times$ energy of particle

$$= 1.5 \times 10^{14} \times 0.5 \times 1.6 \times 10^{-13}$$
$$= 12 \text{ W}.$$

    b) $\lambda = \dfrac{\ln 2}{t_{\frac{1}{2}}}$ $\dfrac{dN}{dt} = \dfrac{dN_o}{dt} e^{-\lambda t} = 1.5 \times 10^{14} \; e^{-\ln 2 \cdot \frac{10}{30}}$

$$= 1.5 \times 10^{14} \; e^{-\ln \frac{2}{3}} = 1.2 \times 10^{14}$$

So power $= 1.2 \times 10^{14} \times 0.5 \times 1.6 \times 10^{-13}$
$$= 9.5 \text{ W}.$$

TUTOR'S QUESTION AND ANSWER

QUESTION

14 a) What conclusions about the structure of atoms were made as a result of α-particle scattering experiment with thin metal foils?   *(5)*
    b) i) What is meant by conservation of mass-energy in nuclear reactions?   *(3)*
       ii) Explain how and why the masses of atoms differ from the sum of the masses of their constituent particles.   *(3)*
    c) Radium (Ra) decays to radon (Rn) by the reaction
$$^{226}_{88}\text{Ra} \rightarrow \,^{222}_{86}\text{Rn} + \,^{4}_{2}\text{He} + \gamma$$

The atomic masses are:
Radium 3.753×10^{-25} Kg
Radon $\;\;3.686 \times 10^{-25}$ kg
Helium 0.066×10^{-25} kg

[Take the Planck constant h to be 6.6×10^{-34} J s, and the speed of light c in vacuum to be 3.0×10^{8} m s^{-1}.]
     i) Estimate the energy (in joules) released when an atom of ^{226}Ra decays.   *(4)*
     ii) Estimate the wavelength of the gamma (γ) photon emitted during this decay given that 4% of the energy released turns to gamma radiation.   *(4)*
     iii) What happens to the remaining 96% of the energy?   *(2)*
    d) Two units of mass-energy used in nuclear studies are the unified atomic mass unit (*u*) and the megaelectronvolt (*MeV*). The unified atomic mass unit is defined as 1/12 of the mass of a carbon-12 atom. Calculate:
     i) the value of *u* in kilograms;   *(3)*
     ii) the equivalent of 1 MeV, in joules;   *(2)*
     iii) the equivalent of 1 u, in MeV.   *(4)*
    [Take the Avogadro constant N_A to be 6.0×10^{23} mol^{-1} and the electronic charge e to be 1.6×10^{-19} C. The molar mass of carbon-12 is 0.012 kg.]
                                           (Oxford 1988)

ANSWER

14 a) The fact that most alphas went straight through the thin foil undeviated suggested that most of the foil was empty space. The fact that about 1 in 8000 were deflected through angles of more than 90° suggested a small positively charged and massive nucleus to each atom.

b) i) If the mass decreases in a nuclear reaction then the mass difference is released as an equivalent amount of energy calculated using the formula $\triangle E = \triangle m\,c^2$.

ii) The masses of atoms are less than the sum of the masses of their constituent particles. Energy is needed to separate the particles and as the energy is greater than the particles are separate, so is the mass.

c) i) Mass decrease $= 3.753 \times 10^{-25} - (3.686 \times 10^{-25} + 0.066 \times 10^{-25})$
$= 1 \times 10^{-28}$

So energy released $= 1 \times 10^{-28} \times (3 \times 10^8)^2 = 9 \times 10^{-12}$ J.

ii) $4\% = 0.04 \times 9 \times 10^{-12} = 3.6 \times 10^{-13}$ J.

If this energy is released as a photon then $hf = 3.6 \times 10^{-13}$

$$f = \frac{3.6 \times 10^{-13}}{6.6 \times 10^{-34}} = 5.45 \times 10^{20} \text{ Hz}$$

$$\lambda = \frac{c}{f} = \frac{3 \times 10^8}{5.45 \times 10^{20}} = 5.5 \times 10^{-13} \text{ m}.$$

iii) The rest of the energy appears as kinetic energy of the Rn and He nuclei.

d) i) Molar mass (contains Avogadro number) of carbon-12 $= 0.012$ kg.

$$\text{So mass of 1 atom of carbon-12} = \frac{0.012}{6 \times 10^{23}} = 2 \times 10^{-26} \text{ kg}$$

$$1 \text{ u} = \frac{2 \times 10^{-26}}{12} = 1.66 \times 10^{-27} \text{ kg}$$

ii) 1 eV is energy gained by 1.6×10^{-19} C accelerated by 1 V.

So 1 eV $= 1.6 \times 10^{-19}$ J and 1 MeV $= 1.6 \times 10^{-13}$ J

iii) $E = m\,c^2$ m $= 1.66 \times 10^{-27}$ kg

$E = 1.66 \times 10^{-27} \times (3 \times 10^8)^2 = 1.494 \times 10^{-10}$ J

$$= \frac{1.494 \times 10^{-10}}{1.6 \times 10^{-13}} = 933 \text{ MeV}$$

1 u $\equiv 933$ MeV

STUDENT'S ANSWER WITH EXAMINER COMMENTS

STUDENT'S ANSWER TO QUESTION 14

> Has not mentioned that mass is concentrated in nucleus. Needs a little more detail and explanation.

> Not a reason.

a) The conclusions were that the atoms were mainly empty space with a small positive nucleus. This was found out because most of the alphas went straight through the foils but a few were deflected through large angles.

> Not clear what this means.

b) i) Energy and mass are conserved in nuclear reactions.

ii) The mass of the atom is less than the total mass of the particles because of the mass defect.

c) i)
Mass on left	$= 3.73 \times 10^{-25}$
Mass on right	$= (3.686 + 0.066) \times 10^{-25} = 3.752 \times 10^{-25}$
Mass change	$= 0.001 \times 10^{-25}$ kg
E	$= m\,c^2$
Energy change	$= (0.01 \times 10^{-25}) \times (3 \times 10^8)$
	$= 9 \times 10^{-12}$ J

ii) $4\% = \dfrac{4}{100} \times 9 \times 10^{-12} = 3.6 \times 10^{-13}$ J

$hf = 3.6 \times 10^{-13}$ $f = \dfrac{3.6 \times 10^{-13}}{6.6 \times 10^{-34}} = 5.45 \times 10^{20}$ Hz

$\lambda = \dfrac{c}{f} = \dfrac{3 \times 10^8}{5.45 \times 10^{20}} = 5.5 \times 10^{-13}$ m

iii) appears as heat

d) i) Mass of 1 atom of C^{12} $= \dfrac{0.012}{6 \times 10^{23}} = 2 \times 10^{-26}$

   $1 \text{ m} = \dfrac{1}{12} \times 2 \ 10^{-26} = 1{,}67 \times 10^{-27} \text{ kg}$

ii) $1\text{eV} = 1.6 \times 10^{-19} \text{J}$ $1\text{MeV} = 1.6 \times 10^{-19} \times 10^{6} = 1.6 \times 10^{-13} \text{J}$

iii) $E = 1 \text{ MeV} = 1.6 \times 10^{-13} \text{ J}$

   $m = \dfrac{E}{c^2} = \dfrac{1.6 \times 10^{-13}}{(3 \times 10^8)^2} = 1.77 \times 10^{-30} \text{ kg}$

   $m = \dfrac{1.77 \times 10^{-30}}{1.67 \times 10^{-27}} \text{ u} = 1.06 \times 10^{-3} \text{ u}$ **This is equivalent of 1 MeV in u.**

Overall comments: Although there is an error at the end and the initial description is a little weak the bulk of the arithmetical answer is clear. This is what might be expected of a B grade candidate.

PRACTICAL TESTS AND DATA ANALYSIS

BEFORE THE EXAMINATION

AT THE EXAMINATION

EXAMINATION QUESTION

OUTLINE ANSWER AND COMMENTS

GETTING STARTED

In GCSE Physics, unless you were a 'private candidate', your experimental work will have been examined by a method of continuous assessment. At A Level is is much more likely that your assessment will be an externally set **practical test**. These vary considerably from Board to Board. It is common to have one or more experiments of an hour or more in duration in which you have to take a range of readings. JMB has this kind of test, but also a **circus practical**, in which the candidates spend a short amount of time at a large number of stations. This allows the Board to put candidates up against more expensive items of apparatus which a Centre would possess in small numbers. There is a similar pattern in Nuffield A Level Physics in the practical problems paper. However, here there is less emphasis on the accurate collection of data than on the ability to think and write about problems of Physics presented on the bench. The London Board also has a circus arrangement, but with three half hour stations. Again the intention is to test a wider range of skills than is possible with the single experiment.

Some Boards also set a **data analysis test** where candidates are provided with some data from an experiment which they must analyse. Sometimes this test is set within a theory paper. London adds this test to its stations in its practical circus. The exercise is quite similar to the analysis which follows the data collection in a longer-type practical test and so the advice that follows about analysis and presentation applies equally to these tests.

ESSENTIAL PRINCIPLES

BEFORE THE EXAMINATION

The main difference between laboratory work in a practical test and laboratory work during your course is that because many candidates will be being tested simultaneously, it is unlikely that you will be presented with sophisticated apparatus. This is particularly the case with the traditional one-and-a-half hour test; less likely with circus arrangements. The list below gives items which may be used and with which you should refamiliarise yourself before the examination.

- Vernier callipers
- Travelling microscope
- Spectrometer
- Top-pan balance
- Multi-range meter (analogue or digital)
- Scalar/counter

- Micrometer screw gauge
- Cathode ray oscilloscope (CRO)
- Slide wire potentiometer
- Stop watch
- Variable frequency signal generator
- Light beam galvanometer

Experience shows that in practical tests, students are most likely to have anxieties over the use of the micrometer, vernier scales and the oscilloscope, and so the use of these in reviewed below.

THE MICROMETER SCREW GAUGE

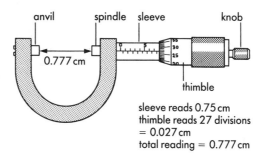

sleeve reads 0.75 cm
thimble reads 27 divisions
= 0.027 cm
total reading = 0.777 cm

Fig. 21.1

The chief features of the **micrometer screw gauge** are shown in Fig. 21.1. When the knob is turned, the spindle moves forward 0.5 mm or 0.05 cm for each complete turn. Before use, the faces of the anvil and spindle should be wiped clean in case there are any particles of dirt which would cause errors. The spindle should be closed up against the anvil by turning the knob. There is usually a clutch mechanism so that the instrument cannot be over-tightened. You should then check whether the instrument has a zero error, note this, and if necessary, apply a + or − correction to your final reading. The item to be measured is then placed between the anvil and spindle and the clutch mechanism is again used to set the micrometer. The sleeve has a scale of 0.5 mm, each of which represents one complete turn of the screw, with fractions of a turn being indicated on the thimble. Each division on the thimble, therefore represents 0.01 cm. The diagram gives an example of how to take a reading, assuming there is no zero error.

CALLIPERS AND VERNIER SCALES

Fig. 21.2 shows a pair of **callipers** used for measuring inside or outside distances on solid objects. As shown they normally have a **vernier scale**. The short scale of ten divisions on the sliding jaw is called a vernier. It enables the accurate determination of the second decimal plate without having to estimate fractions of the division by eye. Verniers are also commonly found on travelling microscopes.

On the callipers illustrated, the vernier is 9 mm long divided into 10 equal parts, so that the difference in length between a vernier division and a scale division is 0.1 mm or 0.01 cm.

Fig. 21.3 shows a scale and vernier giving a reading of 1.35 cm. The fraction of a scale

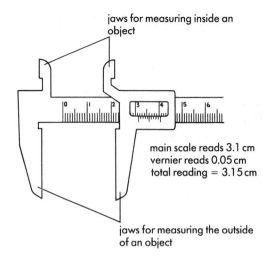

Fig. 21.2

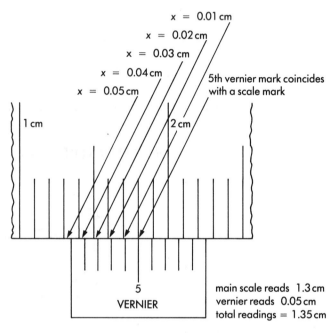

Fig. 21.3

division shown as x is given by a second decimal place. Note that the 5th vernier mark coincides with a scale mark. The second decimal place in the measurement made is given by the number of a vernier mark which coincides with the scale mark.

CATHODE RAY OSCILLOSCOPE

It is the sheer number of controls which cause students anxiety. The ones usually found are:

i) On/off and brightness control
   The brightness control should be kept at the lowest possible intensity suitable for the time-base frequency being used, so that damage to the screen does not occur.

ii) Focus control
   The spot or line trace can be made sharp with this.

iii) X-gain control
   This adjusts the length of the sweep of the spot or line trace in the x direction.

iv) X-shift control
   This bodily moves the whole sweep in either x direction, and can be used to adjust which part of the screen is used for either starting or terminating the sweep.

v) Trig +/− control
   To maintain a stable trace on the screen, each horizontal sweep must start at the same point on the waveform being displayed. This is done by feeding part of the input signal to a trigger circuit which starts the movement of the spot from the left of the screen, and at a point chosen by this control and the trig level control below. The control is normally set in the trig + position, so that the time-base is triggered on a rising waveform.

vi) Time/cm control

This usually has a course control with a number of fixed positions and a fine control to allow further variations. Often the time base can be switched off by turning it fully anti-clockwise.

vii) Stability control

This is turned anti-clockwise until a stable trace is obtained. If turned too far anti-clockwise, the trace will disappear from the screen.

viii) Trig level control

This is used in conjunction with the trig $+/-$ control, and is used to set the voltage level of the trace being displayed which initiates the start of the sweep. However, automatic triggering by the input can usually be obtained. If available this is done by putting the control in the *auto* position. The most easily obtained stationary wave traces are produced in this way.

ix) Volts/cm control

This is an attenuator which enables a vertical deflection amplifier to increase/decrease the potential applied to the Y-plates through the input terminals.

x) Y-shift control

This moves the whole trace bodily in the Y direction in the same fashion as used for the x shift.

xi) D.C./A.C. switch

If D.C. inputs are to be applied this switch must be in the D.C. position, otherwise it is set in the A.C. position. The following procedure should always be followed in order to get a steady trace on the screen.

a) Switch on and turn the brightness control fully clockwise.
b) Apply the signal to the Y input.
c) Turn the stability control fully clockwise.
d) Turn the trigger level control to the auto position.
e) Adjust the Y shift and the X shift until the trace is visible.
f) Adjust the brightness and focus to get a sharp trace.
g) Select a suitable time base and Y amplification, so that all the trace can be seen.
h) Turn the stability control until the trace is just on the point of disappearing. If the trace disappears suddenly turn the stability control clockwise until the trace reappears.

AT THE EXAMINATION

THE FIRST FEW MINUTES

You may have to assemble items for the experiment. Once you have done this spend a few moments getting a feel for the apparatus. If the experiment is about the dependence of one quantity on another, e.g. the input/output characteristics of a small electronic circuit, it is worth getting a rough idea of how the two quantities are related across all the range of measurements before starting to take detailed results. Everything given to you usually has a purpose, so you should try to ensure you have found a use for every item of equipment.

MEASUREMENTS

You will have been taught that in practical work it is important to write down all your measurements. This is particularly the case with external examinations where the examiner can only give you marks for what you have recorded in your paper. So make sure that all your measurements are written down, that you have used an appropriate number of significant figures, and have taken repeat measurements where you think it is necessary. So, if you are timing an oscillation, for example, and measure ten periods, make sure you write down the time clearly for ten periods. Don't simply divide by ten and put that result straight down. If your results are eventually used for a graph, then think about taking at least ten readings. Five ought to be the minimum for a straight-line graph, but if you have a curve, particularly one which has a sharp change of gradient, more readings might be necessary. Sometimes the question may suggest a starting value. This is done to help you but don't make the mistake of recording values only on one side of this starting value.

GRAPHS AND TABLES

Where possible lay out your results in a table with units correctly shown at the head of the column. Use ink for your work except for graphwork where a *sharp* pencil is preferred. If the graph must go through the origin show that you realise this and include it as an assumed experimental point. Be prepared for non-linear effects over part of your curve especially at the ends. Simple scale divisions should be used, using two, five, or ten divisions on the scale for each physical unit. e.g. 2 mm representing 1 μF, 5 mm representing 100 g, 1 cm representing 0.1 V, etc.

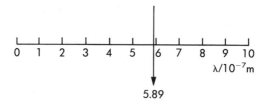

Fig. 21.4

Fig. 21.4 illustrates the convention for showing the variable, the units and the powers of ten. It shows the axis of a graph where values of the wavelength of visible light are to be plotted. Note that the numbers marked on the axis should be between 1 and 10, as a general guideline, rather than a small decimal. Also, the convention is that points on a graph are pure numbers. As an example, the arrow shows the extraction of a value for the wavelength of sodium light. The number on the graph is 5.89. But the axis is labelled $\lambda/10^{-7}$ m. So at the point in question 5.89 = $\lambda/10^{-7}$ m, i.e. $\lambda = 5.89 \times 10^{-7}$ m.

You will often have to measure rates of change on a curve. The best way of doing this is to employ a small plane mirror. The mirror is placed on the line at the point where the gradient is to be taken, and rotated until the line and its image in the mirror seem to be a continuous curve. The mirror is then perpendicular to the curve. A pencil line can be drawn along the mirror and a protractor used to draw a gradient at 90° to the perpendicular line. The gradient line should be at least 10 cm long so that little error is made in reading off y and x values to find the slope. Don't choose experimental points at the ends of a line for slope measurements. This is because the slope should be the mean of a number of experimental points.

COMMENTARY

You will usually be expected to draw a diagram showing the crucial details of your experiment. Remember to do this even if a diagram of some kind is provided in the question. The examiners sometimes give diagrams in order to speed up your setting up of the experiment. It is rare for a description of the experiment to be required. You should check the rubrics of the question on this point and not waste time writing a long account if this is not expected. The examiner will be much more interested in comments you make about special precautions to ensure accuracy.

USE OF TIME

Use your time carefully, remembering that most marks are likely to be allocated for data collected. For a one and a half hour test the following is a suggested scheme. For other lengths of time you should adjust it accordingly.

0–5 minutes	Read the question thoroughly
5–15	Try out apparatus and decide exactly how to do the experiment
15–50	Obtain results
50–70	Draw graphs and tables (where required). Repeat any readings where absences are revealed on your graph.
70–90	Complete the writing up of your experiment and draw any diagrams as necessary. Check your work.

EXAMINATION QUESTIONS

PRACTICE QUESTION

1 The following half-hour test was set by London in 1989 as part of a 2-hour circus. As it is fairly simple to set up you should try it out and compare your results against those of the student in the student's answer and the comments made on that student's answer. Note that in this test the student writes the answer in the spaces provided on the question paper.

The apparatus requirements are:

1 12-V, 24-W lamp, with a suitable power supply. The coiled lamp filament should be straight.
2 Diffraction grating having 300 line mm^{-1} (7500 line inch^{-1}) (e.g. Philip Harris P39462/8 or Griffin XFY–530–B).
3 Stand, at least 80 cm high, with two bosses and clamps.
4 Piece of white paper, about A4 size (210 mm × 297 mm).

Items 1–4 should be assembled above the bench as shown below, with the lamp filament horizontal. The grating should be clamped a few centimetres below the lamp with its rulings parallel to the filament. The paper should be placed on the bench with its shorter sides parallel to the filament.

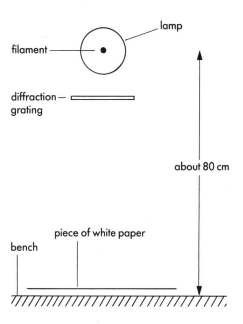

Fig. 21.5

In the experiment the candidate is required to place the lens, 5, on top of the grating and then to move the grating so that a sharp image of the filament is formed on the paper. The Supervisor checks that this will be possible but removes the lens and changes the position of the grating after doing so.

5 Converging lens, focal length 10 cm.
6 Petri dish containing a very dilute solution of potassium manganate (VII) (potassium permanganate) supported on a tripod with balls of Plasticene wedged in the corners to hold the dish. The strength of the solution should be such that when the dish is placed below the grating so as to interrupt the beam of light, the candidate is clearly able to see the presence of an absorption band in the spectra. A few crystals in 100 cm^3 of water should suffice.
7 Metre rule.
8 Card stating: 'Diffraction grating has . . . . . . lines per millimetre'.

The experiment should be performed in a part of the laboratory where there is subdued light.

QUESTION, STUDENT'S ANSWER AND EXAMINER COMMENTS

2   This experiment is concerned with the use of a diffraction grating.
Place the converging lens on top of the diffraction grating and adjust the height of the grating so that a sharp image of the filament of the lamp is focused on the paper on the bench. Measure the following distances:

the distance, u, from the centre of the lens to the filament,

$$12.8 cm; 12.6 cm \quad \text{Mean value } 12.7 cm$$

the distance, v, from the centre of the lens to the bench,

$$53.4 cm; 53.7 cm \quad \text{mean} \quad 53.5 cm$$

> 66 Good values, and credit given for repeats. 99

the distance, D, from the diffraction grating to the bench.

$$53.2 cm$$

> 66 A good value, less than v, but with no repeat. 99

Calculate the power, F, of the lens using the formula

$$F = \frac{1}{u} + \frac{1}{v}$$

where u and v are measured in metres.

$$F = \frac{1}{0.127} + \frac{1}{0.535}$$

$$= 7.87 + 1.87 \quad = 9.74$$

> 66 The calculation is correct, and the final value is within acceptable limits. (Note that F is simply the reciprocal of the focal length of the supplied lens.) However the candidate has failed to spot that F has the units of m^{-1}. 99

Mark on the piece of paper the limits of the first order visible spectrum on either side of the image of the filament.
Sketch the spectra in the box below and record on the sketch the distances between the two red limits and the two violet limits.

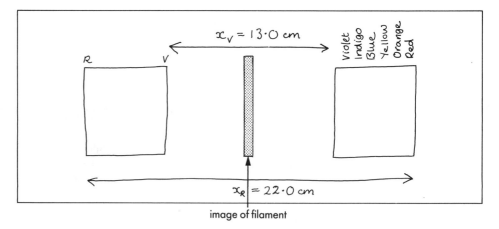

image of filament

> 66 A reasonably drawn diagram. The candidate has interpreted 'limits' correctly i.e. inner limits for violet and outer limits for red. 99

Use your readings, the information on the diffraction grating given on the card, and the diffraction grating formula

$$s \sin \theta = \lambda \quad \text{where } s = 1/N$$
$$\text{and } N = \text{number of lines per metre of the grating}$$
$$\lambda = \text{wavelength}$$

to establish the wavelength limits of the visible spectrum.

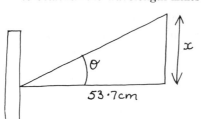

$$x = 6.5 cm \text{ for violet}$$
$$= 11.0 cm \text{ for red}$$

> 66 An error here; probably a slip. 53.7 is the value of v instead of the value of D. 99

$$\theta = \arctan \left(\frac{X}{D}\right)$$

$$\theta_V = \arctan \frac{6\cdot5}{53\cdot7} = 6\cdot9 \text{ degrees}$$

$$\theta_R = \arctan \frac{11\cdot0}{53\cdot7} = 11\cdot6 \text{ degrees}$$

$\underline{N} = 3 \times 105$ lines per metre
So $\underline{\lambda}_V = 4\cdot06 \times 10^{-7}m$ and $\underline{\lambda}_R = 6\cdot70 \times 10^{-7}m$

> **Calculation is clearly set out and the final values are within acceptable limits.**

Carefully insert the tripod and dish containing the purple solution so that the light to one of the first order spectra passes through the solution. Describe any change in the appearance of the spectrum.

> **Answer is a little bare. Some recognition of this being an absorption spectrum is expected of an A-level candidate.**

The green part of the spectrum is no longer seen. Instead there is a black band

Overall Comments: A good answer typical of a bottom grade A or top grade B candidate. All measurements are to an appropriate degree of accuracy, in this case to the nearest mm. Calculations are clearly set out and the final values are in an acceptable range. The final part of the answer is weak on description: the candidate should have linked this with his/her knowledge of absorption spectra.

INDEX